Finding Birds in South Carolina

Finding Birds in South Carolina

Robin M. Carter

University of South Carolina Press

Published in Columbia, South Carolina, by the
University of South Carolina Press

Manufactured in the United States of America

Library of Congress Cataloging-in-Publication Data

Carter, Robin M., 1945–
    Finding birds in South Carolina / Robin M. Carter.
        p.   cm.
    Includes bibliographical references (p.   ) and index.
    ISBN 0–87249–837–9 (paperback : acid-free)
    1. Bird watching—South Carolina—Guidebooks.   I. Title.
QL684.S6C27   1993
598'.07234757—dc20   92-24400

Contents

Contents

Contents

Contents

Contents

Contents

Part A—*General Information*

Interest in finding birds in South Carolina has mushroomed in the last few years. A number of local checklists, pamphlets, and short books have appeared, mostly focusing on the coastal regions of the state, the so-called Low Country—as is appropriate, since many of the best areas for finding birds are near the coast. This book shifts the emphasis, covering the entire state, including not only the Low Country but also what South Carolinians call the Up Country and the Midlands.

South Carolina is a relatively small state and roughly triangular. Its coastline runs generally northeast to southwest for about 220 miles from the North Carolina border near Little River Inlet to the Georgia border at the mouth of the Savannah River. The Georgia border runs roughly southeast to northwest for 270 miles from the mouth of the Savannah River to Ellicott Rock, where South Carolina, North Carolina, and Georgia come together. The North Carolina border is less of a straight line, but it runs approximately west to east for 300 miles or so from Ellicott Rock to the Atlantic Ocean at Little River Inlet. Because of the excellent network of highways in the state, it is quite possible for birders from Columbia or Sumter (near the center of the state) to get up early and travel to any part of the state on a day trip, with a reasonable amount of time spent birding at their destination. Even birders from Charleston or from Greenville can easily go to the mountains or to the coast on a weekend trip.

Although small, South Carolina has a remarkable diversity of natural regions, ranging from the Gulf Stream waters of the Atlantic Ocean a few miles off the coast to the middle elevations of the Blue Ridge Mountains. This diversity of natural regions makes possible a great diversity of breeding birds. Wood Storks, Ruffed Grouse, Sandwich Terns, and Common Ravens all call South Carolina home.

A–1.1—An Overview of the Natural Regions of South Carolina

The complete picture of the natural regions of South Carolina (as used in this book) looks like this:

Atlantic Ocean

offshore Atlantic Ocean *(more than ten miles from land)*
nearshore Atlantic Ocean *(within ten miles of land)*

Coastline

Coastal Plain
    Lower Coastal Plain *(influenced by tides)*
    Upper Coastal Plain *(above the influence of the tides)*

Upper Coastal Plain proper *(flat)*
Sandhills

Fall Line

Piedmont

Foot of the Mountains

Blue Ridge
    Blue Ridge Foothills *(below 2,500 feet)*
    Blue Ridge Mountains *(above 2,500 feet)*

Of course, the most important natural border in the state is the coastline. The land along the coast is part of the broad natural region called the Atlantic Coastal Plain, which stretches from Cape Cod in Massachusetts, across New York's Long Island and New Jersey's Pine Barrens, down the Atlantic Coast to Florida, then westward around the Gulf of Mexico into Mexico to the Yucatan Peninsula. About two-thirds of South Carolina lies within this coastal plain.

From New York City to central Alabama the uphill or inland edge of the Coastal Plain meets another important natural region, the Appalachian Piedmont. The border between these two great natural regions is the Fall Line, so called since colonial times since this line connects the places on rivers where colonial settlers first encountered rapids or falls. Many important cities sprang up on or near the Fall Line: Trenton (New Jersey), Washington (DC), Richmond (Virginia), Raleigh (North Carolina), Columbia (South Carolina), Augusta, Macon, Columbus (Georgia), and Montgomery (Alabama). About 30 percent of South Carolina lies in the Piedmont, a transitional area mediating between the Coastal Plain and the third great natural region of South Carolina, the Appalachian Mountains.

Only a small portion of South Carolina lies within the Appalachian Mountains. All of South Carolina's Appalachian Mountain region is part of the easternmost component of this natural region, which is known as the Blue Ridge.

Thus there are four basic natural regions of the state: the Blue Ridge, the Piedmont, the Coastal Plain, and the Atlantic Ocean. It is often convenient to subdivide the two more diverse regions (the Coastal Plain and the Blue Ridge), in order to understand better the distribution of birds in the state.

The Coastal Plain is often divided into Upper (or Inner) Coastal Plain and Lower (or Outer) Coastal Plain, but there is no general agreement as to where their border should be drawn. The line used in this book is approximately the uppermost reach of the tides on coastal rivers, roughly corresponding to a line along I-95 from the Georgia border to Walterboro, then following US 17 Alternate from Walterboro to Moncks Corner. From Moncks Corner the uphill border of the Lower Coastal Plain follows US 52 north to Lake City, then US 378 east to Kingsburg, and finally SC 41 north from Kingsburg to the North Carolina border near Lake View.

While the Lower Coastal Plain is mostly flat (usually less than one hundred feet above sea level), the Upper Coastal Plain is far less uniform. Much of it is also flat, but near the Fall Line is a discontinuous area of sand hills, some of which reach five hundred feet above sea level. These sand hills are so distinct that many biologists consider them to be another natural region—namely, the Sandhills. But since for the most part the birds of the Sandhills are the same as those of the adjacent flatter portion of the Upper Coastal Plain, we consider the Sandhills to be an interesting subregion of the Upper Coastal Plain.

We have already mentioned that the border between the Upper Coastal Plain and the Piedmont is called the Fall Line, but like most borders of natural regions, this line is hard to draw on a map. Indeed, some geographers prefer to call it the Fall Zone, since it is not so much a line as a band or zone of hard, metamorphic rock at the surface, contrasting with the sedimentary rocks of the Coastal Plain. When you are in central South Carolina, look around you. If the soil is clay or clay loam, with bits of quartz or feldspar rocks mixed in, then you are in the Piedmont. If the soil is sandy with no rocks at all, you are in the Coastal Plain. For this book the Fall Line runs as follows: It crosses the Savannah River at North Augusta, following US 25 north to Johnston. Here the Fall Line follows SC 23 east to Batesburg, where is picks up US 1. It follows US 1 east to Columbia, where it picks up US 21. It follows US 21 north to the Fairfield County line, where it cuts directly east to US 601, just north of Camden. US 601 is followed north to SC 265 just north of Kershaw, thence along SC 265 to SC 268 and SC 109 to the North Carolina border near Mt. Crogan in Chesterfield County.

Like the Fall Line, the border separating the Piedmont natural region from the Blue Ridge natural region is fuzzy. For this book the line runs as follows: From Georgia it follows the eastern border of the Andrew Pickens District of Sumter National Forest in Oconee County. In Pickens and Greenville counties the border is SC 11.

The Blue Ridge Region in South Carolina includes elevations from about 700 feet above sea level to over 3,600 feet. Since bird distribution in the mountains is closely related to elevation, it is convenient to subdivide the Blue Ridge Region into Blue Ridge Foothills (under 2,500 feet) and Blue Ridge Mountains (above 2,500 feet).

A–1.2—An Overview of the Habitats for Birds in South Carolina

There are about as many different ways of classifying natural habitats as there are ecologists and naturalists who are interested in the problem. For those interested in a scientific discussion of the problem, we recommend taking a look at **Natural Vegetation of South Carolina**, by John M. Barry (University of South Carolina Press, 1980), **The Piedmont**, by Michael A. Godfrey, a Sierra Club Naturalist's Guide (Sierra Club, 1980), and **A Field Guide to Eastern Forests**, by John C. Kricher and Gordon Morrison, Peterson Field Guide series (Houghton Mifflin, 1988). This book takes the practical rather than scientific approach, trying to answer the question, What classification of South Carolina's habitats is most useful to help me find birds? We shall consider twenty-three habitats in all, broken down as follows:

Forested Habitats

Dry forests
    oak-hickory forests
    northern pine–oak forests
    southern pine–oak forests
    old-growth pine forests

Moist forests
    cove hardwood forests
    white pine–hemlock forests
    rhododendron thickets
    southern mixed hardwoods
    pocosin and bay swamp thickets

Wet forests
    floodplain forests and swamps

Nonforested Habitats

Inland Aquatic habitats
    alder thickets
    ponds and freshwater marshes
    rocky river shoals
    large lakes

Coastal Habitats
    salt marshes and salt creeks
    ocean beach and nearshore ocean
    vegetated ocean dunes
    rock jetties and groins
    offshore ocean

Disturbed habitats
    old-field habitats
    pastures and meadows
    cultivated farmlands
    urban habitats

Oak-hickory forests

One of the main natural habitats of the South Carolina Blue Ridge and Piedmont is a rather dry forest dominated by oaks and hickories, often with a fair number of pines, especially in young forests. This is part of the great oak-hickory forest of eastern North America, which is found from southern New England and Michigan south to central Georgia and eastern Texas. In South Carolina the oak-hickory forest is characterized by species such as white oak, black oak, red oak, southern red oak, chestnut oak, black gum, mockernut hickory, bitternut hickory, and pignut hickory, as well as other similar species which thrive in somewhat dry soils with a climate of freezing winters and hot summers. A few of the sought-after birds of oak-hickory forests include most of South Carolina's woodpecker species (except Red-cockaded), Brown Creeper (in winter), White-breasted Nuthatch, Summer and Scarlet Tanager, Red- eyed and Yellow-throated Vireo, and Barred Owl, as well as many other common species.

Northern pine–oak forests

On dry, sandy soils in the Blue Ridge region of South Carolina, we can find a few areas dominated by pitch pines or Virginia pines in conjunction with some of the more drought-tolerant oak species, such as blackjack oak, post oak, and black oak. This habitat represents the southern extension of the *northern pine– oak forest*, a forest type which is typical of coastal areas farther north, such as the New Jersey Pine Barrens or parts of Cape Cod in Massachusetts. Here you will find the Scarlet Tanager, Ovenbird, Pine Warbler, and many other species. Rarities of this habitat include breeding Blackburnian Warbler and Red Crossbill.

Southern pine–oak forests

Away from the mountains, the most common forest habitat of South Carolina is one dominated by pines, usually loblolly pines, but including fair numbers of shortleaf pines in the Piedmont or sometimes longleaf- or slash-pines in the Lower Coastal Plain. Where fire recurs, these pines are found almost exclusively, and we will eventually get another type of habitat (old-growth pine forest, covered below). But since for most of the twentieth century fires have been severely suppressed throughout the southeastern United States, the tremendous southern pine forest that once stretched from Virginia to Texas has been converted into a forest in which hardwood species (especially oaks) codominate, hence the name *southern pine–oak forest*. Special birds of this habitat include the Brown-headed Nuthatch, Pine Warbler, and Solitary Vireo.

Old-growth pine forests

In a very few places in South Carolina, mostly on government-owned land, the original southern pine forest still exists. This habitat requires frequent burning (about every four years), or it will quickly turn into a southern pine–oak forest, as oak trees and other hardwood species (such as red maple and sweet gum) gradually crowd out the pines. Old-growth pine forests are rare and cherished places with many unique plant and animal species, including the Red-cockaded Woodpecker. So dependent is the Red-cockaded Woodpecker on the old-growth pine forest that is it futile to look for this species anywhere else. Look here also for all other woodpeckers: the Brown-headed Nuthatch, Pine Warbler, Eastern Wood-Pewee, Summer Tanager, and Bachman's Sparrow.

Cove hardwood forests

This forest type reaches its most impressive development in the Great Smoky Mountains National Park of North Carolina and Tennessee. In the South Carolina Blue Ridge and Piedmont we find similar forests that are almost as impressive, moist forests characterized by a wide diversity of tree species: tulip trees, maples, oaks, hickories, basswoods, buckeyes, and many others. In South Carolina look for tulip trees. An abundance of this magnificent member of the magnolia family quickly tells you that the hardwood forest you are in is more than just another oak-hickory forest, but rather a cove hardwood forest. Sought-after birds of this habitat include the Cerulean Warbler, White-breasted Nuthatch, and many woodpeckers.

4

White pine–hemlock forests

Cove hardwood forests in South Carolina often have a few eastern hemlocks scattered here and there along streams and ravines. But a few stream valleys (such as that of the Chattooga in Oconee County) have large numbers of eastern hemlocks mixed in with eastern white pines, as well as the hardwood species of the classic cove hardwood forest. In some spots this forest approaches a pure white pine forest—an early stage of the succession that eventually leads to a true cove hardwood forest. These moist, cool forests of northern conifers are a unique habitat for birds in South Carolina. Certain species that you would normally expect to breed in spruce-fir forests at a much higher altitude (e.g., six thousand feet in the North Carolina mountains) may breed as low as twenty-five hundred feet in a white pine–hemlock forest in South Carolina. These northern conifer specialists include the Red-breasted Nuthatch, Golden-crowned Kinglet, and Red Crossbill. These species may breed only rarely in South Carolina's northern pine–oak forests, but they are much more common in white pine–hemlock forests.

Rhododendron thickets

Along the streams of the Blue Ridge region, especially in cove hardwood forests, it is very common to find huge thickets of rosebay rhododendron, often mixed in with mountain laurel. These evergreen thickets really stand out in the rather open understory of a cove hardwood forest. In summer they are much darker, moister, and cooler than the surrounding woods and thus provide a special habitat for birds that is somewhat different from the more open areas of the cove hardwood forest. Several species of warbler, including Swainson's Warbler, are common in rhododendron thickets but scarce or absent a few feet away in the open part of the forest. Other warblers common in this habitat include the Hooded, Black-throated Blue, and Worm-eating.

Southern mixed hardwoods

True cove hardwood forests do not occur in the Coastal Plain of South Carolina, but here and there you can find upland forests with a large diversity of tree species. Some pines may be found, especially the spruce pine, but most of the species are hardwoods, including many oaks, hickories, maples, sweet gum, black gum, and other species. Many species are evergreen, including Virginia live oak, southern magnolia, red bay, and a few others. Near the coast you will find many sabal palmettos (South Carolina's state tree). Such southern mixed-hardwood forests are often called maritime forests when they occur near the sea in areas under the influence of salt spray, but very similar forests occur throughout the Coastal Plain. Since the birds of the maritime forest are, for the most part, the same as those of similar forests inland, we call them all southern mixed hardwood forests. Such forests harbor many common bird species, but few rarities.

Pocosin and bay swamp thickets

Pocosins are rather specialized habitats with wide areas of practically impenetrable shrubs—often evergreen. Typical pocosin species include swamp cyrilla, red bay, sweet bay, loblolly bay, zenobia, fetterbush, various hollies, and many other species. Soils are peaty and wet; vines grow everywhere. This habitat is very common in eastern North Carolina but rare in South Carolina, being found only in a few places, such as a few Carolina bays. Much more common in South Carolina are **bay swamp thickets** (also known as bay swamps or bay head swamps). These thickets have many of the same plant species as the classic pocosin of North Carolina but are not so extensive. Bay swamp thickets typically line the banks of small streams in the Sandhills subregion of the Upper Coastal Plain. The main difference is one of extent; a true pocosin covers many acres and often does not have many tall trees aside from a scattering of pond pines, but bay swamp thickets occur as a specialized component of a larger forest, usually a southern pine—oak forest or a floodplain forest. Good birds in this habitat include Swainson's Warbler, Worm-eating Warbler, Ovenbird, Black-and-white Warbler, and Hooded Warbler.

Floodplain forests and swamps

Ecologists usually speak of various types of wet forest in South Carolina, including southern riverine forest, southern mixed-hardwood swamp forest, bald-cypress swamp forest, and other similar forest types, all of which occur in or near fresh water, either along streams or in Carolina bays. Flooding may be intermittent or constant. These forest types merge with the southern mixed-hardwood forests mentioned above. For our purposes we combine all of the wet forest types under one label—*floodplain forests and swamps*—since the birds of one type of swamp are virtually the same as those of all the other types. The size of the forest, more than the species of the trees in it, influences what birds breed there. In the South Carolina Piedmont the White-breasted Nuthatch is rare or absent from floodplain forests, whereas this bird is rather common in similar forests in the Coastal Plain. This main difference between Piedmont and Coastal Plain floodplain forests is size. Piedmont floodplain forests are often just a narrow strip along a river, while a floodplain in the Coastal Plain may spread out for a mile or more from the river. Thus, White-breasted Nuthatches and other forest-interior species are much more common in Congaree Swamp National Monument than they are just a few miles upstream in a similar (but smaller) Piedmont floodplain forest. Other good species of this habitat include Swainson's and Kentucky Warblers, all woodpeckers (except for Red-cockaded), and migrant thrushes.

Alder thickets

Tag alder occurs along streams throughout South Carolina, but in the Blue Ridge region the thickets formed by this species have a special meaning for breeding birds. Some species, such as Yellow Warbler, breed almost exclusively in alder thickets in the Blue Ridge region and a bit into the adjacent Piedmont region. A typical pasture in the Blue Ridge region will have a more or less continuous alder thicket along any stream that runs through it. Because of its pervasiveness and its unique breeding birds, we recognize *alder thickets* as a separate habitat in the Blue Ridge region. Here look for American Woodcocks, Yellow Warblers, and Willow Flycatchers.

Ponds and freshwater marshes

Small ponds are common throughout the state and often have at least a small amount of marsh at one end, usually near the inlet of the pond. Since South Carolina was not glaciated, nor does it have the limestone karst of Florida, almost all ponds in the state are artificial or have been created by beavers. Freshwater marshes occur along the upper reaches of tidal rivers in the Lower Coastal Plain, but most freshwater marshes in the state are artificial. Many such marshes are found on old rice plantations and were originally constructed by slave labor. Rice is no longer grown in South Carolina, but many old plantations have been converted to wildlife refuges, waterfowl management areas, or private hunt club areas. This is the habitat for ducks, herons, and rails.

Rocky river shoals

As the great rivers of the South Carolina Piedmont cut their way from the mountains to the Coast Plain, they often encounter regions of more resistant rocks. Here, a river such as the Savannah, the Saluda, the Broad, or the Catawba will encounter a series of rocky rapids or small waterfalls, locally called shoals.

Many of the best of these shoals have been inundated by the numerous large reservoirs built on these rivers in the last sixty years or so, but a few good river shoals remain, providing a special habitat for birds. For example, Bald Eagles often use these shoals for feeding.

Large lakes

Throughout the Piedmont and Upper Coastal Plain regions of the southeastern United States, many large lakes have been constructed by the Corps of Engineers or by various power companies. These lakes have destroyed huge tracts of floodplain forest and covered many river shoal areas, but they have also given South Carolina something that nature did not—large inland flatwater areas. The lakes include many different habitat types—deep water, shallow water, marshes, and mud flats. Even the long highway bridges built over these lakes have created a new microhabitat for South Carolina's birds. Cliff Swallows, for example, nest in South Carolina almost exclusively under highway bridges over large lakes in the Piedmont.

Salt marshes and salt creeks

The height of tides along the Atlantic coast of South Carolina ranges from about six feet at the mouth of the Savannah River to about three feet at the North Carolina border. Such a high rise and fall of the sea twice daily sends water far inland along the marshy tidal estuaries of the Lower Coastal Plain, so broad areas along these estuaries are marshes. The uppermost marshes are quite fresh, but as one approaches the sea, the water becomes more saline, and the marshes become brackish and finally true salt marshes. These marshes are dominated by various species of cordgrass (**Spartina**) and needlerush (**Juncus**), with their drier margins hosting shrubs such as marsh elder and various species of baccharis. The marshes are drained by a network of salt creeks, which combine into larger and larger waterways, eventually leading to the main tidal estuary and the Atlantic. The birds of South Carolina typically resident in salt marshes include Clapper Rail, Marsh Wren, Common Yellowthroat, and Seaside Sparrow.

Ocean beaches and nearshore ocean

There are many miles of sandy ocean beaches in South Carolina, most of which are highly developed and overrun with people throughout the year. But on the remote barrier islands, and even on Myrtle Beach's Grand Strand in winter, you can find quiet sandy beaches visited by hordes of birds, especially shorebirds, gulls, and terns. Of course, most of these same birds can been seen flying over the nearby ocean, which is why we combine nearshore ocean with ocean beaches as a habitat for birds.

Vegetated ocean dunes

On a classic barrier beach there is a system of sand dunes back from the beach, first a field of dunes covered by various grasses, and then a shrubby zone characterized by plants such as wax myrtle, yaupon, and eastern red cedar. Finally, beyond the shrubs, begins a maritime forest of Virginia live oak, sabal palmetto, and many other species. We have already covered the maritime forest (as a special type of southern mixed-hardwood forest). The shrubby and grassy habitats between the forest and the sandy beach we combine under the la-bel *vegetated ocean dunes,* even though a good case can be made for separating the grassy dune field habitat from the shrub-covered dunes just beyond it. Vegetated dunes are good places to look for Painted Bunting and Common Ground-Dove.

Rock jetties and groins

There are no naturally occurring rocky ocean shores in South Carolina, but humans, in their sometimes futile efforts to control the shifting sands of barrier islands, have constructed many rock barriers along the sandy shores. The most impressive of these (and one that is very accessible by birders) are the two half-mile-long rock jetties that keep Murrell's Inlet from being closed by shifting sands. The south jetty at Murrell's Inlet is in Huntington Beach State Park and is easily bir-ded. (There is a paved roadway on top of the jetty.) From this jetty, especially in winter, birders can find species that are more typical of Maine's rocky coast than of South Carolina, notably Purple Sandpiper. This northern species is common on the jetty in winter but rarely seen away from its rocks. Other rarities found along the jetties in winter include Harlequin Duck, scoters, Great Cormorant, and perhaps an alcid or rare gull.

Offshore ocean

The Gulf Stream lies thirty to sixty miles off the South Carolina coast. In or near this tropical ocean current are found bird species which rarely are visible from shore, including various shearwaters, storm petrels, terns, and perhaps even a tropicbird. This habitat is little visited by birders but is fairly easily accessible by party boat (fishing boats which take tour-ists offshore for a day of fishing). Party boats leave from Charleston, Murrell's Inlet, Little River Inlet, and elsewhere along the coast. Find out from the captain how far out he intends to go. Trips that do not go at least twenty miles off shore usually turn up few, if any, pelagic birds.

Old-field habitats

Old-field succession is a favorite topic of plant ecologists. An abandoned field might be bare earth one year, then covered with weedy annuals the next, which within a few years are replaced by a predictable succession of plants, culminating in tree species such as loblolly or Virginia pine, eastern red cedar, winged elm, and black locust, depending upon the part of the state. Closely related to this kind of natural old field succession are various human-created habitats. Much of South Carolina is planted in pines, usually loblolly pines. When a pine plantation is clear-cut, it is usually re-planted in pines. The first few years of a young pine plantation's growth closely resembles old-field succession. Another artificial habitat that falls into this type is that of utility rights-of-way. A power company will not let its electric or natural gas line grow up into a forest but will maintain a more or less open right-of-way, a permanent old-field habitat. Typical old-field bird species include the Indigo Bunting, Yellow-breasted Chat, Prairie Warbler, Carolina Wren, White-eyed Vireo, Common Yellowthroat, Field Sparrow, Chipping Sparrow, and Bachman's Sparrow.

Pastures and meadows

There are no natural prairies in South Carolina, but we have created somewhat similar habitats. These are pastures, meadows, airports, golf courses, and the like. These habitats attract bird species such as the Grasshopper Sparrow, which would rarely occur in any natural habitat in the state. But since hayfields are common in the Piedmont and Upper Coastal Plain, the Grasshopper Sparrow is now fairly common in summer in South Carolina.

Cultivated farmlands

Row crops are very common in South Carolina, especially in parts of the Upper Coastal Plain, where there are huge fields planted in tobacco, soybeans, corn, cotton, peanuts, and other crops. Despite heavy pesticide spraying, birds are still very common on or near these huge open fields. In some parts of the state cultivated fields are separated by hedgerows, which are extremely useful for wildlife, especially breeding birds. The drastic reduction in numbers of the Loggerhead Shrike in the eastern United States is probably related to the widespread destruction of hedgerows and corresponding increases in the use of pesticides. Fortunately there are still quite a few hedgerows bordering fields in South Carolina, and birds such as the Loggerhead Shrike are still common, at least in some parts of the state.

Urban habitats

Most of us live in cities or large towns, and we see birds every day. Tree-lined suburban streets may even superficially resemble a forest, though the bird species are greatly reduced from the number of species you would find in a true forest, since many birds require large tracts of woods in order to be successful. There are a few species, however, which thrive in cities—Rock Dove, House Sparrow, House Finches, Song Sparrows, and a few others. For this reason we lump all the various habitats to be found in South Carolina's cities into a catchall category, **urban habitats**.

A–2—HOW TO USE THIS BOOK

A–2.1—Organized by County

This book is divided into three main parts (Parts A through C):

Part A   General Information
Part B   Site Information
Part C   Species Accounts

Part B is the heart of the book—a section for each of the forty-six counties of the state, arranged in alphabetical order.

State-maintained secondary roads in South Carolina are numbered with a combination of the county number (1 through 46, in alphabetical order) and a road number. Throughout the state you will find small black-and-white rectangular signs labeling secondary roads at intersections. For example, you might find a road labeled "S-32-68," which means Road 68 in Lexington County, since Lexington is county number 32.

Throughout this book we will refer to state-maintained secondary roads by road number. For example, in the Abbeville County section, since Abbeville is county number 1, a reference to Road 10 means secondary road S-1-10 (the full name that you will find on state road signs).

9

Of course, most roads have names as well as state numbers, and you will often find green-and-white road name signs as well as black-and-white road number signs. This book will often give the road name as well as the road number. Since many roads do not have names, or the names change frequently, the state secondary road numbers are more reliable.

One by-product of South Carolina's road numbering is that it is easy to find out what county you are in. Simply go to the nearest secondary road intersection and look at the sign. The county number will be identified in Part B of this book.

A–2.2—The Best Birding Areas in South Carolina by Season

Birds are where you find them, but it helps to be in the right place at the right time. A winter trip to the mountains might be very interesting as an outdoor experience, but you will find few birds there. Likewise a June trip to the coast will not produce many shorebirds.

The following areas provide the best chances for seeing a wide variety of bird species and numbers by season. (NWR = National Wildlife Refuge; WMA = Wildlife Management Area.)

Winter (November through March)

Winter is a great season for birding in South Carolina. The relatively mild winter climate means that many species which breed farther north spend the winter in our state. The best winter birding is on the coast, but there are quite a few inland spots that are worth checking. Here are the best winter locales, with the section number in Part B which covers the area:

Areas in the Lower Coastal Plain:
  Huntington Beach State Park (B-23)
  Brookgreen Gardens (B-23)
  Bulls Island in the Cape Romain
    NWR (B-10)
  Magnolia Gardens (B-10)
  Bear Island WMA (B-15)

Hunting Island State Park (B-7)
Pinckney Island NWR (B-7)
Hilton Head Island (B-7)
Savannah NWR (B-27)
Corps of Engineers spoil area near
  Savannah (B-27)

Areas in the Upper Coastal Plain:
  Santee NWR (B-14)
  Carolina Sandhills NWR (B-13)
  Congaree Swamp National Monu-
    ment (B-40)

Areas in the Piedmont:
  Broad River WMA (B-20)
  Lake Hartwell area (B-4, B-37, B-39)

Spring (April and May) and Fall (August through October)

Spring is great wherever you are, but it is particularly impressive in the Blue Ridge and Piedmont natural regions in late April and early May, when large numbers of migrant land birds pass through. The land bird migration is less evident on the coast, but you can find good numbers of egrets, shorebirds, terns, and other species which love wetlands. Fall migration is better on the coast than is the spring, but even in fall the inland areas are better.

Here is a list of the best areas in migration:

Areas in the Lower Coastal Plain:
  Huntington Beach State Park (B-23)
  Bulls Island in the Cape Romain NWR
    (B-10)
  Magnolia Gardens (B-10)
  Folly Island (B-10)
  Edisto Beach State Park (B-15)
  Bear Island WMA (B-15)
  Hunting Island State Park (B-7)

Hilton Head Island (B-7)
Savannah NWR (B-27)
Corps of Engineers spoil area near Savannah (B-27)

Areas in the Upper Coastal Plain:
Carolina Sandhills NWR (B-13)
Santee NWR (B-14)
Orangeburg Sod Farms (B-38)
Congaree Swamp National Monument (B-40)
Aiken State Park (B-2)
Webb Wildlife Center (B-25)

Areas in the Piedmont:
lower Saluda River (B-32 and B-40)
Flat Creek Natural Area (B-29)
Landsford Canal State Park (B-12)
Woods Ferry area (B-12)
Broad River Recreation Area (B-44)
Kings Mountain (B-46)
Paris Mountain State Park (B-23)

Bunched Arrowhead Heritage Preserve (B-23)
Broad River WMA (B-20)
Enoree River WMA (B-36)
Lynches Woods (B-36)
Townville (B-4)
Lake Hartwell area (B-4, B-37, B-39)
Clemson area (B-39)
Fury's Ferry (B-19)
Parsons Mountain (B-1)
Pumkintown (B-39)

Areas in the Blue Ridge:
Caesar's Head State Park (B-23)
Jones Gap State Park (B-23)
Sassafras Mountain (B-39)
lower Eastatoe Creek (B-39)
Walhalla Fish Hatchery (B-37)
Tamassee Road (B-37)
Oconee State Park (B-37)
Burrell's Ford (B-37)

Summer (June and July)

June and July is the breeding season for many birds in South Carolina. Shorebirds (except for local breeders) are scarce on the coast, but the resident species of water-loving birds more than compensate. June and early July are good times to visit the mountains. Here, amidst the cool forests, you will find a wide variety of breeding land birds, especially warblers. Here is a list of the best areas in summer:

Areas in the Lower Coastal Plain:
Huntington Beach State Park (B-23)
Santee Delta WMA (B-23)
Francis Marion National Forest (B-10)
Bear Island WMA (B-15)
Savannah NWR (B-27)
Corps of Engineers Savannah spoil area (B-27)

Areas in the Upper Coastal Plain:
Carolina Sandhills NWR (B-13)

Congaree Swamp National Monument (B-40)
Aiken State Park (B-2)
Webb Wildlife Center (B-25)

Areas in the Piedmont:
Flat Creek Natural Area (B-29)
Landsford Canal State Park (B-12)
Woods Ferry area (B-12)
Broad River Recreation Area (B-44)
Townville (B-4)
Fury's Ferry (B-19)
Parsons Mountain (B-1)

Areas in the Blue Ridge:
Caesar's Head State Park (B-23)
Jones Gap State Park (B-23)
Sassafras Mountain (B-39)
lower Eastatoe Creek (B-39)
Walhalla Fish Hatchery (B-37)
Tamassee Road (B-37)
Oconee State Park (B-37)
Burrell's Ford (B-37)

A–2.3—Birding near Major Highways

South Carolina is on several important cross-country highways. Interstate 95, the "Main Street" of the eastern United States, runs through South Carolina for two hundred miles. Other important highways include I-85, I-77, I-26, I-20, and US 17. Birders passing through the state on any of these highways should stop off for an hour (or a week) and sample what South Carolina has to offer.

How to Use This Book

Here is a list, by highway, of relevant sections of this book:

Interstate 95 (north to south):
Dillon County (B-17)
Marlboro County (B-34)
Darlington County (B-16)
Florence County (B-21)
Lee County (B-31)
Sumter County (B-43)
Clarendon County (B-14)
Orangeburg County (B-38)
Dorchester County (B-18)
Colleton County (B-15)
Hampton County (B-25)
Beaufort County (B-7)
Jasper County (B-27)

Interstate 85 (northeast to southwest):
York County (B-46)
Cherokee County (B-11)
Spartanburg County (B-42)
Greenville County (B-23)
Pickens County (B-39)
Anderson County (B-4)
Oconee County (B-37)

Interstate 77 (north to south):
York County (B-46)
Lancaster County (B-29)
Chester County (B-12)
Fairfield County (B-20)
Richland County (B-40)
Lexington County (B-32)

Interstate 26 (northwest to southeast):
Spartanburg County (B-42)
Greenville County (B-23)
Laurens County (B-30)
Union County (B-44)
Newberry County (B-36)
Richland County (B-40)
Lexington County (B-32)
Calhoun County (B-9)
Orangeburg County (B-38)
Dorchester County (B-18)
Berkeley County (B-8)
Charleston County (B-10)

Interstate 20 (east to west):
Florence County (B-21)
Lee County (B-31)
Kershaw County (B-28)
Richland County (B-40)
Lexington County (B-32)
Aiken County (B-2)
Edgefield County (B-19)

US 17 (northeast to southwest):
Horry County (B-26)
Georgetown County (B-22)
Berkeley County (B-8)
Charleston County (B-10)
Dorchester County (B-18)
Colleton County (B-15)
Beaufort County (B-7)
Hampton County (B-25)
Jasper County (B-27)

A–3—OTHER SOURCES OF INFORMATION

This book can be used in conjunction with any good South Carolina road map. Free road maps are available at all South Carolina Welcome Centers, which are on all interstate highways near the North Carolina and Georgia borders and also on US 301 near the Georgia border and on Interstate 95 (southbound) near Santee.

The maps in this book are sketches, designed to help you find birds. They are not drawn to scale, and are not meant as substitutes for proper county road maps.

If you are eager to explore the back

roads of South Carolina beyond what is covered in this book, you will need a county map atlas. An excellent atlas, **South Carolina County Maps**, is available from

County Maps
Puetz Place
Lyndon Station, WI 53944

If you are interested in finding birds along any of the many miles of hiking trails in South Carolina, then you should get a copy of **South Carolina Trails**, by Allen de Hart, 2d ed. (Chester, CT: Globe Pequot, 1989). **South Carolina Trails** and **South Carolina County Maps** are both

Other Sources of Information

available at bookstores in major South Carolina cities.

Maps of the national forests of South Carolina are available from

National Forests in South Carolina
Supervisor's Office
   1835 Assembly Street
   (Post Office Box 2227)
   Columbia, SC 29202
   (803) 765-5222

Many of the best birding areas in South Carolina are in wildlife management areas and heritage preserves managed by the South Carolina Wildlife and Marine Resources Department. Information on specific areas can be obtained by writing

South Carolina Wildlife and Marine
   Resources Department
   Division of Information and Public
   Affairs
   Dennis Building
   (Post Office Box 167)
   Columbia, SC 29202
   (803) 734-3888

The Nature Conservancy protects many extremely valuable natural areas in South Carolina. Information on visiting Nature Conservancy preserves may be obtained from

The Nature Conservancy
South Carolina Field Office
   Post Office Box 5475
   Columbia, SC 29250
   (803) 254-9049

The National Audubon Society has chapters in many South Carolina cities which offer monthly field trips to interesting local natural areas. You can usually get a current address for the local Audubon societies from a local public library or chamber of commerce. Chapters are currently organized in the following cities:

Charleston (Charleston Natural History
   Society)
Columbia (Columbia Audubon Society)
Greenwood (Long Cane Audubon
   Society)
Hilton Head (Hilton Head Island Audubon
   Society)
Myrtle Beach (Waccamaw Audubon
   Society)
Spartanburg (Piedmont Audubon Society)

The Columbia Audubon Society sponsors a telephone information service that you can call for news of upcoming meetings and field trips, and you can also leave a message. You can usually get in contact with local birders by leaving a message on the Columbia Audubon Infoline: (803) 748-9066.

The Carolina Bird Club is the ornithological society for North and South Carolina. It publishes a quarterly magazine (**The Chat**) and a newsletter, and it sponsors a rare bird alert for North and South Carolina: (704) 332-2473. The club has three general meetings a year as well as other field trips at irregular intervals. For more information, write:

Carolina Bird Club
Post Office Box 27647
Raleigh, NC 27611

Part B—*Site Information*

B–1—ABBEVILLE COUNTY

Abbeville County lies in the Piedmont in the northwestern part of the state. The western border of the county is the Savannah River, impounded as the Richard B. Russell Lake. The southern part of the county contains part of the Sumter National Forest. Within the National Forest lies an interesting Piedmont monadnock (isolated mountain), Parsons Mountain, which rises some 500 feet from the surrounding countryside to an elevation of 832 feet. While this elevation is not enough to give its birdlife a truly Appalachian flavor—in its breeding species—the surrounding forests are an excellent example of Piedmont oak-hickory and cove hardwood forests.

B–1.1—Parsons Mountain, Sumter National Forest

Winter   *
Spring   **
Summer   *
Fall   **

See letter A on Map B–1.1.

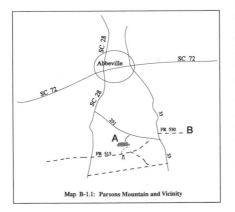

Map B-1.1: Parsons Mountain and Vicinity

The national forest recreation area at Parsons Mountain Lake and the three-mile-long trail from the lake to the top of the mountain are good for finding birds typical of Piedmont hardwood and mixed forests. To reach Parsons Mountain from the center of Abbeville, go southwest on SC 72 (toward Calhoun Falls) to the junction with SC 28. Turn left (south) onto SC 28, and continue 1.8 miles to the junction with Road 251 at Rock Buffalo Church. There should be a sign for Parsons Mountain Lake at this intersection. Go left (southeast) on Road 251 for about 1.7 miles to the entrance to the recreation area on the right (south). Follow the entrance road past the picnic area to the lake's dam, where the trail to Parsons Mountain begins. In winter the recreation area may be closed, in which case use the following directions to find the upper end of the trail.

The hiking trail crosses a forest road about four-fifths of the way up the mountain. To drive to this point, pass by the entrance road to the recreation area (which is closed in winter anyway) and continue on Road 251 for 1.1 miles more (or 2.8 miles east of SC 28). Here turn right (southwest) onto FR 515, Parson Mountain Road (unpaved). About 0.4 mile from the paved road, FR 515 crosses a small creek which has been dammed by beavers. The standing dead trees here are excellent for Red-headed Woodpecker.

Go a total of about 1.5 miles on FR 515 to the trail crossing. There is no parking area here, but there is plenty of room to park on the shoulder of the road. From here you can go downhill to the lake or uphill to the mountain top. To rejoin SC 28, continue west on FR 515 for about a mile.

This is for the most part a heavily wooded

area. Thus spring and fall migrants, while perhaps quite numerous, are difficult to find, since there is so much good habitat for them to spread out in.

B—1.2—Long Cane Natural Area, Sumter National Forest

Winter *
Spring **
Summer *
Fall **

See letter B on Map B—1.1.

Long Cane Creek begins in the woods and farmlands east of the town of Abbeville and flows for about fifteen miles, mostly through the Sumter National Forest, until it becomes an arm of Strom Thurmond Lake, an impoundment of the Savannah River. Along much of its course it is a slow-flowing, silted stream with a wide flood plain—much like a Coastal Plain stream. One of the more interesting portions of the floodplain of Long Cane Creek is preserved as the *Long Cane Natural Area* in Sumter National Forest in the southeastern portion of Abbeville County.

This part of Long Cane Creek does have a few good stands of switch cane, the plant that gives Long Cane Creek its name, but the canebrake is neither extensive nor impenetrable. Just as interesting from a botanist's viewpoint is the fact that the chalk maple, one of the sugar maple group, is common here.

The Long Cane Natural Area is also known for its large hardwoods—a true cove hardwood forest found here in the Piedmont instead of in the Appalachian Mountains. South Carolina's state champion shagbark hickory—a giant 135 feet high and 10.5 feet in circumference—grows along the trail through the natural area.

Birdlife in the Long Cane Natural Area is similar to that described for nearby Parsons Mountain (see Section B-1.1), though certain species are easier to find along the creek than in the dry woods along the trail to the top of Parsons Mountain. Breeding species common in floodplain forests, such as the Acadian Flycatcher and Prothonotary Warbler, are much more common along Long Cane Creek. The canebrakes are probably not extensive enough to attract Swainson's Warbler, but the creek is an excellent area to look for Wild Turkey, especially in late summer.

To reach the Long Cane Natural Area, follow the directions for Parsons Mountain; from the center of the town of Abbeville go southwest on SC 72 (toward Calhoun Falls) to the junction with SC 28. Turn left (south) onto SC 28 and continue 1.8 miles to the junction with Road 251 at Rock Buffalo Church. There should be a sign for Parsons Mountain Lake at this intersection. Go left (southeast) on Road 251. In about 1.7 miles you will pass the entrance to Parsons Mountain Lake recreation area on the right (south). Continue southeast on Road 251 until it ends at Road 33, 3.0 miles southeast of SC 28. At Road 33 turn left (north), and go 0.3 mile. Look on the right for the turnoff for FR 530, a dead-end forest road. Follow FR 530 about one mile to its end. Look for an unmarked trail away from the cul-de-sac at the end of FR 530, and follow it 125 yards to the well-marked Long Cane Trail, a 25-mile-long horse trail.

You will hit the Long Cane Trail just west of where it crosses Long Cane Creek and enters the Long Cane Natural Area. There is a footbridge for hikers a few yards upstream from the horse ford. Cross the bridge, and enter the Natural Area. From the parking lot to the state champion shagbark hickory is about one mile. The trail passes through the Natural Area for a bit more than two miles until it emerges at FR 505 on the east side of the Natural Area. The best canebrake is a bit beyond the champion shagbark hickory, which is marked by a conspicuous sign.

15

The Long Cane Natural Area gives you a bit of Coastal Plain habitat in the Piedmont, and nearby Parsons Mountain gives a bit of mountain habitat. It is quite possible to explore both areas from the Parsons Mountain Lake campground on foot on the same day. This truly points out the fascination of the Piedmont for the naturalist; it is the transition from the mountains to the Coastal Plain.

B–1.3—Lowndesville Park on Lake Russell

Winter *
Spring *
Summer *
Fall   *

The public fishing pier on Lake Russell in Lowndesville is a good place to take a quick look at a narrow arm of Lake Russell. This is a great place for Cliff Swallow (mid-April through early August). From Calhoun Falls follow SC 81 north for 9 miles to the bridge over Lake Russell. From Anderson go south on SC 81 for about 24 miles to the bridge. Or from Abbeville go west on SC 71 for 14 miles, to its end at SC 81, and then continue north on SC 81 less than a mile to the bridge. The fishing pier is right beside the main road, on the northwest side of the bridge. From the fishing pier you can easily examine the underside of the SC 81 bridge, where there are numerous Cliff Swallow nests. This is one of the easiest places in South Carolina to watch Cliff Swallows at their nests.

B–2—AIKEN COUNTY

Aiken County is on or near the Fall Line (the transition from Upper Coastal Plain to Piedmont) and the Savannah River, which forms the Georgia border. Aiken County combines tourism, agriculture, and light industry, centered on the city of Aiken. Tourists come to Aiken for golf and horseback riding, while Graniteville, about 5 miles west of Aiken, is the site of the first cotton mill in the southern United States. As a natural area, Aiken has the typical Upper Coastal Plain mixture of pine-covered hills alternating with river swamps. The hills can best be explored at Hitchcock Woods, a private park open to the public on the west edge of Aiken. The river swamps are represented by Aiken State Park. Although most of the county is in the Sandhills subregion of the Upper Coastal Plain, there are a few areas which are best described as in the Piedmont region, and the part of the county along the Savannah River downstream from the city of North Augusta lies in the Upper Coastal Plain proper. The Piedmont part of Aiken County may be explored at Savannah Bluffs Heritage Preserve, while the non—Sandhills Upper Coastal Plain region may be investigated at Redcliffe State Park and the Beech Island—Silver Bluff area.

B–2.1—Savannah River Bluffs Heritage Preserve

Winter   *
Spring   **
Summer *
Fall   **

See Map B–2.1.

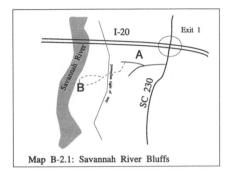

Map B-2.1: Savannah River Bluffs

Savannah River Bluffs Heritage Preserve
is a small area (110 acres) of great interest to the botanist along the Savannah
River just downstream from the I-20
bridge. It protects 1,076 feet of river frontage on one of the last remaining rocky
shoals of the Savannah River. (Most of the
other shoal areas have been flooded by
impoundments.)

Birding at the Bluffs is not particularly
spectacular, although you may see
something interesting on the rocks of
the river shoals or flying up the river. The
best time to come is in the spring, when
migrants are common and the wildflowers are at their peak. Among the
many plants growing here are some
extreme rarities—relict trillium, bottle-
brush buckeye, and upland swamp
privet. And since the site is right on the
Fall Line, you will see species typical of
both these regions. The trees are covered with spanish moss. Dwarf palmetto is
common, making the area look like the
Coastal Plain.

To reach the Savannah River Bluffs from
I-20, leave the interstate at the last exit
before crossing over to Georgia (Exit 1),
and go south on SC 230 (Martintown
Road). At 0.5 mile south of the interstate
turn right onto the first paved road (Old
Plantation Road). Go 0.2 mile to a fork.
Here keep right and continue for another
0.3 mile. Park just before you see the
signs indicating private property. From
where you park (letter A on Map B–2.1)
continue on foot along the road into the
private property. After about eight hundred feet look for a well-marked trail off
to the left. Follow this trail downhill about
a mile to the river. The last part of the
trail is a loop through the heart of the
preserve.

The trail first goes through a quarter mile
of second-growth pine-oak woods and
then emerges onto a power line right-of-
way, along which is some of the best
birding. Look for hawks and sparrows in
winter, but beware of chiggers in late
spring and summer.

After following the power line for a quarter mile, the trail turns downhill toward the
river. The main part of the preserve is a
heavily wooded ravine with a creek. This
is a great area for breeding warblers,
including Louisiana Waterthrush along
the creek. In about a half mile the trail
reaches the river (letter B on Map B–2.1),
where you can check out the rocks for
species such as Killdeer, Spotted and Solitary Sandpipers, and perhaps other
sandpipers in migration. Bald Eagle is
possible in winter.

From the river the trail loops back uphill
along the creek, before the loop closes,
just before you get back to the power
line right-of-way.

B–2.2—Aiken State Park and Vicinity

Winter   *
Spring   **
Summer **
Fall   **

See letter B on Map B–2.2.

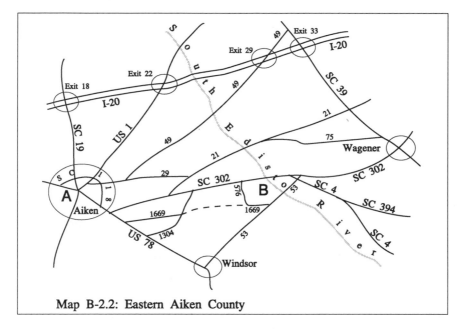

Map B-2.2: Eastern Aiken County

Aiken State Park follows the pattern of many state parks in South Carolina. It is a 1,067-acre park centered on a small swimming lake, with picnicking and camping. But this park is special for birding because it is along the upper reaches of the South Edisto River. The floodplain of the South Edisto, as it flows through the Sandhills, has some of the best bay swamp thickets in South Carolina. Small birds, especially warblers, are readily found in this habitat from April through October. Even in winter there are plenty of Yellow-rumped and Pine Warblers, and you might scare up an Orange-crowned, Yellow-throated, Palm, or Black-and-white Warbler.

To reach *Aiken State Park* (letter B on Map B–2.2) from I-20 westbound, use Exit 33, and go south on SC 39 for 13 miles to the town of Wagener. In downtown Wagener turn right (west) onto SC 113—SC 302. Immediately after this turn, SC 302 branches off to the right. Keep on SC 302 (a right turn off of SC 113), and go west for 9 miles to the junction with Road 53, which is just before the junction with SC 4. Here the three roads form a small triangle. SC 302 turns right and merges with SC 4 about 0.1 mile beyond the junction with Road 53. Instead of turning right and keeping on SC 302, keep straight ahead (which is actually a left turn off of SC 302), and get onto Road 53. You will cross SC 4 in about 0.1 mile. If you miss the turnoff and find yourself at the junction of SC 302 and SC 4, turn left onto SC 4, go 0.1 mile, and then turn right onto Road 53.

From I-20 eastbound get off at Exit 18, and go south on SC 19 for about 5 miles to downtown Aiken. Turn left (east) onto US 78 (Richland Avenue), and go about 3 miles to the eastern edge of town. Here turn left (east) onto SC 4—SC 302 (the back road to Columbia) and go about 13 miles east to the point where SC 302 turns off to the left. About 0.1 mile beyond this junction, turn right (south) onto Road 53.

From the intersection of SC 4 and Road 53, go south on Road 53. In about one mile you will enter Aiken State Park. The first birding stop is just before the *Road 53 bridge over the South Edisto River*. Since this is not a busy road, it is easy to walk out onto the short bridge to look the area over. A jeep road joins Road 53 just before the bridge. If you wish to avoid crowds, walk about two hundred yards on the jeep road until you notice a trail off to the left. This is the trail to the primitive campground. It loops around for about a half mile, giving good access to the swamps on the north side of the South Edisto River. Unless the area is overrun with a youth group camp-out, you will have the place to yourself. The birds here are about the same as on the Jungle Nature Trail in the main part of the park.

To reach the main part of the park, cross the bridge and turn right almost immediately, then turn right again at the main gate of the park. From the main gate enter the main park loop road. At the Y-junction you can go left to the swimming lake, picnic ground, and campground. The best birding is to the right. Take the right fork, and park at the small picnic area (the Cypress Stump picnic area). Here you will see the paint blazes of the two-mile-loop Jungle Nature Trail.

The best birding in the park is along the Jungle Nature Trail, which, true to its name, leads you into (and hopefully out of) the junglelike thickets along the river. This trail has been relocated from time to time, with the result that parts of it are poorly marked. You may well get lost, but if you come between mid-April and early October, you will also find lots of birds. If you lose the trail, backtrack until you pick it up again or until you get back to your car. (Plenty of insect repellent is advised.) If you do not wish to chance the poorly marked trail, most of the birds of the park can be observed from the loop road.

You will find plenty of birds in winter (the Aiken Christmas count usually finds between seventy and eighty species), but the breeding season is the time to come to Aiken State Park.

B–2.3—Hitchcock Woods in the City of Aiken

Winter   *
Spring   **
Summer *
Fall   **

See letter A on Map B–2.2.

Hitchcock Woods is a 2,252-acre park maintained by the Hitchcock Foundation (P.O. Box 930, Aiken, SC 29802). It is right on the edge of downtown Aiken and is open to the public for hiking and horseback riding during daylight hours.

Birding at Hitchcock Woods is fair. The park is in a hilly area cut by a small stream (Cuthbert Branch). The habitat is a typical Sandhills mixture of loblolly- and longleaf-pine forest on the upper slopes, with a bay-swamp thicket along the creek.

To reach *Hitchcock Woods* from I-20, go south on SC 19 at Exit 18. In about 5 miles you will enter the city of Aiken, where SC 19 becomes Laurens Street. Continue south on SC 19 to the intersection with US 1—US 78 (Richland Avenue), in the heart of downtown Aiken. Here SC 19 turns east, but to reach Hitchcock Woods, continue south on Laurens Street. About 0.4 mile south of Richland Avenue you will reach the intersection of Laurens Street and South Boundary Avenue. Turn right (west) onto South Boundary, and go 0.2 mile to the Hitchcock Woods parking lot. (If you miss the turnoff at South Boundary, you will soon be at the end of Laurens Street, at its intersection with Coker Spring Avenue. Turn around and try again.)

Trail maps for Hitchcock Woods are usually available at the parking lot. If you do not find a trail map, here is a suggested route for a short walk:

From the parking lot go straight ahead on Devil's Backbone Road to the Memorial Gate. Here turn left. Soon you will cross a dry creek bed (marked as a "sand river" on the trail map). Take the first trail to the right (downstream), and follow this trail westward (downhill) to the

Horse Show Grounds. At the extreme southwest corner of the Horse Show Grounds, pick up another trail (called Peek-a-Boo Lane on the trail map), and follow this trail downstream to the first trail off to your left (south). Turn left and go a few yards to a bridge over the creek (Barton's Pond Bridge over Cuthbert Branch). From this point you can explore the pine-covered hillside uphill to the south. Eventually you should backtrack to the bridge and then retrace your steps uphill and eastward to the parking lot.

There are at least twenty miles of trails in Hitchcock Woods. This is a delightful place to hike, especially in early spring, when wildflowers are common. The best birding is in September and October, when a fair number of migrant warblers can be found.

B–2.4—Beech Island to Silver Bluff

Winter	**
Spring	***
Summer	**
Fall	**

See Map B–2.3.

From the Fall Line at North Augusta, the Upper Coastal Plain portion of Aiken County widens from a few hundred yards to several miles. Two outstanding birding areas may be found in the low floodplain of the Savannah River in the southwestern part of Aiken County: Gum Swamp (privately owned) and Silver Bluff Plantation (a sanctuary of the National Audubon Society).

To reach the Gum Swamp and Silver Bluff from I-20 westbound, leave the interstate at Exit 5 and follow US 25 to downtown North Augusta. From I-20 eastbound use Exit 1, and go south on SC 230 to downtown North Augusta. In North Augusta pick up SC 125, and follow this highway south toward the Savannah River Site of the U.S. Department of Energy. A couple of miles from downtown North Augusta, SC 125 crosses over US 1. The first birding area on this tour is just a bit south of US 1.

From US 1 follow SC 125 south for about a mile. The four-lane highway crosses a bridge over Horse Creek. Just beyond the bridge turn right (west) onto the entrance road for *Horse Creek Wastewater Treatment Plant* (letter A on Map B–2.3). This sewage treatment plant is closed to the public, but the entrance road passes through an interesting area of flooded woods. This is a good place to find Wood Ducks and Red-headed Woodpeckers. After checking out the flooded woods, turn around near the gate of the sewage treatment plant, and return to SC 125. Turn right (south) onto SC 125. SC 125 reaches the community of Beech Island 3.9 miles south of US 1. Here the directions are a bit tricky. Turn right (west) onto Road 781, following signs for US 278. Immediately after turning right, you will reach a stop sign at SC 28. Go straight ahead, crossing SC 28, and you will find yourself on Road 5. Follow Road 5 southwest out of Beech Island.

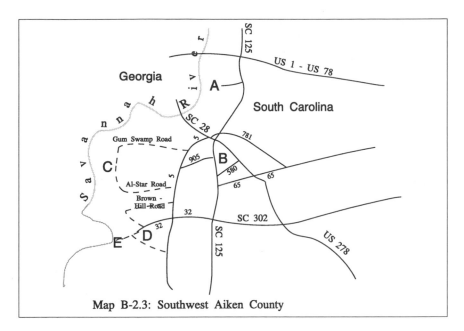

Map B-2.3: Southwest Aiken County

About 1.9 miles south of SC 28 turn right (west) onto *Gum Swamp Road*, a good (although unpaved) road (letter C on Map B–2.3). Follow this road as it loops around through Gum Swamp and then through agricultural fields along the Savannah River. This is private property, so all birding must be done from the roadside. Nonetheless, you will find lots of birds, including most species of the Upper Coastal Plain floodplain forest. The open areas are a great place to find Mississippi Kites (late April through late August), and Wild Turkey are common in the woods.

The road loops around counterclockwise. Halfway around it changes its name to Al-Star Road. You will rejoin Road 5 (the paved road) in about 8.5 miles.

Once back on Road 5, go south for 1.0 mile to the first unpaved public road to the right. This is Brown-Hill Road. Turn right (west) onto Brown-Hill Road, which leads through agricultural areas and pinewoods. You will soon reach the edge of the National Audubon Society's *Silver Bluff Sanctuary*. This sanctuary is set up primarily to do research and to provide a feeding area for Wood Storks, not for the public to visit. This tour remains on the public roads. If you wish to visit Silver Bluff Sanctuary proper, advance arrangements must be made. Call (803) 827-0781 well in advance of your proposed visit, and ask for assistance.

Follow Brown-Hill Road counterclockwise for about 3.8 miles to its end at Road 32 (paved). Turn right (southwest) onto Road 32. In just 0.3 mile you will see impoundments off to the left (letter D on Map B–2.3). Look for an unmarked roadside overlook on the left. Park along Road 32 and check out the ponds and marshes, but do not cross any fences. This is the best birding spot along Silver Bluff Road. In summer these impoundments attract Wood Storks, White Ibis, and most of the common herons and egrets. In winter look for Double-crested Cormorants, a few ducks, and perhaps a Bald Eagle.

After overlooking the impoundments, continue straight ahead on Road 32. You will pass more impoundments. The pavement ends, but continue straight ahead on a good unpaved road through pinewoods and farmlands. The road passes the headquarters of the Silver Bluff Sanctuary about a mile beyond the end of the pavement and reaches a boat launch on the Savannah River 2.4 miles beyond the end of the pavement (letter E on Map B–2.3).

To return to North Augusta, backtrack along the unpaved road to the beginning of the pavement (Road 32). Follow Road 32. In 2.1 miles you will reach Road 5. Cross Road 5, and go straight ahead on Road 32. At 1.8 miles east of Road 5 you will reach SC 125. Turn left (north) and go about 10 miles back to North Augusta.

While you are in the neighborhood, you might want to drop by *Redcliffe Plantation State Park* (letter B on Map B–2.3). The lawns and gardens of this historical park attract many birds, including Ruby-throated Hummingbirds in summer and Great Horned Owls year-round.

B–3—ALLENDALE COUNTY

Allendale County is a small, predominately rural county in the Upper Coastal Plain along the Savannah River. Its county seat is the city of Allendale (population 4,400), which is on US 301 about forty-three miles southwest of Orangeburg and thirteen miles northeast of the Georgia border (defined by the Savannah River).

The best birding in Allendale County is along the Savannah River, which is easily reached at any of several boat-launching ramps.

B–3.1—A Savannah River Tour (North of US 301)

Winter	*
Spring	*
Summer	**
Fall	*

See Map B–3.1.

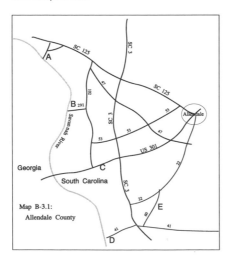

Map B-3.1:
Allendale County

For most of this tour you will be passing through farm county, with scattered woodlots, pine plantations, pastures, cultivated fields, and small swampy areas near streams. This is a very birdy area, especially for the common species of open farmlands. just about anywhere you can find a good, wide shoulder or other pulloff, and you will find birds in any season.

The tour starts at the *South Carolina Welcome Center* on US 301, which is three miles northeast of the Georgia border (the Savannah River) or ten miles southwest of downtown Allendale. (See letter C on Map B–3.1.) This welcome center is very lightly visited, since most of the tourist traffic uses I-95 instead of US 301, which was a main route to Florida twenty years ago. If the welcome station has not been closed, it makes a good short rest stop. The grounds of the welcome station usually have quite a few birds, often including Red-headed Woodpeckers and Eastern Bluebirds. Be sure to check the sewage ponds by walking to the rear of the area and peering through the fence. This looks like the sort of place that might attract some vagrant bird in the fall or winter.

From the welcome station drive southwest on US 301 toward Sylvania, Georgia. In about two miles the four-lane divided highway narrows to two lanes. Currently only one bridge over the Savannah River is open to traffic, which is the old Georgia-bound bridge. The old South Carolina-bound bridge is closed.

You can get a good view of the Savannah River by driving along the existing US 301 causeway to the river. There is an informal boat-launching area on the South Carolina side of the river and a more developed launching area on the Georgia side. These are good places to look for kites (late April through August). Mississippi Kites are quite common here, and this is currently about as far upstream on the Savannah River as you have a reasonable chance to see an American Swallow-tailed Kite. Do not venture away from the state-owned right-of-way, however, since all other land here is privately owned and posted.

To continue the tour, get back onto US 301 and go the other way, returning toward the welcome station (and the city of Allendale). At 2.9 miles from the river (just before you return to the welcome station), look for a paved secondary road off to the left (north). This is Road 102. Turn left onto Road 102, and go north for 3.5 miles until you reach the first state secondary road to the left (west), Road 291. This is the road to *Johnson's Landing*, a small boat-launching area on the Savannah River. (See letter B on Map 3.1.) If you want to visit this area, turn left and follow Road 291 for about 1 mile to its end. This area does not give a particularly good view of the river, so you may wish to skip this side trip, especially if you are in a hurry.

To continue the tour, keep going north on Road 102, passing the Sandoz chemical plant on your left (west, toward the river). About 9 miles north of US 301 you will enter the village of Martin. Here Road 102 ends at SC 125. (To return to US 301 in Allendale, turn right onto SC 125 and go east for about 11 miles.)

Once on SC 125 headed north (toward North Augusta), you will immediately cross over Lower Three Runs Creek on an elevated bridge. About 3.5 miles beyond this high bridge you will reach a lower bridge over Furse Mill Creek. The old mill (still in operation) is on the left (west) side of the road, and the millpond is on the right (east). Furse Mill Pond is one of the more interesting millponds in the area for birding. Pull off onto the shoulder of the road, and scan the pond. There are always a few Wood Ducks and Common Moorhens around. From April through October you can usually spot an Anhinga or two, either swimming in the pond or drying their wings while perched on a nearby dead snag. Other species of interest are found in warm weather (especially late summer)—herons, egrets, White Ibis, and an occasional Wood Stork.

At the bridge over Furse Mill Creek get turned around on SC 125 (carefully!), and look for Road 17, coming in from the southwest right beside the old mill. Go toward the river on Road 17. In 1.4 miles you will reach the village of Millet. Here Road 17 turns hard to the right (northwest). Go 0.4 mile more on Road 17 until you see a state secondary road coming in from the left (southwest). This is Road 368, which goes 2 miles to a boat-launching area on the Savannah River (*Little Hell Landing*). (See letter A on Map B–3.1.)

Road 368 is a good birding road. The first mile or so goes through interesting pasture land, which is good for Cattle Egrets (in summer) as well as the usual birds of the open country. As you near the river, you will pass through a swampy area (good for swamp birds in summer; Prothonotary Warblers are very common here.)

Little Hell Landing at the end of Road 368 gives a good view of the Savannah River. In summer look for Mississippi Kite, Anhinga, White Ibis, and Wood Stork.

Return to Road 17. Here you have a choice of routes to use to return to SC 125. If you are going farther north on SC 125 (toward Aiken or Augusta), turn left. This turn will put you on Road 12, and you will reach SC 125 in 1.4 miles. At SC 125 turn left (north) for Augusta or right for Allendale. The shortest way back to Allendale is to retrace your path along Road 17 through Millet and then back to SC 125 at Furse Mill. Here turn right (east) to return to US 301 in Allendale.

B–3.2—A Savannah River Tour (South of US 301)

Winter   *
Spring   *
Summer **
Fall   *

See Map B–3.1.

The following tour makes a good side trip from US 301 if done on its own, or it makes a great way to go from US 301 to the excellent birding areas along the Savannah River in Hampton County, the next county downstream from Allendale County (see Section B–25).

The best season for this tour is summer, and the species of most interest are hawks. In summer you might see most of the following species of hawks along the way: Black Vulture, Turkey Vulture, Osprey, American Swallow-tailed Kite (uncommon, but increasing), Mississippi Kite (common), Cooper's Hawk (rare), Red-shouldered Hawk, Broad-winged Hawk, Red-tailed Hawk, and American Kestrel (rare). Few other places in South Carolina can boast of so many breeding hawks.

This tour starts at the intersection of SC 3 and US 301, which is 7 miles southwest of Allendale on US 301 or about 2.5 miles northeast of the South Carolina Welcome Center on US 301. (See letter C on Map B–3.1.) From US 301 go south on SC 3 toward Estill and Hardeeville. This part of SC 3 (US 301 to the Hampton County line) roughly parallels the Savannah River at a distance of one to four miles.

Soon after leaving US 301, you will find yourself in plantation country—flatter and more wooded than the farm country characteristic of Allendale County northwest of US 301. Roadside birding here is good, but usually not quite as good as along the Savannah River in Hampton County, the next county to the south. If you are on your way to Hampton County, do not tarry too long in Allendale County.

About 9 miles south of US 301 look for the first state secondary road off to the right (west) toward the river. This is Road 41, which ends at an excellent boat-launching area on the Savannah River, known as *Cohen's Bluff Landing* (see letter D on Map B–3.1). Turn right onto Road 41, and follow it to its end (1.4 miles from SC 3). In about a mile you will cross Pipe Creek, which is a great place to see Prothonotary Warblers and other swamp birds in summer. Cohen's Bluff Landing at the end of Road 41 is probably the best boat-launching area for birding along the entire Savannah River. There is a large parking lot and a twenty-foot bluff overlooking the river. In midsummer at this place it is a very good bet that you will be able to see kites of both species as well as Anhinga, White Ibis, Wood Stork, and a good number of herons and egrets. Set up your lawn chair in a shady spot, and watch the sky, especially from midmorning through early afternoon. American Swallow-tailed Kites breed in the area and are usually not too hard to see between early April and late August.

From the intersection of Road 41 and SC 3 continue across SC 3 on Road 41 for just 0.1 mile. Here turn left (north) onto Road 60, and follow this road for 1.3 miles until you see a water-lily—covered pond on your right (letter E on Map B–3.1). Here, from the roadside, you can usually find a Wood Duck or two. Purple Gallinules are usually present from mid-

April until mid-September, but you must be a bit patient or lucky to see one.

Retrace your route to SC 3. If you are not going on to Hampton County, you might as well turn back at this point. (To return to US 301, turn left onto SC 3.) To continue on to Hampton County, go right (southeast) on SC 3 for 6.4 miles to the Hampton County line. Here turn right onto Road 104. See Section B-25 for a detailed description of the tour through the Savannah River plantation country of Hampton County.

B–4—ANDERSON COUNTY

Anderson County is a rather densely populated county in the Piedmont region in the northwestern part of the state. The county seat is the city of Anderson, a manufacturing and commercial center with a population of about thirty-five thousand. The Savannah River and its impoundments (Lake Hartwell and Lake Russell) form the western edge of the county and provide good birding, especially during migration and in winter.

Anderson County is probably best known to South Carolina birders for the Townville area, with its breeding Dickcissels and Black Rails, and wintering longspurs, Lincoln's Sparrows, and Brewer's Blackbirds.

Interstate 85 runs through the northern portion of Anderson County, from the Georgia border almost to the city of Greenville. Directions to birding areas will be given from this highway.

B–4.1—Sadler's Creek State Park

Winter **
Spring **
Summer *
Fall **

Sadler's Creek State Park is on a 395-acre peninsula on the east shore of Lake Hartwell. Its second-growth woods of Virginia pine, oaks, and hickories are not particularly good for birding, although you can find most of the species of Piedmont southern pine—oak forests there. The boat launch area and the main picnic area are worth checking out in fall, winter, or early spring. Horned Grebes can be abundant in winter, and you might find a few Common Loons and ducks as well. There is a half-mile walking trail which begins at the main picnic area.

Follow the signs for the pavilion and look for the beginning of this loop trail near the rest rooms. (One of the more curious aspects of this trail is that it features a rustic wooden love seat at a rest stop.)

To reach Sadler's Creek State Park, leave I-85 at Exit 14, and go 1.3 miles south on SC 187 to SC 24. Here turn left (east), and stay on SC 187. SC 24 and SC 187 cross an arm of Lake Hartwell and then split about 3 miles beyond this point. Bear right (south) onto SC 187, and go about 7 miles to the entrance road to the park, on the right (west).

Winter   **
Spring   ***
Summer **
Fall   **

See Map B–4.1.

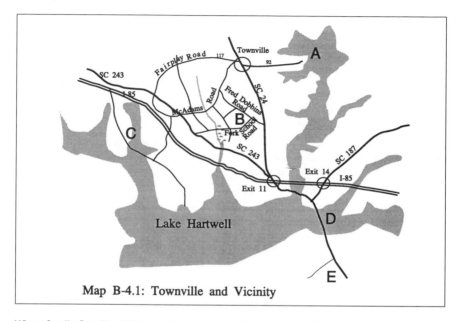

Map B-4.1: Townville and Vicinity

When South Carolina birders refer to the great open-country birding near Clemson, they are usually speaking of the *Townville* area, which is a few miles southwest of Clemson but still in the Clemson Christmas Count circle. Here, in most years, you might find up to a half dozen singing Dickcissels from early May through early July as well as numerous breeding Grasshopper Sparrows, a few Horned Larks, and the species usual in Piedmont agricultural areas.

To reach *Townville* from I-85, leave at Exit 11, and go northwest on SC 24 for about 4 miles to the village of Townville. At 3.6 miles north of the interstate look for Road 92 off to the right (east). This road leads 1.6 miles to a park on Lake Hartwell, *Townville Recreation Area* (letter A on Map B–4.1).

After exploring the lakeshore at the recreation area, return to SC 24 and turn right (northwest). You are now in the village of Townville. In about a half mile, look for Road 117, Fairplay Road, which veers off to the left (west). (If you reach the Oconee County line, you have gone too far.) Turn left onto Fairplay Road, and go about 0.1 mile to the first left, Fred Dobbins Road. Go south on Fred Dobbins Road for about 2 miles to the third paved county road on the right. This is Fork School Road. Turn right (south) onto *Fork School Road* (letter B on Map B–4.1). This stretch of road from Fred Dobbins Road to the bridge over Little Beaverdam Creek, about one mile down the hill, is the best area for Dickcissel. In 1988 at least six males were singing here from late April into June. This is the most dependable place in South Carolina for breeding Dickcissel.

At the bottom of the hill Fork School Road crosses Little Beaverdam Creek. Stop just before the bridge. There is a small marshy area near the bridge which attracts migrant Sora and Virginia Rails and an occasional breeding Least Bittern. Another interesting breeding species here is the Yellow Warbler, a rare breeder this far from the mountains.

This is a good area for wintering sparrows, including White-crowned. Lincoln's Sparrow has been found in the brush near the creek, but this elusive species is not to be expected.

To continue the Townville area tour, backtrack from the bridge to Fork School and turn left (west) onto Gaines Road. (You get to this road before you get to the bridge. If you go right (east) onto Gaines Road, it will reach a dead end in a half mile at an observation point for ducks and geese.) To continue the tour, go west on Gaines Road until it ends at a T-junction with McAdams Road. Here turn left (south) onto McAdams Road. In about a quarter mile you will approach Little Beaverdam Creek again. Just before you cross the creek, look for a farm road to the left (an entrance road for Beaverdam Creek Waterfowl Management Area). Park here and explore the area downstream along the creek. This is a good area for migrants. (This area may be closed during the winter.)

A few yards into the waterfowl management area from McAdams Road there is a gate. Carefully cross this gate and explore the wet meadows, marshes, and beaver ponds in front of you. In some years Black Rails have bred here, but they are usually not around if the weather has been too dry. The Black Rails, if present, might be heard calling at dawn or dusk in May or June. Do not count on this species here, but it is something to hope for.

After exploring the marsh area, return to McAdams Road and backtrack to the north. Keep on McAdams Road. Within a mile of the creek you will pass two farm ponds on the left, each with convenient pulloffs. Do not cross any fences here. These ponds are great for migrant ducks and shorebirds. Horned Larks might visit the muddy edges at any time of year, and there may well be American Pipits or a Lapland Longspur in winter. These pastures are among the best places in South Carolina to find wintering Brewer's Blackbirds, but this primarily western species is rare even here.

About 1.5 miles north of Little Beaverdam Creek, McAdams Road ends at Fred Dobbins Road. Here you may turn left to return to the village of Townville or turn right and follow Fred Dobbins Road south and east to SC 24 between I-85 and Townville.

B-4.3—Big Beaverdam Creek

Winter	**
Spring	**
Summer	*
Fall	**

See letter C on Map B-4.1.

When Lake Hartwell is a bit low, great mud flats emerge in the backwaters of the lake. One such place, which has proved very productive over the years, is *Big Beaverdam Creek*, just south of I-85 in extreme northwestern Anderson County. To reach the area from I-85, leave the interstate at Exit 4, and go southeast on Road 23 for about 2.3 miles. Park along the road at either end of the bridge, and

overlook the area from the bridge. If the water is very low, it may be possible to explore some of the area on foot, but expect mud and briars.

At low water this is a great birding area. Shorebirds are common during migration (April through May and August through October), and look for waterfowl in winter. Rarities found here in recent years include Baird's and Buff-breasted Sandpipers, Lesser Golden-Plover, and Snow Goose.

When the lake is high, do not expect as many shorebirds, but waterfowl may be common in winter. Canada Geese are common permanent residents here.

B–4.4—The Anderson Airport Area

Winter   *
Spring   *
Summer *
Fall   *

See Map B–4.1.

Airports are often good areas for unusual birds, but they are also usually not very accessible. The *Anderson Airport* is easily birded from roadsides or parking lots around its perimeter. It is relatively easy to scan the runways and grassy areas for birds. Horned Larks, Killdeer, and Eastern Meadowlarks are common year-round. From mid-April through September, Grasshopper Sparrows are present in the grassy areas of the airport proper and also in weedy fields nearby. If you scan the airport after a rain in the migration season (March through April and August through September), you may well find a migrant shorebird or two. Lesser Golden-Plovers and Upland Sandpipers are both regular.

The airport is on the west side of the city of Anderson, just south of SC 24. From I-85 leave at Exit 14, and go south on SC 187. In 1.3 miles you will reach the junction with SC 24. Here turn left (southeast), and continue toward Anderson on SC 24—SC 187.

Soon after joining SC 24, you will pass over an arm of Lake Hartwell. There is a pulloff on the left midway across the lake causeway where you can stop and scan the lake for geese, loons (in winter), and gulls (at letter D on Map B–4.1). Cliff Swallows breed under nearby bridges.

To continue on to the airport, keep going southeast on SC 24. At about 4 miles beyond the lake turn right (south) onto Road 1028, which is the entrance road to the airport (letter E on Map B–4.1).

B–5—BAMBERG COUNTY

Bamberg County is a small, rural county in the Upper Coastal Plain. The town of Bamberg, the county seat, is on US 301 about 17 miles south of Orangeburg. The northeastern border of Bamberg County is the South Edisto River, and the southwestern border is the Salkehatchie River. The swamps and floodplain forests of these two rivers provide the best birding in the county. Between the two rivers you will find a typical mixture of agricultural fields, woodlots, and pine plantations quite typical of South Carolina's Upper Coastal Plain.

The best birding area on public land in the county is Rivers Bridge State Park, on the Salkehatchie River in the extreme southern part of the county. The other birding area on public land in Bamberg County is Cathedral Bay, an 80-acre Carolina bay near Olar, in the southwestern part of the county.

Winter   *
Spring   **
Summer *
Fall   **

See letter B on Map B–5.1.

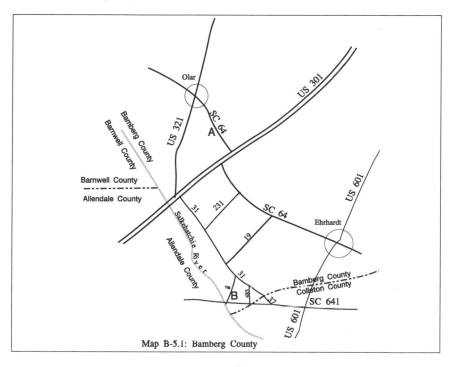

Map B-5.1: Bamberg County

To reach *Rivers Bridge State Park* from I-95, use Exit 57, near Walterboro in Colleton County. Go west on SC 64 for 19 miles, then turn off to the left onto SC 641. Go 6.0 miles west on SC 641 to US 601. Cross over US 601, and continue west on SC 641 for 0.7 mile to Road 37 (still in Colleton County). Following signs for the state park, turn right onto Road 37 and go northwest for 0.5 mile to the Bamberg county line. At the line Road 37 becomes Road 31 in Bamberg County. Go northwest on Road 31 for 3 miles to Road 8, on the left. Turn left (south) onto Road 8, and follow the signs to the main entrance of the park.

To reach the park from US 301, go south from the town of Bamberg or north from Allendale to the intersection of US 301 and US 321. This intersection is just north of the Allendale county line, but in Bamberg County. A few yards north of the intersection, turn east onto Road 31, and go 6.4 miles southwest on Road 31 to Road 8. Turn right (south) onto Road 8, and follow the signs to the main entrance to the park.

The best birding area in the park is along the edge of the floodplain forest of the Salkehatchie River. From the main park entrance go south on Road 8 to the Confederate Breastworks, which are on the right (west) about 0.8 mile south of the main entrance road. Turn onto the side road, and go a few yards to the parking area.

There are no trails into the floodplain forest, but you can see a bit of it by exploring the historic breastworks, site of a Civil War battle. Birds here are typical of floodplain forests in the Coastal Plain.

Rivers Bridge State Park is not a great birding area, but it is a quiet place for a rest stop or a good base for camping. It is reasonably close to places with very good birding along the Savannah River or along the coast, but it is far enough inland to avoid the crowds of the coastal campgrounds.

B–5.2—Cathedral Bay

Winter	**
Spring	**
Summer	**
Fall	**

See letter A on Map B–5.1.

The Heritage Trust program of the South Carolina Wildlife and Marine Resources Department (SCWMRD) has preserved a small number of Carolina bays—those mysterious oval-shaped depressions that are common in the Coastal Plain of North and South Carolina. Cathedral Bay is one of the more accessible of these protected bays.

Cathedral Bay is an eighty-acre pond-cypress and black-gum swamp near the town of Olar. To reach the bay from the Columbia area, leave I-26 at Exit 115, and go south on US 321 for about 50 miles to the town of Olar. In Olar turn left (east) onto SC 64. Go east on SC 64 for 1.7 miles. Look for the white, diamond-shaped property markers of the Heritage Trust program on the south (right) side of SC 64, on the edge of a pond-cypress swamp (which is Cathedral Bay).

From I-95 exit at the SC 64 exit (Exit 57), which is the Walterboro exit, and go west on SC 64 for about 36 miles to the intersection with US 301. (This point on US 301 is about 2.6 miles north of Road 31, a turnoff for Rivers Bridge State Park—see Section 5.1 above). To reach Cathedral Bay, continue west on SC 64 for 0.7 mile west of US 301, then look for the Heritage Trust property markers on the left (south) side of the road.

Cathedral Bay is an impressive place. Its water comes from unchanneled runoff,

so it is a swamp without a stream or spring. In wet seasons (such as late spring or early summer) there may be as much as three feet of water in the swamp. In fall and early winter the swamp may be almost dry. When it is dry, it is an easy place to visit. Once you work your way through a few yards of catbriers and vines at the edge of the bay, you will find yourself in a beautiful pond-cypress swamp. If the swamp is filled with water, you may still enjoy the bay by working your way around on the high ground on its rim, or wade right in (in clothes you don't mind getting wet, of course).

The birdlife of the bay is typical of species that breed in cypress swamps. In late spring or early summer you can expect to find most of the following summer residents:

Green-backed Heron; Yellow-billed Cuckoo; Chimney Swift; Ruby-throated Hummingbird; Eastern Wood-Pewee; Acadian and Great Crested Flycatchers; Fish Crow; Blue-gray Gnatcatcher; Wood Thrush; White-eyed, Yellow-throated, and Red-eyed Vireos; Northern Parula; Yellow-throated, Pine, Prothonotary, and Kentucky Warblers; Summer Tanager; and Indigo Bunting.

Typical winter residents include the American Woodcock; Yellow-bellied Sapsucker; Eastern Phoebe; Brown Creeper; House and Winter Wrens; Golden-crowned and Ruby-crowned Kinglets; Hermit Thrush; American Robin; Solitary

Vireo; Yellow-rumped and Palm Warblers; Chipping, Field, Fox, Song, Swamp, and White-throated Sparrows; Red-winged and Rusty Blackbirds; and American Goldfinch.

Common year-round residents include the Great Blue Heron; Black and Turkey Vultures; Red-shouldered Hawk; Mourning Dove; Barred Owl; Red-bellied, Downy, Hairy, and Pileated Woodpeckers; Northern Flicker; Blue Jay; American Crow; Carolina Chickadee; Tufted Titmouse; Carolina Wren; Northern Mockingbird; Brown Thrasher; Northern Cardinal; Rufous-sided Towhee; and Common Grackle.

The bay is relatively undisturbed by hu-

man activity except for a water hole or small pond which has been dug on the south side of the bay. This pond has water even in dry periods. In the fall and winter (or whenever the rest of the bay is dry) the pond is a focus of bird activity. Everything comes here to drink. Sit quietly for an hour at the edge of the pond during a dry spell, and you will see an amazing number of birds of most of the species listed above.

In spring and early summer, when the bay is flooded, the concentration of nesting Prothonotary Warblers is incredible. It is easy to have six to ten Prothonotaries in view at once. But also the mosquitoes can be very thick in the wet season, so be prepared for insects.

B-6—BARNWELL COUNTY

Barnwell County is a predominantly rural county in the Upper Coastal Plain, stretching from the Savannah River to the South Edisto River. The western third of the county is part of U.S. Department of Energy's Savannah River Site and is therefore

off-limits to casual bird watching. The rest of the county is typical Upper Coastal Plain farm country, with a mixture of cultivated fields, hayfields, pastures, loblolly-pine plantations, river-bottomland swamps, and floodplain forests.

B-6.1—Barnwell State Park and the Blackville Turf Farms

Winter   *
Spring   **
Summer *
Fall   **

See letters A and B on Map B-6.1.

Barnwell State Park (letter A on Map B-6.1) is on SC 3 about 2.5 miles south of the intersection of SC 3 and US 78 in Blackville, or about 7 miles north of the intersection of SC 3 and SC 70 in the town of Barnwell.

The park is small (307 acres), and like many South Carolina state parks it consists mostly of picnic and camping areas on the shore of a small lake. In the case of Barnwell State Park there are actually two lakes, a lower lake and an upper lake separated by a dike. A nature trail goes around the lower lake.

The best birding in the park is from the nature trail or in the floodplain forest below the dam of the lower lake. There is a bit of marsh along the edge of the lower lake where you can scare up a Common Yellowthroat at any time of the year or a Swamp Sparrow or two in the winter. Birding here is pleasant but unremarkable. You can expect species typical of southern pine-oak forest and perhaps a Pied-billed Grebe on the lake in winter or an Osprey in spring or fall.

For a change of pace from the state park, take an hour to visit the nearby agricultural areas, including the *Blackville turf farms* (letter B on Map B-6.1). From

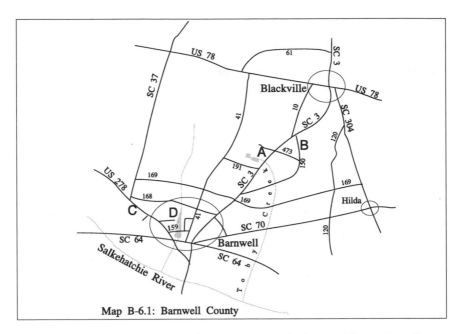

Map B-6.1: Barnwell County

the state park entrance road turn left (north) onto SC 3, and go 0.8 mile. Here SC 3 turns off to the right. (The road straight ahead becomes Road 10.) Keep on SC 3 for a few yards, then turn right onto Road 150. In less than a half mile Road 150 skirts the western edge of the best of the turf grass fields. Park on the shoulder, and overlook the broad fields with a telescope. During spring and fall migration look for migrant shorebirds, including both yellowlegs, Lesser Golden-Plover, and Upland Sandpiper. At any time of year you might find Killdeer, East-

ern Meadowlark, and Horned Lark. The Horned Larks are on the southern edge of their breeding range here.

Once you have looked over the main turf farm area, continue on Road 150, which rejoins SC 3 in about 2.9 miles. When you get to SC 3, you will be about 1.8 miles south of the entrance to Barnwell State Park. The route is through typical Upper Coastal Plain farmland, with a few pastures, weedy fields, and small turf farms as well.

B–6.2—Barnwell Airport Wildlife Management Area

Winter	**
Spring	**
Summer	*
Fall	**

See letter C on Map B–6.1.

Airports are well known to birders as good places to find open-field birds, but most airports are not very accessible to birders. Barnwell Airport is a pleasant exception to this generalization and offers

some of the best sparrow birding in the South Carolina Coastal Plain in winter.

To reach the *Barnwell Airport Wildlife Management Area* from the town of Barnwell, go northwest on US 278. About 0.8 mile beyond the intersection of US

278 and SC 64 you will pass the main entrance road for the airport on the left (south). About 0.2 mile beyond the entrance road you will pass an attractive cemetery (distinguished by a beautiful grove of longleaf-pine trees). Just past the cemetery look for a sign and an entrance road for Barnwell Airport Wildlife Management Area. (This entrance road is almost directly opposite the intersection of US 278 and SC 37.) Drive in on the entrance road as far as the locked gate, and proceed on foot. The wildlife management area is primarily a dove-hunting area. During the short dove season it is best left to the hunters, but for most of the year it is a great place to bird.

The present Barnwell Airport lies on a small part of a World War Two military airfield. Many of the old runways and taxi areas are partially overgrown with grasses (mostly broom sedge). The rest of the area is a delightful mixture of cultivated fields, weedy fields, hedgerows and briar thickets, loblolly-pine plantations, and pine-oak woods. The area covers several hundred acres. It is possible to walk for miles along old runways and abandoned roads. Be sure to keep clear of the active runways so that this great area will continue to be open to the public.

Birding is best here during the winter, when great numbers of sparrows are present. A visit to the area during the period from mid-November to mid-March will yield most of the following species:

Chipping, Field, and Savannah Sparrows (hundreds of each species), as well as good numbers of White-throated, Song, and Swamp Sparrows. Vesper Sparrows are here in small numbers. Other sparrow species may also be around. There is good habitat for wintering Grasshopper, LeConte's, and Henslow's Sparrows, but count yourself fortunate if you find these rarities.

Also here in winter are large numbers of American Pipits, a few Palm Warblers, Eastern Meadowlarks, Northern Mockingbirds, Brown Thrashers, House and Carolina Wrens, Loggerhead Shrikes, and other species typical of weedy fields and hedgerows. This is a good area for hawks. In winter you can expect numerous Red-tailed Hawks and American Kestrels, and an occasional Northern Harrier, Sharp-shinned Hawk, or Cooper's Hawk.

The Barnwell Airport area is good for sparrows, buntings, and the like during the breeding season as well. Chipping and Field Sparrows are common, as are Blue Grosbeaks and Indigo Buntings. With a bit of luck you might also find Bachman's Sparrows, Grasshopper Sparrows, and Painted Buntings. The habitat looks great for Dickcissel, but none have been found so far.

B—6.3—Lake Edgar Brown

Winter *
Spring **
Summer *
Fall **

See letter D on Map B—6.1.

Lake Edgar Brown is a hundred-acre lake within the city limits of the city of Barnwell. It is one of the South Carolina Wildlife and Marine Resources Department's state fishing lakes and is also a fairly good birding area.

From downtown Barnwell go northwest on US 278. In about 0.6 mile after the intersection with SC 64 (or, if you are coming from the northwest, 0.2 mile toward town from the entrance road to the Barnwell Airport), look for Road 159, Wellington Drive, on the east (right, as you leave town). Turn east onto Road 159, and go 0.4 mile to the lake. Park in the lot on the left just before Wellington Drive crosses the lake on a causeway.

The best way to bird Lake Edgar Brown is from the fishing dike, which runs north and south from Wellington Drive, paralleling the west shore of the lake and separating the lake into two unequal portions. The part of the lake east of the fishing dike is about a quarter mile wide and is relatively deep. The lake west of the fishing dike is narrow (little more than a canal) and very shallow.

Walk the fishing dike north for 0.7 mile to the north end of the lake. There is a cattail marsh along the dike, which varies from fifty to two hundred yards wide—a very unusual habitat for the Upper Coastal Plain of South Carolina. Check

the marsh for wintering Pied-billed Grebe, American Bittern (rare), Sora (fairly common), and Virginia Rail (rare). Wood Ducks and King Rails are present year-round but are seldom seen. From April through October keep an eye out for Least Bittern, which may breed here. The upper end of the marsh has standing dead trees, which are used year-round by Red-headed Woodpeckers.

The main body of the lake is usually birdless aside from a few Ring-billed Gulls in winter, but check it out for Buffleheads and other ducks (late fall and early spring).

B–7—BEAUFORT COUNTY

The city of Beaufort (pronounced "BYOU-firt"; the city of "BOE-firt" is in North Carolina) is a beautiful old port city with historic houses, live oaks, spanish moss, and lots of atmosphere—the essence of the South Carolina Low Country. Beaufort is also a busy industrial city and the seat of a major military base (Parris Island Marine Base and Beaufort Marine Air Corps Station). East and south of Beaufort are some of the most famous of South Carolina's Sea Islands: Hunting Island, Fripp Island, Hilton Head Island, and Daufuskie Island. Many of these islands are highly

developed resort areas, but it is still possible to find natural areas to explore.

Many areas covered briefly or not at all in this account are described in great detail in the book *Birder's Guide to Hilton Head Island and Low County*, compiled by Graham C. Dugas, Jr., and published by the Hilton Head Island Audubon Society P.O. Box 6185, Hilton Head Island, SC 29938 ($3.00). If you are planning a vacation at Hilton Head, this sixty-five-page book is a must.

B–7.1—Victoria Bluff Heritage Preserve

Winter	*
Spring	**
Summer	*
Fall	**

The 1,255 acres of *Victoria Bluff Preserve* protect a kind of habitat known as Florida scrub—flatwoods of slash- and longleaf-pine with saw-palmetto understory—alternating with wetter areas of almost impenetrable bay-swamp thickets and also a few higher areas with oaks and hickories. This type of woods is common in north Florida and south Georgia and just barely enters South Carolina in the extreme southern part of the state.

To reach the Victoria Bluff Preserve from I-95, leave the interstate at Exit 8, just north of Hardeeville, in Jasper County. Go east on Road 88 for 1.5 miles to a T-junction with Road 141. Here turn left (east), and continue for 7.5 miles to US 278—SC 170, in Beaufort County. Here turn right (south), and follow US 278 toward Hilton Head. In 3.4 miles US 278 makes a hard left turn (east), while SC 170 continues south. Keep on US 278 toward Hilton Head. In 7.7 miles turn left (north) onto Road 744.

Road 744 runs northward for 3.3 miles, finally ending at a public boat ramp on the Colleton River. The first two-thirds of Road 744 goes through the Victoria Bluff Preserve. There are numerous firebreak trails, mostly off to the right, which allow easy access on foot to the preserve. The boat launch at the end of the road gives a good view of the Colleton River and

brackish marshes along its border. Here look for gulls and terns year-round, and Common Loons, Horned Grebes, and a few ducks in winter.

Birding at Victoria Bluff is fair. You will find many of the common species of oak-pine forests. Fall is the best season for a wide variety of birds here, but you will find something of interest in any season. Be prepared for hordes of insects, even in winter.

B–7.2—Pinckney Island National Wildlife Refuge

Winter   **
Spring   ***
Summer ***
Fall   ***

Pinckney Island National Wildlife Refuge in one of a chain of refuges in coastal Georgia and adjacent South Carolina known as the Georgia Coastal Complex. Although Pinckney Island NWR is less well known than the Savannah NWR (see Section B-27.2), it is very accessible and offers good birding.

To reach Pinckney Island from I-95, follow the directions for Victoria Bluff Preserve (see Section B-7.1), but continue east toward Hilton Head. At about 10 miles east of the intersection of US 278 and SC 170 you will reach the salt water and cross a salt creek (Mackays Creek). You are now on Pinckney Island. The entrance to the refuge is on the left (north). If you get to the high bridge over the Intracoastal Waterway, you have gone too far.

Pinckney Island NWR consists of over four thousand acres of salt marsh, maritime forest, pine flatwoods, agricultural fields, brushy scrub, and freshwater ponds. This great diversity of habitats makes for excellent birding.

About two-thirds of the refuge is salt marsh or salt creek. As you drive along the entrance road, you will pass through a great salt marsh, with views of Mackays Creek to the west and Skull Creek to the east. Soon you will reach the parking lot in the midst of a beautiful grove of live oaks. There is a display and bulletin

board near the parking lot where you can pick up a refuge map and a bird checklist.

The main refuge road beyond the parking lot is closed to automobiles, so you will have to walk or ride a bicycle. The road goes for 2.5 miles to the ranger's residence. Several walking trails branch off from this central road, including a half-mile trail to White Point on Port Royal Sound at the extreme northern end of the island.

The best birding on the island is less than a mile from the parking lot, along the main refuge road. Here you will find Ibis Pond, which is the site of a major heronry. Here, in late spring and early summer, you will find several species of herons and egrets breeding. The Yellow-crowned Night-Heron is common here. In fact, this is probably the best place in South Carolina to observe this species breeding. Other species breeding in the heronry typically include Snowy Egret, Cattle Egret, Tricolored Heron, Little Blue Heron, and Black-crowned Night-Heron. The breeding herons are joined in summer by a few nonbreeding Wood Storks. Other species of interest here include Common Moorhen, White Ibis, and some large alligators. In winter you will still find a few egrets and perhaps a duck or two. Nineteen species of ducks have been found on the refuge.

The Painted Bunting Is a frequent summer resident of the island and is easily seen in late spring or early summer in brushy spots throughout the area. In fall and early winter look for warblers among the live oaks and in the brush. Yellow-rumped Warblers are abundant in winter, but you may also find six or seven other species of warbler: Orange-crowned Warbler, Yellow-throated Warbler, Pine Warbler, Palm Warbler, Black-and-white Warbler, and Common Yellowthroat. Keep an eye out for a rarity, especially in fall.

B–7.3—Hilton Head Island

Winter   **
Spring   **
Summer *
Fall   ***

Although Hilton Head is a heavily developed resort area, there are still quite a few good birding areas on the island. Two of the best (Sea Pine Forest Preserve and the Port Royal Mud Flats) are covered here.

The *Port Royal Mud Flats* is the name given to the flats that are exposed at the north end of Hilton Head Island *at low tide*, when they are well worth a visit. At high tide you will find few birds. To reach the flats from the high bridge over the Intracoastal Waterway, continue east on US 278 for four miles. Here turn left (north) onto Road 44, Beach City Road. Follow Beach City Road to its end and park. To your right (amidst the large live oaks) you will find an undeveloped trail to a jeep road. Follow the jeep road about two hundred yards to the beach.

Except in early summer the Port Royal Mud Flats provide feeding and loafing habitat for most of the herons, shorebirds, gulls, and terns of the South Carolina coast, but you will need a telescope (or a willingness to get your feet wet) to see them well. American Oystercatchers appear year-round, and this is a particularly good spot for wintering Marbled Godwits.

The other first-rate birding area on Hilton Head Island is the Sea Pines Forest Preserve. This 572-acre private wildlife preserve with over five miles of trails is an important part of Sea Pines Plantation, a development near the southwestern end of the island. Follow US 278 to its end at a large traffic circle. From the circle take Greenwood Drive west to the Sea Pines Plantation gate. (Visitors must pay a small fee here.) Continue 1.0 mile west to the main parking lot for the preserve. A trail map is available at the parking lot.

The preserve contains a marvelous mixture of swampy woods, marshes, small lakes, weedy fields, and pine plantations. This is a great birding spot all year round, but it is at its best during migration and in early winter. In addition to the common species of coast plains woods, be alert for rails, bitterns, and herons in the marshes and a few wintering ducks on the lakes. If you explore this area for a day, you can easily find fifty to seventy species of birds at any time of year—many more than that during spring or fall migration.

Winter	**
Spring	**
Summer	*
Fall	**

See Map B–7.1.

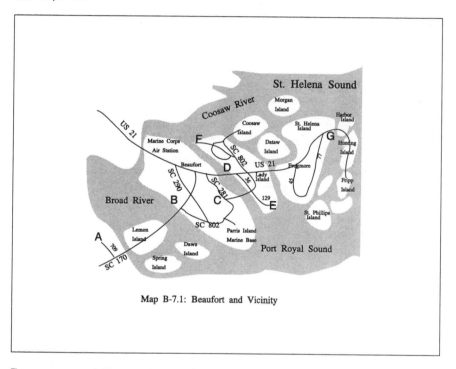

Map B-7.1: Beaufort and Vicinity

There are many fairly good birding spots in or near the city of Beaufort, since the city is built on a bluff above a tidal estuary (Beaufort River). We will mention a few of the more easily accessible, although other spots may be just as good. If you are in the area, get a map and do a bit of exploring. From downtown Beaufort go east on US 21 (Carteret Street) toward Hunting Island State Park. As you leave the city, you will cross the Beaufort River on Woods Memorial Bridge. There may be a gull or two on the bridge as well as a wintering or migrant Ruddy Turnstone. Immediately after crossing the bridge, look for the turnoff on your left for a boat landing on *Factory Creek* (letter D on Map B–7.1.), a branch of Beaufort

River. Here you can park and backtrack along the shoulder of the road to a point where you can overlook the salt marshes along the river as well as the river itself. At low tide sizable mud flats are exposed here. Look for shorebirds, including American Oystercatchers, on the flats, as well as cormorants, Brown Pelican, loons, grebes, and ducks in the river itself. This area can be good at low tide in migration or winter, or dull at high tide or in summer.

From Factory Creek continue east on US 21 (Sea Island Parkway) for 1.6 miles to the intersection with SC 802. Here turn left (north) onto SC 802, which soon merges with Sams Point Road. Go north on SC

802 for 2.4 miles. Here turn left (northwest) on Road 72 (Brickyard Point Road). Follow Road 72 for 6.2 miles to the boat launch area at *Brickyard Point* (letter F on Map B–7.1). From the public boat launch area you can overlook a good portion of Brickyard Creek and the Coosaw River. This is a good spot in winter to look for the Common and Red-throated Loon, Horned Grebe, Double-crested Cormorant, Brown Pelican, and a few ducks, especially Buffleheads, Lesser Scaup, Hooded Mergansers, and Red-breasted Mergansers.

From Brickyard Point retrace your route back to SC 802, and go south on SC 802. Soon you will cross US 21. At 1.5 miles south of US 21 turn left (southeast) onto *Island Causeway*, a paved county road that goes for about three miles to a dead end at a private development (letter E on Map B–7.1). Birding is good from the roadside along Island Causeway, which winds through salt marshes and maritime forest. This is all private property, so do not leave the roadside. Expect many of the birds of salt marshes and oak-pine woods.

When you get to the dead end, backtrack to SC 802, and turn left (south). You will soon cross over the Beaufort River on McTeer Memorial Bridge. In 1.6 miles from Island Causeway, SC 802 reaches a T-junction with SC 281 (Ribaut Road) in the city of Port Royal. Turn left (south) onto SC 281–802, and go just one short block. Here turn right (west) onto Waddell Road. Follow Waddell Road west to a T-junction at Battery Creek Road. You are now back in the city of Beaufort. Turn right onto Battery Creek Road, and immediately look for *Arthur Horne Nature Park* on your right (letter C on Map B–7.1). When you have finished exploring this small city park (good for migrants and wintering birds), go right (north) on Battery Creek Road, which winds it way back to SC 281 in about 2 miles. Once back at SC 281, you can return to the starting point of this tour (downtown Beaufort) by turning left (north) onto SC 281.

B–7.5—Broad River and Chechessee River Estuaries

Winter   **
Spring   ***
Summer **
Fall   ***

See Map B–7.1.

West of the city of Beaufort one encounters a series of broad tidal estuaries interspersed with salt marshes. Two of these (the Broad River and the Chechessee River) are fairly easily birded from land.

From US 21 on the north side of the city of Beaufort, go southwest on SC 170 toward Hilton Head Island. In 5.0 miles you will reach the marshes along the Broad River. This tidal estuary is really the continuation of the Coosawhatchie River and is not at all connected to the Broad River of the South Carolina Piedmont.

Just before the SC 170 bridge over the Broad River (Edward Rogers Burton Bridge), turn off to the right, and park at *Broad River Landing* (letter B on Map B–7.1). A public fishing pier here provides an excellent platform from which to overlook the estuary. This area is good from fall through spring for Brown Pelicans, gulls, terns, loons, and ducks. Rarities seen here include the Surf Scoter. If the tide is right, you might encounter hundreds of terns feeding on bait fish in the estuary. Just about any gull or tern species in South Carolina might show up here.

The back side of the parking lot borders a salt marsh where you might find any of the birds typical of South Carolina salt marsh without getting your feet wet!

When you are done at Broad River Landing, return to SC 170, and continue west across the bridge. Here the road traverses *Lemon Island*, which is currently

(1992) relatively undeveloped. The sand flats and salt creeks along the highway on Lemon Island harbor hundreds of shorebirds at high tide. Wilson's Plovers, American Oystercatchers, and Willets breed here and are joined during most of the year by many species of migrant or wintering shorebirds, including numerous Dunlin, Short-billed Dowitchers, Black-bellied Plovers, and Whimbrels.

In about a mile SC 170 leaves Lemon Island and crosses the Chechessee River, a much smaller tidal estuary than the Broad River. Just west of the bridge over the Chechessee look for Road 709 to the right (north). This half-mile-long road leads through the salt marsh to *Red Bluff Island* (letter A on Map B—7.1), a small pine island with many vacation homes. There are often hundreds of shorebirds in the marshes and sand flats along Road 709. Since this is a dead-end road, the traffic is much less than that on SC 170. Keep in mind that Red Bluff Island is private property. Only the public road to the island is of particular interest to the birder.

B—7.6—Hunting Island State Park

Winter	**
Spring	***
Summer	**
Fall	***

See Map B—7.1.

To reach *Hunting Island State Park* from downtown Beaufort, go east on US 21 for 18 miles to the main park entrance on the left.

The birding starts along US 21 before you get to the state park. About 7 miles east of Frogmore (known to the post office as St. Helena Island) US 21 emerges onto a causeway through a broad salt marsh, leading up to a bridge over a salt creek known as Harbor River. Just before you get to the bridge over Harbor River, look for a boat ramp in a small county park on the right (south) side of US 21. This is *Butch's Island* (letter G on Map B—7.1). At high tide there are often hundreds of shorebirds here as well as the usual species of the salt marsh. At low tide the birds scatter, and you won't see much.

After checking out the shorebirds at Butch's Island, continue east on US 21 to the state park.

Hunting Island State Park consists of about five thousand acres of beach, dunes, salt marsh, salt creek, and maritime forest. It is the most popular South Carolina state park, crowded in summer and busy even in the dead of winter. Despite the crowds, Hunting Island State Park is an excellent birding area well worth a visit any time of year.

There are several good birding areas in the park. We will cover four general areas in this account: the lighthouse to Johnson Creek Inlet; the lagoon and Fripp Inlet; the Marsh Boardwalk Trail; and the fishing pier.

(1) To reach the lighthouse, use the main park entrance, and follow the signs to the lighthouse or North Beach parking lot. Park near the lighthouse, and look for the beginning of the *Lighthouse Trail*, a one-mile trail that begins at the edge of the parking lot on the far (north) side of the lighthouse. This trail goes to the beach through a thicket and brushy slough. This swampy slough is great for birds, especially in migration. In winter this swampy area will be overrun with hundreds of Yellow-rumped Warblers. In spring or fall migration look for migrant land birds. This is an excellent place to observe warblers in migration. The Northern Waterthrush is especially fond of this swamp.

Once you come to the beach, turn left and follow the beach northward to *Johnson Creek Inlet*. Along the way you will encounter a large freshwater marsh which is good for migrant rails (Sora, Virginia Rail, and King Rail) and breeding

Least Bitterns. In summer Painted Buntings are common in the brushy thickets just inland from the dunes. Keep in mind how fragile the dunes are, and walk only along the beach.

In about a mile you will reach Johnson Creek Inlet. This is good place for shorebirds, especially on the sandbars and tidal flats on the other side of the creek. With a good telescope you will be able to pick out numerous species of gulls, terns, sandpipers, and plovers. The Black Skimmer is common here, and sometimes American Oystercatchers winter here by the hundreds. After you have checked out the inlet, backtrack to the lighthouse parking lot. If you are camping, you will find that Johnson Creek Inlet is close to the campground and that the freshwater marsh is south along the beach from the campground.

(2) To reach *the lagoon* and *Fripp Inlet,* go to the main park entrance, and follow the sign for the cabin area. The road to the cabins leads past the east side of the lagoon, a former salt creek which has been dredged out for better fishing. The lagoon is usually better for fishing than birding, but you can sometimes find a few birds here such as Red-breasted Merganser, Brown Pelican, and a few shorebirds. Follow the road all the way to the end, past all the cabins, and park at the end. From here you can overlook another part of the Lagoon and explore the live oak and cabbage palmetto woods.

After checking out the lagoon, backtrack on foot along the road for a few yards to a point where you can get to the salt marsh and sand flats along the north side of Fripp Inlet. Here you will find a few shorebirds, gulls, terns, and perhaps other species.

(3) The third good birding spot in the park is the *Marsh Boardwalk.* To reach the boardwalk parking lot, do not enter the main park road, but rather continue south on the road to Fripp Island. You will find two pulloffs to the right. The first leads to an overlook of the salt marshes along Johnson Creek. The second pulloff leads to the parking lot for the Marsh Boardwalk Trail. (If you get to the private bridge leading to Fripp Island, you have gone too far.)

The Marsh Boardwalk Trail consists of a boardwalk over the marsh; it leads to a small pine-and palmetto-covered island. This is an excellent place from which to study the salt marsh without getting your feet muddy. Look and listen for the common birds of the salt marsh: Clapper Rail, Marsh Wren, and Seaside Sparrow as well as numerous herons, egrets, gulls, and terns. The pine island is great for Yellow-rumped Warblers in winter and a few migrants in the fall.

(4) The fourth good birding spot in the park is *the fishing pier,* which juts 1,120 feet out into Fripp Inlet. This is a great place to sit and wait for the birds to come to you, especially when the tide is going out or at sunset. To reach the pier, follow the road toward Fripp Island. Just before the private bridge over Fripp Inlet turn left toward the ocean, and follow the fishing pier entrance road a few dozen yards to the parking lot. This pier is run by a private concessionaire, and there may be a small entrance fee.

B–8—BERKELEY COUNTY

Berkeley County is a large county on the Lower Coastal Plain, just inland from Charleston County. At present (1992) it is still mostly rural, but it is rapidly growing in population as the Charleston metropolitan area grows.

Strictly speaking, Berkeley County is not a coastal county, although the rivers flowing out of the county (the Santee, the Cooper, and the Wando) are influenced by the tides and may be somewhat brackish (especially the Wando).

Berkeley County has great opportunities for the birder. Most of the eastern half of the county lies within Francis Marion National Forest (which spills over into Charleston County—see Section B-10). Birders from all over the world come here to see the specialties of the pine forests of the southeastern United States: Brown-headed Nuthatch, Pine Warbler, Bachman's Sparrow, and Red-cockaded Woodpecker. All of these species are permanent residents of Francis Marion National Forest.

In addition to the pine forests, Berkeley County has a long stretch of the flood-plain of the Santee River. This is kite country. From mid-April until mid-August the Mississippi Kite is common, and the American Swallow-tailed Kite occurs in small numbers here near the northern edge of its breeding range.

Rounding out the picture are two large artificial lakes—Lake Marion and Lake Moultrie, South Carolina's inland seas. All of Lake Moultrie and the eastern third of Lake Marion fall within Berkeley County. Thus the county has a great variety of habitats for birds, many of which are on public lands; this is a birder's paradise.

B–8.1—Cainhoy

Winter	**
Spring	**
Summer	**
Fall	**

See letters G and H on Map B–10.1 (p. 55).

Cainhoy is a community on the Wando River, in the southeastern part of Berkeley County. The combination of tidal river, mature pine forest, and marshy ponds makes this area an excellent birding destination all year round. From the end of I-26 In Charleston go north on US 17 for 11 miles to the intersection with SC 41. Turn left (north) onto SC 41. In 4.7 miles you will enter Berkeley County just before you get to the bridge over the *Wando River*. There is a boat launch area on the right where you can park and overlook the river (letter G on Map B–10.1).

The Wando here is tidal but fresh (or only slightly brackish). In winter look for loons, grebes, and waterfowl. Expect Double-crested Cormorants, Anhingas, herons, and gulls anytime.

To continue the tour, cross the Wando River on SC 41. About 2.5 miles north of the river turn right (east) onto Forest Road 183 (*Hoover Road*; see letter H on Map B–10.1). This road goes about three miles through well-managed pine forest. Since there are several active Red-cockaded Woodpecker cavity trees along this stretch, this is an excellent area to find this endangered woodpecker as well as all of the other South Carolina wood-peckers. Bachman's Sparrows are common residents of the open pine forest but are difficult to find when they are not singing. The sparrows' song season lasts from mid-March until early September. Other species commonly seen along Hoover Road include Wild Turkey, Brown-headed Nuthatch, and Pine Warbler. Keep an eye out for Cooper's Hawk, which nests in the neighborhood and is a permanent resident.

In about 3 miles Forest Road 183 ends at a T-junction with a paved road (Road 598). Turn left (north) onto Road 598, which goes 7.2 miles before it ends at SC 41. In about two miles from Forest Road 183 you will reach a bridge over the upper end of a small pond. From this bridge you can overlook the pond, which is a good spot for marsh species, such as Anhinga, Little Blue Heron, White Ibis, Osprey, and Common Moorhen.

When you reach SC 41, you have a choice. To return to Cainhoy and US 17, turn left (south). There are several Red-cockaded Woodpecker colonies along SC 41 before you reach Cainhoy and the

Wando River. To reach the community of Huger and explore another part of the Francis Marion National Forest, turn right. (See Section B-8.2 for details.)

B–8.2—Witherbee Road, Francis Marion National Forest

Winter   *
Spring   **
Summer *
Fall   **

This tour of the Francis Marion National Forest starts at the intersection of SC 41 and SC 402 in Huger (pronounced "YOU-jee"). This intersection is 17 miles north of US 17, along SC 41.

Go north on SC 402 past the Huger Recreation Area (camping, boat launching). At 2.9 miles from SC 41 turn off to the right onto Road 125. Follow Road 125 north for 2.2 miles to a T-junction. Here turn left, and go just 0.2 mile, where you will turn right (northwest) onto Road 171, *Witherbee Road*. This road soon crosses a railroad track. Just beyond the railroad track look for a pond on the right. This is Little Hellhole Reserve, which may harbor a Wood Duck or a Little Blue Heron.

Witherbee Road is a great place for the species typical of old-growth pine forests.

Red-cockaded Woodpeckers are fairly common here, as are all other South Carolina woodpeckers and other species of the pine forest. Check for summering American Kestrels in dead trees standing in clear-cut areas. The bay-swamp thickets along the creeks harbor breeding Swainson's Warblers. Bachman's Sparrow and Wild Turkey are both common along Witherbee Road.

About 1.5 miles beyond Little Hellhole Reserve look for Forest Road 130 on the left. Turn left here, and then turn right onto Forest Road 130-C in about two miles. Forest Road 130-C loops back to Road 171 (Witherbee Road). Here turn left onto Road 171, and go another three miles to SC 402, just southeast of Moncks Corner. At SC 402 turn left to return to the start of the tour in Huger.

B–8.3—Guilliard Lake, Francis Marion National Forest

Winter   *
Spring   **
Summer **
Fall   **

To reach *Guilliard Lake Scenic Area*, go west from SC 45 on Forest Road 150. This turnoff is 4 miles south of US 17-A in Jamestown or 16 miles north of US 17 in Mc-Clellanville. Follow Road 150 east for three miles to the entrance road for the Scenic Area, on the left (north). This road leads to a campground on the shore of Guilliard Lake, an oxbow lake of the nearby Santee River.

The woods near the campground have most of the common species of coastal plain floodplain forest. Look for American Swallow-tailed Kites in summer. There is no trail to speak of, but you can explore the area a bit by following fishermen's paths or by backtracking along the entrance road. Look for kites in summer anywhere you can see a bit of the sky.

B—8.4—Sandy Beach Waterfowl Area

Winter   *
Spring   **
Summer **
Fall   **

Sandy Beach Waterfowl Area is a medium-sized duck management area (several hundred acres) on the north shore of Lake Moultrie. Sandy Beach consists of freshwater impoundments, marshes, and pine flatwoods. It is adjacent to the North Dike Unit of Moultrie Wildlife Management Area. Moultrie WMA consists of 8,093 acres of pine flatwoods, swampy hardwood forest, dikes, and canals along the north shore of Lake Moultrie.

To reach Sandy Beach Waterfowl Area from the east or south (Charleston or McClellanville), go to the intersection of US 52 and SC 45 in the town of St. Stephen. Head west on SC 45 toward the Santee Dam. At 8.9 miles west of US 52 look for the Pineville Lookout Tower on the right (north). The entrance road for Sandy Beach Waterfowl Area is directly opposite the tower.

Coming from the north on US 52, cross the Santee River from Williamsburg County (see Section B-45). At 4.0 miles south of the bridge, US 52 makes a sweeping turn to the left. This is also the intersection with Road 6. Turn right onto Road 6, and keep to the right to remain on Road 6. This road will intersect with SC 45 in the village of Pineville. Turn right (west) onto SC 45, and follow it for 2.9 miles to the Pineville Lookout Tower (on the right). The entrance road to Sandy Beach is opposite the tower.

Coming from the west, take SC 6 or SC 45 to the point where SC 45 splits off from SC 6. Stay on SC 45, which soon crosses the canal that links Lake Marion with Lake Moultrie. From this point continue east on SC 45 for about 7 miles, until you reach the Pineville Lookout Tower, on the left (north) side of SC 45. The entrance road to Sandy Beach is directly opposite the tower.

Drive south along the sand entrance road. In 2.4 miles you will reach a dike (the main dike along the north shore of Lake Moultrie). Park just before the dike, and continue on foot. The land along the dike is part of the North Dike Unit of Moultrie Wildlife Management Area. This area is mostly pine flatwoods with thick undergrowth, interspersed with swampy hardwoods in low spots.

Just north of the dike is a wet power line right-of-way, which might be worth exploring in winter for sparrows, including the elusive Henslow's Sparrow. (For a better spot for Henslow's Sparrow, see Section B-8.5.)

Once you have reached the dike, you are about ten minutes' walk north of the edge of *Sandy Beach Waterfowl Area.* Be advised that the waterfowl area is closed (except by special permit) from November 1 until March 1, so this is not an area to visit in winter in hopes of seeing ducks. At other times of the year, cross the dike on the service road and walk south. The service road goes through wet woods which are good for breeding Swainson's Warbler (mid-April through early September). These wet areas also allow mosquitoes to breed, so bring along plenty of repellent.

In about a half mile you will reach the waterfowl area, marked by a sign. From March 1 through the end of October you may walk beyond the sign. Here the road becomes a causeway between a large marsh on the left and an even larger freshwater impoundment on the right. Here you can expect species such as Pied-billed Grebe; Double-crested Cormorant; Anhinga; Least Bittern (rare); Great Blue Heron, Great and Snowy Egret; Tricolored Heron; Cattle Egret; Green-backed Heron; White Ibis; Wood Duck; Mallard; Common Moorhen; American Coot; Killdeer; Forster's Tern; and other species common to freshwater marshes. The service road eventually ends at Lake Moultrie. There are various side trails that you might explore.

Sandy Beach Waterfowl Area is almost never birded, so there is no list of rarities that have been found here. But there is a lot of good habitat, especially for marsh species. When you are done exploring, backtrack to the parking area along the dike.

B–8.5—The Santee Dam (South Side)

Winter **
Spring **
Summer *
Fall **

To reach the *south side of the Santee Dam* from the north, east, or south, first follow the directions to the Pineville Lookout Tower (given at the beginning of Section B-8.6). From the tower continue west on SC 45 for 3.6 miles to the turnoff for Road 31, on the right. Turn onto Road 31, and follow it to its end. Road 31 takes a hard right turn in 1.7 miles, then continues for 2.8 miles to an informal parking area near the dam.

To reach the south side of Santee Dam from the west, take SC 6 or SC 45 to the point where SC 45 splits off to the left. Keep left on SC 45 for 3.0 miles beyond the split. (This takes you over the canal that connects Lake Marion with Lake Moultrie). Look for Road 708 to the left. Follow Road 708 for 0.4 mile to a T-junction with Road 23. Turn left onto Road 23 for about 0.5 mile, to Road 31. Turn left onto Road 31, and follow it to its end (being careful to remain on Road 31 at the point where it turns sharply to the right). There is an informal parking area at the end of Road 31.

From the parking area you can overlook Santee Dam and the floodplain of the Santee River below the dam. This is a good lookout from which to observe hawks, including Mississippi Kites in the late spring and early summer.

Winter is the best season to visit this area, because that is when its specialty bird, the Henslow's Sparrow, may be found. From late October until early April one or more Henslow's Sparrows can sometimes be found along the power line right-of-way that you pass under just before you reach the end of Road 31. From the end of the road backtrack a few hundred yards to the right-of-way, and explore it to the east, away from the dam.

As you walk along, you will flush numerous sparrows. Most will be Savannah, Swamp, and Song Sparrows, but keep an eye out for an elusive olive-colored sparrow. With luck you will flush it into a bush, where you can observe it at leisure. After a hundred or so Savannah Sparrows you may be lucky enough to find one Henslow's. Other good sparrow species to be alert for here are Grasshopper Sparrow (perhaps more common than Henslow's) and LeConte's Sparrow. LeConte's Sparrow has not yet been found here, but the habitat is similar to its wintering habitat in north Florida and Louisiana, so be alert to the possibility. Henslow's, LeConte's, and Grasshopper Sparrow are not easy to find, and you must be prepared for failure. But there is a reasonable chance. Birders, like anglers, are eternally optimistic.

B—8.6—Cypress Gardens

Winter   *
Spring   **
Summer **
Fall   **

Cypress Gardens is a 162-acre public garden and natural area best known for its azalea displays in early spring. It is also a fairly good birding locale, especially for species of cypress swamps. A walk around the garden's main trail in late spring or early summer will yield species typical of cypress swamps, such as Prothonotary Warbler, Northern Parula, and Yellow-throated Warbler. Swainson's Warblers breed in the dense vegetation at the far end of the property (not in the cypress swamp). Other species of interest include herons (especially Green-backed Heron, Little Blue Heron and Yellow-crowned Night-Heron) and woodpeckers (especially Red-bellied and Pileated).

To reach Cypress Gardens from I-26, leave at Exit 208, and get onto US 52 north, toward Moncks Corner. After about 8 miles turn right (east) onto Cypress Gardens Road, and follow the signs to the gardens. An admission fee is charged.

Cypress Gardens was severely damaged by Hurricane Hugo in 1989. Most of the large pine and oak trees were blown down, but most of the bald-cypress trees survived. The area is now much more open to the sky than before the hurricane, but it is still a good birding spot.

B—8.7—Old Santee Canal State Park

Winter   *
Spring   **
Summer *
Fall   **

Old Santee Canal State Park is one of the newest of South Carolina's state parks, having opened in July 1989, but it promises to be a fairly good bird-finding area. This historic park preserves part of the Santee Canal (in operation from 1800 through about 1850), one of the first such canals in the United States.

The park is on the south side of the city of Moncks Corner (the seat of Berkeley County) along the east bank of the modern Tail Race Canal that connects Lake Moultrie to the Cooper River. To reach the park, go to the junction of US 52 and US 17-A in Moncks Corner. Here follow US 52—17A northeast toward Kingstree or Georgetown. At 0.6 mile from the junction turn sharply right onto bypass road P-0801, Rembert C. Dennis Boulevard. Go 1.0 mile southwest on Dennis Boulevard to the entrance road of the park, on the left (southeast). Follow the entrance road for about a mile to the parking lot.

The park has about three miles of excellent trails, including several boardwalks. The trails lead roughly northwest from the Stony Landing House (the main house of the old Stony Landing Plantation). You will have the choice of walking along the banks of the new Tail Race Canal or through the woods and swamps of Biggin Creek. Several boardwalks lead to wildlife observation points where you can observe breeding Ospreys, Little Blue Herons, and perhaps an alligator or two. There is a canoe rental point at the far end of the foot trail, where you can take a canoe for a ride on a restored portion of the old canal.

Do not neglect the open fields and live-oak areas near the parking lot. These should be good for migrants and wintering warblers and sparrows. Painted Bunting breed in the brush along the entrance road. Mississippi Kites breed nearby (in suburban neighborhoods of

45

Moncks Corner), so keep an eye out for this species (late April through August).

Old Santee State Park is too new to have a list of rarities sighted, but the habitat looks good, and you should be able to find lots of birds there at any time of the year.

The park was heavily damaged by Hurricane Hugo in September 1989. Most large trees were blown down, and the boardwalks, which had just opened a few months before, were largely destroyed by falling timber. The park has reopened, however, and the boardwalks have been rebuilt.

B–9—CALHOUN COUNTY

Calhoun County is a rural county about forty miles southeast of Columbia. Thousands of travelers pass through the county on I-26. Those who leave the interstate are treated to a delightful ride through the gentle wooded hills of the western part of the county (which is in the Sandhills subregion of the Upper Coastal Plain) or the farm country of the eastern part of the county (which lies in the flatter part of the Upper Coastal Plain). The county seat of St. Matthews calls itself the Purple Martin Capital. From mid-March through August birders will

find hundreds of Purple Martins in and around St. Matthews.

Calhoun County is usually visited by birders who are en route to other destinations such as Santee National Wildlife Refuge in nearby Clarendon County (see Section B-14) or Congaree Swamp National Monument in Richland County (see Section B-40). For this reason two tours are detailed here, one in the Sandhills and one in the Upper Coastal Plain. Almost all of Calhoun County is private property, so birding should be done from the roadside.

B–9.1—A Calhoun County Sandhills Tour

Winter   **
Spring   **
Summer   *
Fall   **

See Map B–9.1.

The northwestern part of Calhoun County lies in the Sandhills subregion, that mysterious part of the Upper Coastal Plain which lies between the flat lands of the true Coastal Plain and the Piedmont. The Sandhills are a remnant of ancient beach dunes now stranded a hundred miles inland from the sea. The Sandhills of Calhoun County have been completely altered by human activity. The great longleaf-pine forest is gone, but in its place is a fascinating mixture of farmlands, pine plantations, and swampy floodplains along creeks—all set in a hilly landscape that seems more like parts of the Piedmont than the Coastal Plain.

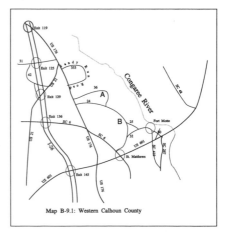

Map B-9.1: Western Calhoun County

B–9—Calhoun County

The following tour gives you a laid-back alternative to driving on I-26 from the Columbia area to the edge of the flat parts of the Upper Coastal Plain at US 601. From US 601 the tour continues as described in the next section (Section B-9.2).

From I-26 eastbound get off at Exit 119 in Lexington County. (This is the end of the Old State Road tour, described in Section B-32.7.) Go south on US 21—US 176. You will soon pass the entrance of the Carolina Eastman plant and begin driving through the farm country of the community of Sandy Run in Calhoun County. At 7.8 miles from I-26, US 21 turns off to the right. Keep straight ahead on US 176. US 176 passes an interesting farm pond on the left and then crosses a small creek (Sandy Run). At 0.8 mile south of the turn-off of US 21, which is immediately after crossing Sandy Run, turn left onto Road 353, Sandy Run Road. This road loops clockwise for 5.6 miles before rejoining US 176. Along the way are some interesting clear-cut areas, where you might spot a Red-headed Woodpecker. Road 353 comes close to the Congaree River (near the Teepak plant, a small chemical factory), so be alert for Mississippi Kites in summer along this stretch. In fact this entire tour route is great for hawks, including Broad-winged Hawks in summer, American Kestrels in winter, and Red-tailed and Red-shouldered Hawks year-round.

Once back at the T-junction with US 176, turn left (southeast) onto US 176. In about two miles you will pass over Big Beaver Creek. There is a large pond on the right (west) here, where you might be able to spy a Wood Duck or two. The wooded hills here are attractive to summering Broad-winged Hawks.

From Big Beaver Creek continue southeast on US 176. In about another 1.5 miles turn left onto the first secondary road, Road 36. This road loops clockwise for 5.0 miles. Along the way it passes by

Geigers Pond, a large millpond on the right side of the road. (See letter A on Map B–9.1.) This is a good spot for migrating ducks and in summer Wood Ducks or Mississippi Kites.

When Road 36 ends at a T-junction, turn left onto Road 24, and drive through an area of small farms and pine plantations. At 4.8 miles from Road 36, Road 24 crosses *Bates Mill Creek*, just before a small church (Mount Carmel Church). (See letter B on Map B–9.1.) The floodplain woods along this creek are great for birds, including breeding Louisiana Waterthrush. Just past the church turn left onto Road 25, which ends in 1.5 miles at a T-junction. Here turn left (still Road 25; to the right is Road 32). Road 25 becomes SC 419 in about three miles, when you enter the historic old village of Fort Motte, site of a skirmish between British and American troops on May 12, 1781. If you follow the unpaved road along the railroad to the left (north), you will reach the Congaree River floodplain in about 2 miles. This is a great place for Mississippi Kites in summer.

To continue the tour, take SC 419 east. At 1.1 miles from the railroad tracks in Fort Motte, turn left onto Road 80. Road 80 leads through an area of large, open fields. Horned Larks are found in these fields year-round and are joined in summer by a few Grasshopper Sparrows. About here you leave the Sandhills and enter the true Upper Coastal Plain.

In 1.6 miles Road 80 reaches US 601 directly opposite the intersection of US 601 and SC 267. If you go left onto US 601, you will reach the bridge over the Congaree River, the starting point for the tour described in the next section, or you may wish to pick up that tour here, at the intersection of US 601 and SC 267 (see Section B-9.2). To return to I-26, turn right onto US 601, and follow it for about 17 miles to Exit 145 near Orangeburg.

B–9.2—A Calhoun County Farmlands Tour

Winter   **
Spring   **
Summer *
Fall   **

See Map B–9.2.

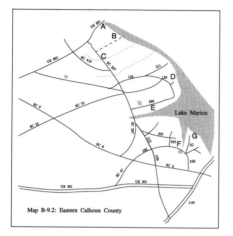

Map B-9.2: Eastern Calhoun County

This tour is designed to lead you through typical Upper Coastal Plain farm country as you travel from the Congaree Swamp in Richland County to the birding areas around Lake Marion (such as Santee State Park, in Orangeburg County, or Santee National Wildlife Refuge, in Clarendon County). The tour works equally well in either direction. Road and birding details will be given first for those going west to east; then for those going east to west, just so you won't have to follow directions backward.

The tour begins at the south end of the *US 601 bridge over the Congaree River,* at the Richland County—Calhoun County line (letter A on Map B–9.2). (See Section B-40 for details about Richland County). After crossing the bridge from Richland County, pull over onto the shoulder of the road, and walk back to the bridge. From this point you can overlook a huge portion of the floodplain forest along the Congaree River, because the Calhoun (or south) side of the Congaree is bordered by a high bluff ranging from forty to two hundred feet above the river.

There is little or no swamp along the Congaree or Santee Rivers in Calhoun County because of this high bluff.

Watch for birds soaring over the swamp. You might see a Red-shouldered Hawk or a Great Blue Heron anytime, but the best time to watch is in late summer (July or August), when you may also see Anhinga, White Ibis, Wood Stork (rare), Mississippi Kite (common), American Swallow-tailed Kite (rare), and hundreds of Chimney Swifts, which nest in hollow trees in the swamp.

From the bridge go south on US 601 for 2.0 miles to the first paved crossroads. Here turn left (east) onto SC 267. (This is the *eastern end of the Calhoun County Sandhills tour,* described in Section B-9.1.) The habitat here is broad croplands with hedgerows and small woodlots, a few pecan groves, and a few small pine plantations. This is a good area to see common birds of the open county. If you pass through this area at night, be alert for Barn Owls. These magnificent raptors thrive in farm country such as this. In the daytime you will see species such as Eastern Bluebird (abundant), Loggerhead Shrike (fairly common), Northern Mockingbird, Brown Thrasher, and Eastern Meadowlark. These permanent residents are joined in winter by large numbers of hawks (mostly Red-tailed Hawk, American Kestrel, and Northern Harrier), as well as American Pipit, Palm Warbler, and sparrows, including Savannah and Vesper. Common summer residents include the Purple Martin, Barn and Northern Rough-winged Swallow, Fish Crow, Eastern Kingbird, and Orchard Oriole. Rare breeders to hope for include Dickcissel and Horned Lark.

At 1.0 mile from US 601 look for a sign indicating the side road to *Trevezant Landing* (letter B on Map B–9.2). If the weather has been dry, you may wish to turn left (north) along this road and follow it a mile or so to a boat-launching ramp on the Santee River. The road becomes difficult in wet weather and is not recommended. If you take the side trip, you will cross open fields for a half mile or so, then enter a cutover area. Red-headed Woodpeckers are sometimes found in dead trees here, especially in the woods to the right of the road. After about a half mile of oak-pine-hickory woods you will reach the bluff, more than one hundred feet above the Santee River. The road descends rather steeply to the riverside. Do not attempt this descent unless the road is dry, or you may not get back up again in your car. If in doubt, park at the top (there is a small, informal parking area at the top of the bluff), and walk down. Like the US 601 bridge, this bluff provides an excellent lookout for watching birds fly up and down the river. The advantage here is that you won't have to dodge huge trucks zipping along at sixty-five miles an hour.

If you go to Trevezant Landing, return to SC 267 to resume the tour. Continue east on SC 267. At about 3 miles from US 601 the road descends slightly to the bridge over *Squirrel Creek* (letter C on Map B–9.2). The shoulder of the road near the bridge is narrow, but if you go up the hill a few yards, you can usually find a place to pull off. Be sure to park completely off the road, since SC 267 is heavily used by people going to and from Lake Marion.

The prime attraction at Squirrel Creek is the huge bamboo grove along the creek, on the south side of the road. From the bridge you can hear the songs of warblers that breed in this bamboo or along the creek—Hooded and Swainson's Warbler, and also Louisiana Waterthrush. The songs of these species are quite similar, so you can have a bit of practice in separating them in the field.

To continue the tour, follow SC 267 east from Squirrel Creek. At 4.3 miles from US 601 you will pass SC 419 on the right. At 4.9 miles you will descend to another creek, Warley Creek. This is a good birding spot, but it is difficult to find a parking spot here. There is one spot about a hundred yards beyond the bridge, on the

right. Be careful, and do not stop if you cannot park completely off the road. The best birds at Warley Creek are Red-headed and Hairy Woodpeckers (year-round), and a good variety of common warblers, vireos, and Summer Tanager in the breeding season.

From Warley Creek continue on SC 267 east to the intersection with Road 129. This intersection is 6.2 miles from US 601, just beyond St. Marks Church. Look for a sign for the *Low Falls Landing* boat ramp. Turn left (north) onto Road 129. Follow Road 129 toward Low Falls Landing. In 0.6 mile (6.8 miles from US 601) the road to Low Falls Landing turns hard to the right. Straight ahead is Road 221. Go a few yards straight ahead on Road 221 and park. The woods here are good for Hairy Woodpecker (year-round), and Summer Tanager, Wood Thrush, and Eastern Wood-Pewee in the breeding season.

To continue the tour, return to Road 129. At 8.5 miles from US 601 you will reach a stop sign. Turn left to continue on Road 129. At 10.3 miles from US 601 you will reach the intersection with Road 286, which comes in from the right. This is where you want to go to continue the tour, but in the meantime go 0.2 mile farther on Road 129 to *Low Falls Landing* (letter D on Map B–9.2). This boat launch area is popular with anglers, and there are usually no birds. If you are lucky, you may spot a Pied-billed Grebe in the lake (Lake Marion), or a Double-crested Cormorant or Anhinga drying its wings in a tree on the opposite shore.

To continue the tour, return to the intersection of Roads 129 and 286 (10.7 miles from US 601). Turn left onto Road 286 (the road you did not come in on). This leads through a delightful wooded area great for woodpeckers, including Northern Flicker. At about 2.3 miles from Road 129 (13.0 miles from US 601) look for a grove of longleaf pines on the left (letter E on Map B–9.2). Park on the shoulder, and examine this grove. Pine Warbler, Brown-headed Nuthatch, and Red-headed Woodpecker are common here, and there used to be a family of Red-cockaded Woodpeckers here, but the birds' habitat was destroyed by Hurricane Hugo in 1989, and they have not been seen since.

After trying for the Red-cockaded Woodpeckers, continue ahead on Road 286. At 13.5 miles from US 601 look for a small pond on the right, where there is often an Anhinga in summer. At 14.0 miles you will reach a T-junction with SC 267. If you wish to return to US 601, turn right here. To continue the tour, turn left (east) onto SC 267.

At 15.2 miles from US 601, turn left onto Road 203. After turning, keep an eye out for the Loggerhead Shrike that lives in this area. Soon you will pass through a small peach orchard. This is a good area for Vesper Sparrow in winter. Continue east on Road 203. At 16.4 miles from US 601, Road 203 becomes narrower, and Road 215 goes off to the right. To continue the tour, be sure to keep straight on Road 203.

At 18.9 miles from US 601 turn right onto Road 563 in Orangeburg County. (If you miss this turn, you will come to a dead end in 1.1 miles. Turn around and come back to Road 563.) The rest of the tour is in Orangeburg County (see Section B-38) but is covered here for the sake of completeness. At 19.6 miles from US 601 you will reach a T-junction. Turn left (east) onto Road 105. After about a mile on Road 105 you will be going through a beautiful longleaf-pine forest, which the landowner maintains with controlled burns. There used to be a family of Red-cockaded Woodpeckers near the road in this area (letter F on Map B—9.2), but they were apparently wiped out by Hurricane Hugo. The woods have breeding Bachman's Sparrows, which may be heard singing from early April until September. Confine your birding to the roadside. Hopefully this land will not be cut over, since it is the best longleaf-pine forest in Orangeburg County.

To continue the tour, go east on Road 105. At 20.6 miles from US 601 you will cross over Big Poplar Creek. There is a great millpond on the right. The signs here indicate, "No Parking," but you can usually pull over onto the shoulder for a minute or two to scan the millpond. Com-

mon Moorhens are permanent residents here, as are Pied-billed Grebes and Wood Ducks. In summer look for herons, especially Green-backed Heron, and an Anhinga or two.

Continuing on Road 105, you will soon enter *Santee State Park* (letter G on Map B—9.2; see Section B-38 for details). You will reach a stop sign. Here turn right to continue on Road 105. (Straight ahead or left both go into the state park.) This stop sign is 22.8 miles from US 601. At 25.2 miles from US 601 you reach the T-junction with SC 6. Turn left (east) onto SC 6, and go into the town of Santee. You will reach Exit 98 of I-95 at 26.5 miles from US 601. This ends the tour.

Since the tour route is quite complicated, we will now give brief directions to those going from east to west. Birding details will not be repeated. From Exit 98 of I-95 at Santee go west on SC 6 for 1.3 miles to Road 105. Turn right onto Road 105 and go 2.4 miles to a stop sign in Santee State Park. Here turn left to continue on Road 105. Go 2.2 miles from the stop sign to the intersection of Road 563. Go north on Road 563 for 0.7 mile to the Calhoun County line. Here turn left at the stop sign onto Road 203. Go straight ahead on Road 203 for 3.7 miles to a stop sign at SC 267.

Go right (northwest) on SC 267 for 1.2 miles, then turn right (north) onto Road 286. Go 3.3 miles on Road 286 to Road 129. Here turn right, and go 0.2 mile to *Low Falls Landing* (letter D on Map B—9.2). From Low Falls Landing go west on Road 129 for 2.1 miles to a tricky right turn. You must turn right here to continue on Road 129. Straight ahead is Road 326. Continue on Road 129, reaching the intersection with Road 221 in 1.7 miles (turn left to keep on Road 129) and returning to SC 267 in 0.6 mile more.

Turn right (northwest) onto SC 267, and go 6.2 miles to US 601. Here turn right (north) and go 2.0 miles to the bridge over the Congaree River, which is the western end of this tour. See Section B-40 for more details on Richland County, on the north side of the river.

B–10—CHARLESTON COUNTY

Located on the Atlantic Coast about midway between the North Carolina and Georgia borders, Charleston County is named for its principal city—Charleston, the best-known city in the state. The Charleston metropolitan area is one of three (along with Columbia and Greenville) that are approximately the same size—each about 250,000 people. Ask a local booster which is the largest city in the state. You will get three different answers—a Low Country, a Midlands, and an Up-Country answer.

In addition to being a cultural, military, and economic focus for the South Carolina Low Country, Charleston County has many outstanding natural areas. Other counties of the state have good birding areas, to be sure, but none can equal Charleston for year-round birding excellence combined with easy public access.

The main part of the city of Charleston sits on a peninsula formed by two rivers, the Ashley to the west and the Cooper to the east. The Ashley and Cooper Rivers flow together into Charleston Harbor.

These bodies of water divide Charleston County into three unequal parts.

East of the Cooper River lies the city of Mount Pleasant and a delightful area of barrier islands, swamps, and pine forests. Here are Cape Romain National Wildlife Refuge (including Bulls Island), a portion of Francis Marion National Forest, and the readily accessible barrier islands of Sullivans Island and the Isle of Palms.

Between the Cooper and the Ashley is the city of Charleston itself, heavily urbanized but still affording good birding along the waterfront and from boat tours of the harbor.

West of the Ashley River are two main types of habitat—the plantations along the west bank of the Ashley River (including Magnolia Gardens), and the salt marshes and beaches of a number of islands—James, Folly, Johns, Kiawah, and Seabrook islands. Edisto Island is partially in Charleston County, but in 1975 the town of Edisto Beach was annexed to Colleton County, so we shall cover Edisto Island in Section B-15.

B–10.1—The City of Charleston and Charleston Harbor

Winter   **
Spring   **
Summer   *
Fall   **

The proximity of Charleston Harbor and of the Ashley and Cooper Rivers makes the city of Charleston a good birding area. Birding from land is best along the Battery and along the Ashley River in the Brittlebank Park area. In addition, boat tours of Charleston Harbor and Fort Sumter National Monument leave at regular intervals from the City Marina.

To reach Brittlebank Park, follow I-26 to its eastern terminus at US 17. Take the exit for US 17 South. US 17 soon ceases to be a freeway but becomes the Crosstown Expressway, which has traffic lights but

moves quickly. Follow the Crosstown, which becomes Spring Street in about a mile. Look for Lockwood Drive, the last exit before the bridge over the Ashley River. Here turn right (north) onto Lockwood Drive, which goes along the eastern edge of a riverfront park. This is Brittlebank Park. Turn in and explore the area on foot.

Brittlebank Park is an open area on reclaimed land along the Ashley River. It has a small amount of salt marsh where you may find Marsh Wrens, Clapper Rails, and perhaps a heron or two, but the best birding is on the lawns and parking lots. Here, in late summer or early fall, you will find a wide variety of shorebirds, especially after a rain. After exploring the park proper, take a few minutes to explore the vacant lots, parking areas, and athletic fields of the Citadel (South Carolina's military college), which lie just east of Brittlebank Park along Fishburne Street. To reach Fishburne Street, follow Lockwood Drive to its northern end and turn right.

Brittlebank Park and the Citadel athletic fields may have little more than a few Killdeer and Boat-tailed Grackles on a slow day, but on a good day you may might find a rarity. Hudsonian Godwit and Baird's Sandpiper have been found here by a lucky few.

From Brittlebank Park return to Lockwood Drive and go south. About a mile south of US 17 look for the City Marina on the right. Here boats leave several times a day for tours of *Charleston Harbor* and Fort Sumter National Monument. Although you will see some birds any time of year, the harbor is best in winter. Then the permanently resident Brown Pelicans and Laughing Gulls are joined by loons, ducks, gulls, and other species. At Fort Sumter you might find a few shorebirds. Ruddy Turnstones and Spotted Sandpipers are common, and there is a slight

chance that a Purple Sandpiper will be on the rocks in winter.

Many of these same species may be seen from land, from the seawall walkway along the Battery, near White Point Gardens. To reach this area, go south on Lockwood Drive until it turns into Broad Street. Go one short block east on Broad Street, and turn right (south) onto Chisholm Street, skirting the Coast Guard station. After one block on Chisholm Street turn right (west) onto Tradd Street, which turns left (now named Murray Boulevard) along the waterfront. Follow Murray Boulevard to White Point Gardens, a park at the tip of the Charleston peninsula. As you walk along the seawall here, be sure to check out the low island in the harbor to the southeast. This is Shutes Folly Island, site of the ruins of Castle Pinckney and a magnet for shorebirds, herons, gulls, terns, and ducks.

From mid-March until June a small breeding colony of Yellow-crowned Night-Herons is usually in Washington Park, a small city park just northeast of the intersection of Broad Street and Meeting Street, in the heart of downtown, a few blocks north of White Point Gardens. If the birds are there, you will be able to get good sightings. This is the most accessible heronry in the state.

B—10.2—Mount Pleasant

Winter	***
Spring	***
Summer	**
Fall	***

Just across the Cooper River Bridge from Charleston is the city of Mount Pleasant, a delightful old village that has, in recent years, mushroomed in population. There are two good birding locations within Mount Pleasant, each with a view of the Charleston Harbor and at least a bit of salt marsh—Patriot's Point and the Pitt Street Causeway. The starting point for directions to these places will be the east end of the Cooper River Bridge, the US 17 bridge from Charleston.

To reach Patriot's Point from the Cooper River Bridge, keep right and use the US 17 Business exit. Once you are off of the bridge, follow US 17 Business (Coleman Boulevard) to the first stop light. Here turn right onto Patriot's Point Road. A few yards from the turn you will be passing the edge of a golf course on your left and a large vacant lot on your right. Look for a place to park on the right and stop.

The area to the right, back toward the

direction of the Cooper River Bridge, is currently (1992) a weedy vacant lot, but this may well be developed in the near future. If the lot still exists and is not posted, it may well be a good birding spot. The weeds here harbor numerous sparrows in winter and breeding Painted Buntings in summer. From May through August 1988 several pairs of Dickcissels were here, a rare occurrence of this species breeding on the coast.

If you make your way to the back of the vacant lot, you will reach a good overlook of the Charleston harbor as well as a small spoil area which sometimes has a few birds. The best time of year to work over this area is in the fall, when anything might turn up.

Return to the road, and look over the ponds near the edge of the golf course. There small ponds have American Coots in winter and Common Moorhens year-round. When you have finished looking over the golf course (from the roadside; do not enter the golf course itself), drive or walk along Patriot's Point Road for its half-mile length to a dead end at the golf course parking lot. The thickets of wax myrtle, baccharis, chinaberry, and mulberry along the road are great for small birds all year long. This area is especially attractive in the spring, when hundreds of Cedar Waxwings and other species feed on chinaberry flowers and the ripening mulberries. This is a great place for birds, and many rarities have been seen (mostly in fall migration).

The other main birding spot in Mount Pleasant is the Pitt Street Causeway. To reach this area from the Cooper River Bridge, bear right, taking the US 17 Business exit. Once off the bridge, go straight ahead on US 17 Business (Coleman Boulevard). Pass by Patriot's Point Road. About a mile from the Cooper River bridge you will pass over Shem's Creek. Immediately after crossing Shem's Creek, US 17 Business swings a bit to the left. Here turn off to the right onto Royall Street. Follow Royall Street through the old village portion of Mount Pleasant. In about a mile Royall Street comes to a dead end at William Street. Turn right (west) onto William Street, and go one block to Pitt Street. Turn left (south) onto Pitt Street. Pitt Street emerges from the village and begins crossing a salt marsh on a causeway. This is Pitt Street Causeway, one of the best birding spots on the South Carolina coast.

The causeway no longer leads completely across the marshes to Sullivans Island. The old causeway is now a city park popular with crabbers, sightseers, and birders. To the left (east) is a large salt marsh; to the right is a shallow cove connected with Charleston harbor. At low tide, huge mud flats emerge here. These flats are popular with shorebirds. Just about all the gulls, terns, herons, and shorebirds of the South Carolina coast have been seen here, especially in migration. American Oystercatchers are present year-round, and a few Marbled Godwits may usually be found in winter.

A visit to the Pitt Street Causeway is good at any time of year, but for best results try to arrive at or near low tide. At high tide the mud flats are inundated, and you will find far fewer birds.

B—10.3—Sullivans Island

Winter	**
Spring	**
Summer	*
Fall	**

Sullivans Island is a barrier island just southeast of downtown Charleston. The island is almost completely urban, but it still retains a couple of good birding areas—Fort Moultrie at the west end of the island (on Charleston harbor) and Breach Inlet at the east end.

To reach Sullivans Island from Charleston, go north on US 17 toward Mount Pleasant. From the Cooper River Bridge exit to the right onto US 17 Business. Follow US 17 Business (Coleman Boulevard) for 2.6 miles to the intersection with SC 703 (Ben Sawyer Boulevard). Here turn south onto SC 703 toward the beach.

SC 703 soon crosses an extensive area of salt marshes and salt creeks. This area can be good for herons, egrets, and shorebirds, if you can find a safe place to pull off onto the shoulder of this busy road. When you get to the island (Sullivans Island, 2.9 miles from US 17 Business), look for signs for Fort Moultrie, and turn right (west) onto Middle Street. In about three blocks you will reach a park on your right—*Sullivans Island Recreation Area*.

A prominent feature of this park is a huge mound of earth, an old gun emplacement. Turn off of Middle Street, and park to explore this area on foot. On the mound has grown up brushy vegetation which is attractive to Prairie Warblers and Painted Buntings in summer. In winter look for sparrows and wintering warblers. Most will be Yellow-rumped Warblers, but there is always a chance for the odd Orange-crowned Warbler or even something better. Exploring around toward the back of the earth mound, you will find a sports field which is wet at certain times of the year. This is a good place to look for wintering Sedge Wren in the low sedges and rushes in the wetter parts of the field. You can even work your way over to the edge of the salt marsh to look for typical salt marsh species, including Marsh Wren and Seaside Sparrow (year-round).

When you are done at the recreation area, return to Middle Street and continue west. At 1.5 miles from SC 703 you will reach Fort Moultrie, which is administered by the National Park Service as part of Fort Sumter National Monument. Park in the visitors' center parking lot, on the right, and explore on foot.

Fort Moultrie can offer some good birding at times, but sometimes it is dull. At the back (north) side of the parking lot is a small dock that overlooks the salt marshes. But the best birding is across the street, on the beach behind the old fort. Here you will find rocky groins, a sandy beach, vegetated dunes, and a view of Charleston Harbor and the Atlantic Ocean. This can be an excellent area for loons, grebes, cormorants, pelicans, sea ducks, and shorebirds. Ruddy Turnstones are common on the rocky groins for much of the year, and you have a slight chance of finding a Purple Sandpiper in winter. Other good birds to look for include a few breeding Wilson's Plovers, Black Terns (late summer), Red Knots (during migration and in winter), and an occasional Common Ground-Dove.

When you are done at Fort Moultrie, backtrack on Middle Street, following this street all the way to the inlet at the east end of Sullivans Island. Here, just before the bridge to the Isle of Palms, is a small parking lot for Breach Inlet. Park and look for birds. This area is good for birds all year round. In winter look for scoters and other sea ducks. During the warmer part of the year look for terns. This is an excellent place for most of the tern species of the South Carolina coast, including Sandwich Terns (fairly common in summer) and even a few Gull-billed Terns (occasional in spring and summer).

When you are done at Breach Inlet, you can follow SC 703 back to the mainland, or you might consider staying on a few days at one of the many resorts on the Isle of Palms, directly across the narrow inlet from Sullivans Island.

While you are on the island, keep an eye out for flocks of cowbirds. South Carolina's first Shiny Cowbirds were seen at a feeder on Sullivans Island, and there might be one around at any time of year.

B–10.4—Palmetto Islands County Park

Winter   **
Spring   **
Summer *
Fall   **

To reach *Palmetto Islands County Park* from Charleston, take US 17 north toward Georgetown. About 7 miles beyond the Cooper River Bridge look for Road 97, Long Point Road, on the left. If you are coming from the north on US 17, look for Road 97 at 1.2 miles south of the junction of US 17 and SC 41. From US 17 turn north onto Road 97, and go about a mile to the park entrance road, following the signs.

Palmetto Islands County Park is a 943-acre natural jewel consisting of salt

marsh and oak-pine-palmetto maritime forest. This is a great spot for a picnic, and although it is not a birding hot spot, you can find many of the common species of the salt marsh (including breeding Osprey) and oak-pine woods.

Two short trails invite the birder. At the east end of the park is the half-mile-long Marsh Trail. The other trail is the 1.5-mile-long nature trail, which begins at the Park Center and crosses a salt marsh on a boardwalk before looping around a small island.

B–10.5—The Cape Romain National Wildlife Refuge

Winter   ***
Spring   ****
Summer **
Fall   ****

See letters A and B on Map B–10.1.

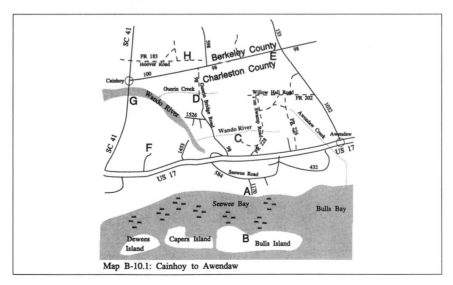

Map B-10.1: Cainhoy to Awendaw

Cape Romain National Wildlife Refuge consists of about thirty-four thousand acres of maritime forest, dunes, salt marsh, freshwater impoundments, mud flats, and salt creeks along the Atlantic in the northeastern part of Charleston County. It is probably the best-known birding destination in South Carolina. The most famous part of the refuge is Bulls Island, a barrier island some five miles long and about one mile wide lying three miles from the mainland. Most of the 338 species of birds on the refuge checklist have been found on Bulls Island.

On the night of September 21—22, 1989, the Cape Romain National Wildlife Refuge was hit by the worst part of Hurricane Hugo. The area suffered from winds over 135 miles per hour and a storm surge of some seventeen feet. The refuge headquarters was completely destroyed. Most of the maritime forest on Bulls Island was either blown down or killed by salt water. The area will show the effects of Hugo for at least a century. Despite this damage, Cape Romain NWR is still a good birding spot. The most striking effect is that the trees are gone. The old-growth pine forest along Seewee Road no longer exists, and the maritime forest on Bulls Island is much changed, if not destroyed.

To reach Cape Romain National Wildlife Refuge from the intersection of SC 41 and US 17 on the eastern edge of the city of Mount Pleasant, take US 17 northeast toward Georgetown for 7.2 miles. Here turn right (east) onto Road 584, Seewee Road. Follow Seewee Road east for 3.5 miles to the intersection with Road 1170, Moores Landing Road (also known as Bulls Island Road). Along the way you will pass through what used to be an old-growth pine forest, part of the Francis Marion National Forest. Before Hurricane Hugo you could find all of the common species of this habitat, including Red-cockaded Woodpecker, Brown-headed Nuthatch, Pine Warbler, and Bachman's Sparrow. Some of these species are still around, but you will find them much more readily in areas less affected by Hurricane Hugo, such as the Santee Coastal Reserve (see Section B-10.7).

As you drive along Moores Landing Road, keep an eye out for a nest in a snag on the left side of the road that is being actively used by Bald Eagles. The eagles' old nest tree was destroyed by Hurricane Hugo, but the birds are still trying to nest in the neighborhood, even though there are no tall trees left. The birds are usually here from late winter through early spring.

Moores Landing Road ends at the landing in 1.6 miles. *Moores Landing* (letter A on Map B—10.1) itself is a great birding area. Here, in addition to a boat landing (usable at high tide only) you will find a two-hundred-yard-long fishing pier jutting out into the salt marsh of Seewee Bay. From this pier you can overlook one of the best spots in South Carolina to observe birds, especially shorebirds. The tides on Seewee Bay are critical for finding birds. At high tide there may be little here aside from a few Laughing Gulls and Brown Pelicans, but at low tide (especially in winter or during the shorebird migration periods) you should see hundreds of shorebirds of several different species. American Oystercatchers are common year-round, and this is about the best spot in South Carolina to observe Marbled Godwits. In winter or early spring it is not unusual to spy fifty or more godwits. Keep an eye out for rarities, such as a wintering Long-billed Curlew or American White Pelican.

The breeding season is a relatively slack time at Moores Landing, but you can almost always find a Painted Bunting or two in the brush near the parking lot. Barn Swallows breed under the pier and have been joined in the past by a pair or two of Cliff Swallows—rare on the coast.

The pier at Moores Landing is reason enough to come to Cape Romain National Wildlife Refuge, but for a special treat plan a visit out to Bulls Island. Currently (1992) a concessionaire runs a ferry service (hikers only—no cars or bicycles) for day trips out to Bulls Island. (There is no camping allowed on Bulls Island.) For reservations and information, contact

Captain John Pryor
1222 Calais Drive
Mount Pleasant, SC 29464
(803) 884-0448

If Captain Pryor is no longer ferrying people to the island, contact the refuge headquarters for information:

Cape Romain National Wildlife Refuge
390 Bulls Island Road
Awendaw, South Carolina 29429
(803) 928-3368

A day on Bulls Island can be a real birding adventure. Be sure to take everything you need: food, water, insect repellent, sun screen, rain gear, and a watch (so you won't miss the boat back to the mainland). The three-mile ride out to the island will give you a good look at the creeks, salt marshes, and mud flats which make up Seewee Bay. Here you will get fairly good looks at many of the birds which were only specks as seen from the pier at Moores Landing. American Oystercatchers are virtually guaranteed at any time of year.

Your time on the island will begin at the *Visitor Contact Station* near the boat landing (letter B on Map B–10.1). Here you will find rest rooms, picnic tables, and a place to hide from the rain, but no drinking water. It is time to study the map and plan your excursion. Be aware that there is more on the island than you can see in a single visit, so you will just have to come back again.

B–10.6—I'on Swamp

Winter	**
Spring	***
Summer	**
Fall	*

See letter C on Map B–10.1.

To reach *I'on Swamp Road* (pronounced "EYE-on") from the intersection of SC 41 and US 17 on the northeast side of Mount Pleasant, go northeast on US 17. In 7.2 miles you will pass Road 584 (Seewee Road) on your right. (This is the road to Moores Landing; see Section B-10.5 above). Keep going northeast on US 17 for an additional 4.2 miles. Here look for Forest Road 228, I'on Swamp Road, on the left (north).

Turn north onto I'on Swamp Road. This famous road leads through pinewoods and hardwood swamps for about 3.8 miles to a T-junction with Forest Road 202, Willow Hall Road. Here turn right, and follow Willow Hall Road east for about 3.7 miles to its end at a paved highway (Road 1032). Turn right onto Road 1032 to return to US 17 in about 1.9 miles. This point on US 17 is in the community of Awendaw, about 6.5 miles northeast of the junction of US 17 and I'on Swamp Road.

The I'on Swamp Road loop gives you a great cross section of the birding habitats of the Francis Marion National Forest. Along this route you can find most of the specialties of the forest, including American Swallow-tailed Kite, Wild Turkey, Red-cockaded Woodpecker, Brown-headed Nuthatch, Black-throated Green Warbler, Swainson's Warbler, and Bachman's Sparrow. Many birders come here in early spring to search for the legendary Bachman's Warbler. There have been no reliable records of this species in South Carolina since the 1960s, so your chances of finding it alive here (or anywhere else) are slim to none.

At 0.6 mile north of US 17 along I'on Swamp Road there is a spur road to the left (west): *Forest Road 239, Clayfield Road* (letter C on Map B–10.1). Six species of owl have been found along Clayfield Road or I'on Swamp Road just north of Clayfield Road: Barn Owl, Eastern Screech-Owl, Great Horned Owl, Barred Owl, Long-eared Owl (winter and early spring), and Northern Saw-whet Owl (winter and early spring). This is also one of the few places in Charleston County where you might hear a Whip-poor-will in the spring (along with numerous Chuck-will's-widows).

Winter   **
Spring   ***
Summer **
Fall   ***

See letter A on Map B–10.2.

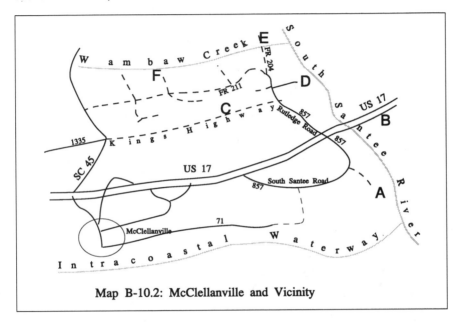

Map B-10.2: McClellanville and Vicinity

To reach the *Santee Coastal Reserve* from the intersection of SC 45 and US 17 on the north side of McClellanville, go northeast on US 17 for 2.9 miles to Road 857, South Santee Road. Here turn right (east). (There is a Red-cockaded Woodpecker colony in the middle of the Y formed by US 17 and Road 857. Keep an eye out for the woodpeckers' roost trees, live pine trees with lots of white sap oozing from sap wells drilled by the woodpeckers around the entrance holes to the roost cavities.)

At 3.2 miles east of US 17 you will reach the community of South Santee. Look for the community center building on the right. Just beyond this building an unpaved road leads off to the right. This is the entrance road to the Santee Coastal Reserve.

If you are southbound from Georgetown on US 17, look for the other end of South Santee Road at 1.0 mile southwest of the bridge over the South Santee River. Here you can turn right to visit Hampton Plantation State Park (see Section B-10.8, below) or turn left (south) to go to the Santee Coastal Reserve. Go south on Road 857 for 1.5 miles to the entrance road to the reserve, on the left (southeast).

Bear in mind that the Santee Coastal Reserve is open to the public only from March 1 to October 31 from 8 A.M. until 5 P.M. The telephone number is (803) 546-8665.

The Santee Coastal Preserve protects some twenty-three thousand acres of outstanding Lower Coastal Plain and coastal habitats, including saltwater, brackish, and freshwater marshes, freshwater impoundments, bald-cypress—water-tupelo swamps, maritime forest, and old-growth pine forest. Up to fifty thousand waterfowl winter here, and many interesting bird species may be found, especially in the early spring, when visiting conditions are most pleasant. From May through October the area is often infested with mosquitoes and biting flies. Only the most dedicated of birders will hike the trails here in late summer.

Birding highlights of the Santee Coastal Reserve include hundreds of breeding herons, egrets, and ibis, Wood Storks in summer, permanent resident Mottled Ducks (introduced here in the 1970s), thousands of wintering ducks, breeding American Swallow-tailed Kites, resident Bald Eagles, hundreds of migrant shorebirds, breeding Black-necked Stilts, Red-cockaded Woodpeckers, Bachman's Sparrows, and many other species.

The entrance road goes through an old-growth longleaf-pine forest great for Bachman's Sparrow and Red-cockaded Woodpecker. At 1.8 miles into the reserve, look for a nature trail off to the left (north). This trail follows an old roadbed in the shape of a figure 9 for a 1.2-mile loop. The beginning of the trail is through old-growth pine forest, but the trail also leads through an area of mixed hardwoods which is quite good for warblers.

After exploring the nature trail, return to the entrance road. At 2.7 miles into the reserve you will reach the beginnings of the Washo Reserve Trail on the right (south). This 2.5-mile loop trail goes past an active heronry, then loops through maritime forest to a saw-grass marsh and eventually back to the main road through the reserve. This is a good trail for herons, ducks, shorebirds, and Bald Eagles.

The other main trail in the reserve is the five-mile-long Hike-Bike Trail. As its name implies, this trail is best explored on bicycle, but it is open to hikers as well. From the parking lot near the beginning of the Washo Reserve Trail keep going east on the continuation of the entrance road. The first few hundred yards of this trail are the same as the end of the Washo Reserve Trail. When you get to the point where the Washo Reserve Trail turns off to the right, keep going straight ahead on the service road (closed to automobiles). Follow the service road east through the marshes and freshwater impoundments for about two miles to a T-junction of dikes at the Intracoastal Waterway. Here turn left (north) and follow the dikes for a broad loop along first the Intracoastal Waterway and then the South Santee River, before finally completing a large figure 9.

The Hike-Bike Trail is good for ducks (including Mottled Ducks), shorebirds, herons, and Bald Eagles. For most of its length it follows dikes through open marshland and by freshwater impoundments, but along the Intracoastal Waterway you will find numerous thickets and small groves of trees—islands of trees in a sea of marsh. These tree islands are great migrant traps, but be warned: the biting insects along this trail are often bad. You might find a Gray or Western Kingbird here in September or October, but you will pay a toll in blood donated to the local mosquitoes.

B—10.8—A Hampton Plantation and Wambaw Creek Tour

Winter	**
Spring	***
Summer	**
Fall	***

See Map B—10.2.

This section features a tour of *Hampton*

Plantation State Park and the *Wambaw Creek Wilderness* area of the Francis Marion National Forest in extreme eastern

Charleston County. The tour begins at the intersection of US 17 and SC 45 on the north side of McClellanville. Go northeast on US 17 toward Georgetown. In 2.9 miles you will reach Road 857, South Santee Road, veering off to the right. This is the turnoff for the Santee Coastal Reserve (see Section B-10.7). To follow the present tour, however, keep on US 17. Just beyond Road 857, on the right (south) side of US 17, is an area of mature longleaf-pine forest. Red-cockaded Woodpeckers roost in living pine trees here and are relatively easy to find, especially early in the morning or late in the afternoon, when they are leaving or returning to their cavity trees. Bachman's Sparrows are permanent residents in these woods but are extremely difficult to find when they are not singing. The song season extends from late March until early September, especially at dawn and dusk.

At 6.5 miles from SC 45 you will reach a second intersection with Road 857. To the right the road is the other end of South Santee Road; to the left Road 857 is known as Rutledge Road in honor of Archibald Rutledge, late poet laureate of South Carolina. Rutledge's plantation, Hampton Plantation, is preserved as a South Carolina state park.

To follow the tour, turn left (north) onto Road 857, Rutledge Road. In about 1.8 miles from US 17 there is a sand road on the left. This is the historic Kings Highway, a colonial road. You may wish to take a short side trip here, following the sand road west for about 2 miles to historic *St. James Santee Church* (letter C on Map B–10.2). The quiet churchyard is a good place for birds. Red-cockaded Woodpeckers nest in the old pines near the church. The main tour continues north on Road 857. At 2.6 miles north of US 17 you will reach the entrance road for *Hampton Plantation State Park* on the right (letter D on Map B–10.2). Turn in and follow the park road about a mile to the parking lot. The plantation grounds have grassy lawns and ancient live oaks, and are a great place for a picnic (if the mosquitoes are not too hungry). There is no formal trail, but you can find most of the common species of southern gardens by exploring the grounds. Early in

the morning you might well find a flock of Wild Turkeys strolling around the grounds. These birds are truly wild, since Wild Turkeys in this part of Charleston County have never been hunted out. Another species to watch for at Hampton Plantation is the Pileated Woodpecker, which is common and conspicuous here.

There are a few old rice fields (now freshwater marsh) along Hampton Creek, a backwater of the nearby South Santee River. You will find Common Yellowthroats in the marsh year-round and a variety of sparrows in the winter, but this is not a good marsh for rails and bitterns.

When you have finished exploring the state park, return to Road 857 and turn right (north). In 0.7 mile the pavement ends. Continue straight ahead on Forest Road 204. If you keep going on Forest Road 204, you will soon cross Wambaw Creek into Berkeley County. There is a boat launch near the *Forest Road 204 bridge over Wambaw Creek* (letter E on Map B–10.2). The swamp near the bridge is a great place for species of floodplain forests, including Swainson's Warbler (mid-April until August). This bridge is at the eastern end of the *Wambaw Creek Wilderness* of Francis Marion National Forest. There are no roads or trails in the wilderness area, which is best explored by canoe. (However, this area was heavily damaged by Hurricane Hugo, and the canoe trail has numerous obstacles.)

The Wambaw Creek Wilderness is the best place in Charleston or Berkeley counties for finding American Swallow-tailed Kites in the breeding season. Keep an eye out for this magnificent species, especially if you find a place where you can see a bit of the sky.

To continue the tour, turn around when you get to the boat launch near the Forest Road 204 bridge and backtrack just a bit to the first forest road to your right (west), Forest Road 211, Mill Branch Road. Here turn and follow Forest Road 211 as it winds around for about five miles, until it reaches SC 45. Soon after getting onto Forest Road 211, you will pass Elmwood Wildlife Center on your right (formerly a campground, now a wildlife management area work center). Forest Road 211 leads through a variety of habitats—old-growth pine forests with Red-cockaded Woodpeckers, wildlife clearings which offer feeding areas for deer and Wild Turkey, young pine plantations, and brushy cutover areas. Notice that many of the cutover areas within the National Forest are selectively cut, not clear-cut. A number of pines have been left standing to help reseed the forest and to insure continuing habitat for Red-cockaded Woodpeckers. The cutover areas often abound with birds, including Sedge Wrens in the winter, American Swallow-tailed Kites in summer, and Red-headed Woodpeckers year-round.

After about 2.5 miles on Forest Road 211 you will reach the turnoff for another boat launch area on the right (north). This is *Still Boat Landing*, on the edge of the Wambaw Creek Wilderness (letter F on Map B—10.2). This is a good place to get a close look at the Wambaw Swamp, even if you do not have a canoe.

Once you reach SC 45, turn left (south) and go about five miles to return to US 17. This completes the loop.

B—10.9—Guerin Bridge Road

Winter   **
Spring   **
Summer *
Fall   **

See letters D and E on Map B—10.1.

To reach Guerin Bridge Road from the intersection of SC 41 and US 17 on the northeast side of Mount Pleasant, go northeast on US 17. In 7.2 miles you will pass Road 584 (Seewee Road) on your right. (This is the road to Moores Landing; see Section B-10.5 above). Keep going northeast on US 17 for an additional 0.8 mile. Here look for Road 98, *Guerin Bridge Road*, on the left (north).

Guerin Bridge Road leads through a wide variety of habitats: mixed-hardwood forest with many species of breeding warbler, salt marshes with resident Seaside Sparrows and with Black Rails in spring migration, clear-cut areas where you might spy an American Swallow-tailed Kite in the spring or early summer, and old-growth pine forests with Bachman's Sparrows and Red-cockaded Woodpeckers.

From US 17 follow Road 98 (Guerin Bridge Road) north. Within the first four miles the road crosses two salt marshes. This first is at Ward Bridge over the Wando River; the second is at Guerin Bridge over Guerin Creek. At the second bridge Road 98 becomes the Charleston County—Berkeley County line (letter D on Map B—10.1).

At 5.5 miles from US 17 you will reach the intersection with Road 100 on the left, in Berkeley County. (You can turn left here to get to SC 41 at Wando in 4.1 miles). To continue with the present tour, continue on Road 98, which here runs along the county line (Berkeley County on the left; Charleston County on the right). Follow Road 98 east for another 7.6 miles. At 1.2 miles beyond Road 100 is the intersection with Road 598. Keep going east on Road 98 through old-growth pine forest. This area was heavily damaged by Hurricane Hugo in 1989, but it is still a great birding area. At about 7 miles east of Road 100 you will reach *Halfway Creek*, a forest service campground (letter E on Map B—10.1). At 7.6 miles you will reach the intersection with a paved road (known as Road 1032 in Charleston County, to the right, or as Road 133 in Berkeley County, to the left). Here you may turn right to return to US 17 in Awendaw in 4.7 miles or turn left to return to SC 41 in Huger in 7.4 miles.

B–10.10—East Cooper Airport

Winter   **
Spring   **
Summer *
Fall   **

See letter F on Map B–10.1.

The East Cooper Airport is a quiet general-aviation airport just north of US 17 between Mount Pleasant and McClellanville. While it is not a major birding destination, it is well worth a twenty-minute stop if you are passing by on US 17. The road to the airport goes north from US 17 at 2.0 miles northeast of the intersection of US 17 and SC 41, which is about 8 miles northeast of the Cooper River Bridge.

The best birding is along the airport entrance road. The clear-cut here attracts hawks in all seasons, including an occa-sional Mississippi or American Swallow-tailed Kite in the summer. This area is a good place to find Red-headed Woodpecker, a decreasing species in Charleston County.

Just before you reach the airport buildings, you will notice marshy areas on both sides of the road. This is a great area for wintering Common Snipe and Sedge Wren. Look for other shorebirds in migration, American Bittern (rare) and perhaps a rail (Virginia Rails have been found in winter). All birding should be done from the roadside, well away from any airport operations. Please do not cross any fences.

B–10.11—Folly Island

Winter   ***
Spring   ***
Summer **
Fall   ***

Folly Island is a barrier island just southwest of the city of Charleston. Except during the summer beach season, Folly Beach offers great birding opportunities. To reach Folly Beach from the end of I-26 in Charleston, take US 17 south. Immediately after crossing the Ashley River, turn left onto SC 171, Folly Beach Road, which leads ten miles to Folly Island.

An interesting side trip, either going to or coming from Folly Beach, is to nearby James Island County Park. See Section B–10.14 for directions.

After passing through a residential and commercial area (the James Island neighborhood of the city of Charleston), the road to Folly Beach reaches a vast salt marsh area. There are good mud flats along the road. By pulling off onto the shoulder you can examine the mud flats and sand flats for shorebirds, herons, and waterfowl. Rarities found here include a Long-billed Curlew (early April). Whimbrels are common in the spring, and at least a few shorebirds are here all year round.

For an interesting side trip into the salt marsh, look for Road 632 (Sol Legare Road), which turns off to the right (west) about 8 miles south of US 17. Road 632 runs through a residential area for a mile or so, then enters the salt marsh. The road ends at a boat launch on the Stono River, 2.7 miles west of Folly Beach Road. From the boat launch look for the usual gulls, terns, and herons of the salt marsh. In winter look for Hooded Mergansers, which are quite common in salt creeks.

The salt marshes along Sol Legare Road look like proper habitat for Black Rails, but this elusive species is seldom found here. Still, this might be a good area to listen for them on calm June nights.

Return to Folly Beach Road, which crosses the Folly River and reaches the center of the city of Folly Beach. There is a traffic light at the intersection of Folly Beach Road and Ashley Avenue. Here you may turn left to explore the west end of the island or turn right to reach the east end.

The best birding is often at Folly Beach County Park, at the west end of the island. Turn right onto West Ashley Avenue, and follow it to the park entrance in about one mile. Folly Beach County Park is open year-round from 10 A.M. to 7 P.M. in summer, 6 P.M. in spring and fall, and until 5P.M. in winter.

The county park preserves a bit of wild beach, vegetated sand dunes, and salt marsh. The dunes are the best place in Charleston County to look for the dainty little Common Ground-Dove, a species which is getting quite hard to find in South Carolina. From mid-April until October the dune scrub is home to numerous Painted Buntings.

The park has four thousand feet of ocean beach and two thousand feet of salt creek frontage. Walk west along the beach to Stono Inlet. Across the inlet you will see Bird Key, a South Carolina Heritage Preserve. This twenty-acre island is little more than a high sandbar with a few vegetated dunes, but it is a major nesting area for seabirds. Common nesters on Bird Key include Brown Pelican (up to two thousand pairs), Snowy Egret, Tricolored Heron, and the following species of tern: Royal, Sandwich, Least, and Gull-billed. Uncommon or rare breeders here include Common Tern (one or two pairs each year) and Sooty Tern (very rare; not every year).

After exploring the county park, return to Ashley Avenue, and follow it east. About two miles east of Folly Beach Road, East Ashley Avenue passes a narrow part of the island called the Washout. There is a pulloff here, where you can overlook the ocean as well as the rock groins and seawalls that people have built in a effort to keep the Washout from becoming a new inlet. In winter look for sea ducks, loons, and Northern Gannets in the ocean, and Ruddy Turnstones on the rocks. This looks like a spot for Purple Sandpipers, but they are rarely found here.

In another mile or so East Ashley Avenue ends at an abandoned Coast Guard station. There is limited parking along the public street here, and also a very small parking lot. From the small public parking lot you can either follow a public walkway to the beach or explore the old Coast Guard station. If you follow the public walkway to the beach, walk east along the beach for about two hundred yards to Lighthouse Inlet. Across the inlet is Morris Island, a low barrier island, the site of the Morris Island Lighthouse. The part of the island near the lighthouse is really just a sandbar. The lighthouse is in the water at high tide. There are usually numerous gulls, terns, skimmers, and Brown Pelicans idling on the sandbar (unless it is completely underwater). This is a good place to look for a Great Black-backed Gull. Rarities seen here include Greater Flamingo, Lesser Black-backed Gull, and Roseate Tern.

If the grounds of the old Coast Guard station are still open to the public (i.e., if there are no signs telling you to keep out), spend an hour or more exploring the dunes, woods, and marshes of this great birding area. Look for Painted Buntings in summer and Common Ground-Doves year-round. This area attracts numerous migrants, especially in the fall. Rarities found here in fall include Western Kingbird, Lark Sparrow, and Clay-colored Sparrow.

Winter   **
Spring   **
Summer *
Fall   **

Kiawah Island (pronounceed KEE-a-wah") is a popular resort area on a barrier island about twenty miles southwest of the city of Charleston. Most of the island is open only to property owners and guests of the resort. If you are vacationing at Kiawah Island, inquire about guided tours by jeep or canoe, which will give you a taste of this great natural area. For day-trippers Kiawah Island does have a public park—Beachwalker County Park, one of the excellent parks of the Charleston County Park system. Beachwalker County Park is open from 10 A.M. to 7 P.M. every day during June, July, and August, and also on the weekends during April, May, September, and October. It is closed from November to March. The best birding at Beachwalker Park is during the shorebird migration (April through early June and also late August through early October). Winter birding is probably similar to that at Folly Beach (see Section B-10.11) but is restricted to residents and guests of the resort.

To reach Beachwalker County Park on Kiawah Island from Charleston, follow US 17 south over the Ashley River. Immediately after crossing the river, turn left onto SC 171, Folly Beach Road. After a mile on SC 171 you will cross the drawbridge over the Intracoastal Waterway at Wappoo Cut. Just beyond this bridge turn right (west) onto SC 700 (Maybank Highway). Follow SC 700 over the Stono River. (Just before reaching the river, look for Riverland Drive; this is the turnoff for James Island County Park—see Section B-10.14.)

At 4.2 miles from SC 171 turn left (southwest) onto Road 54 (River Road on Johns Island). Go southwest on River Road. At 3.1 miles from SC 700 you will pass the entrance road for Charleston Executive Airport. The grassy fields along the entrance road to the airport are worth checking for migrating shorebirds in spring or late summer. You will probably not see anything other than Cattle Egrets, Killdeer, and Eastern Meadowlarks, but there is a slim chance of finding an Upland Sandpiper or a Lesser Golden-Plover, especially just after a rain.

Continue south and west on River Road, which is a county road once you pass the airport. Two miles past the airport River Road improves and becomes Road 91. Keep straight ahead on Road 91 for 6.3 miles to a T-junction at Road 20 (Bohicket Road). Turn left onto Road 20, and go another 3.0 miles. Here turn left onto Kiawah Island Parkway, the entrance road for Kiawah Island. This road goes over a salt marsh and creek (Kiawah River), where you may find Whimbrel and other species typical of salt marshes. Follow Kiawah Island Parkway onto Kiawah Island. Just before you get to the security gate, turn right onto Beachwalker Drive, which leads to Beachwalker County Park in about a mile.

The parking lot at the county park gives you a good overlook of the Kiawah River and its salt marshes. At low tide a few sandbars emerge, which are used by several species of shorebirds, including American Oystercatcher (common) and Marbled Godwit (rare). Follow the boardwalk over the dunes to the beach. Once on the beach, walk to your right (southwest) for about a mile to the mouth of the Kiawah River. This is Captain Sam's Inlet, one of the best shore birding spots on the South Carolina coast. Here you will find gulls, terns, and shorebirds. A few Wilson's Plovers nest here, and you might be lucky enough to see a Piping Plover in migration.

On your way to and from the inlet be alert for birds in the thick beach scrub behind the main dunes. Painted Buntings are common here (mid-April though September), and you might find a Common

Ground-Dove (uncommon permanent resident) or a migrating Palm Warbler. Keep off the fragile dunes themselves; if you do cross them, then only on the boardwalk. It is possible to get into the

scrub from the parking lot without disturbing the dunes, but it is probably not worth the effort. You will be able to see enough from the beach.

B—10.13—Magnolia Gardens

Winter	***
Spring	***
Summer	**
Fall	***

To reach *Magnolia Gardens* from Charleston, cross the Ashley River on US 17 southbound. Immediately after crossing the river, bear right onto SC 61, and follow SC 61 (Ashley River Road) about ten miles north to the gardens' entrance on the right.

From I-26 eastbound leave the interstate at Exit 199, and take US 17 Alternate south through downtown Summerville. At 3.2 miles from I-26 turn left (south) onto SC 165. Follow SC 165 for 4 miles to SC 61. Here turn left (southeast) toward Charleston. You will reach the entrance to Magnolia Gardens in about 7 miles.

Magnolia Gardens is a popular tourist attraction, and an admission fee is charged. It is also an excellent birding area. This five-hundred-acre area has a formal garden, freshwater and brackish marshes, ponds, a cypress swamp, a few weedy fields, and many acres of mature oak-hickory-pine forest. Local birders often purchase an annual pass to the Gardens and come here every chance they get.

With your admission you will receive a small map of the Gardens. A bird list is available as well. Ask for one at the snack bar near the main parking lot.

The main birding spot at Magnolia Gardens is the old rice field area. There are two ways to explore the ponds and freshwater marshes of this 125-acre portion of the gardens. You can rent a canoe (inquire at the snack bar), or you can circle the marsh on foot by following a trail on the dikes.

To view the area on foot, enter the formal gardens from the parking lot, and make your way over to the Ashley River, on the northern edge of the formal gardens. Here follow the trail along the river to your left (northwest). You will soon reach the beginning of the dikes, which is also where the canoe landing is. Follow the trail counterclockwise around the marsh. After about a mile you will reach a junction where one trail continues along the river and another trail goes left. Take the trail to the left, which follows a dike separating a pond on your right from the main rice field marsh on your left. By keeping left, you will eventually reach an observation tower on the edge of the marsh. After overlooking the area from the tower, you can follow the signs back to the formal gardens.

Birding along the old rice field dikes is good to excellent. In winter you can expect to find most of the species of puddle ducks that occur in South Carolina as well as a few other ducks: Wood Duck, Green-winged Teal, American Black Duck, Mallard, Northern Pintail, Blue-winged Teal, Northern Shoveler, Gadwall, American Wigeon, Ring-necked Duck, Lesser Scaup, Hooded Merganser, and Ruddy Duck. American Coot and Common Moorhen are common year-round as well as a good selection of herons, egrets, White and Glossy Ibis, and other species of freshwater marshes.

In fall and winter keep an eye out for Fulvous Whistling-Duck. This is one of the most dependable spots in the state for this elusive species. The best way to see a whistling duck is to watch the marsh from the observation tower until one or two fly up from the reeds. Other goodies include rails (especially in winter and in migration) and bitterns. The American Bittern is occasionally seen in winter, and the Least Bittern is fairly common and often seen during the warmer months (April through August).

The other outstanding birding spot at Magnolia Gardens is the Audubon Swamp Boardwalk. To reach this area, walk or drive from the main parking lot toward the exit. Just before you get back to the fee station, you will reach a parking lot for the swamp boardwalk. Follow the trail from the parking lot onto the boardwalk, which leads along the edge of a bald-cypress swamp and eventually to a small pond. This area always has

Anhingas and Wood Ducks. From early April through late August you will also find many of the typical swamp-breeding warblers. Prothonotary Warblers are abundant, and you will also see or hear Northern Parula, Yellow-throated Warbler, and probably a Hooded Warbler or two. In winter you will find lots of Yellow-rumped Warblers.

There are many other trails crisscrossing the gardens. It will take you several visits to explore them all. Along these trails you will be able to find (at one time or another during the year) almost all the bird species of the Coastal Plain of South Carolina. All in all, Magnolia Gardens offers some of the best birding opportunities in South Carolina.

B—10.14—James Island County Park

Winter	**
Spring	**
Summer	*
Fall	**

James Island is the district of the city of Charleston that you pass through on your way to Folly Beach (see Section B-10.11). In 1990 a new, 640-acre county park opened on the western edge of James Island, which promises to be a fairly good birding area. To reach *James Island County Park* from US 17, follow SC 171 (Folly Beach Road) south toward Folly Beach. In about a mile you will cross over the Intracoastal Waterway on a high drawbridge over Wappoo Cut. Just south of the drawbridge turn right (west) onto SC 700 (Maybank Highway), the road to Johns Island, Rockville, and Kiawah Island (see Section B-10.12). Follow SC 700 west for about 1.3 miles. Here turn left (south) at the traffic light onto Riverland Drive. Go south on Riverland Drive for about 2 miles to the park entrance on the right (west).

James Island County Park has live-oak woods, meadows, salt marsh, and the "lagoon"—a sixteen-acre shallow freshwater lake. There are many miles of hiking trail, paved bike paths, and roads. This is a good spot for a picnic. There is

also a large campground and a limited number of cabins for rent.

The park is too new to have much of a track record as a birding location, but it promises to be fairly good. You can find good numbers of common land birds along the trails. The lagoon has a few ducks in winter (mostly Bufflehead and Ruddy Duck), as well as egrets year-round. And there is a crabbing pier which allows you to get out over the salt marsh along the Stono River. Here look for typical salt marsh species as well as Ospreys, Bald Eagles, and other birds of prey flying over the broad marshes.

If you are going on to Folly Beach from the park, turn right onto Riverland Drive and follow it for about two miles, to Grimball Road. Here keep left on Grimball Road, which reaches SC 171 (Folly Beach Road) in a few hundred yards. Here turn right (south) to reach Folly Beach in about four miles.

To reach the park from Folly Beach, take SC 171 north for about five miles, and watch for directional signs which will show you where to turn left onto Camp Road, which leads to Riverland Drive and the park entrance.

B–11—CHEROKEE COUNTY

The industrial heartland of the Carolinas lies along a 250-mile lazy arc, from Raleigh, North Carolina, in the east, through the cities of the North Carolina Piedmont—Durham, Greensboro, Winston-Salem, Charlotte, and then southwest into South Carolina, to Spartanburg and Greenville. This is the so-called Piedmont Crescent of cities, which enters South Carolina just a few miles west of Charlotte, in Cherokee County. The Main Street of the Piedmont Crescent is I-85, which crosses Cherokee County from northeast to southwest.

Cherokee County is a typical part of the Piedmont Crescent. It has a mix of small cities (notably Gaffney), suburbs, well-kept small farms, woodlots, a few pine plantations, and few truly wild areas. Cherokee County is in the heart of the Carolina peach-growing county. From I-85 in Gaffney you can gawk at the Peachoid, a water tower painted to resemble a peach.

The largest wild area in the county is part of Kings Mountain National Military Park, along the eastern border of the county. Since most of this park is in York County, it is covered in Section B-46 below. A few miles west of Kings Mountain, near the Cowpens National Battlefield, is another Piedmont ridge, similar to, but not as high as, Kings Mountain. This is Thicketty Mountain.

Cherokee County has the eastern end of SC 11, the Cherokee Foothills Highway. This is a scenic, but quick, route that skirts the South Carolina mountains, rejoining I-85 at the Georgia border. A birder traveling through South Carolina on I-85 might well consider taking SC 11 as an alternate route. The other counties on SC 11 are Spartanburg (see Section B-42), Greenville (Section B-23), Pickens (Section B-39), and Oconee (Section B-37).

B–11.1—Cowpens National Battlefield

Winter   **
Spring   **
Summer *
Fall   **

Cowpens National Battlefield is one of three areas in the Piedmont of South Carolina administered by the National Park Service that interpret significant battles of the American Revolution. (The others are Kings Mountain National Military Park, covered in Section B-46, and Ninety Six National Historic Site, covered in Section B-24.) The 842 acres at Cowpens National Battlefield afford good birding at any time of year. Unlike nearby Kings Mountain, Cowpens has open fields and brushy areas in the early stages of succession as well as a hardwoods forest. The auto tour road goes through great areas for species such as sparrows

(Song, Field, and Chipping year-round; others in winter) as well as breeding Yellow-breasted Chat, Prairie Warbler, Brown Thrasher, Rufous-sided Towhee, and similar species of thickets and hedgerows.

To reach Cowpens National Battlefield from I-85 southbound, get off at Exit 92 in Gaffney, and follow SC 11 west for about 10 miles to the park entrance on the left (south). From I-85 northbound use Exit 83, and go north on SC 110 for about 6 miles to SC 11. Turn right (east) onto SC 11, and go a quarter mile to the park entrance on the right (south).

Follow the entrance road 0.5 mile to the visitor center. Here you can view the historic museum and pick up a park map. The easiest way to bird the park is to drive the three-mile tour road and to stop at the various pulloffs.

At 1.3 miles from the visitor center there is a picnic area. Here is the best place to explore the woods. From the west end of the picnic area (the end nearest the visitor center) walk west along an abandoned roadway a few yards. Soon this old road intersects another old road. Turn left (south) onto this second old road, and walk two or three minutes. You will notice a trail crossing the old road. This is (or will be) the park's nature trail, but as of the late 1980s this trail, although cleared, had not been blazed. Turn right onto the nature trail, which soon leads into a large grove of bamboo and then into second-growth oak woods with a few Virginia pines mixed in. You will soon reach a fork in the trail. (To the right the trail goes toward the visitor center.) Take the left fork. The trail loops back to the old road, crosses it, and then goes in a wide loop along Long Branch of Island Creek. The habitat here is mature cove hardwoods. The trail eventually winds back up the hill to the picnic area after a total of about two miles.

B–12—CHESTER COUNTY

Chester County is in a mostly rural part of the Piedmont, in the north-central part of the state; the county seat is the small industrial city of Chester. Interstate 77 runs north to south through the eastern part of the county, affording easy access from nearby urban areas such as Charlotte, Rock Hill, and Columbia.

Chester County has a variety of Piedmont habitats. There are loblolly-pine plantations, many small farms, and open fields. Here and there creeks and small rivers have cut impressive valleys, the slopes of which are often covered with oak-hickory forests. Just north of the city of Chester is an extensive area of poorly drained, sandy soil similar to parts of the Upper Coastal Plain (see Section B-12.5).

From the birder's point of view Chester County is dominated by two rivers, the Broad and the Catawba. The Broad River forms the western boundary of the county. Much of the land here is in the Sumter National Forest. While pine plantations are the rule, there is also a bit of floodplain forest as well as mature oak-hickory forests on the steeper slopes of ravines that drop about three hundred feet from ridgetop to river.

The eastern border of Chester County is the Catawba River (including Fishing Creek Reservoir, which is an impoundment of the Catawba River). The land here is less wild than that along the Broad River, but some moist hardwood slopes can be found, such as at Landsford Canal State Park.

In the middle of the county is the small city of Chester. This area of small farms and suburbs has the county's other state park—Chester State Park. A few miles north of the city is Lake Oliphant, a small public fishing lake with good birding in winter and during migration.

B–12.1—Woods Ferry Recreation Area, Sumter National Forest

Winter   *
Spring   ***
Summer **
Fall   **

See letter A on Map B–12.1.

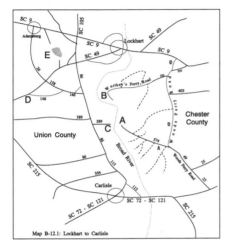

Map B-12.1: Lockhart to Carlisle

Woods Ferry Recreation Area has a developed campground (closed in winter) and boat-launching area on the Broad River in a rather wild part of the Sumter National Forest. There is a one-mile-loop hiking trail from the picnic area through floodplain forest. Nearby forest roads give good access to wooded ravines and other parts of the Broad River floodplain.

To reach the area from the north, turn south from SC 9 onto Road 49, Woods Ferry Road. This intersection is 4.7 miles east of the SC 9 bridge over the Broad River at Lockhart (Union County), or it is about 9.5 miles west of the intersection of SC 9 and US 321 Bypass, on the west side of the city of Chester. Once on Road 49, go about 5.7 miles south to the intersection with Road 574. There should be a national forest sign at this intersection, which is near the Leeds Lookout Tower. Turn right (west) onto Road 574, and follow it to its end at the recreation area (3.5 miles from Road 49).

To reach Woods Ferry Recreation Area from the south, turn north from SC 72—SC 121 onto Road 25, Woods Ferry Road. This turn is 2.7 miles east of the bridge over the Broad River near Carlisle, or it is 11.1 miles west of the intersection of SC 72 and SC 9 Bypass, on the southwest side of the city of Chester. Follow Road 25 north. In 2.1 miles Road 25 becomes Road 49, but it is still Woods Ferry Road. At 5.8 miles north of SC 72—SC 121, turn left (west) onto Road 574, which goes another 3.5 miles to the recreation area.

This is rugged country, with deep, wooded ravines cut into the Piedmont Plateau. The change in elevation is impressive, ranging from 686 feet at the beginning of Road 574 to about 320 feet at the Broad River at Neals Shoals. Some of the steep hillsides and bluffs will remind you of the mountains. The flatter areas are planted in loblolly pine, but the steep ravines support a mature oak-hickory forest, with a cove hardwood forest along the streams which flow down to the Broad River. The result is a good place for birds.

Numerous well-maintained forest roads branch off of Road 574. Three of these roads deserve special mention.

About a mile down Road 574 from the fire tower look for Forest Road 304 on the left (southwest). This road goes for a bit more than a mile to a parking area overlooking the Broad River just below the Neals Shoals hydroelectric plant and dam. The rocks in the river below the dam attract a few shorebirds in migration. This is also a good area for swallows, especially Barn Swallows and Northern Rough-winged Swallows, which breed on the grounds of the hydroelectric plant across the river.

A bit beyond the turnoff for Forest Road 304, look for another gravel road off to

69

the left from Road 574. This is Forest Road 305D, which goes about a mile to a parking area near a quiet backwater of the lake formed by Neals Shoals Dam. This is a good spot for breeding Wood Ducks and Prothonotary Warblers. Great Blue Herons are common here and may breed nearby. A jeep trail continues a short way from the parking area, which allows easy access to the river. There is a thick pine grove along this jeep trail, which is good for owls. The Eastern Screech-Owl breeds here, and other owls are possible in winter.

The third good side road from Road 574 turns off to the right (north) about a half mile beyond the turnoff for Forest Road 305D. This is Forest Road 305, which unlike the other two forest roads is not a dead-end road. Forest Road 305 winds for about three miles and eventually reaches Road 49. A half mile north of Road 574 this forest road crosses Clarks Creek on a low bridge. The floodplain of Clarks Creek is a great place for birds, including most of the species of Piedmont floodplain forest. Eastern Phoebes breed under the bridge, and American Woodcocks are fairly common in the moist woods along the creek. This is an excellent place for Wild Turkey, especially in late summer.

B–12.2—Worthey's Ferry Wildlife Station

Winter	*
Spring	***
Summer	*
Fall	**

See letter B on Map B–12.1.

Worthey's Ferry Wildlife Station is another area along the Broad River in the Sumter National Forest, but it differs from the Woods Ferry Recreation Area (see Section B-12.1) or the Broad River Recreation Area in Union County (see Section B-44.2) in one important respect. In addition to having great floodplain forest, the Worthey's Ferry area has several dozen acres of open fields which have been planted with corn, lespedeza, and other crops designed to encourage wildlife. The result is an extremely diverse area attractive to birdlife.

To reach Worthey's Ferry Wildlife Station from the Woods Ferry area, start from the intersection of Road 574 and Road 49 near the Leeds Lookout Tower, and go north on Road 49 for 5.5 miles. Here turn left (west) onto Road 535, Worthey's Ferry Road.

To reach this point from SC 9 in Chester, follow SC 9 west from the intersection with US 321 on the western edge of the city of Chester. At 9.1 miles west of US 321 turn left onto Road 535, which joins Road 49 in about a half mile.

From Road 49 follow Road 535 westward. The pavement ends in 1.4 miles; here Worthey's Ferry Road becomes Forest Road 301. Follow Forest Road 301 to its end. At about three miles from Road 49, Forest Road 301 descends into the floodplain of the Broad River and reaches the open fields of the wildlife station. You will find several trails off to the right toward the river.

Note: this area is popular with hunters. During the hunting season it is best to visit only on Sunday (since there is no hunting in the national forest on Sundays).

Winter *
Spring *
Summer *
Fall *

The 523 acres of *Chester State Park* provide a pleasant picnicking and fishing area in the southern suburbs of the city of Chester. There is a 160-acre lake, a campground, and a short nature trail, but no swimming. The habitats in the park include loblolly pine plantation, mixed oak-hickory-pine woods, and a small area of moist woods just below the dam of the lake.

To reach Chester State Park, find the intersection of SC 9 Bypass and SC 72 on the southwest side of the city of Chester, and go 1.8 miles south on SC 72 to the park entrance, on the left (east).

The lake at the park sometimes has a few waterfowl. A few Canada Geese may stop by in late fall or early spring, and you may spot a Pied-billed Grebe in winter. The picnic grounds are good for Chipping Sparrow (mostly spring through fall; only a few in the winter). This is a great place to study the differences between two similar pine species—the loblolly- and the shortleaf-pines. The loblolly pine has needles six to nine inches long in clusters of three. The shortleaf has needles three to five inches long, mostly in clusters of two. Both species are common in the picnic area. The loblolly is essentially a tree of the Coastal Plain, but it has been planted extensively in all parts of South Carolina. The shortleaf pine occurs throughout the state, but it is most common in the Piedmont.

To find the nature trail, walk right (counterclockwise) around the lake from the picnic area until you start seeing the painted trail blazes. The trail leads to the dam of the lake but does not go around the lake. The area below the dam is good for wildflowers in early spring and usually has a breeding pair of Louisiana Waterthrushes (late March through July). The other birds along the trail will be birds typical of oak-pine woods anywhere in South Carolina.

B—12.4—Landsford Canal State Park

Winter *
Spring ****
Summer **
Fall ***

The expansion of the United States in the early nineteenth century has left us an unusual legacy of natural areas. Many canals were built then to connect the eastern cities with the western frontier. Most of these were dug alongside Piedmont rivers. Today, in New Jersey, Maryland, Virginia, and also South Carolina, the remnants of these canals are preserved in state or national historic parks. These parks also preserve the natural environment, in some cases protecting Piedmont floodplain forest which has not been cut in 150 years. The most famous of these canal parks is the C & O canal towpath in Washington, DC, and Maryland—a national trail that stretches for over a hundred miles through the Maryland Piedmont and mountains along the Potomac River.

The South Carolina park which protects a bit of Piedmont riverside wilderness is Landsford Canal State Park, along the Catawba River in eastern Chester County. Here we find three miles of trail, not a hundred, but it is still a special place.

The Landsford Canal was constructed

between 1819 and 1823 to circumvent rapids in the Catawba River. Due to extremes of flooding and drought as well as the coming of the railroad, the canal was soon abandoned. Today this scenic area is a state park protecting two hundred acres of floodplain climax forest and adjacent wooded slopes.

Landsford Canal State Park is famous as one of the best sites in South Carolina for spring wildflowers. From early March through late May you can find a succession of flowers such as trout lily, spring beauty, jack-in-the-pulpit, crane-fly orchid, Atamasco lily, and columbine. At the same time, the birder will be looking up, not down, to find some of the numerous migrating warblers, vireos, thrushes, and other species that can be found here in late April to early May.

There is nowhere in South Carolina that gets the kind of songbird migration that can be observed farther north (such as at Point Pelee, Ontario) or along the Gulf Coast from west Florida to Texas. But here at Landsford Canal there is a pretty good selection of migrants—both spring and fall. The combination of the river, the hillside, and the mature woods attracts many of the following as transients in April, May, late August, and September: Osprey; Bald Eagle (rare); Sharp-shinned and Cooper's Hawk; Spotted Sandpiper; Ring-billed Gull; Black-billed Cuckoo (rare); Common Nighthawk; Veery; Swainson's and Gray-cheeked Thrush; Cedar Waxwing; Solitary Vireo; Philadelphia Vireo (fall); Blue-winged, Golden-winged, Tennessee, Orange-crowned, Chestnut-sided, Magnolia, Cape May, Black-throated Blue, Yellow-rumped, Black-throated Green, Blackburnian, Bay-breasted, Blackpoll, Worm-eating, and Canada Warblers; Northern Waterthrush; Rose-breasted Grosbeak; and Northern Oriole.

In addition to these transients, which are seen only in migration, quite a few species stay to breed along the canal. These include the Green-backed Heron; Wood Duck; Red-shouldered Hawk; Killdeer; American Woodcock; Yellow-billed Cuckoo; Chimney Swift; Ruby-throated Hummingbird; Belted Kingfisher; Red-bel-

lied, Downy, Hairy, and Pileated Woodpecker; Northern Flicker; Eastern Wood-Pewee; Acadian and Great Crested Flycatcher; Eastern Phoebe; Purple Martin; Northern Rough-winged and Barn Swallow; Blue Jay; American and Fish Crow; Carolina Chickadee; Tufted Titmouse; Carolina Wren; Blue-gray Gnatcatcher; Wood Thrush; American Robin; Gray Catbird; Brown Thrasher; White-eyed, Yellow-throated, and Red-eyed Vireo; Northern Parula; Yellow-throated, Pine, Black-and-White, Prothonotary, Kentucky, and Hooded Warbler; Ovenbird; Louisiana Waterthrush; Common Yellowthroat; Summer and Scarlet Tanager; Northern Cardinal; Indigo Bunting; Rufous-sided Towhee; Chipping Sparrow; Common Grackle; Brown-headed Cowbird; and Orchard Oriole.

To reach Landsford Canal State Park from I-77, use Exit 65, and go east on SC 9 toward Fort Lawn for 1.3 miles to the junction with SC 223. Turn left (northeast) onto SC 223, and go 6.7 miles to US 21. (This intersection is 5 miles north of the intersection of SC 9 and US 21 in Fort Lawn or 13 miles south along US 21 from the intersection of US 21 and I-77 in Rock Hill.) Turn left (north) onto US 21, and go about 1.3 miles to Road 327, where there is a sign for the park. Turn right (east) onto Road 327, and go 1.7 miles to the main park entrance road. (There is another entrance road some 1.3 miles farther on Road 327.)

As you drive along Road 327, stop and look over the pastures. This is a good spot for the Eastern Meadowlark all year long. From late April until August you can usually find a Grasshopper Sparrow in the pasture on the north side of Road 327 about a mile east of US 21. This is private land, so confine your birding to the roadside. Keep an eye out for Wild Turkeys also, which have been reestablished in recent years on private property south of the state park. Once you get to the main parking lot, you can easily explore the park on foot. There are two trails, one along the river and one along the canal going south from the picnic ground. These trails connect, so you can make a three-mile circuit to the south end of the park and back.

B–12.5—Lake Oliphant

Winter   **
Spring   **
Summer *
Fall   **

The state of South Carolina has built a series of small lakes for public fishing at various places around the state. One of the better of these lakes for birding is *Lake Oliphant*, a forty-acre lake about 7 miles north of the city of Chester.

To reach Lake Oliphant from Chester, get onto SC 132, which is a bypass around the northern edge of the city. Go to the intersection of SC 132 and Road 1, Old York Road. Here turn north onto Road 1, and follow this road for about three miles until you get to the turnoff for SC 909 east (a right turn onto Aaron Burr Road). There is a sign for the lake at this turnoff. Follow SC 909 for 1.4 miles. Here turn left (north) onto Road 190, and go about 0.1 mile to the entrance road for Lake Oliphant.

You can overlook the entire lake from a fishing pier near the parking lot. This lake is good for wintering waterfowl. Expect the Pied-billed Grebe, Canada Goose, Mallard, Ring-necked Duck, and Ruddy Duck.

There is a two-mile loop trail around the lake. If you follow the trail counterclockwise over the dam and along the north shore of the lake, you will reach the edge of a public dove-hunting area in about a half mile. This is a large area of open fields and hedgerows, good for sparrows and of course Mourning Doves. Do not enter the dove field during the dove-hunting season. Another good sparrow field lies along the short entrance road to the fishing lake.

B–13—CHESTERFIELD COUNTY

Chesterfield County is a predominately rural county in the Sandhills subregion of the Upper Coastal Plain in the northeastern part of the state, along the North Carolina border. Its largest city is the lovely old town of Cheraw, which lies at the junction of US 1 and US 52 in the eastern part of the county.

Though Chesterfield County lies between two important rivers—the Great Pee Dee

River on the east and Lynches River on the west—it is the Sandhills area between these rivers which attracts birders to the county. Along US 1 lie four adjacent public areas: Carolina Sandhills National Wildlife Refuge, Sand Hills State Forest, Cheraw Fish Hatchery, and Cheraw State Park. These areas protect over 140,000 acres of sandhills habitats. All four areas have Red-cockaded Woodpeckers as well as many other less rare bird species.

B–13.1—Carolina Sandhills National Wildlife Refuge

Winter   **
Spring   **
Summer **
Fall   ***

See Map B–13.1.

The auto tour route through *Carolina Sandhills National Wildlife Refuge* gives

the visitor a good introduction to the Sandhills. To reach the southern end of the tour road from US 1 northbound, follow US 1 to its intersection with SC 151 in

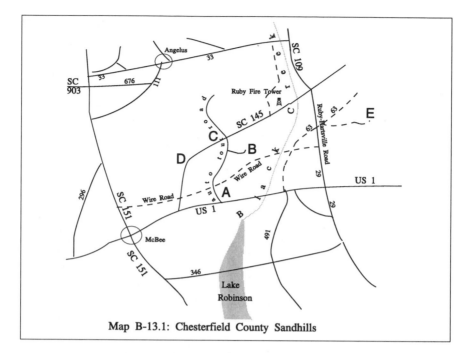

Map B-13.1: Chesterfield County Sandhills

the town of McBee. Continue northeast on US 1 for another 3.4 miles. The *refuge headquarters* (letter A on Map B–13.1) and the beginning of the tour road are on the left (northwest). If you are southbound on US 1, starting from the junction of SC 9 and US 1 in the western part of the town of Cheraw, follow US 1 southeast for about 23.5 miles to the refuge headquarters, on the right.

Look for the visitor contact station at the beginning of the auto tour route. Here you can pick up refuge brochures, including a map and a bird list. Go north on the auto tour route. In about one mile you will reach Pool A, one of several small ponds in the refuge. Just beyond the pond, on the left (west), is a parking area of the Woodland Pond Trail. This trail is one-mile loop trail along Little Alligator Creek. Here you find the common species of bay-swamp thickets and oak-pine woods.

After exploring the Woodland Pond Trail, continue north on the auto tour road. In about 0.2 mile you will cross Wire Road,

an east-west sand road. You may wish to take a side trip to Black Creek in the eastern part of the refuge. To check out Black Creek, turn right (east) onto Wire Road, and go about three miles to the bridge over Black Creek, one of four fishing access points on this interesting creek. Black Creek is one of the better places in the refuge to find migrant and wintering birds. It is especially good from late August through early October for migrating warblers. When you are done at Black Creek, return to the main auto tour road, and continue north.

About two miles north of Wire Road the auto tour route reaches the turnoff for *Martin's Lake* (letter B on Map B–13.1) on the right. This is the best birding area on the refuge. Turn right (east) onto the Martin's Lake Road, which winds about a mile to a parking area. There are several Red-cockaded Woodpecker cavity trees along this stretch of road, and the chances of finding this rare woodpecker here are pretty good.

From the Martin's Lake parking area follow the trail downhill toward the lake. In about a quarter mile you will join another trail, the four-mile-long Whitetail Trail. Turn left (northwest) onto this trail, which parallels the southwest shore of Martin's Lake. You will quickly come to an observation deck giving you a good view of the lake. About ten minutes' walk from the observation deck you will come to a lake-level photo blind on the lake shore, an excellent place to observe the waterfowl on the lake.

Permanent residents on Martin's Lake include a flock of introduced Canada Geese as well as several Wood Ducks and a few Mallards. These species are joined in winter by other ducks, mostly American Wigeons, American Black Ducks, Ring-necked Ducks, and Hooded Mergansers as well as a few coots and Pied-billed Grebes.

From the photo blind rejoin the Whitetail Trail for a few yards until you reach a service road. Turn left onto the service road, which leads to the parking area in about a quarter mile.

The bay-swamp thickets and Atlantic white-cedar bogs along the Whitetail Trail are great birding places, especially in fall migration. Common migrants here include the following warblers: Blue-winged, Chestnut-sided, Magnolia, Black-throated Blue, Black-and-white, American Redstart, and Ovenbird.

From Martin's Lake rejoin the auto tour route, which goes north another two miles to SC 145. Here, just beyond SC 145, is the Lake Bee picnic area (letter C on Map B–13.1). There are numerous Red-cockaded Woodpecker roost trees in this area.

If you are looking for Red-cockaded Woodpeckers and other species of the pinewoods and you did not find them at Martin's Lake, the May's Lake Loop Road is a good one to try. From the Lake Bee picnic area return to the auto tour route, cross SC 145, and drive southeast, back

toward the refuge headquarters. In about one mile you will reach a point where the paved auto tour route turns sharply to the right. An unpaved road goes straight ahead at this point. This is the May's Lake Loop Road, which wanders in a long loop to May's Lake, a popular fishing spot.

The May's Lake Loop Road makes about a six-mile loop though a variety of habitats. The last mile or so of this loop runs through a superb old-growth longleaf-pine forest where Red-cockaded Woodpeckers are fairly common. During much of the year the May's Lake Loop Road is closed to traffic, but you can still reach an excellent longleaf-pine forest in a few minutes' walk. From the gate at the entrance to the road to May's Lake, walk straight ahead for a few yards, then turn left at the first sand road (which is the end of the May's Lake Loop Road). Walk north on this road, going clockwise around the loop. You will reach the longleaf-pine forest in about a quarter mile. This is a good area for Red-cockaded Woodpeckers year-round and for Bachman's Sparrow March through September.

Many other spots on the refuge offer fairly good birding. Use the refuge fishing map to explore the refuge, if you have time.

From Lake Bee go south on SC 145 toward McBee. In about three miles you will leave the refuge and come out into an area of peach orchards and broad cultivated fields (letter D on Map B–13.1). Horned Larks are fairly common permanent residents here and are most easily found in late winter or early spring, when they are singing. Listen for their tinkling song, which is often sung high in the air.

At five miles south of Lake Bee, SC 145 ends at US 1. Here you can turn right to go on to the town of McBee or left to return to the beginning of the refuge auto tour route.

B—13.2—Sugar Loaf Mountain, Sand Hills State Forest

Winter   *
Spring   *
Summer *
Fall   **

See letter E on Map B—13.1.

Sand Hills State Forest includes about ninety thousand acres of pine-covered hills between the Carolina Sandhills National Wildlife Refuge and Cheraw State Park. *Sugar Loaf Mountain*, a 160-foot-high sandstone outcropping, is one of the most interesting areas in the forest.

Directions will be given from the headquarters of Carolina Sandhills National Wildlife Refuge (see Section B-13.1 above). From the south end of the auto tour road, go northeast on US 1, toward Cheraw. In 6.5 miles you will reach the intersection with Road 29, the Ruby-Hartsville Road. Turn left (north) onto Road 29. In about two miles you will cross Wire Road, a sand road. (Black Creek is about three miles to your left (west); see Section B-13.1.) Continue north on Road 29.

At about a half mile north of Wire Road there is a power line right-of-way which crosses Road 29. This is a good area to look and listen for Bachman's Sparrow, which in this part of the state is often found in brushy clear-cuts, power line rights-of-way, and other brushy, open areas.

At 2.9 miles north of US 1 turn right (northeast) onto Road 63, Scotch Road, an improved, although unpaved, road. Follow Road 63 for 0.3 mile to the entrance road of Sugar Loaf Recreation Area (fishing and picnicking, but no camping).

Sugar Loaf Recreation Area has a small lake, a short nature trail (across the road from the lake), and a short trail to the top of Sugar Loaf Mountain. Rising only 160 feet above the surrounding area, Sugar Loaf is not much of a mountain, but there is a great view from the top. Birds here are the common species of pinewoods and oak-pine woods. When you are done here, backtrack to US 1.

B—13.3—Cheraw State Park and Fish Hatchery

Winter   **
Spring   **
Summer **
Fall   **

Cheraw State Park is South Carolina's oldest (established 1934) and one of its largest (7,361 acres). It is a delightful place to camp, picnic, fish, or swim. The main entrance is along US 1 about 4 miles south of the town of Cheraw or 24 miles north of McBee.

The best birding in the park is in the Dogwood Picnic Area, which is along the main park road between the US 1 entrance and the campground. This is a fairly open area with trees in which Red-cockaded Woodpeckers actively roost. For a one-mile walk take the Dogwood Nature Trail (brochure available at the park office). Birds here are the common species of Sandhills oak-pine woods.

The main park lake (Eureka Lake) is large enough to attract a few Pied-billed Grebes, coots, and ducks in winter. There is a permanently resident flock of Canada Geese on this lake. If you cannot find the Red-cockaded Woodpeckers at Cheraw State Park, return to the US 1 entrance and turn left (south). Go about a mile toward McBee to the *Cheraw State Fish Hatchery* on the left. Red-cockaded Woodpecker cavity trees are along the entrance road to the fish hatchery. The hatchery ponds attract a few birds as well. Look for Wood Duck year-round, a few Great Egrets in summer, and perhaps some other ducks in winter. The Canada Geese from Cheraw State Park often use this area.

B–14—CLARENDON COUNTY

Clarendon County is a predominately rural county in the Upper Coastal Plain, near the center of the state. Interstate 95 runs through the center of the county. The county seat is Manning, a pleasant town of about five thousand. Clarendon County is primarily an agricultural county with a typical coastal-plains mixture of cultivated fields, pastures, pine plantations, and floodplain forest along the larger rivers (the Black and Pocotaligo Rivers in this case).

From the naturalist's point of view Claren-don County is dominated by the flood-plains of the Black and Pocotaligo Rivers in the north and by Lake Marion on the southern border of the county. In addition, Clarendon County has numerous Carolina bays—those strange oval-shaped depressions which mark the Coastal Plain of North and South Carolina. The north shore of Lake Marion is the site of Santee National Wildlife Refuge, one of the best birding areas in South Carolina (see Sections B-14.1, B-14.2, and B-14.3).

B–14.1—The Bluff Unit of Santee National Wildlife Refuge

Winter ****
Spring ***
Summer **
Fall ***

See letter A on Map B–14.1.

Santee National Wildlife Refuge lies on the north shore of Lake Marion. The refuge has 74,352 acres, of which 70,940 acres are lake and marsh, while 3,412 acres are in upland areas. Santee Refuge is the most dependable place in South Carolina to find geese and swans in winter, when there are always a few hundred wintering Canada Geese, and usually a few dozen Snow Geese and a handful of Greater White-fronted Geese and Tundra Swans. Santee Refuge may well be the most dependable spot along the east coast of the United States to find a Greater White-fronted Goose in winter.

The refuge is divided into four disjunct units, which are (from west to east) Bluff Unit, Dingle Pond Unit, Pine Island Unit, and Cuddo Unit.

The *Bluff Unit* is the best known of the four, since it has the refuge headquarters and visitors' center, and a nature trail (Wright's Bluff Wildlife Trail) which is open year-round. The Bluff Unit is also the unit most conveniently reached from I-95 (letter A on Map B–14.1).

If you plan to visit the refuge from November 1 through the last day of February, you will be limited to visiting either the Wright's Bluff area of the Bluff Unit or the Dingle Pond Unit. The current management plan prohibits use of the western part of the Bluff Unit or of any of the Pine Island or Cuddo Units during this period. The only common exception to this policy is the day of the Santee Christmas Bird Count, when birders are allowed on the entire refuge.

To reach the Bluff Unit from I-95, exit at North Santee (Exit 102). Take the service road west a short distance to the old road (US 15—301). At US 15—301, turn

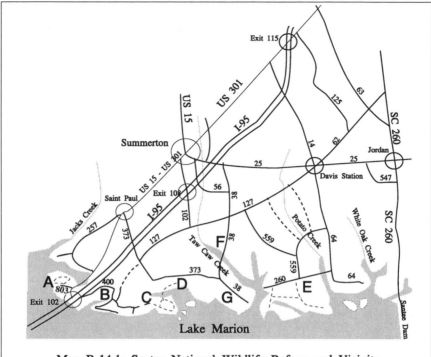

Map B-14.1: Santee National Wildlife Refuge and Vicinity

right (north) toward Summerton, and go about 0.3 mile to Road 803, the main entrance road into the refuge. The visitors' center is about a half mile down this road. Although the center is usually open only from 8:30 A.M. to 4:30 P.M. Monday through Friday, refuge leaflets (including maps and a bird list) are available seven days a week.

After picking up refuge leaflets and overlooking Lake Marion from the deck of the visitors' center, return to Road 803 and follow it another half mile to the parking lot for the Wright's Bluff Wildlife Trail. This is as far as you may drive.

The Wright's Bluff Wildlife Trail is a 1.1-mile-long nature trail through a pine plantation to an observation tower and a short boardwalk over a marsh. Most of the pines were blown down by Hurricane Hugo in September 1989. As a result, the former pine plantation is now in the process of succession, with lots of brushy tan-

gles. From the parking lot take the trail clockwise. You first enter the former loblolly-pine plantation, now a brushy field. After crossing a small bald-cypress slough (usually dry), the trail leads to an observation tower. From the tower you can overlook the open fields and distant ponds and marshes of the western part of the Bluff Unit. This area is closed in winter, when it is the winter home of several hundred migratory Canada Geese as well as small numbers of Snow Geese and usually a Greater White-fronted Goose or Tundra Swan or two as well. A telescope is helpful in studying the geese.

If you see no geese from the observation tower, continue around the trail. In a few more minutes the trail leads along the side of Canty Bay, a backwater of Lake Marion. This is the best place in the refuge to observe wintering waterfowl. In the bay, especially on the distant mud flats, you should find at least a few geese as well as ducks. Duck species typically seen here include Green-winged Teal, American Black Duck, Mallard, Northern Pintail, Northern Shoveler, American Wigeon, Ring-necked Duck, Bufflehead, and Hooded Merganser. Other species appear but are either more likely in other parts of the refuge (especially the parts closed in winter) or are rare anywhere. The common breeding duck of the refuge is the Wood Duck, which may be encountered anywhere. (A few Mallards also breed, but note that all the geese are migrants—there is no permanently resident Canada Goose flock here.)

The mud flats of Canty Bay attract shorebirds year-round, but especially in spring and fall migrations. The Killdeer is common all year and is joined from fall through spring by Common Snipe (frequent), both yellowlegs (mostly Greater), Least Sandpiper, and a few Dunlin. Common migrants which do not appear in winter include Solitary, Spotted, and Pectoral Sandpipers. Other species are rare but possible.

Hawks are also commonly seen along the trail. Ospreys are common during the warmer part of the year. Winter brings Northern Harriers and a few Bald Eagles. Red-tailed and Red-shouldered Hawks are seen all year.

From the boardwalk over the marsh at Canty Bay the trail loops back to the parking lot. If you are in a hurry, you can go more directly to the marsh by taking the trail counterclockwise from the parking lot.

A summertime visit to the Bluff Unit gives you a chance to walk into the agricultural areas along the edge of the lake, which are closed during the winter. Just after you leave the observation tower, you will cross a refuge road leading out into cornfields. If you walk a mile or so along this road, you will reach an area of lakeside willow trees where up to four Warbling Vireos were spotted in June of 1989, 1990, and 1991. You might not find the vireo, but you will find many common species of Coastal Plain farms and brush, including numerous Painted Buntings.

B–14.2—The Dingle Pond and Pine Island Units of Santee National Wildlife Refuge

Winter	****
Spring	***
Summer	*
Fall	***

See Map B–14.1.

The *Dingle Pond Unit of Santee NWR* is one of two areas (the other being the eastern part of the Bluff Unit) which are open year-round. Dingle Pond is a Carolina bay about a half mile long along its main axis. The interior of this bay has low, scrubby growth—pocosin—alternating with more open areas. Unlike most Carolina bays, Dingle Pond has water in it most of the year, probably because it is right next to Lake Marion.

The *Pine Island Unit of Santee NWR* probably has the best birding on the refuge, but this unit is closed from November 1 though the end of February. (Pine Island may be open in winter; check with the refuge manager.) Pine Island has upland areas, marsh, small ponds, and an arm of Lake Marion (Savannah Branch). It also has a Red-cockaded Woodpecker colony and is a great place to observe alligators.

To reach Dingle Pond and Pine Island from I-95, exit at North Santee (Exit 102), which is also the exit for the refuge headquarters and the Bluff Unit of the refuge. Instead of going west, go east from the interstate on Road 400. Road 400 first goes by a large truck stop, then turns sharply left for a half mile and then sharply to the right. Soon after turning right, you will be driving along the northern edge of the *Dingle Pond Unit*. At about 1.7 miles look for a gated road on the right (letter B on Map B—14.1). Park along the paved road (being careful not to block the gate).

This gated road is the northern end of the Dingle Pond Trail, a 0.7-mile trail that skirts the eastern and southern edges of Dingle Pond. Dingle Pond is a bit difficult to observe without getting your feet wet, but from the trail you can spy a bit of it. It often has quite a few ducks in winter: Wood Duck, Mallard, Green-winged Teal, and American Wigeon. Other wintering species include numerous Swamp and Song Sparrows, Virginia Rail, and American Bittern. The rail and the bittern are found every two years or so. A bit of loud hand clapping may encourage a rail to call, but you will be lucky to see it.

One interesting species that can been seen here in winter is the American Woodcock. At dawn and dusk this large sandpiper flies to and from Dingle Pond and the nearby woods. You may flush one in the daytime along the trail, but don't count on it.

After reaching the end of the Dingle Pond Trail, backtrack to Road 400, and continue driving east on this road. In less than a mile you will reach the intersection with Road 556, a paved road to the right. (This intersection is the center of the Santee NWR Christmas Count circle.) Continue straight ahead on Road 400. In about two miles beyond Dingle Pond, the paved road takes a sharp right turn. Here continue straight ahead on a sand road, which soon enters the Pine Island Unit of the refuge (letter C on Map B—14.1). There is a boat-launching area at the end of this sand road (open all year). Beyond the boat launch is a gate. From March 1 through October 31 you may ride a bicycle or walk beyond this gate into the main part of the *Pine Island Unit*. Pine Island may now be open in winter. If you see no "AREA CLOSED" sign, you may enter.

To explore the Pine Island Unit on foot, cross the gate, and continue straight ahead on the main service road. Within a few yards you will emerge from a pine grove into an area of open fields, with a few trees along the service road. Go east for about a half mile to an intersection. This is the southwestern corner of a one-mile loop. To circle the loop clockwise, turn left, and walk north about a quarter mile. In March and April the low spots on either side of this part of the trail usually have at least a little water, creating mud flats and rain pools in the cultivated fields. These pools are excellent for shorebirds. In March it is not unusual to flush twenty to fifty Common Snipe from these wet areas. The snipe are joined in late March and April by other migrating shorebirds, including Greater and Lesser Yellowlegs, Pectoral, Solitary, Spotted, and Least Sandpipers, and perhaps other species. Killdeer are also common.

When the service road approaches the edge of Lake Marion (about a quarter mile from the intersection where you turned left), marshes come into view. These marshes are home to Common Moorhens in the summer, and American Coots year-round. (They are also home to several large alligators, which feed on the coots and moorhens.) You will encounter a second intersection. To continue the loop, you will turn right, following another service road along the edge of the lake.

Before you turn back, you may wish to explore the swampy woods in front of you. Instead of turning right, go straight ahead over a short causeway and into the woods. The road continues into the woods for about a mile to a dead end at the end of the refuge lands. This stretch of road is great for migrant and breeding warblers. Common breeders include Northern Parula, Yellow-throated and Pine Warblers, American Redstart, Prothonotary, Hooded, and Kentucky Warblers. With luck you might hear a Swainson's Warbler or a Louisiana Waterthrush.

This road also runs past an active Red-cockaded Woodpecker colony, where you can also find other typical pine-woods breeding species: Pine Warbler, Brown-headed Nuthatch, Bachman's Sparrow (a few), Summer Tanager, Eastern Bluebird, and Eastern Wood-Pewee (letter D on Map B—14.1).

After exploring the woods, return to the intersection by the marshes, and continue the clockwise loop. When you return to the main service road, backtrack to the parking lot.

The Pine Island Unit is an excellent area for birds, especially in migration. In spring or fall you should find most of the following species (some of which are here also in summer): the Pied-billed Grebe; Double-crested Cormorant; Anhinga; American and Least Bittern (both rare); Great Blue Heron; Great and Snowy Egret; Little Blue and Tricolored Heron (rare); Cattle Egret; Green-backed Heron; Black-crowned Night-Heron (rare); White Ibis; Wood Duck; Mallard; Black and Turkey Vulture; Osprey; Bald Eagle (rare); Sharp-shinned, Cooper's, Red-shouldered, and Red-tailed Hawk; American Kestrel; Northern Bobwhite; Common Moorhen; American Coot; Killdeer; Greater and Lesser Yellowlegs; Solitary, Spotted, Least, and Pectoral Sandpiper; Dunlin; Common Snipe; Laughing, Ring-billed, and Herring Gull; Forster's and Least Tern; Mourning Dove; Belted Kingfisher; Red-headed, Red-bellied, Downy, and Hairy Woodpecker; Northern Flicker; Pileated Woodpecker; Eastern Wood-Pewee; Eastern Phoebe; Eastern Kingbird; Purple Martin; Tree, Northern Rough-winged, and Barn Swallow; Blue Jay; American and Fish Crow; Carolina Chickadee; Tufted Titmouse; Carolina and House Wren; Golden-crowned and Ruby-crowned Kinglet; Blue-gray Gnatcatcher; Eastern Bluebird; Gray Catbird; Northern Mockingbird; Brown Thrasher; Loggerhead Shrike; European Starling; White-eyed, Solitary, Yellow-throated, and Red-eyed Vireo; Northern Parula; Yellow, Magnolia (fall only), Black-throated Blue, Yellow-rumped, Pine, Prairie, Palm, and Black-and-white Warbler; American Redstart; Prothonotary Warbler; Common Yellowthroat; Yellow-breasted Chat; Blue Grosbeak; Indigo Bunting; Rufous-sided Towhee; Chipping, Field, Savannah, Song, Swamp, and White-throated Sparrow; Bobolink; Red-winged Blackbird; Eastern Meadowlark; Common Grackle; Brown-headed Cowbird; Orchard Oriole; and American Goldfinch.

B—14.3—The Cuddo Unit of Santee National Wildlife Refuge

Winter	*
Spring	**
Summer	*
Fall	**

See Map B—14.1.

The Cuddo Unit is the least known to birders of all the areas of Santee NWR, since it is relatively inaccessible and much larger than the Pine Island Unit (thus forcing the birder to walk farther to get to the marsh and lakeshore). But Cuddo has much the same habitats as Pine Island (except that it lacks Red-cockaded Woodpeckers) and should provide excellent birding, especially in the spring and fall. The Cuddo Unit is the only part of the refuge which has a resident flock of Wild Turkeys (though these wary birds are seldom seen).

To reach the Cuddo Unit from I-95, use the Summerton exit (Exit 108), and go south on Road 102 for 1.7 miles to a T-junction with Road 127. Here turn left (east), and go on Road 127 for 2.1 miles, until you encounter Road 559. Turn right (southeast) onto Road 559. This road reaches a sharp right turn in about 3.8 miles. In 4.1 miles Road 559 ends at a T-junction with Road 260. Road 260 is the northern border of the *Cuddo Unit* (letter E on Map B—14.1). Turn right (west) onto Road 260, and immediately on your left (south) you will see a gated road with refuge markings. This is the entrance to the Cuddo Unit.

(If you continue west on Road 260, you will reach Log Jam Landing, a boat launch area on Taw Caw Creek, in about one mile. Log Jam Landing is open year-round. There is a small marsh near the parking lot and also a good view of the Taw Caw Creek arm of Lake Marion. If you go east on Road 260, you will soon cross over Potato Creek and reach Potato Creek Landing. A Eurasian Wigeon was on Potato Creek one winter in the late 1970s.)

To explore the Cuddo Unit, enter at the gate, and walk or bicycle south. In about two miles you will reach Lake Marion.

There are refuge service roads and jeep trails crisscrossing the area in a pattern that seems to correspond only roughly to the refuge leaflet's map of the area. The majority of these roads loop around and rejoin the main road eventually, so you will not get too lost by following whichever trail strikes your fancy. Be prepared for an all-day hike with plenty of mosquitoes for company. In other words, the Cuddo Unit is a place for the adventuresome, a place to get away from the crowd for a day.

B—14.4—Taw Caw Creek and the Goat Island Area

Winter	**
Spring	**
Summer	*
Fall	**

See Map B—14.1.

The *Goat Island area* of Lake Marion is a highly developed resort area, but there are some good birding spots nearby, especially near a cattle feedlot and at *Taw Caw Creek County Park*. To reach the Goat Island area from I-95, use the Summerton exit (Exit 108), and go south on Road 102 for 1.7 miles to a T-junction with Road 127. Here turn left (east), and go on Road 127 for 1.5 miles, where you will encounter a stop sign at Road 38. Road 38 continues for 5.0 miles to Goat Island Landing on Lake Marion. Along the way it passes agricultural fields, a cattle feedlot, a major arm of Lake Marion, and some good habitat of marsh and mud flats.

Go right (south) on Road 38 from where you turned onto it from Road 127. In a bit over two miles you will reach *Taw Caw Creek County Park* (letter F on Map B—14.1) on your right (west). This day-use park has picnicking and an interesting boardwalk which leads to a small island in Taw Caw Creek (here widened to form an arm of Lake Marion). Two fishing piers on this island provide a good overlook of the lake. Back on the mainland take a few minutes to check out the swampy woods near the parking lot. This is a good place for small birds year-round.

Return to Road 38, and continue south. About a half mile south of the bridge over Taw Caw Creek look for a place where a small arm of Lake Marion comes up to the road. There are often mud flats on the left here, and on the right is a small marsh easily visible from the roadside.

About 4.5 miles south of Road 127 you will see a group of four silos on the right side of the road (letter G on Map B—14.1). The cattle feedlots and pastures near these four silos are a great place to bird. In winter look for large flocks of blackbirds. Most of the birds will be European Starlings, Red-winged Blackbirds, Common Grackles, and Brown-headed Cowbirds, but keep an eye out for rarer species. Several Brewer's Blackbirds were here in the winters of 1988—89 and 1989—90, and they are probably regular here.

At 5.0 miles south of Road 127 you will reach Lake Marion at *Goat Island Landing*. In winter scan the lake for the usual Ring-billed Gulls and Forster's Terns. Bald Eagle and Peregrine Falcon have been seen here in winter. When you are done here, retrace your path to Road 127, where you can pick up the road to the Cuddo Unit of Santee NWR (see Section B-14.3) or return to I-95.

B–15—COLLETON COUNTY

Colleton County is a largely rural coastal county lying between Charleston and Beaufort. Interstate 95 cuts through the northern part of the county. On I-95 is the county seat of Walterboro, a convenient rest stop for many travelers. The northern part of the county is in the Upper Coastal Plain, while the part south of I-95 (west of Walterboro) or US 17 Alternate (east of Walterboro) are in the Lower Coastal Plain. The good birding areas of Colleton County lie in the Lower Coastal Plain.

From a naturalist's point of view, Colleton County is dominated by the two rivers which form its eastern and western borders—the Edisto and the Combahee (called the Salkehatchie north of I-95). These two rivers (along with the Ashepoo River) form the so-called ACE Basin (an acronym for *Ashepoo-Combahee-Edisto*).

The dark swamps and floodplain forests

of the ACE basin are good birding spots, accessible at Colleton State Park and the Edisto Nature Trail at Jacksonboro. As the rivers reach the sea, they form vast marshes, which are mostly freshwater marshes at first and eventually become salt marshes along the tidal estuaries which are the mouths of these rivers. These marshes are best viewed along the road to Bear Island, one of the top birding areas in South Carolina.

Finally, there is an accessible barrier island in Colleton County: Edisto Beach. The island is best explored at Edisto Beach State Park, which protects a bit of beach and dune community as well as salt marshes and one of the finest maritime forests in South Carolina. Edisto Beach is a good birding spot, especially in spring and fall.

B–15.1—Bear Island Wildlife Management Area

Winter   ****
Spring   ****
Summer **
Fall   ***

See Map B–15.1

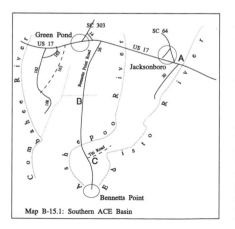

Map B-15.1: Southern ACE Basin

Bear Island Wildlife Management Area provides some of the most exciting birding in South Carolina at any time of year. Though best known for its wintering waterfowl, it is also a good place to find shorebirds in spring and fall, nesting Bald Eagles, Wood Storks, ibis, and herons in summer, and marsh birds (such as moorhens and rails) all year long.

If you are coming on I-95 southbound, get off at Exit 57, and follow SC 64 into Walterboro. In about 2 miles SC 64 merges with US 15 (Jeffries Boulevard). Keep straight ahead on Jeffries Boulevard. In less than a half mile US 17A merges with Jeffries Boulevard. Keep straight ahead on US 17A for another half mile, until you get to SC 303, on the left. Turn left (south) onto SC 303, heading toward the town of Green Pond, which is about 14 miles south of Walterboro. Keep on SC 303 until you reach its end at US 17. Here turn left (northeast) onto US 17 toward Charleston. Go 2.5 miles northeast on US 17 to Road 26, Bennetts Point Road, on the right. There should be a sign here for Bear Island. Road 26 leads to the wildlife management area in another 13 miles.

If you are coming on I-95 northbound, get off at Exit 33 and take US 17 northeast toward Charleston. In about 21 miles you will pass the intersection with SC 303 on the left. Go another 2.5 miles to Road 26, on the right. This is the road to Bear Island.

From the Charleston area go southeast on US 17. In about 30 miles you will cross over the Edisto River and enter Colleton County. Go another 8.3 miles to Road 26, on the left. Road 26 is about a mile beyond the bridge over the Ashepoo River.

From the intersection of US 17 and Road 26 (Bennetts Point Road), go south on Road 26. Road 26 passes through mostly second-growth oak-hickory-pine woods. At 6.0 miles south of US 17 the road passes over a brackish marsh at *Social Hall Creek* (letter B on Map B–15.1). There is usually plenty of room to park on the shoulder, near a little bridge. This is a good spot for marsh birds. Soras and Virginia Rails winter here, and a Least Bittern is often seen in late spring or early summer. Scan the trees along the edge of the marsh for Bald Eagles, which nest nearby and are often here.

At 10.8 miles south of US 17 you will cross over the high bridge over the Ashepoo River and enter *Bear Island Wildlife Management Area* (letter C on Map B–15.1). This area consists of about twelve thousand acres of freshwater marsh and impoundment, tidal marsh, maritime forest, and agricultural lands. Bear Island is a great birding spot. It is fairly good even on slow days and can be fantastic at times. The best time to visit is late winter, when thousands of ducks are here, or spring, when hundreds of shorebirds, herons, ibis, and Wood Storks visit the mud flats of the freshwater impoundments.

Bear Island is primarily a duck-hunting area, so visits during the duck season (October to January) are usually limited to viewing the marshes along Road 26. Also, the gates may be locked on Sunday, when the area is closed to fishing. If you want to visit during the duck season or on a Sunday, please call ahead for instructions ((803)-884-8952). In fact, it is always a good idea to call ahead to let refuge personnel know that you are coming and to get an up-to-date briefing on the condition of refuge roads.

The first birding spot in the refuge is immediately after crossing the high bridge over the Ashepoo River. On the right are extensive salt marshes with resident Clapper Rails, Marsh Wrens, and Seaside Sparrows. The bridge is attractive to swallows. At least one species is here any time of year. In midsummer you can often find dozens of Bank Swallows here, mixed in with Barn, Tree, and Northern Rough-winged Swallows and Purple Martins. Cliff Swallows sometimes appear in fall, and Tree Swallows are common in winter.

On the left is an access point to the dikes along the edge of a large freshwater impoundment. You can walk for miles along these dikes (except during hunting season, when they are usually closed). Most birders give this spot a quick look and then drive on to the main part of the refuge.

From the high bridge Road 26 goes south for about a mile, with salt marsh on the right and a freshwater impoundment on the left. Then the road passes through 0.3 mile of maritime forest (Nancy Hill), before emerging to a point where there are impoundents on both sides of the paved road. The impoundment to the right often has some of the best birding in the refuge. It has hundreds of ducks in winter and at least a few ducks all year-round. Bear Island is one of the places where Mottled Ducks were introduced in the early 1970s. Now there are several hundred Mottled Ducks resident on the refuge. In winter they are joined by good numbers of American Black Ducks, so a winter trip gives you the chance to try to tell these two species apart. This is not easy, and you may give up and say, "They're black or mottled."

This same impoundment (on the right of the paved road as you enter) is great in spring, when water is drawn down, exposing extensive mud flats. In May you might find hundreds of shorebirds—mostly Greater and Lesser Yellowlegs, but also species such as Semipalmated Plover, Killdeer, Black-necked Stilt, Solitary and Pectoral Sandpipers, and four species of peeps: Semipalmated, Western, Least, and White-rumped Sandpipers. Other species are possible but not so common. Herons and egrets are abundant, and there are usually White and Glossy Ibis and a few Wood Storks as well.

Soon you will reach the main refuge road, *Titi Road*, to the left. Turn here, and go to the building with the tall radio mast. This is the "radio shack," which also functions as the field headquarters for the refuge. If there is anyone on duty at the "radio shack," stop by and tell that person what you are up to. There are usually maps of the area available, and you can ask where you can drive safely and where you must walk.

Titi Road is the only unpaved road on the refuge that is open in all weather, and even it might be washed out by a storm. This road forms a spine, with ribs of other roads and dikes branching off from it. You can usually drive on Titi Road east for about two miles to the beginning of private property beyond the wildlife management area. If this is your first trip to Bear Island, this is a good way to get the lay of the land. Titi Road goes past several impoundments and marshes, as well as through the cropland area of the refuge, so that it is an excellent birding road, even if you do not walk (or cautiously drive) on any of the dike roads.

As you drive on Titi Road from the "radio shack," you will pass impoundments on both sides. The first one on the right (south) is often the best one for wintering ducks in the entire refuge. The best spot to overlook this duck area is from the picnic tables near the maintenance sheds that you soon pass on your right. As you eat lunch here in February, hunkering down to keep warm in the chilly wind, you might well watch several hundred ducks of a half dozen species.

The first notable side trip from Titi Road starts in the maintenance area. A dike road goes off to the right (south). This road is usually passable by car for a short distance. To be safe, however, all dike roads should be walked, rather than driven on. Follow this road south for about a half mile into an oak-pine woods. Soon after entering the woods (White House Island on the refuge map), look for a turn to the left. Take this turn, and go northeast into an area of salt marsh on the right and fresh marsh on the left. After crossing a salt creek, but before you get to the next wooded island, look for a dike road off to the right toward the Edisto River. This dike leads (in about a quarter mile) to an extensive impoundment which is excellent for wintering ducks.

After returning to Titi Road at the maintenance area, go east on the good road. In about a quarter of a mile you will see a dike road off to the left, leading to a popular fishing spot. This road is one of the best in the refuge, but as always it may not be passable by car, so it is best to walk. (Bald Eagles actively nest in this area, which is posted during the eagles' breeding season).

After about a quarter mile of farmlands, you reach a dike between two impoundments. Pied-billed Grebes are abundant here year-round. In winter look for Ruddy Ducks and other bay ducks. In August you will be treated to a tern show. As many as eighty Black Terns have been counted here from a single spot in August. Other terns in late summer include Least, Caspian, Common, Forster's, and Royal. Marsh Wrens are common residents in the reeds, and Common Moorhens are abundant year-round, being joined in winter by hundreds of American Coots.

In about a half mile you will reach an informal parking area for fishermen. From this parking area (which may not be accessible by car in winter) go left toward the wooded island. The oak woods here have a resident Great Horned Owl, which is often seen flying away from you in daylight. In spring and fall there may be a few migrant warblers about, as well as millions of mosquitoes and lots of poison ivy—a spot only a birder could love.

From this oak woods you have a choice—either return by the same route, going right along a short dike road back to Titi Road, or go left along several miles of dike road to the Ashepoo River and eventually back to Titi Road at the eastern border of the refuge.

Once you are back on Titi Road, you will notice numerous side-road and dike trails, mostly passable only by foot or four-wheeled drive vehicle. This is your chance to explore, limited only by time, stamina, and the amount of blood you wish to contribute to the local mosquitoes—birding at its best!

There are also numerous dike roads *west of the paved road*. These are little known to birders, since most birders spend their time east of the paved road, along Titi Road. One good dike road west of Road 26 takes off about a quarter mile south of the intersection of Road 26 and Titi Road. Follow the overgrown road into the pinewoods for about two hundred yards until you reach an intersection with another dike road going west, directly away from the paved road. This dike road gives you a good view of two large freshwater impoundments and is good for ducks in winter and Wood Storks in summer.

Road 26 continues another two miles beyond Titi Road to the fishing village of

Bennetts Point. Birding is good along this road, especially for land birds in fall migration. The area looks good for a summering Gray Kingbird or for a fall Western Kingbird, but these species are rare and should not be expected. A Lark Sparrow was found here in November, 1991.

Any time you visit Bear Island, be alert for birds of prey. Bald Eagles nest here, and are found all year-round. Great Horned Owls are often seen in the woods. Also found (mostly in winter and migration) are Red-tailed and Red-shouldered Hawks, Northern Harriers, Merlins, Peregrine Falcons, American Kestrels, Sharp-shinned and Cooper's Hawks, and Ospreys.

Late summer brings thousands of swallows to Bear Island. All six species found in South Carolina can be found. Most common are Tree, Barn, and Bank Swallows. In fact, Tree Swallows can be found every month of the year (except perhaps June), although they do not breed here. Other migrants that are common in late summer are Eastern Kingbirds and Eastern Wood-Pewees, often by the dozens or even hundreds.

In short, birding at Bear Island is great all year round. A slow day will be good, and a good day will be fantastic. No place else in the state has so much marshland so easily accessible on public land, and here, as everywhere in the world, marshlands mean good birding.

B-15.2—Colleton State Park

Winter	*
Spring	*
Summer	*
Fall	*

Colleton State Park is a small area (thirty-five acres) on the Edisto River, little more than a picnic- and campground, but it does have some nice floodplain woods and makes a good rest or lunch stop.

From I-95 get off at Exit 68, and go southeast (toward Canadys and Charleston) on SC 61. In 3 miles you will reach US 15.

Turn left (north) onto US 15, and go 0.5 mile to the park entrance, on the left.

There is a trail of sorts that begins opposite the picnic ground and leads a short way into the woods. Birds here are the common species of Coastal Plain floodplain forests. This is a particularly good trail for seeing a Barred Owl in the daytime.

B—15.3—The Edisto Nature Trail at Jacksonboro

Winter   *
Spring   **
Summer *
Fall   **

See Map B—15.1.

The Timberlands Division of Westvaco Corporation maintains two loop trails through the floodplain forest along the Edisto River near Jacksonboro. These trails (a half-mile-long loop and a one-mile-long loop) give easy access to the woods and are excellent places to observe most of the species of Lower Coastal Plain floodplain forest. Species to look for here include Wild Turkey (year-round), Mississippi Kite (late April through August), and Yellow-crowned Night-Heron (April through September).

If you are going southbound on I-95, get off at Exit 57, and follow SC 64 southeast through the city of Walterboro. (Be careful to take the left turn in downtown Walterboro and thus to stay on SC 64.) About

14 miles southeast of Walterboro SC 64 ends at US 17. Go left (northeast toward Charleston) on US 17. The nature trail is on the left (north) just before the bridge over the Edisto River. This is about a mile from the intersection with SC 64.

If you are going northbound on I-95, get off at Exit 33, and follow US 17 toward Charleston for about 31 miles to Jacksonboro. The nature trail is on the left (north), about a mile beyond the intersection with SC 64.

From Charleston follow US 17 southwest toward Savannah. In about 30 miles you will cross over the Edisto River and enter Colleton County. The nature trail is on the right (north), just beyond the bridge over the Edisto (letter A on Map B—15.1).

B—15.4—Edisto Beach State Park

Winter   **
Spring   **
Summer *
Fall   **

Edisto Beach State Park protects 1,255 acres of beach, dunes, salt marsh, and maritime forest on the Atlantic near the southwestern corner of Edisto Island, one of South Carolina's sea islands, about 45 miles southwest of Charleston.

From Charleston go southwest on US 17 for about 20 miles to the intersection with SC 174. Turn left (south) onto SC 174, and go about 25 miles to the park border.

From I-95 follow the directions for the Edisto Nature Trail (Section B-15.3 above). From Jacksonboro follow US 17 toward Charleston, crossing the Edisto River into Charleston County. Go about 6 miles northeast from the bridge to the intersection with SC 174. Here turn right (south),

and go about 25 miles to the park border.

There are three principal roads off of SC 174 leading to birding areas in the park. The first road (Road 1461, Palmetto Road) is at the northern edge of the Park, leading about 1.5 miles to a boat-launching ramp on Big Bay Creek. This area gives you access to part of the park's extensive salt marsh and a good view of a tidal creek.

The next road into the park is about a half mile from Road 1461. This is the road to the cabin area (State Cabin Road); it turns off to the right (west) directly opposite the road to the overflow campground. Follow the cabin road west for about 0.2 mile to the trailhead of the Indian Mound Trail on the right.

The Indian Mound Trail wanders through the park's maritime forest, a wonderful area of live oaks, cabbage palmetto, and various other interesting trees. This is a great place for small birds from fall through spring, with the best concentrations in October and early April. At about 0.1 mile there is a split in the trail. Keep to the left here. At 0.4 mile the trail forks. Here you may wish to take the right fork, which returns directly to the road. The Indian Mound Trail continues to the left for another 1.4 miles to an old shell mound on the edge of the salt marsh.

The third main road into Edisto Beach State Park is the one taken by most park visitors—the turnoff to the left for the beach parking lot and beachside campground. Park in the beach parking lot. From here you have a choice of ways to explore the beach and dunes. You can go directly to the beach and follow it east about a mile to Jeremy Inlet, or you can wander through the campground, exploring the heavily forested dunes. In spring and fall migration you might find a few migrant warblers on these dunes. In winter the place is overrun with Yellow-rumped Warblers. After about a half mile the forested dunes end, and you can follow the beach to the inlet with good views of a broad salt marsh to the north and of the Atlantic Ocean to the south. Expect to find most of the common species of the salt marsh, beach, and open ocean.

On the whole, birding at Edisto Beach State Park is good but not as good as at Huntington Beach State Park (see Section B-22 below) or at Hunting Island State Park (see Section B-7 above). Edisto Beach is much better for shelling than the other state park beaches, however.

Once you are done at the park, consider visiting a couple of interesting places in the town of Edisto Beach. From the beach parking lot turn left, and continue on SC 174 (McConkey Boulevard) through the town. In about 2.4 miles SC 174 comes to an end at a marina parking lot. Just before this lot there is a road off to the left (Yacht Club Road), which leads a short way to a public beach access point on the shore of St. Helena Sound, where you might find loons or sea ducks in winter. At low tide look for large flocks of gulls, terns, skimmers, and shorebirds on the mud flats.

At the end of SC 174 look for a road continuing back to your right, looping back to SC 174. This is Road 683 (Dock Site Road), which parallels a small salt creek. This road leads to a golf course with several artificial freshwater ponds clearly visible from the public road. In spring and fall migration look for grass-loving shorebirds and also shorebirds that prefer fresh water to salt. You will probably find Killdeer and Black-bellied Plovers on the grass and Spotted Sandpipers along the shores of the ponds. In about a mile Road 683 rejoins SC 174.

B–15.5—Combahee River Plantations

Winter	**
Spring	**
Summer	*
Fall	**

See Map B–15.2.

The Combahee (pronounced "CUMbee") River, which separates Colleton County from Beaufort County to the west, was important as a rice-growing area in the nineteenth century. The following tour

takes you through several of the old rice plantations and gives you a few places to overlook extensive freshwater marshes from the roadside.

The tour goes from I-95 on the north to US 17 on the south and is easily combined

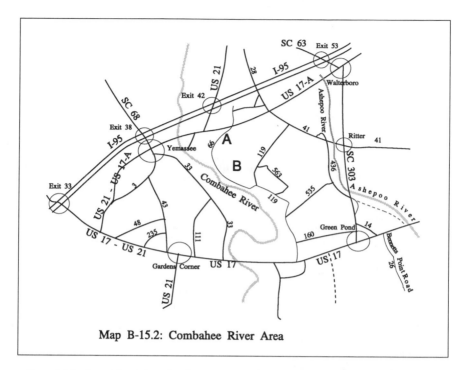

Map B-15.2: Combahee River Area

with a visit to Bear Island (see Section B-15.1 above).

Directions for going north to south:

Leave I-95 at Exit 42, and go south on US 21 for 2 miles to US 17 Alternate. Turn left (east) onto US 17 Alternate toward Walterboro, and go 3.4 miles to Road 66, a crossroad. Turn right (south) onto Road 66. In about a mile you will reach the first marsh at the bridge over *Calfpen Creek* (letter A on Map B–15.1). King Rails are fairly easy to hear at this marsh, but don't expect to see one.

Continue south on Road 66, which winds through many old plantations. At about 8 miles from US 17 Alternate you will pass through an area of extensive tidal freshwater marshes—the old rice fields of Combahee Plantation (letter B on Map B-15.2). There is an impoundment on the right (north) side of the road which often has a few ducks, Anhingas, and Common Moorhens. All birding must be done from the roadside, since this is private property.

At 9.2 miles south of US 17 Alternate, Road 66 ends at Road 119. Turn right onto Road 119. If you keep straight ahead on this road, you will reach US 17 just west of Green Pond in 4.5 miles. To continue the tour, however, go just 2.4 miles south on Road 119. Here turn left (northeast) onto Road 535. Follow Road 535 for 4.9 miles to a T-junction with Road 436. Here turn right and go 0.9 mile to the intersection with SC 303. (If you turned right onto SC 303, you would reach US 17 at Green Pond; to the left you would reach US 17 Alternate in Walterboro). To continue the tour, however, do not turn onto SC 303, but keep straight ahead. A few yards beyond SC 303 the paved road ends. (Ignore the paved road to your right). Keep straight ahead on a good unpaved road.

This unpaved road leads for about 3 miles through plantations along the west bank of the Ashepoo River. The road passes over a small bald-cypress swamp and then leads through a delightful combination of farmland and southern mixed-hardwood forest. The unpaved road ends at US 17 just west of the bridge over the Ashepoo River. Here you can turn left toward Jacksonboro (7 miles) or right toward Green Pond (3 miles).

Directions for going from south to north:

Begin at the US 17 bridge over the Ashepoo River, which is about 7 miles west of Jacksonboro, or 3 miles east of Green Pond. Just west of the river look for an unpaved road off to the north. Turn here, and follow this delightful road for about three miles to SC 303.

At SC 303 keep straight ahead (northwest) on Road 436. Go 0.9 mile on Road 436, and then turn left (southwest) onto Road 535. Follow Road 535 for 4.9 miles to its end at Road 119. Here turn right (north) onto Road 119, and go for 2.4 miles.

Here you will reach the intersection with Road 66. Turn left (west) onto Road 66. You will soon enter an area of extensive freshwater tidal marshes. Go north on Road 66 for 9.2 miles to US 17 Alternate. Turn left onto US 17 Alternate, and go 3.4 miles west to US 21. Turn right (north) onto US 21, and go two miles to Exit 42 of I-95.

B–16—DARLINGTON COUNTY

Darlington County has a typical mixture of agricultural lands and light industrial development in the northeastern part of South Carolina. Its northwestern edge is in the Sandhills subregion of the Upper Coastal Plain, but most of the county is in the true Upper Coastal Plain. The city of Darlington, the county seat, is 8 miles northeast of Florence on US 52—401. Interstate 95 just touches a part of the southeastern edge of the county, and I-20 cuts through the southern part of it.

Birding in Darlington County is dominated by the Great Pee Dee River, which is the eastern border of the county, and by tributaries of the Great Pee Dee. Black Creek provides fairly good birding; it flows from Lake Robinson in the north-central part of the county, through Kalmia Gardens near the town of Hartsville, and then on to the river.

The Great Pee Dee River is one of the better rivers in the Coastal Plain for birding. Many birders come to this river in summer to look for Mississippi Kites. This beautiful species breeds in Darlington County and may be found in the town of Society Hill (on US 52—401—15 in the northern part of the county) and along SC 34.

B–16.1—Kalmia Gardens

Winter *
Spring **
Summer **
Fall **

Kalmia Gardens is a delightful garden and small natural area administered by Coker College in the small college town of Hartsville. The area is only twenty-eight acres, but it is nevertheless a fairly good birding spot.

To reach Kalmia Gardens, first go to the intersection of US 15 and SC 151 just south of Hartsville.

To get to this spot from the west, leave I-20 at Exit 116 near Bishopville in Lee County, and follow US 15 northward for about 18 miles to SC 151.

From I-95 take US 52 north from Exit 164 near Florence in Florence County. Soon you will enter Darlington County. Stay on US 52 Bypass around Darlington. About 9 miles north of I-95 you will encounter SC 151. Turn left (west) onto SC 151, and go

12 miles to the intersection of SC 151 and US 15, south of Hartsville. (Stay on Bypass 151, and do not get onto Business 151, which goes into downtown Hartsville.)

From the intersection of SC 151 and US 15 south of Hartsville, go northwest on SC 151 for 3.4 miles to Road 12 (Kellytown Road). Turn right (east) onto Road 12, and follow it for 0.6 mile until it ends at Business 151 (West Carolina Street). The entrance to Kalmia Gardens is less than one block east on West Carolina Street, so turn right at the stop sign, and look for the entrance on the left (north) side of West Carolina Street. Since Kalmia Gardens is relatively small, it is easy to explore all the grounds. The best birding is usually in the natural area, along the creek. From the parking lot go downhill and to the right (northeast). You will find many of the species of Sandhills forests, including breeding Swainson's Warbler.

B–16.2—I-95 Detour to the Great Pee Dee River

Winter   *
Spring   **
Summer **
Fall   **

See Map B–16.1.

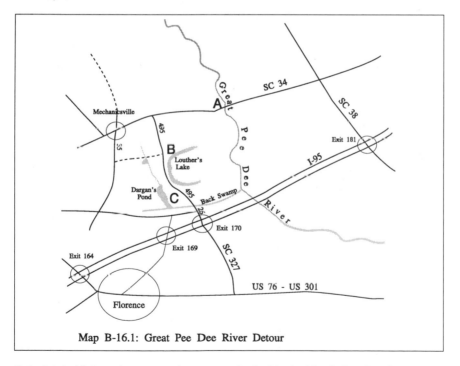

Map B-16.1: Great Pee Dee River Detour

Out-of-state birders who are passing through South Carolina on I-95 should consider the following short detour to the SC 34 crossing of the Great Pee Dee River. This route gives a good brief look at typical South Carolina Coastal Plain habitats. From late April until late August there is a fairly good chance of finding a few Mississippi Kites along the way.

Brief directions will be given for a north-to-south tour, then a more detailed description will be given for a south-to-north tour.

Going on the tour north to south: If you are going south on I-95, leave the interstate at Exit 181, which is 18 miles south of the North Carolina border, in Dillon County. Go northwest on SC 38 toward Bennettsville. You will enter Marlboro County and intersect with SC 34 in about 5 miles. Turn left onto SC 34, and go west for 5.6 miles to the *bridge over the Great Pee Dee River* (letter A on Map B–16.1). Cross the bridge, and look for a paved road to a boat launch (Road 900). Road 900 turns off to the right (north) about 0.4 mile beyond the bridge.

After exploring the boat launch area (the best area for Mississippi Kites in summer), return to SC 34 and continue west. At 2.5 miles beyond Road 900 you will pass the intersection with Road 495 on the left. Keep on SC 34 for 0.9 mile more to Road 35 in Mechanicsville. To continue the tour, turn left (south) onto Road 35, and go south for 1.3 miles to the first county road (unpaved) on the left. Turn left onto the unpaved road, cross a creek, and go 1.5 miles to the end of the unpaved road at Road 495 (paved). Turn right (south) onto Road 495, and go just 0.3 mile. Look for a dirt road off to the left (east). This turnoff is rather inconspicuous. The dirt road leads 0.3 mile to a boat launch on *Louther's Lake*, an oxbow lake of the Great Pee Dee River (letter B on Map B–16.1).

After checking out Louther's Lake, return to the paved road (Road 495), and turn left (south). In 2.0 miles you will pass the entrance road to *Dargan's Pond* (letter C on Map B–16.1), on the right (west). This area is open only on Saturdays and Wednesdays (April through October; closed in winter).

From the Dargan's Pond entrance road keep on south on Road 495. In 1.2 miles Road 495 crosses over Back Swamp and enters Florence County, where it becomes Road 26. Continue south on Road 26 for 1.3 miles to reach Exit 170 of I-95.

Going on the tour south-to-north: From I-95 northbound leave at Exit 170, the Myrtle Beach exit, but do not follow SC 327 south toward the beach. Instead, go north on SC 327, which quickly becomes Road 26. At 1.3 miles north of I-95, Road 26 enters Darlington County, where it continues as Road 495.

The creek at the Florence County–Darlington County line is Back Swamp. This looks like a fairly good birding spot, except that there is no good spot to park along the road. If you do manage to find a place to pull over, you will probably find lots of birds. This is private land, so do not leave the roadside. Between mid-April and early July listen for Swainson's Warbler in the swamp. Common breeding warblers here are those typical of South Carolina's Coastal Plain floodplain forests: Northern Parula; Yellow-throated, Prothonotary, Kentucky, and Hooded Warblers.

About 1.2 miles north of the bridge over Back Swamp you will pass a dirt road on the left (west) that goes to a boat-launching area on *Dargan's Pond* (letter C on Map B–16.1). This road is open only on Wednesdays and Saturdays. Continue north on Road 495. About 2.0 miles north of the side road to Dargan's Pond look for an inconspicuous dirt road off to the right (east). This side road goes 0.3 mile to an informal boat-launching area on *Louther's Lake* (letter B on Map B–16.1), which is a long, narrow oxbow (old river channel) of the Great Pee Dee River.

The old riverbank area is a good birding spot. Here you can find Blue-gray Gnatcatcher, Acadian and Great Crested Flycatcher, and Hooded Warbler in summer. Permanent residents include White-breasted Nuthatch, which is a swamp species in the South Carolina Coastal Plain. In fall migration (late August thought late October) this is a good area for warblers, including Worm-eating, Magnolia, Chestnut-sided, and Black-throated Blue Warbler. In September you might find just about anything.

From Louther's Lake return to the paved road, and turn right (north). Just 0.3 mile from the Louther's Lake side road, turn left (west) onto an unpaved county road.

This first mile or so of this road leads through open county. In summer look for Indigo Bunting, Blue Grosbeak, and Orchard Oriole. In winter look for sparrows and hawks. If any of the fields are fallow, from April through August look and listen for Grasshopper Sparrow. Its insectlike song is sometimes heard along this stretch of road. Other breeding sparrows are the Field Sparrow and the Chipping Sparrow.

About 0.8 mile west of Road 495 the county road crosses a creek which has been dammed on both sides of the road. The pond on the north side is most interesting, since it has standing dead trees and lots of water lilies. Wood Ducks are usually in this pond. The habitat looks good for other species (such as Common Moorhen), but I have not found them there (yet). The pond on the south side of the road is deeper and may attract a duck or two in winter. This is private property, so do not leave the roadside.

Continue west on the unpaved county road. At 1.5 miles from Road 495 you will come to a paved road, Road 35. Turn right (north), and go north for 1.3 miles, to the intersection with SC 34 in the community of Mechanicsville. (This is where you would join the tour if you are coming from the city of Darlington.)

Turn right (east) onto SC 34. In 0.9 mile you will pass Road 495. (To return directly to I-95, turn right onto Road 495 and go south to the interstate.) To continue the tour, keep going east on SC 34. You will soon descend a short hill down onto the floodplain of the Great Pee Dee River. Most of the floodplain forest has been cut here, leaving large open fields interspersed with woodlots.

Soon after entering the floodplain of the Great Pee Dee, you will pass an area of standing dead trees on your right (south). This "dead swamp" is particularly attractive to Red-headed Woodpeckers.

Just before the *bridge over the Great Pee Dee River* (letter A on Map B–16.1) look for a road off to the left. This is Road 900, which leads to a boat launch on the Darlington County side of the river. From late April until late August you have a fairly good chance of seeing one or more Mississippi Kites at this boat launch area.

Return to SC 34, and go east across the river into Marlboro County. In 6.6 miles SC 34 intersects SC 38 just before the Dillon County line. Turn right (southeast) onto SC 38, and go about 5 miles to return to I-95 at Exit 181 in Dillon County.

B–17 DILLON COUNTY

Dillon County is the first part of South Carolina that most out-of-state visitors see. Interstate 95 enters the state from North Carolina at the northern edge of Dillon County, at South of the Border, a truly world-class tourist trap which is probably the best known resort in the state.

Visitors who form their impressions of South Carolina from Dillon County, as seen from I-95 at sixty-five miles per hour, will not be very impressed with the state as a natural area. Most of Dillon County is heavily agriculturalized. Tobacco and other row crops occupy most of the land. Here and there are small woodlots and

pine plantations. Only along rivers will you find extensive woods.

Despite its heavily developed countryside, there is fairly good birding in Dillon County, especially in winter, when you can find many hawks, sparrows, and other birds of open fields (such as American Pipits). Horned Larks are permanent residents of large, open fields. The hedgerows between fields provide cover for many species: Northern Mockingbird, Brown Thrasher, Northern Bobwhite, Loggerhead Shrike, and others. To find these species (and many others), simply leave the interstate and drive a few miles on any country road—better unpaved.

Little Pee Dee State Park preserves an interesting area of floodplain forest and turkey-oak barrens. This is a fair birding area, and about the only sizable public area in the county.

Winter   *
Spring   *
Summer *
Fall   **

To reach *Little Pee Dee State Park* from I-95 southbound, go southeast on SC 57 from Exit 193. In 2.1 miles you will be in the center of the town of Dillon, at the intersection of Second Avenue and Main Street. Here turn left onto Main Street, keeping on SC 57.

From I-95 northbound exit onto SC 34 at Exit 190, and go 3.3 miles east, into the town of Dillon. Here, at the intersection of Main Street and Second Avenue, keep straight ahead on SC 57 (Main Street).

From downtown Dillon go southeast on SC 57. In one mile SC 9 keeps going straight ahead; be sure to bear right, staying on SC 57. At about 8.4 miles from the point where SC 9 and SC 57 split (9.4 miles from downtown Dillon), look for Road 22, and turn left (north), following signs for Little Pee Dee State Park. In about 0.8 mile you will cross over the Little Pee Dee River and enter the state park.

Just after you cross over the river, look for a dirt road to the right, which goes through a short section of public land before ending at private residences along the river. Just north of this road, in the park, is a fascinating natural area of brilliant white sand with turkey oaks, rosemary, and other Sandhills plants alternating with bay-swamp thickets along creeks and low areas. This is almost a desert; temperatures may reach 110 degrees Fahrenheit on a sunny summer afternoon. Few birds are to be found in the turkey-oak barrens, but the thickets abound with birds, especially in fall migration. On a good day in late summer or early fall you might easily find a dozen species of warblers, including Worm-eating and Blue-winged. When warblers are common, keep an eye out also for their predators. Sharp-shinned Hawks are common in fall and winter, and Cooper's Hawks occur year-round.

After exploring the turkey-oak barrens, return to Road 22, and drive north to the main park entrance road. Little Pee Dee State Park offers camping, lake swimming, fishing, and picnicking. A short nature trail (Beaver Pond Nature Trail) starts from the main park road about 0.3 mile before you reach the picnic area. Another entrance to the trail is from the campground. As its name implies, this trail leads to a small beaver pond at the upper end of the park lake. The habitat is typical oak-hickory-pine forest, with a bit of floodplain forest as well. This trail is good for typical birds of Coastal Plain forests.

Another good birding area is the dam of the park lake. A stroll here will let you check out the lake for waterfowl as well as give you a bird's eye view of the thick second-growth vegetation just below the dam.

B—18—DORCHESTER COUNTY

Dorchester County lies just northwest of the city of Charleston, so that like its neighbor, Berkeley County, it is undergoing rapid development. Nevertheless, there are wild places left in the county.

The Francis Beidler Forest has a virgin bald-cypress swamp, and Givhans Ferry State Park preserves floodplain forest and upland oak-pine forest along the Edisto River.

B—18.1—Francis Beidler Forest (Four-Hole Swamp)

Winter **
Spring ***
Summer **
Fall **

The National Audubon Society and the Nature Conservancy have combined to protect almost six thousand acres of bald-cypress—tupelo swamp and adjacent forest along the *Four Hole Swamp* in the northeastern part of Dorchester County. A modern visitors' center and a mile-long boardwalk into the heart of the swamp make this an extremely easy place to get into a cypress swamp.

Please note that the Beidler Forest is closed on Mondays, Thanksgiving Day, December 24, 25, and 31, and January 1, and that a modest admission fee is charged. For more information contact Sanctuary Manager, Francis Beidler Forest, Route 1, Box 600, Harleyville SC 29448; telephone (803) 462-2150.

The swamp was heavily damaged by Hurricane Hugo in September 1989. Many large trees came down, and the boardwalk was mostly destroyed. But the boardwalk has since been rebuilt, and the walk on it into the swamp is probably even more interesting now than before the hurricane. Very few of the large cypresses came down in the storm, and the cypress swamp is essentially intact.

The Beidler Forest is a good place to bird anytime, but the swamp is at its best in the spring, when warblers abound. Many species occur as migrants, while some—

including good numbers of Northern Parula, Prothonotary, and Swainson's— remain to breed. Even in the depths of winter you can find a few species of warbler as well as good numbers of woodpeckers, chickadees, Carolina and Winter Wrens, and an occasional Solitary Vireo.

To reach the forest from I-26 eastbound, leave at Exit 177, and follow SC 453 south into the town of Harleyville. Here turn left (east) onto US 178, and go 6.1 miles to the intersection with Road 28. Turn left (north) onto Road 28, and go over the interstate (no exit here). In about 4.4 miles you will reach a sand road on the right. Follow this sand road for about a mile to the sanctuary entrance road, on your right.

To reach Francis Beidler Forest from I-26 westbound, exit at Exit 187, and go south on SC 27 for 1.0 mile to US 78. Here turn right (west), and follow US 78 for 2.8 miles to its junction with US 178. Bear right onto US 178, and go another 0.8 mile to Road 28. Here turn right (north) onto Road 28, and go 4.4 miles to a sand road. The sand road goes straight ahead at a point where the paved road (Road 28) turns left. Turn onto the sand road, and follow it north for about a mile to the sanctuary entrance road, on your right.

B—18.2—Givhans Ferry State Park

Winter   *
Spring   **
Summer *
Fall   **

Givhans Ferry State Park is a 1,235-acre park along the Edisto River. Most of the park is in Dorchester County, while a small part is across the river in Colleton County.

The Edisto River is a blackwater river—a river which rises in the Sandhills rather than in the Piedmont or Blue Ridge of South Carolina. Its waters are black from the tannic acid of the vegetation along its border, chiefly bald cypress and tupelo as well as oaks. The longer rivers of South Carolina—the Pee Dee, the Santee, and the Savannah—start well up in the mountains and flow through the Piedmont, picking up sediments that turn these rivers brown.

The Edisto has a charm that is evident along its entire length. The section at Givhans Ferry is no exception. The river is cool, placid, and lazy. Givhans Ferry State Park shares these attributes. It is a great place to camp, even in summer.

There is a mile-long nature trail that begins at the picnic area and loops through typical oak-hickory-pine forest. While this is not a great place for birds, there are always at least a few around. This trail is worth an hour, if you are in the neighborhood.

To reach Givhans Ferry State Park from I-26, leave the interstate at Exit 187, and go south on SC 27. Follow SC 27 for about 9 miles to its intersection with SC 61. Turn right (west) onto SC 61, and go 3.2 miles to Road 30. Turn right (north) onto Road 30, and go a few yards to the park entrance.

From I-95 use Exit 68, and go east on SC 61 for about 18 miles. Just after crossing the Edisto River, look for Road 30. Here turn left (north), and go a short way to the park entrance, on your left.

B—18.3—Old Dorchester State Park

Winter   *
Spring   *
Summer *
Fall   *

Old Dorchester State Park is a small (ninety-seven-acre) historical park in the suburbs of Summerville commemorating the first settlement in Dorchester County, which a group from Dorchester, Massachusetts, established in 1696. The park is along the Ashley River but well upstream from the wide, tidal marshes that are typical of the Ashley from Middleton Place down to Charleston. There is a short nature trail where you will find a few of the common birds of oak-hickory-pine forests.

To reach Old Dorchester State Park from I-26, use Exit 199, and take US 17-A south into the city of Summerville. Here pick up SC 165, on the left. Follow SC 165 for 3 miles to SC 642. Turn left (east) onto SC 642, and go 2.0 miles to Road 373, the entrance road to the park.

B–19—EDGEFIELD COUNTY

Edgefield County is a predominately rural county along the Georgia border in the west-central part of the state. The southeastern third of the county is in the Sandhills subregion of the Upper Coastal Plain and is devoted to peach growing. In a good year Edgefield County can produce more peaches than the entire state of Georgia, the Peach State. The northwestern portion of the county lies in the Piedmont region. A good portion of this Piedmont area is within the Sumter National Forest. Logging roads and hiking trails in the National Forest offer good birding opportunities for typical forest species.

One bird species that is rapidly expanding in Edgefield County is the Wild Turkey. Appropriately enough, the National Wild Turkey Federation has its headquarters in the town of Edgefield.

B–19.1—Lick Fork Lake Recreation Area, Sumter National Forest

Winter **
Spring **
Summer **
Fall **

Lick Fork Lake Recreation Area has facilities for camping and picnicking on a small lake on Lick Fork Creek in the Edgefield District of Sumter National Forest. To reach this area from I-20, leave the interstate at Exit 1, and go north on SC 230. In 0.4 mile you will enter Edgefield County. Continue north on SC 230. At 13.5 miles north of I-20 you will pass through the community of Colliers. Continue north on SC 230. In another 0.8 mile (14.3 miles north of I-20) you will pass Road 263 on the right. Ignore this end of Road 263, and continue north on SC 230 for another 2.6 miles. Here you will encounter the northern end of Road 263. There should be a sign for Lick Fork Lake at this intersection (16.9 miles north of I-20). Turn right (east) onto Road 263. (If you reach the intersection of SC 230 and SC 23, you have gone too far. Backtrack 0.5 mile to Road 263, and follow the signs for Lick Fork Lake.)

Follow Road 263 south for 2.1 miles to the paved entrance road to the recreation area. This stretch of Road 263 goes through an extremely attractive open loblolly-pine forest. These woods are managed for Red-cockaded Woodpeckers by the Forest Service. Red-cockaded Woodpeckers are very rare here—perhaps even extirpated—but with good habitat in this place, they may return. There is a good chance that the woodpeckers will be reintroduced into these woods as part of the Red-cockaded Woodpecker recovery plan. This is one of the few areas in the South Carolina Piedmont where you have even a remote chance of spotting a Red-cockaded Woodpecker.

Even if there are no Red-cockaded Woodpeckers around, you will find plenty of birds. Other woodpeckers, Pine Warblers, and Brown-headed Nuthatches are common permanent residents. In summer listen for the elusive Bachman's Sparrow. This beautiful songster is most often found in clear-cut areas that are just beginning to grow up in brush, but it may also be heard singing in the open pinewoods.

If the *Lick Fork Lake Recreation Area* is open (it is sometimes closed during the winter), it makes an excellent place to picnic, camp, and hike through typical Piedmont woods. Two loop trails begin from the parking area: a 1.7-mile-long loop around the lake (this is the Lick Fork Lake trail) and a 5.4-mile loop south of the lake (the Horn Creek trail). Either trail will give you a chance to see typical species of Piedmont oak-hickory-pine woods. It is best to avoid this area from October through December, during the deer-hunting season, or limit you visit to Sunday, when there is no hunting in the National Forest, since this is an extremely popular deer-hunting area.

B—19.2—Fury's Ferry Recreation Area, Sumter National Forest

Winter   **
Spring   **
Summer **
Fall   **

See letter A on Map B—35.2 (p. 00).

Fury's Ferry Recreation Area is a boat-launching ramp and picnic area (tables only—no toilets) on the Savannah River at the McCormick County—Edgefield County line. To reach this area from I-20, go to exit 65 in Georgia, and go north on GA 28. In about 11 miles the highway crosses the Savannah River and becomes SC 28 in McCormick County. Once in South Carolina, go north on SC 28 for about 2 miles to the intersection with Road 112. Here turn right (southeast) onto Road 112, and go about one mile to the turnoff for Forest Road 660-E. Here turn right (south), and follow the road for 0.7 mile to a parking lot, which is just inside Edgefield County.

Fury's Ferry is about two miles upstream from Steven's Creek Dam, a minor dam on the Savannah. The Steven's Creek Dam impounds the river into a shallow lake. Fury's Ferry is at the base of a peninsula in this lake. To the west is the main channel of the Savannah River. To the east of the peninsula is a marshy backwater, very attractive to herons, ducks, and water birds of all sorts. The peninsula itself is a low-lying floodplain forest harboring birds typical of Piedmont floodplain forests.

To explore the forest, follow an overgrown logging road southeast from the parking lot into the woods. This old road is passable on foot for about a half mile. Along the way you will see a couple of spots where you can bushwhack through the woods for two hundred yards to the edge of the slough. Here you will find birds typical of Piedmont marshes and small lakes. Wood Ducks are present year-round and are joined in winter by a variety of puddle ducks, Pied-billed Grebe, and American Coot. With luck you might even find a bittern or a rail. Be aware that there are no trails in this area, so you must find your way through the woods to the marsh as best you can.

Even if you are not in the mood to explore the forest interior, there is good birding along the edge of the woods near the parking lot, or you might spot something flying up or down the main channel of the Savannah River.

There is a public dove field with numerous trails and hedgerows, along the forest road between Fury's Ferry and Road 112. During hunting season this area should be left to the hunters, but outside of the short dove season it is a good birding area. Expect species typical of Piedmont brush and hedgerows, including, of course, the Mourning Dove.

The combination of river, floodplain forest, marsh, and brushy fields so close together makes Fury's Ferry one of the better birding spots along the Piedmont portion of the Savannah River.

B–20—FAIRFIELD COUNTY

Fairfield County, in the Piedmont about twenty-five to fifty miles directly north of Columbia, was a major cotton-producing area in the nineteenth century. Early in the twentieth century the fields were largely abandoned and replaced by huge loblolly-pine plantations. In recent years industry has moved into Fairfield County, including a nuclear power plant at Lake Monticello and a major automo-

tive factory (Mack Trucks) in Winnsboro. But the county remains mostly rural and mostly pinewoods.

Fairfield County lies between two major rivers, the Broad River on the west and the Catawba/Wateree River (two names for the same river) on the east. The best birding areas in the county are along these rivers or at Lake Monticello, which is near the Broad River.

B–20.1—Broad River Waterfowl Area

Winter   ***
Spring   ***
Summer *
Fall   **

See Map B–20.1.

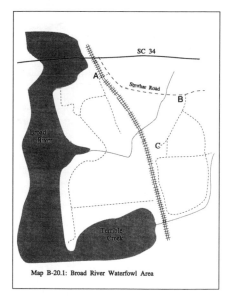

Map B-20.1: Broad River Waterfowl Area

The best place to observe ducks in the South Carolina Piedmont is the *Broad River Waterfowl Area*, a wildlife management area along the Broad River in Fairfield County where a small stream (Terrible Creek) comes down from the

hills and flows into the Broad River, forming a large bay with mud flats. Dams have created an extensive marsh—rare in the Piedmont—as well as a swampy woods, which together make a so-called green-tree reservoir. This combination of habitats is almost unique in the South Carolina Piedmont and an excellent birding area.

Broad River Waterfowl Area is closed to birders from November 1 to February 1, so the best time to visit to see large numbers of ducks is in early February, just before the ducks fly north. Typically there are several hundred ducks here in early February. Three waterfowl species— Canada Goose, Wood Duck, and Mallard—remain to breed.

Other seasons are also rewarding. Spring and fall migrations along the Broad River are usually fair to good for warblers, vireos, Bobolinks, and other small birds. The diversity of species is highest in early May and late September.

A species to be hoped for here is the Wild Turkey, of which Fairfield County has large numbers. These great beasts commonly use the agricultural fields of the waterfowl area. The best time of year to see Wild Turkeys at Broad River is in August or September, when the young, unwary birds of the year form large flocks and feed tamely in the open fields.

To reach the Broad River Waterfowl Area from I-26, leave the interstate at Exit 74 in Newberry County, and head east on SC 34. In 12.0 miles SC 34 crosses the Broad River and enters Fairfield County. At the east end of the SC 34 bridge over the Broad River look for Strother Road, a gravel county road to the right (southeast). (There should be a sign for Broad River Waterfowl Area at this turn.) Turn right onto Strother Road, and follow it east.

To reach the Broad River Waterfowl Area from I-77, go west from Exit 41 on Road 41. In 4.4 miles Road 41 merges with SC 200. Continue west on SC 200 for 2.3 miles. Here SC 200 merges with SC 34, on the north side of the town of Winnsboro. Continue west on SC 34 for about 19 miles. Just before the SC 34 bridge over the Broad River, turn left (southeast) onto Strother Road.

Since the Broad River Waterfowl Area is divided by a busy railroad, directions will be given to two access points, one for the portion of the waterfowl area west of the railroad (i.e., between the railroad and the Broad River), and a second access point for the portion east of the railroad, away from the river.

To reach the western part of Broad River Waterfowl area, follow Strother Road southeast from SC 34. At about 0.4 mile from SC 34 you will see a farm road off to the right. This farm road crosses the railroad just a few yards from Strother Road and then disappears into second-growth woods. Turn right onto this farm road and park just before crossing the railroad. (See letter A on Map B–20.1. This turnoff may be marked by a sign for a public dove field.)

On foot follow the farm road through private property for about two hundred yards to the edge of the waterfowl management area. Here take the road off to the right, which goes down a short hill and then bears left, paralleling the Broad River. In about five minutes' walk you will reach a well-maintained trail off to the right, toward the river. This side trail offers good birding, especially in migration. It winds first through a loblolly-pine plantation and then through swampy woods and a marshy area, before ending on the banks of a backwater of the Broad River.

After exploring the side trail, return to the main trail, which continues for more than a mile, eventually leading to large agricultural fields, which are flooded in winter to attract ducks. After exploring this area and all obvious side trails, return to your car to reach the second access point, that for the eastern portion of the waterfowl management area.

Once back to your car, return to Strother Road and continue southeast. At 0.8 mile from SC 34 you will ford a small creek (be careful if the water is high). At 1.2 miles from SC 34 you will reach the *main entrance road* to the waterfowl area (letter B on Map B–20.1). This is a side road to the right, which is almost always gated. Park along Strother Road, and walk in on the entrance road. In less than a mile you will pass a maintenance area on your right and then descend into the waterfowl management area proper.

If you are visiting in February, you should begin finding flocks of ducks at this point. Most will be Mallards and American Black Ducks, but other puddle ducks are often here as well. Expect most of the following duck species: the Wood Duck, Green-winged Teal, American Black Duck, Mallard, Northern Pintail, Northern Shoveler, Gadwall, American Wigeon, Ring-necked Duck, Lesser Scaup, and Hooded Merganser.

Soon the trail becomes a dike road paralleling the railroad. Follow the road counterclockwise, turning always to the left. In about a mile you will return to the point where you first descended from the hill with the maintenance sheds. Backtrack to Strother Road.

Once back on Strother Road, you have a choice either to backtrack to SC 34 or to continue east. Strother Road ends at

Road 99 in about another two miles to the east. Here you can turn right and follow the directions given in the next section to visit Lake Monticello.

B–20.2—Lake Monticello

Winter **
Spring **
Summer *
Fall **

Lake Monticello is a bit unusual compared to most other impoundments in the South Carolina Piedmont. It was constructed in the 1970s as the water source for a nuclear power plant. It impounds several small creeks, not a major river (even though the Broad River is just a mile or so to the west). Most of the lake's water is pumped from the Broad River. As a result, the water is clear, which makes the lake quite attractive to certain wintering species of birds, especially the Common Loon.

To reach Lake Monticello from I-26, follow the directions for Broad River Waterfowl Area (see Section B-20.1 above) to get to the east end of the SC 34 bridge over the Broad River. From the bridge continue east on SC 34 for 3.2 miles to Road 99. Turn right (south) onto Road 99. At about 0.2 mile south of SC 34 you will reach the east end of Strother Road, the road to Broad River Waterfowl Management Area. See Section B-20.1 for details. At 3.3 miles south of SC 34 turn left (continuing on Road 99). In another 0.7 mile (that is, 4.0 miles from SC 34) you will reach a fork in the road at the intersection of Road 99 and Road 347. All further directions will be given from this intersection.

To reach Lake Monticello from I-77, follow the directions for Broad River Waterfowl Area (see Section 20.1), but go only 12 miles west from Winnsboro on SC 34. Here you will find the intersection with SC 215, in the community of Salem Crossroads. Turn left (south) onto SC 215, and go 1.4 miles. Here turn right (southwest) onto Road 347. Follow Road 347 for 2.4 miles until it ends at Road 99.

From the intersection of Road 347 and Road 99 you have two choices. If you go northeast on Road 347 for a hundred yards or so you will come to the entrance to a picnic ground and boat ramp on the northern end of Lake Monticello. This is not a particularly good birding area, but it is a great place for a swim in summer (at the picnic ground, which has a sandy beach). The boat ramp area has toilets which are open all year.

The better birding is along Road 99. A few yards east of the intersection with Road 347, Road 99 passes the entrance road of a boat launch area on the right. This is a good area from which to overlook the northern half of Lake Monticello. From the parking lot look for an indistinct fisherman's trail going to a point that juts out into the lake. (This trail begins a few yards to the left of the boat ramp, as you look from the parking lot.) From this point you can survey most of the lake.

Return to Road 99, and continue east. The road crosses the upper end of the lake on a causeway dividing Lake Monticello into two areas, the main lake (to the south) and the so-called Lake Monticello subimpoundment (to the north). There is a pulloff just beyond the causeway where you can look for ducks and Canada Geese (introduced; here year-round).

To continue the tour of Lake Monticello, go east on Road 99 to its junction with SC 215 about two miles east of the causeway over the upper end of the lake. At SC 215 turn right (south). In 1.0 mile you will enter the village of Monticello. Just south of town look for a gravel road (Lakeside View Road) off to the west, toward the lake. This road is a half-mile loop through pastures on a hill overlooking the lake. This is the place where you are most consistently likely to see the introduced Canada Geese, and it is an excellent place to look for Common Loon, Horned and Pied-billed Grebe, and ducks in winter.

Return to SC 215. At about 2 miles south of the village of Monticello you will pass another boat launch area. Do not stop here, but go just a few yards farther south, and turn right into a small park. (There is a sign here which says, "Ball field and overlook.") There is a short, grassy peninsula jutting into the lake from this park. From this vantage point you can overlook most of the southern half of Lake Monticello. Here, in winter, you will find at least a few Common Loons (perhaps as many as twenty) and usually a few Horned and Pied-billed Grebes as well. Other birds wintering on the lake include Double-crested Cormorant, Bufflehead, Lesser Scaup, Hooded Merganser, and gulls—Ring-billed, Herring, and Bonaparte's. Dress warmly. The windchill here in winter can make you think this is the coldest place in South Carolina.

The overlook park is the end of our tour of Lake Monticello. If you are going on south to Columbia, follow SC 215 south. It reaches I-20 on the north side of Columbia in about 26 miles.

B–20.3—Lake Wateree State Park

Winter   **
Spring   **
Summer   *
Fall   **

The main part of *Lake Wateree State Park* is a 238-acre island lying along the western shore of Lake Wateree. Lake Wateree is a large lake (13,710 acres; 242 miles of shoreline) touching Lancaster, Fairfield, and Kershaw counties. The river flowing into the lake is called the Catawba, and the river flowing out of it is called the Wateree.

To reach Lake Wateree State Park from I-77, go to Exit 41, and then go east on Road 41. At 2.6 miles from the interstate you will reach US 21. Turn left (north), and go 2.2 miles. Here turn right onto Road 101, following signs for the park. The entrance to the park is about 5 miles east of US 21 on Road 101. Just before reaching the park, Road 101 crosses over an arm of Lake Wateree (Taylor Creek). A few Cliff Swallows have recently started breeding under the bridge over Taylor Creek. Other Cliff Swallows breed under the next bridge of Road 101—over Dutchman Creek, which is about a half mile south of the park entrance road.

Lake Wateree has a fair number of ducks in winter, but never in the numbers at Broad River Waterfowl Area in the western part of Fairfield County (see Section B-20.1 above). The best place to look for ducks in the park is from the causeway that connects the island to the mainland. Drive in on the entrance road. Just before the causeway there is a small parking area on the right. Park here and walk out onto the causeway.

In spring and fall the best birding in the park is along the nature trail, which begins at the main parking lot opposite the park store. This trail winds for about a mile through moist woods. Here you will find the common birds of Piedmont oak-pine woods as well as Prothonotary Warblers and Northern Parulas along the lakeshore. This trail is best in fall migration (late August through early October). On a good day in September you might find numerous migrants, including Veery, Swainson's Thrush, and the most of the following warblers: Blue-winged, Tennessee, Northern Parula, Chestnut-sided, Magnolia, Black-throated Blue, Yellow-rumped, Blackburnian, Yellow-throated, Pine, Bay-breasted, Blackpoll, Black-and-white, American Redstart, Prothonotary,

Worm-eating, Ovenbird, Northern Water-thrush, Kentucky, Common Yellowthroat, Hooded, and Canada Warblers. Some of these species are also found in spring, but the migration in spring is not as exciting as in fall (as is the case in most of South Carolina).

When you are done with the park, return to Road 101, and turn left (southeast). If you drive a few miles on this road, you will most likely find a recently clear-cut pine plantation, where you can find most of the birds of Piedmont old fields. The main attraction here is the Bachman's Sparrow. It is fairly common from April through early September and easily found as it sings from a low perch in the middle of a large clear-cut.

B–21—FLORENCE COUNTY

Florence County is a part of South Carolina seen by thousands of out-of-state travelers daily, since two major interstate highways cross it. Interstate 95 runs through the western part of the county, and Interstate 20 has its eastern terminus at the city of Florence, just east of its intersection with I-95. With about thirty-five thousand residents, the city of Florence is an important industrial and commercial center, while the rest of Florence County is typical Upper Coastal Plain farm county, important for cotton, tobacco, and other row crops. Two large rivers cross the county. The Great Pee Dee River forms the northern and eastern border of the county, while the Lynches River flows through the southern part.

The best birding in the county is probably at Lynches River State Park, a few miles from I-95 off of US 52. Travelers in a hurry might see a few species from the interstate itself. In particular the I-95 rest areas just south of the Great Pee Dee River sometimes have a Mississippi Kite soaring overhead during the heat of the day in summer.

B–21.1—Lynches River State Park

Winter	**
Spring	**
Summer	**
Fall	**

Lynches River State Park is a day-use park (no camping) on the south side of Lynches River, a typical Coastal Plain river. From I-95 exit at Exit 164, and follow US 52 south through the city of Florence. About 12 miles south of the interstate, US 52 crosses Lynches River. Just beyond the bridge turn right (west) onto Road 147, and go another 3.5 miles to the park entrance road, on the right (north).

Follow the park road to its end in a parking lot near the picnic area. A 1.7-mile nature trail begins at this parking lot, giving good access to the floodplain forest along Lynches River. This is a fairly good area to find species typical of Coastal Plains floodplain forests. For some reason this is not a particularly good area for Mississippi Kites, which are more easily seen along the Great Pee Dee River. (See Section B-16, Darlington County, for a description of a side trip from I-95 which is better for kites.)

B–21.2—Pee Dee Station Boat Ramp

Winter   *
Spring   *
Summer *
Fall   *

See letter A on Map B–33.1 (p. 00).

Birders traveling from the Florence area toward the South Carolina coast might want to take a brief rest at this public boat ramp on the Great Pee Dee River, especially in summer, when it is an excellent area for Mississippi Kites. From I-95 exit at Exit 170, and go south on SC 327 for 5 miles to US 76—US 301, east of the city of Florence. Go east on US 76—US 301 for 1.7 miles, and then turn right (south) onto SC 327 at the campus of Francis Marion College. Go south on SC 327 for 4.8 miles to the intersection with Road 57, the back road to US 378 at Kingsburg. Follow Road 57 for 17.5 miles through typical Coastal Plain farm country. You may well spy a kite or two along this stretch during the summer. At 17.5 miles from SC 327 turn left (east) onto Road 66, and go 0.4 mile to a boat-launching area on the Great Pee Dee River. Scan the sky for soaring kites (late April through mid August).

To continue on toward the coast, return to Road 57, and turn left (south). In another 4.2 miles you will reach US 378. Here you can go east toward the coast. (See Section B-33, Marion County, for a description of additional birding areas on the other side of the river.)

B–22—GEORGETOWN COUNTY

The city of Georgetown lies on the main coastal highway (US 17) about thirty-five miles south of Myrtle Beach and sixty miles north of Charleston. This delightful town is an industrial and tourist center, and the seat of Georgetown County. Georgetown County has some of the best birding in South Carolina, offering beach, salt and fresh marsh, maritime forest, pinewoods, and river-swamp habitats easily accessible to visitors.

The coast north of Georgetown is called the Waccamaw Neck since it is on a triangular peninsula formed by the Waccamaw River, Winyah Bay, and the Atlantic. This is the southern end of the great tourist area centered on Myrtle Beach—the Grand Strand (see Section B-26 below, Horry County). The Georgetown County portion of the Grand Strand is less developed than the Horry County portion and contains the best birding spot in the state, Huntington Beach State Park.

South of the city of Georgetown there is no easy access to the beach. A system of fresh, brackish, and salt marshes dominates the scene. This is the Santee delta area. (Part of the Santee delta is in Charleston County—see Section B-10 above.) The best birding areas of the Santee delta are on private plantations, which regrettably are not usually open to the public. But there are many good spots that are on public land or can be birded from the public road.

Directly north of Georgetown, along US 701, is the delta of the Pee Dee river system, which includes the Black and Waccamaw Rivers as well as the Great Pee Dee River itself. This area is similar to the brackish and fresh marshes of the Santee Delta. Public access is limited, but birding is good along the roads or at Samworth Wildlife Management Area. The marshes at Brookgreen Gardens are a readily accessible part of the Waccamaw River marshes, which are part of the Pee Dee delta.

B–22.1—Huntington Beach State Park

Winter ****
Spring ****
Summer ***
Fall ****

See Map B–22.1.

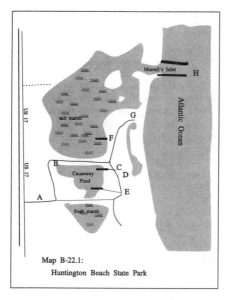

Map B-22.1:
Huntington Beach State Park

The best single birding destination in South Carolina is probably Huntington Beach State Park. The park combines ocean beach, inlet and rock jetty, beach dunes and scrub, salt and freshwater marsh, and maritime forest—all in one relatively compact area (2,500 acres), open to the public all year long.

From downtown Georgetown go about 17 miles north on US 17 to the park entrance on the east (right). From the junction of US 17 Bypass and US 17 Business, at the Horry County—Georgetown County line, go south for about 4 miles to the park entrance on the left. The entrance to Huntington Beach State Park is marked by inconspicuous signs easily missed in the heavy traffic on US 17. Look for the entrance to Brookgreen Gardens, marked by a huge statue of two rearing horses. The entrance to the state park is

directly across US 17 from the main entrance to Brookgreen Gardens.

Driving into the park, you will pass an entrance-fee station (see letter A on Map B–22.1). Once past the entrance station, the main park road turns left and passes through several hundred yards of maritime forest. The live oaks here harbor lots of small birds, including permanently resident Yellow-throated Warblers. From late March until September the Northern Parula is abundant here. This is a good spot to hear Eastern Screech-Owls calling after dark, especially in late summer and early fall. There is a small parking lot on the right just before the entrance road leaves the woods and crosses the causeway. Park here to explore either the woods or the causeway. (See letter B on Map B–22.1.)

Leaving the woods, the main road crosses a half-mile-long causeway. This is an excellent birding area in all seasons. To the left (north) is an extensive salt marsh with many mud flats. Shorebirds are here year-round but are most abundant in August and May. Willets, Seaside Sparrows, Marsh Wrens, Clapper Rails, and Boat-tailed Grackles are common permanent residents and are joined in winter by a few Sharp-tailed Sparrows.

On the right (south) side of the causeway is a freshwater pond with a marshy border, which you can overlook from an observation deck or from either of two boardwalks. This pond has a few alligators and is excellent for birds. In winter look for Common Loon, Pied-billed Grebe, American Wigeon, Canvasback, Ring-necked Duck, both scaup species, Oldsquaw (rare), Surf Scoter (rare), Hooded and Red-breasted Merganser, Bufflehead, and Ruddy Duck. In summer look for Least Tern, White Ibis, and Great and Snowy Egrets. Black-crowned Night-Herons roost in the shrubby vegetation along the back side of the pool and are seen year-round, especially at dawn and dusk. A few Least Bitterns nest in the marsh, but you will be lucky to catch a glimpse of one.

One of the best ways to view the fresh-water pond next to the causeway is to continue across the causeway, turn right at the T-junction, and then look for a small parking area on the left immediately after turning right. (See letter C on Map B-22.1.) Park here and follow the short trail which begins just across the road from the parking area. This trail goes about seventy-five yards to a boardwalk and deck overlooking the pond. (This trail is accessible by wheelchair.)

Farther along the road from this parking lot is the *campground* (see letter D), the *South Beach parking area* (see letter E on Map B-22.1), and Atalaya, Anna Hyatt Huntington's former art studio, modeled after the royal court in the Spanish province of Granada (open for tours in the summer). For now, however, turn around and go north on the main park road. You will soon reach the Marsh Boardwalk area and the North Beach parking area.

For the best birding in the park, go toward the North Beach parking area. The road goes through thick scrub of small pines, eastern red cedar, wax myrtle, and other species typical of southeastern beach dunes. This thicket abounds in birds. From mid-April through early September the thicket harbors many Painted Buntings. The males sing from conspicuous perches in May and June but may be difficult to find in late summer. A few are here into early November. Other common species of the thickets include Common Ground-Dove (this is the one of the best places in South Carolina to find this beautiful little dove), Prairie Warbler (March through September), Gray Catbird (abundant year-round), Rufous-sided Towhee, and Carolina Wren.

Soon after turning onto the North Beach road, you will reach a parking lot on the left (west) for the *Marsh Boardwalk* (see letter F on Map B-22.1). This is an excellent place to observe the salt marsh.

At the *end of the North Beach road* is a parking lot and picnic ground (letter G on Map B-22.1). Park here for the one-mile walk to the jetty. On the south side of the parking lot is a freshwater pool (Sandpiper Pond), which usually has a few ducks and Pied-billed Grebes in winter and Common Moorhens year-round. After checking out this pool, head out on the main trail to the beach. In the dunes on your right (north) just before reaching the beach is a small rain-fed pool which is attractive to White Ibis, especially from late summer to early winter.

Once you reach the beach, you will see the *jetty* (letter H on Map B-22.1) about a mile to the left (north). At this point you have a choice. If you walk south, away from the jetty, you will skirt Sandpiper Pond (the freshwater pool near the parking lot that you may have checked out earlier). In about a third of a mile you will reach the southern end of the pond. Cut over the dunes on the path that goes from the beach to the campgrounds, and you will find a delightful spot with freshwater marsh and mud flats. This is a good place to look for sandpipers and marsh birds, especially American Bittern (winter) and Least Bittern (summer).

Most birders pass up the walk south in favor of going to the jetty immediately, since this portion of the park is most likely to have rarities. A good way to walk to the jetty is along the edge of the salt marsh, behind the dunes. Just after passing the small rain pool favored by White Ibis and before you get the open beach, look for an indistinct trail along the back of the dunes. Follow this trail to the edge of the marsh, and walk north. By zigzagging into the marsh and then back out again to the edge of the dunes, you can find quite a few species of birds. The upper edge of the marsh is an excellent place to find Sedge Wren in winter, while Marsh Wrens and Seaside Sparrows are permanent residents in the wetter parts of the marsh out among the juncus or needlerush plants. Other sparrows found here in winter are the Savannah (abundant), the Sharp-tailed (uncommon), and the LeConte's (rare and difficult to see well).

A new (as of 1989) nature trail begins directly opposite the entrance to the South Beach parking lot and leads a quarter mile through maritime forest to a boardwalk and observation deck on the freshwater marsh on the edge of the causeway pool. The observation deck gives you another perspective on the waterfowl in this pool in winter as well as a good place to sit and wait for species of freshwater marshes, such as Least Bittern (summer), Marsh Wren (year-round), and rails (Virginia Rail and Sora in migration and winter, King Rail year-round).

B–22.2—Brookgreen Gardens

Winter   ***
Spring   **
Summer *
Fall   ***

Brookgreen Gardens are a natural companion piece to Huntington Beach State Park; both were at one time part of the estate of Archer M. and Anna Hyatt Huntington. In 1960 about 2,500 acres of the estate on the ocean side of US 17 became Huntington Beach State Park, while the remainder of the estate became Brookgreen Gardens, a unique area combining formal gardens, fine art, and natural beauty.

Brookgreen Gardens are best known as an outdoor sculpture garden. Over 350 sculptures of nineteenth and twentieth century artists—mostly American—are exhibited in the midst of a formal garden. In addition, there are picnic areas, a native wildlife zoo (including a flight cage for native birds), and hiking trails along the dikes of an old rice plantation. The creeks and marshes of the old rice fields are good for marsh birds, while the formal gardens are good for resident and migrant species of woodland and garden birds.

The entrance to Brookgreen Gardens is hard to miss. Anna Hyatt Huntington's huge sculpture, *Fighting Stallions,* marks the entrance road on the west side of US 17 about 17 miles south of Myrtle Beach or 17 miles north of Georgetown. (This is directly across US 17 from the entrance to Huntington Beach State Park.)

To reach the best birding area, proceed straight ahead past the entrance-fee station to the parking lot for the sculpture gardens. Pass through the visitors' pavilion and go straight ahead into an open portion of the gardens. Look for the giant sundial in front of you and slightly to your left. From the sundial area you can cut across the lawn to the edge of the old rice fields. After passing by a small, fenced-in sewage lagoon, you will reach the rice fields. Here follow the road around to the right. In a hundred yards or so you will see a path along an old rice field dike going west toward the main part of the Waccamaw River marshes. This dike is good for marsh birds. Rails are commonly heard here but seldom seen. King Rails are common permanent residents and are joined in winter (October through May) by a few Virginia Rails and Soras. Other marsh species to look for here include Marsh Wrens (common year round), Least Bitterns (April through October), and American Bitterns (October thorough early May).

At the end of the dike is an observation deck built over Brookgreen Creek, a backwater of the Waccamaw River. From here you may spot a few ducks, coots, or Common Moorhens. Wood Ducks and Mallards are found year-round and are joined in winter by a few American Black Ducks, American Wigeons, and perhaps other duck species as well as migratory Canada Geese. Check the distant trees along the edge of the marshes for hawks and an occasional Bald Eagle.

To continue exploring the marshes at Brookgreen Gardens, retrace your steps to the road past the sewage lagoon, and go the other direction (south). In about two hundred yards you will see another observation deck and more marshes. The marshes by this second deck are great for Common Moorhens and a few American Coots. From April through September this is a good place to look for the elusive Least Bittern. If you follow the path around to the left, you will go up a small bank to the edge of the sculpture gardens.

The sculpture gardens are a good birding area, especially in fall and winter. In winter look for a mixed flock of small birds. When you find a flock, you will usually encounter most of the following species: the Red-bellied and Downy Woodpeckers, Yellow-bellied Sapsucker, Eastern Phoebe, Carolina Chickadee, Tufted Titmouse, White-breasted Nuthatch, Carolina Wren, Golden-crowned and Ruby-crowned Kinglets, Blue-gray Gnatcatcher, Eastern Bluebird, Hermit Thrush, American Robin, Brown Thrasher, Solitary Vireo, and the following warblers: Orange-crowned (rare), Yellow-rumped, Yellow-throated, Pine, Palm, and Black-and-white Warblers, and Common Yellowthroat. Common wintering sparrows include Chipping, Field, Song, Swamp,

and White-throated. This is a good place to look for Lincoln's Sparrow in winter, but this species is elusive and seldom noticed.

Because of the large numbers of small birds in winter, the sculpture gardens are a good place to look for wintering hawks. American Kestrel and Sharp-shinned Hawk are often seen, and Cooper's Hawk is not too unusual (though less common than the Sharp-shinned Hawk). These bird-eating hawks in the formal gardens combine with other species more often seen hunting over the marshes or soaring high overhead: Black and Turkey Vulture, Osprey (rare in midwinter; common in spring), Bald Eagle, Northern Harrier (winter), Red-tailed and Red-shouldered Hawks, Merlin (rare), and Peregrine Falcon (rare).

Another raptor common at Brookgreen Gardens is the Great Horned Owl. At closing time in winter you will hear one or more owls hooting from the live oaks, where they nest. With luck you may spy a nest or catch a glimpse of an owl flying from tree to tree.

B–22.3—The Santee River Delta

Winter	**
Spring	**
Summer	*
Fall	**

See letter B on Map B–10.2 (p. 58).

The Santee River is one of the main rivers of South Carolina. It begins in the Blue Ridge Mountains of North Carolina as the *Broad River*, flows into the South Carolina Piedmont, and is joined at the Fall Line (at Columbia) by the Saluda. Here the river becomes the *Congaree*. The Congaree River meanders through the Upper Coastal Plain for some forty miles, until it is joined by the Wateree River. Here the river becomes the *Santee*. Just below the confluence of the Congaree and Wateree, the Santee flows into a huge artificial lake—Lake Marion. Below Lake Marion some of the water of the Santee is di-

verted into Lake Moultrie, another large artificial lake. But most of the water flows down the final stretch of the Santee River, forming the Santee Swamp—the northernmost stronghold of the American Swallow-tailed Kite. In its last few miles the Santee River forms a great tidal estuary system with marshes along its course. The upper marshes are freshwater marshes, but then they become more and more brackish. This area of freshwater and brackish marshes is known as the Santee River delta and is one of the outstanding areas for waterfowl, waders, and marsh birds in the state.

Most of the marshes of the Santee delta

are on private plantations and are usually closed to the public, but two areas are open (at least at some times of the year). One of these is the Santee Coastal Reserve in Charleston County (see Section B-10 above), the other, the Santee Delta Wildlife Management Area. This fifteen-hundred-acre area is conveniently located along US 17 in Georgetown County just north of the South Santee River (letter B on Map B–10.2).

There is a parking lot on the east side of US 17 just south of the bridge over the North Santee River. From this lot you can walk the main dike of the wildlife management area. (Observe posted restrictions, however. Much of this area is closed during the duck-hunting season,

December 1 through January 20.) The dike continues for several miles, but it may be overgrown and impassable. At first it parallels the North Santee River, but then it turns southward into the heart of the delta. This is essentially an out-and-back walking trip, since to loop back to US 17 requires about a seven-mile walk. Be prepared for biting insects at any time of year. In summer and fall the mosquitoes can be incredible. This is not a particularly good area to see great numbers of birds, but the lure of rarities (such as Sandhill Crane or Ruff in fall or winter, American Swallow-tailed Kite in summer, or Bald Eagle anytime) keeps a passionate birder going, even in the face of horrendous insect attacks.

B–22.4—The Great Pee Dee River

Winter   **
Spring   **
Summer *
Fall   **

There is good birding along the Great Pee Dee and Black Rivers just north of the city of Georgetown. In most areas forests and marshes such as those along the Great Pee Dee system would be prime attractions to birders, but in Georgetown County they are overshadowed by the more spectacular habitats of the Santee delta and so are relatively neglected.

From the intersection of US 17—US 17A and US 521—US 701 in downtown Georgetown go north on US 701 toward Conway. In about 7 miles you will reach the marshes along the Black River. Look for the old, abandoned road, which turns off to the right (east) about 0.2 mile before the new bridge of the Black River. Park by the "Road closed" sign, and walk along the old road to the river.

This old road is a great place from which to observe the brackish marshes and old rice fields along the Black River, a tributary of the Great Pee Dee River. The birds here are much the same as in the Santee delta. Look for puddle ducks and Bald Eagle in the winter, herons and

White Ibis year-round, and a few shorebirds in the spring or from late summer into October. Ospreys are common from March through November (and rare in winter). King Rails are common permanent residents of this marsh but are more often heard than seen.

To continue the tour, cross the Black River, and continue north on US 701 for about 0.2 mile to the intersection of Road 4. Turn right (east) onto Road 4. For the next 15 miles or so the road passes through plantation country similar to that along the Santee River, south of Georgetown. In swampy areas listen for Swainson's Warbler (mid-April though July) as well as many other species typical of Coastal Plain swamps. Where you find open pinewoods or young pine plantations with small trees, listen for the song of the Bachman's Sparrow (late March through September); with luck you will detect this singer, perhaps perched on a low bush. Mississippi Kites are common late April though late August.

The only public access to the marshes along the Great Pee Dee River is at Samworth Wildlife Management Area. From US 701 just north of the Black River go east 2.4 miles on Road 4. Here the road turns hard left (north) and becomes Road 52. Go north on Road 52 for 3.9 miles. Look for the well-marked entrance road to Samworth Wildlife Management Area on the right (east), and follow the entrance road for about a mile to a parking area and boat-launching ramp along the Great Pee Dee River.

You can see a bit of the marsh from the boat launch. For a better view, follow the path north from the parking lot. It goes into the woods and past a small pond overgrown with tupelos and bald cypress. Just past this pond turn right onto a dike along an overgrown rice field. (Do not go straight ahead; this is Arundel Plantation, private property).

You will probably not be able to follow the dike more than a few yards before being turned back by blackberry brambles, but this dike gives a better look at the marsh than you have from the boat-

launching ramp. During spring and fall keep an eye out overhead for migrating ducks and other species. White Ibis are common year-round, as are King Rails (usually only heard). Rarities seen here include Lincoln's Sparrow (early April).

Backtrack to the parking lot and return to Road 52. Go right (north) on Road 52 for 4.5 miles to the intersection with Road 264. Turn right (north) onto Road 264, and follow this road about 4.9 miles to US 701 at Yauhannah Creek. This is about as far north as the American Swallow-tailed Kite is regularly seen in South Carolina, but do not expect this species here; the Santee delta area is a much better place for this beautiful raptor.

At US 701 you may turn left (south) to return to Georgetown or go right (north) to go to Conway. If you head north, you will pass through a good bald-cypress—tupelo swamp where US 701 crosses the Great Pee Dee River into Horry County. This is an excellent place for Mississippi Kites late April through late August.

B–22.5—The Georgetown Sewage Treatment Plant

Winter   **
Spring   **
Summer *
Fall   **

See letter B on Map B–22.2.

Sewage treatment plants are famous among birders as good places to find birds. Unfortunately most such areas are closed to the public for safety reasons. The sewage treatment plant of the city of Georgetown is closed to casual entry, but many of its ponds are visible from a nearby public road. Here you will find shorebirds, herons, egrets, and a few ducks. Migration and winter are the best seasons, but even in summer there may be something around.

To reach the sewage ponds from downtown Georgetown, go west on US 521 toward Andrews. This is Highmarket Street. Look for a stoplight at Merriman Street, about one mile west of the intersection

of US 521 and US 17 in downtown Georgetown. From Merriman Street go west on US 521 for 1.8 miles. Here look for a sign for the Georgetown Animal Shelter, on the left. (The animal shelter is directly across the street from the sewage treatment plant, so if you can find the one, you can find the other.)

Turn left (south) onto Ridge Road. Follow Ridge Road to its end at a T-junction. Here turn right, and cross the railroad tracks. You will see the sewage treatment plant straight ahead. This is about a mile south of US 521.

The unpaved street running along the northern edge of the sewage treatment plant is West Street. By walking or driving along West Street, you can peer through

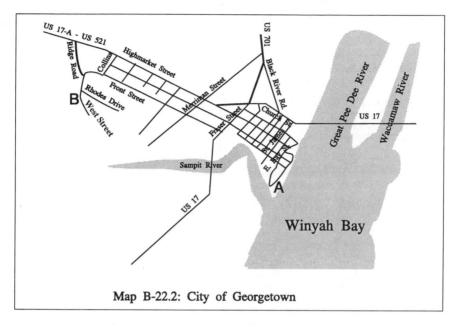

Map B-22.2: City of Georgetown

the fence at several of the ponds of the plant. West Street may be blocked by a closed gate, but you can still see the first sewage pond quite well.

Birding here can be good in spring and fall migration, when you can expect a good number of shorebirds, including Semipalmated Plover, Killdeer, both yellowlegs, and the following sandpipers: Solitary, Spotted, Semipalmated, Least, and Pectoral. In winter look for ducks (mostly Ring-necked Duck, Lesser Scaup, and Bufflehead), coots, and gulls (including Bonaparte's Gull). Mallard, Wood Duck, and Common Moorhen stay to breed. Common land birds here include Fish Crow and Boat-tailed Grackle.

B–22.6—East Bay and Morgan Parks, Georgetown

Winter   **
Spring   **
Summer *
Fall   **

See letter A on Map B–22.2.

Four rivers (the Waccamaw, the Great Pee Dee, the Black, and the Sampit) converge near the city of Georgetown to form a tidal estuary called Winyah Bay, which winds seaward for another dozen miles before reaching the open ocean. At Georgetown the bay is not very salty; in fact it is mostly fresh except during dry periods or storms. The shores of Winyah Bay near Georgetown are lined with a

marsh of juncus, phragmites reeds, and cattails. This marsh is home to typical marsh-dwelling species such as Marsh Wren, Least Bittern (summer), and rails. Large rails are common permanent residents of the marshes along the shore of Winyah Bay. Most ornithologists would call these Clapper Rails, but some would call them King Rails. In fact the rails here are intermediate between Clapper and King Rails, informally called "Kling" Rails. We may well see a time when the King

Rail is lumped with the Clapper Rail by taxonomists.

Two adjacent parks allow for easy access to the bay shore in Georgetown: East Bay Park and Morgan Park. To reach these parks from US 17, go to the intersection of US 17 and US 521. Here turn off of US 17 to the east toward downtown Georgetown, onto Highmarket Street. In about a mile Highmarket Street comes to East Bay Street. Here jog right a short way to continue straight ahead on Highmarket Street, which becomes Greenwich Drive. Greenwich Drive follows the edge of the marsh, providing an occasional view of Winyah Bay. In about 0.8 mile turn left into the parking lot for Morgan Park. Here a short trail leads over a footbridge to an island on the shore of Winyah Bay. This is a great place to set up a telescope and check out the birds in the bay. Most will be the usual gulls and terns, but you can expect a few ducks and loons in winter, and Black Skimmers in summer. White Ibis and other wading birds often nest on islands in Winyah Bay a few miles below Georgetown and can be seen flying back and forth during the spring and early summer. The few trees on the island attract quite a few migrant land birds, especially in the fall.

B–23—GREENVILLE COUNTY

The city of Greenville is one of the three largest cities in South Carolina, the urban center of what South Carolinians call the Up Country. Greenville County, therefore, is largely urban and suburban, at least in its southern parts. But this typical Piedmont part of the county gives way to mountains in the northern third of the county, culminating in Caesar's Head, Jones Gap, and the Mountain Bridge Wilderness, an area about three thousand feet above sea level along the North Carolina border.

From mid-April until early October the Mountain Bridge Wilderness of northern Greenville County offers some of the best birding in the state. Here the birder can find most of the common breeding species of the Southern Appalachians: Ruffed Grouse, Common Raven, Solitary Vireo, Dark-eyed Junco, and numerous species of warblers, among others.

B–23.1—Caesar's Head State Park

Winter   *
Spring   ****
Summer   **
Fall   ***

See Map B–23.1.

Many people from outside of South Carolina are surprised that the state has any mountains, since the state is so widely known for its coastal resort areas. South Carolina birders know better. More than ten thousand acres of prime mountain habitat are protected by a complex of state parks and wildlife management areas known as the Mountain Bridge Wilderness in extreme northern Greenville County, along the North Carolina border. The two adjacent state parks in the Mountain Bridge Wilderness are *Caesar's Head State Park* (covered here) and Jones Gap State Park (see Section B-23.5).

The gateway to Caesar's Head State Park is the junction of SC 11 and US 276 westbound. These two highways join in the community of Cleveland and run westbound together for 5.7 miles. Just before SC 11 crosses into Pickens County, US 276 branches off to the right (northwest) and zigzags up the mountain. The distance from SC 11 to the overlook parking lot in

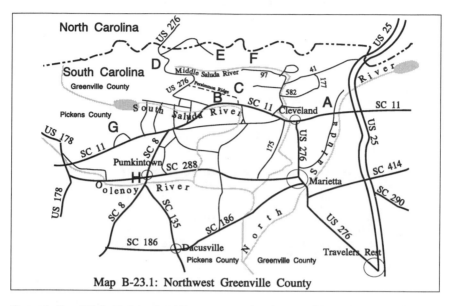

Map B-23.1: Northwest Greenville County

Caesar's Head State Park is about 7 miles. Along the way you will pass through an area of dry pine-oak woods and then enter a wonderful area of steep slopes covered with a mature cove hardwood forest. There are numerous pulloffs and parking areas along US 276 that offer excellent birding with little effort. A drive along this stretch in late April or early May can offer some of the best migration birding in the state. Many warblers stay to breed, including numerous Black-throated Green Warblers, Worm-eating Warblers, Black-and-white Warblers, Hooded Warblers, and Ovenbirds.

The junction of SC 11 and US 276 is about 1,120 feet above sea level. At this elevation the birds are those of the Piedmont more so than those of the Blue Ridge Mountains. After going 2.0 miles farther up the mountain, you will reach Bald Rock, a large granite rock outcropping. Bald Rock covers several acres and is badly marred by litter and debris. You may be able to walk out onto the outcropping and overlook the valley (unless this area has become posted). The elevation here is about 1,700 feet. Birds are scarce here, since the surrounding woods consist mostly of Virginia pine, pitch pine, and various scrubby oak species. This is a hot, dry place, especially on a sunny summer afternoon.

About 3.1 miles up the mountain from SC 11 look for an unpaved county road to the right. This is the western or uphill end of the *Persimmon Ridge Road* (letter C on Map B–23.1; see Section B-23.3). The elevation here is about 2,000 feet. From here up the mountain the dry pine-oak woods of the lower elevations are gradually replaced by a much moister forest of cove hardwoods. Pitch pines gradually give way to tulip trees. There are even a few eastern hemlocks along the creeks that spring from the mountain gulches.

At 4.5 miles from SC 11 you will pass the uphill end of the Oil Camp Creek Trail, a jeep trail that winds down the hill for a few miles to the end of Road 578, Oil Camp Creek Road, near Jones Gap State Park. A short hike down this trail might be good for typical birds of the lower Blue Ridge Mountains. This is a fairly good spot for Wild Turkey; Ruffed Grouse also occur, as do such typical breeding species as Solitary and Red-eyed Vireo, Black-and-white Warbler, Black-throated Green Warbler, Worm-eating Warbler, Ovenbird, Hooded Warbler, and Scarlet

113

Tanager. The elevation at the upper end of the Oil Camp Creek Trail is about 2,300 feet.

From the Oil Camp Creek Trail to the overlook parking lot at Caesar's Head State Park you will gain about 1,000 feet in elevation and reach an area that is definitely part of the Blue Ridge Mountains, as opposed to the Piedmont, with respect to birds. Many mountain species are found near the *Caesar's Head overlook* (elevation 3,208 feet; letter D on Map B–23.1) that are rarely found breeding elsewhere in South Carolina, including Dark-eyed Junco (common), Blackburnian Warbler (rare), Chestnut-sided Warbler (uncommon). Red Crossbills have been found breeding on private property nearby and may be here at any time of year. If you sit at the overlook long enough, a Common Raven will fly by, since ravens breed on cliffs nearby.

The overlook at Caesar's Head is a two-minute walk from the parking lot and has the most dramatic mountain view in South Carolina. You will look down a fifteen-hundred-foot drop into the Great Gulf of Matthews Creek. Table Rock Mountain is clearly visible to the southwest, and on a good day you can see all the way to the city of Greenville and even beyond, more than twenty-five miles away. The park naturalist has organized a fall hawk watch here at the overlook. On a good day in September you might see hundreds of hawks pass by in ones and twos. Most will be Broad-winged Hawks, but other species occur, including Osprey, Cooper's Hawk, Sharp-shinned Hawk, both vultures, American Kestrel, and others. Even Peregrine Falcon is possible. This is about the only place in the South Carolina mountains that has been explored as a hawk watch. Do not expect the numbers of hawks that you might find at a hawk watch in Pennsylvania or New Jersey, but a few hours' watch in September or October will probably not go completely unrewarded.

Once you have checked out the overlook, return to US 276, and drive about 0.7 mile to a trailhead parking lot on the right (east) side of US 276. This is the trailhead for several good birding trails. The Foothills Trail currently has its eastern terminus here. This magnificent trail winds for about a hundred miles through the low mountains of the North Carolina—South Carolina border area, ultimately leading to Oconee State Park.

Two other good birding trails also begin from the trailhead parking lot. The most popular trail in the park is the Raven Cliff Falls Trail. This trail begins across US 276 from the parking lot and goes about 2.3 miles to an overlook of Raven Cliff Falls, a magnificent cascade with a four-hundred-foot drop. This trail is rated easy to moderate with a few steep portions as you near the falls. It is not a loop trail.

Some of the best birding along the Raven Cliff Falls trail is in the first mile. Just downhill from US 276 the trail crosses a power line right-of-way and also an alder swamp, which are both great places for birds. The tall trees along the trail just beyond the alder swamp had summering Cerulean Warblers in 1988. Hopefully this species will be found breeding here in the future. Common breeders here include Black-and-white Warbler, Worm-eating Warbler, Hooded Warbler, Solitary Vireo, and Scarlet Tanager.

The Foothills Trail goes along with the Raven Cliff Falls Trail for a bit more than a mile until it finally branches off to the right. If the trail to the falls is overrun with people, you might consider following the Foothills Trail for a bit. This trail gets a lot less traffic and is quite good for birds. You are much more likely to find a Ruffed Grouse on the Foothills Trail, since it is less traveled.

Numerous unmarked paths and old roads crisscross this area. Do not wander off the marked trail too far unless you have a topographic map and a compass, or unless you enjoy getting lost.

The other good birding trail that begins at the trailhead parking lot is the Jones Gap—Cold Spring Branch Loop Trail. This is a rather strenuous five-mile loop that begins at the north end of the parking lot. Here a short spur trail leads downhill a short distance to the Jones Gap Trail, a five-mile trail from US 276 to the parking lot in Jones Gap State Park at the bottom of the hill. When you get to the Jones Gap Trail, follow this trail down the upper reaches of the Middle Saluda River. In about two miles you will reach a side trail on the right. This is the Cold Spring Branch Trail, which winds back up the mountain for about two miles, until it reaches US 276 a few hundred yards from the parking lot where you started.

A good portion of the Jones Gap—Cold Spring Branch Loop Trail goes along a stream (either the Middle Saluda River or Cold Spring Branch). This means that it is a good trail for birds that are partial to

mountain streams and the streamside rhododendrons, hemlocks, and white pines. Species to look for along this trail in late spring or early summer include Louisiana Waterthrush, Swainson's Warbler (rare), Black-throated Green Warbler (common in hemlocks), and Black-throated Blue Warbler in addition to the species mentioned above for the Raven Cliff Falls Trail.

If you have time when you have finished with Caesar's Head State Park, you might consider going on to Camp Greenville (see Section B-23.2 below) or backtracking down the mountain to the Persimmon Ridge Road (see Section B-23.3).

B–23.2—Camp Greenville (YMCA)

Winter	*
Spring	***
Summer	**
Fall	**

See letter E on Map B–23.1.

To reach *Camp Greenville* from the overlook area of Caesar's Head State Park (see Section B-23.1), turn left (north) onto US 276, and follow this road north toward Brevard, North Carolina. In 2.8 miles you will reach the state line. Just before you get to North Carolina, turn right (east) onto Road 15. This road enters North Carolina almost immediately. Continue straight ahead on this road, now called SR 1559, in Transylvania County, North Carolina. The road reenters South Carolina in 2.6 miles.

The same road continues another 2.5 miles to a dead end. Soon after reentering South Carolina you will reach an overlook on the right. The brush here is good for breeding Black-and-white Warbler and Worm-eating Warbler. Be alert

for Common Ravens, which sometimes drift by on a rising air current.

The last mile of Road 15 is through the middle of *Camp Greenville*, a YMCA Camp. This area is normally closed to the public, unless you get permission from the camp management to hike on the trails. But the camp's chapel, at the end of the road, is open to the public. This is Symmes Chapel, also known as the Pretty Place. From the chapel there is a magnificent view of the valley of the Middle Saluda River, over 1,500 feet below. (The chapel may not be open to the public on Saturdays, especially from May through September, if the chapel has been reserved for a wedding, as it often is then.) Common Ravens sometimes nest on rock cliffs in the neighborhood, so this is the best place in South Carolina to look for this mountain species.

Winter *
Spring **
Summer **
Fall   **

See letter C on Map B–23.1.

The upper (northwest) end of the *Persimmon Ridge Road* is 3.8 miles downhill (south) along US 276 from the overlook at Caesar's Head State Park (see Section B-23.1) or 3.1 miles uphill from the junction of US 276 and SC 11. Persimmon Ridge Road is an unpaved road that winds down Persimmon Ridge for 3.5 miles, reaching SC 11—US 276 at a point 2.2 miles east of their junction.

Persimmon Ridge Road is a rough track through dry pine-oak woods. The road is barely passable for ordinary cars. Unless you have a high-clearance vehicle, you should park near the upper end of the road and walk. This is a great place for breeding Ovenbirds, Pine Warblers, and other species of Piedmont pine-oak woods. With a bit of luck you might find a flock of Wild Turkey.

The rarest birds that have been found along the Persimmon Ridge Road are summering Golden-crowned Kinglets and Red-breasted Nuthatches. These high-mountain species have been found in the groves of Virginia- and pitch-pine near the upper end of the road, even though the elevation here is under 2,000 feet. Another species to look for is Red Crossbill. Crossbills have bred near Caesar's Head, and may also wander in from the high mountains of North Carolina. The best time of year to find crossbills is late summer through early winter, but do not rely this rare species' being here at any time.

You can also explore Persimmon Ridge Road from its lower end. The first mile or so uphill from SC 11 is well maintained. When you reach a spot that looks like a turnaround, park your car, and proceed on foot (unless you have a high-clearance vehicle or enjoy getting stuck in the mud).

The Persimmon Ridge Road skirts two Heritage Trust Preserves, the Chandler Tract and the Ashmore Tract. These wild areas have no developed trails and are better known for their rare plants (including the endangered mountain sweet pitcher plant, *Sarracenia jonesii*) than for their birds.

To explore the Ashmore Tract, park at the circular turnaround (where the Persimmon Ridge Road starts to deteriorate into a jeep trail). A few yards uphill from the parking area look for a gated jeep trail on the right (northeast) side of the Persimmon Ridge Road. Follow this trail. In about 0.5 mile you will cross a creek. Just beyond the creek is a side trail to the left (west). This side trail follows the creek uphill for about 0.3 mile to an interesting waterfall.

Once you have explored the side trail, return to the main trail. This trail ascends a low ridge (ignore numerous side trails here) and then descends, reaching a small pond in about 0.5 mile. The mountain sweet pitcher plant is common along the marshy border of this pond. This pond is the largest pond within the borders of the Mountain Bridge Wilderness. Although its altitude is rather low (about 1,200 feet above sea level), it is a good spot to look for rare mountain species such as summering Least Flycatchers or Red Crossbills. (These species have not yet been found here, but the habitat is right, and so they should be looked for here.)

B–23.4—Wildcat Wayside Park

Winter *
Spring **
Summer **
Fall **

See letter B on Map B–23.1.

Wildcat Wayside Park is a small park (sixty-three acres) on the north side of SC 11 (the Cherokee Foothills Highway) about 10 miles west of US 25 or 0.6 mile east of the junction where US 276 goes up the mountain toward Caesar's Head and the North Carolina line. This park is currently (1992) a South Carolina State Park, but it has been under other jurisdictions in the past and may well be turned over to some other agency in the future.

The park is not well marked. Look for a wide shoulder on the north side of SC 11 and park. There is an indistinct trail leading up Wildcat Branch for about half a mile. This trail is good for breeding warblers, including Black-throated Green Warbler (in hemlocks) and Louisiana Waterthrush (along the creek). Wildcat Wayside is a small gem and hopefully will long remain a quiet place to enjoy the woods and a mountain steam.

B–23.5—Jones Gap State Park and Vicinity

Winter *
Spring ***
Summer **
Fall **

See letter F on Map B–23.1.

Located along the Middle Saluda River in northern Greenville County, *Jones Gap State Park* is part of the Mountain Bridge Wilderness. This park used to be considered part of Caesar's Head State Park but now is administered separately. The park offers picnicking, trailside camping, hiking, and trout fishing in one of the most scenic parts of the state of South Carolina. Furthermore, the road from SC 11 to the park leads through a delightful countryside of small farms, ponds, and woodlots, where you can find most of the bird species of the farmlands of the Blue Ridge foothills. To reach Jones Gap State Park, start at the intersection of SC 11 (the Cherokee Foothills Scenic Highway) and US 276 in the community of Cleveland. (This is the eastern junction of these two highways, five miles west of US 25 and six miles east of the turnoff for Caesar's Head State Park.) Follow SC 11—US 276 west. At 0.6 mile from the junction of SC 11 and US 276 you will cross the Middle Saluda River. Just beyond the bridge is a

road to the left, Road 175, River Road. During spring migration you might want to park along River Road and walk a bit along this riverside road. The tall sycamores along the river here attract many migrant birds, including Cape May Warblers, Rose-breasted Grosbeaks, and Northern Orioles. During the breeding season watch for breeding orioles. Most will be Orchard Orioles, but there is a chance for Northern Oriole breeding here—a rare breeder in South Carolina.

To continue toward the park, return to SC 11—US 276 and go west. At 0.8 mile beyond the SC 11 bridge over the Middle Saluda River turn right onto Road 97. (There should be a sign for Jones Gap State Park here.) Road 97 leads through a delightful farming area. Here you will find breeding species such as American Goldfinch, Yellow Warbler, and other species typical of the farmlands of the Blue Ridge foothills. This is one of the few places in the state where House Wrens breed in the countryside, rather than in suburban gardens.

To reach Jones Gap State Park, follow Road 97 to its upper end, about 6 miles from SC 11—US 276. To enjoy the park, you must hike its trails. The main trail is the Jones Gap Trail, which follows the Middle Saluda River uphill to Jones Gap, near Caesar's Head State Park.

The avian specialty of Jones Gap State Park is Swainson's Warbler. This shy species is rather common in the rhododendron thickets along the river, but you may have trouble hearing its song over the roar of the cascading water.

B–23.6—Pleasant Ridge Park

Winter   *
Spring   **
Summer **
Fall   **

See letter A on Map B–23.1.

Pleasant Ridge Park is a three-hundred-acre Greenville County park on SC 11, the Cherokee Foothills Scenic Highway. From US 25 north of Greenville exit at SC 11 and go west for 2.0 miles to the park entrance road. The park offers fishing in a small lake, picnicking, and camping.

Many of the common species of the lower Blue Ridge Mountains may be found in the park, including such sought-after species as Ruffed Grouse (rare, but possible). The best birding is on the mile-long nature trail, a loop trail which begins at the lower picnic area.

B–23.7—Green Creek and Lake Lanier

Winter   *
Spring   ***
Summer **
Fall   **

See Map B–23.2.

The foothills of the Blue Ridge Mountains near Landrum, South Carolina, and Tryon, North Carolina, offer interesting birding all year long, but especially during spring and fall migrations. Here we will describe a meandering route through some of the South Carolina portion of this area. The Tryon Bird and Nature Club of Tryon, North Carolina, has a bird checklist and frequent outings in this delightful area. Contact the Tryon Chamber of Commerce for the names and addresses of current officers of the club.

To reach this area from I-26, use the Landrum exit (Exit 1), in Spartanburg County. (See also Section B–42.1 below) Go west on SC 14 for 2.0 miles to downtown Landrum. Here turn right (northwest) onto US 176 toward Tryon, North Carolina. In 1.9

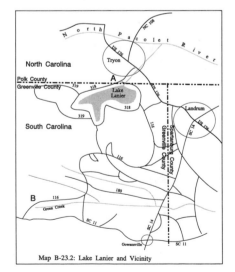

Map B-23.2: Lake Lanier and Vicinity

miles you will enter Greenville County. In another 0.8 mile you will reach the North Carolina state line. Just before you enter North Carolina, you will pass a large stand of tulip trees and other species typical of cove hardwood forests, on the left (west). This is a good area to look for migrants in the spring, and it is possible to come across breeding Cerulean Warblers.

Once in North Carolina, continue north on US 176 for about 0.3 mile. Here turn left at the first paved road. This road leads up the hill for 0.2 mile to the South Carolina border (letter A on Map B–23.2).

When you reach South Carolina, you will find yourself on Road 318 on the north shore of Lake Lanier, a mile-long, narrow mountain lake almost completely surrounded by vacation houses. Take Road 318 to the right (southwest), and follow this road counterclockwise around the lake.

Road 318 is very developed, but the setting is wooded and suburban. Find a place to park, and walk the road for a while. You will find lots of birds, especially during late April or early May.

In about 2.5 miles you will cross the inlet creek for the lake. This is a good spot for migrant and summer resident warblers. Just beyond the inlet creek turn away from Road 318 onto a paved county road to the right (south). Follow this road for about a mile, past Oak Grove Church, to a T-junction with Road 116.

Turn right (west) onto Road 116, and follow it for about 5 miles to its end at SC 11. Along the way you will pass through a wide variety of Blue Ridge foothills habitats: cultivated fields, Virginia-pine groves, peach orchards, small streams, clear-cut areas, and the like. The last few miles of *Road 116* parallel Green Creek (letter B on Map B–23.2). During spring migration you can easily find twenty species of warbler along Road 116, as well as orioles, vireos, tanagers, grosbeaks, and other typical passerine migrants. Keep alert for breeding Solitary Vireos and perhaps even Red-breasted Nuthatches in Virginia-pine groves along Green Creek. When you get to SC 11, you will be about 11 miles east of US 25 or 14 miles west of I-26, between Cleveland and Gowansville.

B–23.8—Paris Mountain

Winter	*
Spring	**
Summer	**
Fall	**

Looming about 1,300 feet above the city of Greenville, *Paris Mountain* (elevation 2,050 feet) is a large Piedmont monadnock which offers good birding, especially during migration. The mountain is mostly privately owned, but 1275 acres have been set aside for Paris Mountain State Park.

To reach the park from the city of Greenville, go north on US 276 to the intersection with SC 291, North Pleasantburg Drive. Here turn right (east), and go just 0.2 mile before bearing left onto SC 253, Paris Mountain Road. Go northeast on SC 253 for 2.3 miles. Here turn left onto Road

344, Reservoir Road, which leads to the park entrance in about a mile.

Once in the park, you have a choice of two trails to hike. The Lake Placid Nature Trail is a mile-long loop trail around the swimming lake, which you will see on the right shortly after entering the park. You can pick up this loop trail near the bathhouse.

For a longer walk through a wild portion of the park, try the four-mile-long hiking trail to the top of Paris Mountain. This trail begins at the Sulphur Springs Picnic Area, which you will find on the left about 1.5

miles into the park along the main park road. The hiking trail can be a long, hot walk, but it leads to an area of old-growth Virginia pines and eventually to the top of the mountain. This is not a loop trail.

B—23.9—Bunched Arrowhead Heritage Preserve

Winter   **
Spring   ***
Summer *
Fall   ***

See letter A on Map B—23.3.

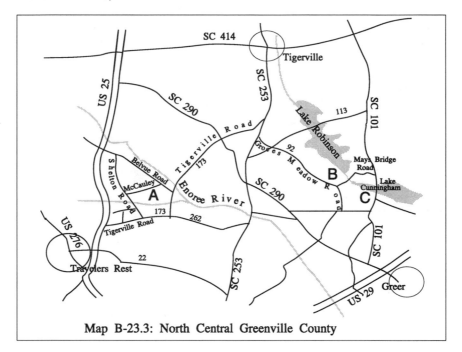

Map B-23.3: North Central Greenville County

The bunched arrowhead (*Sagittaria fasciculata*) is a rare aquatic plant whose range in South Carolina is restricted to a few places in the Piedmont where seeps or springs create small marshes or swamps. Some of these seeps occur in central Greenville County in an area of rapid suburban development. The Heritage Trust program of the South Carolina Wildlife and Marine Resources Department now protects a small site (178 acres) near Travelers Rest which contains a colony of bunched arrowhead.

The preserve, which is under the stewardship of the Greenville Audubon Society, is a good birding area, particularly during migration. It consists of a variety of habitats, including meadows, hedgerows, small hardwood swamps, Virginia-pine thickets, and a small (two-acre) pond. The Greenville Audubon Society has laid out a 1.5-mile trail through the property, giving easy access to all of its habitats.

This is one of the few public areas in the South Carolina Piedmont where birders have access to old fields, meadows, and hedgerows. As a consequence, the preserve is a great place for finding birds of old fields and meadows, especially sparrows. Breeding sparrows include Field, Chipping, Song, and a few Grasshopper Sparrows. In winter these are joined by numerous other species, including White-throated, White-crowned, Fox, and Swamp Sparrows, and Dark-eyed Juncos. Rarities to look for include Henslow's Sparrows (early spring) and Lincoln's Sparrows (late fall and early spring).

To reach the preserve, take US 25 or US 276 north from Greenville to Travelers Rest, where US 276 crosses US 25. From the junction of US 25 and US 276 go north on US 25 for 2 miles to Road 173, Tigerville Road. Here turn right (east), and go about 1.2 miles to the intersection with Shelton Road. Here turn left (north), and go about a mile. Take the first right shortly after crossing a creek (a branch of the Enoree River). This is McCauley Road. The parking area for the preserve

is about a half mile east along McCauley Road. The trail begins at the parking area (letter A on Map B–23.3).

A visit to *Bunched Arrowhead Heritage Preserve* is easily combined with a visit to Lake Robinson (see Section B-23.10 below). To reach the lake, go east on McCauley Road from the parking area for 0.5 mile to its junction with Belvue Road. Turn right and follow Belvue Road southeast for 0.2 mile to a T-junction at Road 173, Tigerville Road. Here turn left, and follow Road 173 northeast. In 1.7 miles you will reach SC 290. Keep straight ahead on Road 173. In another 1.9 miles you will reach an intersection with SC 253. Here turn right (south) and follow SC 253 for 0.9 mile to Road 92, Groces Meadow Road. Here turn left and follow Road 92 southeast for about 3 miles to the intersection with Mayes Bridge Road on the left. The entrance to Smith Park on Lake Robinson is at this intersection (letter B on Map B–23.3).

B–23.10—Lake Robinson and Lake Cunningham

Winter *
Spring **
Summer *
Fall **

See letters B and C on Map B–23.3.

There are no large lakes in Greenville County to rival Lake Hartwell (a few miles west, in Anderson and Oconee counties), but the city of Greer has a reservoir, *Lake Robinson* on the Middle Tyger River, where you might find a few ducks or gulls in winter or in migration.

Lake Robinson is about four miles long and one mile wide at its widest point. Near the dam at the lake's south end the Greer Water Commission maintains a delightful little park, *J. Verne Smith Park*, with rest rooms, picnic facilities, and a boat ramp (letter B on Map B–23.3). From the park you can easily overlook most of the lake. Even if there are few birds on the lake, you will be treated to a panorama of the Blue Ridge Mountains of northern Greenville County a few miles to the north of this Piedmont lake.

To reach Smith Park from the west, follow the directions given in Section B-23.9.

To reach Smith Park from the south, go to the intersection of SC 101 and US 29, on the northwest edge of the city of Greer. Go north on SC 101—SC 290. In 0.3 mile you will reach the split of SC 290 and SC 101. Bear right, keeping on SC 101. At 3.1 miles north of this split (3.4 miles from US 29), SC 101 crosses a narrow portion of another Greer reservoir, *Lake Cunningham*. There is an informal parking area to the right on the south side of the bridge. Park here to have a brief look around.

From the bridge over Lake Cunningham you can overlook a portion of *Lake Cunningham Waterfowl Area*, where you might find a Wood Duck (letter C on Map B–23.3). The willows and alders near the SC 101 bridge over Lake Cunningham are good for breeding Yellow Warblers.

The habitat looks good for breeding Willow Flycatchers, but none have been found there yet.

From the SC 101 bridge over Lake Cunningham keep north on SC 101 for another 1.5 miles. Here turn left (west) onto Mays Bridge Road. Follow Mays Bridge road for 1.5 miles. Soon after you cross the Middle Tyger River, look for the entrance to Smith Park on the right (north).

B–23.11—The Reedy River Falls Greenway in Downtown Greenville

Winter   *
Spring   **
Summer *
Fall   **

In 1797 the village of Pleasantburg was laid out around a mill built near the falls of the Reedy River. In 1831 Pleasantburg became the city of Greenville, and the water power harnessed at the falls of the Reedy River started the new city on its career as an internationally known center of textile manufacturing. Today the falls still exist and are protected by a small park just south of downtown Greenville. Reedy River Falls Historic Park today preserves twenty-four acres of a wild Piedmont landscape and is the beginning of a five-kilometer loop trail through a corridor connecting Reedy River Falls Historic Park with nearby Cleveland Park, a much larger Greenville City Park. This corridor is known as the *Reedy River Falls Greenway*, which provides a fairly good birding area in the middle of one of the largest cities in the state.

The trail through the Reedy River Falls Greenway is paved and has the form of a figure 9. The tail of the 9 is near the falls. From this point you follow the trail downstream toward Cleveland Park (the home of the Greenville Zoo). In about a mile you reach the loop portion of the 9. Since the trail is much used by runners, distances from the beginning are painted (in meters) on the paved walkway, so you can easily tell just how far you have gone on the trail.

Since there is no easy public parking near the falls, the best way to visit the trail is to go to Cleveland Park, where there is ample parking. From the center of Greenville go south on US 29 (Church Street) or US 25 Business (Main Street). In less than a quarter mile from the city center you will reach Washington Street. Turn left (east) onto Washington Street, following signs for the Greenville Zoo. In about a half mile you will reach the zoo entrance. Parking is somewhat limited near the zoo, so proceed east past the zoo entrance for one short block. Here you will encounter Lakehurst Drive. Turn right (south) onto Lakehurst Drive, entering the main part of Cleveland Park. There are numerous parking lots at small picnic areas along Lakehurst Drive. Park at any one of them. From any of the picnic areas you should have little trouble locating the paved trail.

The best way to bird Cleveland Park and the Reedy River Greenway is to follow the paved trail around its entire 5-kilometer course. Early mornings in late April or early May offer the best birding, but at any time of year you will find something of interest.

Look for the 2050-meter mark, which is near the Woodland Way bridge over Reedy River. Across Woodland Way from this point is the beginning of a half-mile loop trail, Fernwood Nature Trail, which winds up a wooded ravine on the edge of the park. The trail was established by the William Bartram Group of the Sierra Club in cooperation with the City of Greenville Parks and Recreation Departments. A brochure describing the trail is usually available from a box at the beginning of this delightful side trip.

Once you have explored the nature trail, return to the main, paved trail, and cross the river along the Woodland Way bridge. Here, just south of Woodland Way, are the Cleveland Park stables. In winter there is often an active bird feeder near the stables. The House Finch is abundant at this feeder, and you can also look for typical urban feeder birds such as American Goldfinch, Pine Siskin, and others.

By following the entire paved trail along its loop, you will encounter many good birding spots. Woodpeckers, including Red-headed Woodpeckers, are fairly common in the wooded areas. Belted Kingfishers often breed along the river and are present year-round. At any time of year you might spy an American Kestrel somewhere along the trail. This is one of the few places in the South Carolina Piedmont where you might find a summering kestrel. During spring migration the tall tulip trees and other species along the way are attractive to migrant land birds, including orioles, tanagers, vireos, and up to twenty-four species of warblers.

B–24—GREENWOOD COUNTY

Greenwood County is a farming and manufacturing county in the west-central part of the state. Its seat is the city of Greenwood, with a population of about twenty-five thousand people. Greenwood County has a typical Piedmont mixture of oak-pine woods, pine plantations, flood-plain forests along streams, and small farms.

Lake Greenwood, an impoundment of the Saluda River, forms the northeastern boundary of the county and offers typical Piedmont reservoir birding (see Section B-24.1, Greenwood State Park). The other notable birding area in the county is Ninety Six National Historic Site, a unit of the National Park system just south of the town of Ninety Six (see Section B-24.2).

B–24.1—Greenwood State Park

Winter *
Spring *
Summer *
Fall *

Greenwood State Park is a 914-acre park on the west shore of Lake Greenwood that offers picnicking, camping, swimming, fishing, and other typical lakeside recreation. To reach the park from I-26, leave the interstate at Exit 74 near Newberry, and follow SC 34 and SC 34 Bypass west for about 24 miles. Soon after crossing the Saluda River just below the Lake Greenwood dam, turn right (north) onto SC 702, and go 1.7 miles to the main park entrance road (on the right).

Greenwood State Park has mostly second-growth oak-pine woods and a few loblolly-pine plantations, which are not particularly good for birding. The best birding is along the lakeshore, especially from October through April, when you might see a few Common Loons, Horned or Pied-billed Grebes, ducks, and gulls in or over the lake. There is good access to the shore from the main picnic area or from the boat launch area. Follow park signs.

Winter **
Spring **
Summer *
Fall **

Ninety Six was a colonial settlement. It was called Ninety Six because it was ninety-six miles from Oconee Station in the Cherokee country in what is now northwestern South Carolina. Here, on November 18, 1775, a major battle of the American Revolution was fought. *Ninety Six National Historic Site* is one of three national parks (along with Kings Mountain National Military Park and Cowpens National Battlefield) which commemorate the American Revolution in South Carolina.

This is a relatively new park, established in 1976, so it still retains much of the aspect of a Piedmont farm. There is a small lake, also hayfields, overgrown fields coming up in pines, oak-pine woods, and even a floodplain forest along Ninety Six Creek. The result is a varied collection of habitats and good birding opportunities.

To reach the park from I-26, leave at Exit 76, and go west on SC 34 for about 30 miles to the modern town of Ninety Six. Here turn left (south) onto SC 248, and go 2.1 miles to the park entrance on the left. at the visitors' center for a look at a small museum, a free slide show, and a map of the park.

The self-guided trail through the historic area of the park might yield a few birds, but the best birding is in the back part of the park, little used except by a few horseback riders. Follow the trails indicated on the park map to explore the park.

A horse trail parallels the old Charleston Road (now mostly overgrown). Follow this trail to the Gouedy Cemetery on the south side of the park. Just beyond the cemetery the trail leaves the open fields and enters the floodplain woods along Ninety Six Creek, where you can always find birds typical of Piedmont floodplain forests.

As you explore the park, be alert for Wild Turkey. This species has been reintroduced into most of South Carolina in the last twenty years and is increasing rapidly. Since there is no hunting on park property, the area acts as a refuge for turkeys and other wildlife, such as white-tailed deer.

Another good birding area in the park is Star Fort Lake, in the eastern part of the park. The swampy woods below the dam and also at the upper end of the lake are especially good areas for common species. Look for Canada Geese on the lake itself. This species, like the Wild Turkey, has been reintroduced widely in the South Carolina Piedmont and is increasing rapidly.

B–25—HAMPTON COUNTY

The swamps and pine forests along the lower stretch of the Savannah River between the US 301 bridge south of Allendale and the I-95 bridge near Hardeeville offer us some of the best birding in South Carolina at any time of year. Some of this area is in Allendale County (see Section B-3 above) or in Jas-per County (see Section B-27), but the best parts of the lower Savannah are in the plantations and wildlife management areas of Hampton County.

Hampton is a rural county in the Upper Coastal Plain. Its general aspect is that of the deep South; more like parts of south

Georgia or north Florida than it is like most of the rest of South Carolina. Its most interesting birds are also the birds of the deep South: Mississippi and American Swallow-tailed Kites, Red-cockaded Woodpecker, Swainson's Warbler, Painted Bunting, and Bachman's Sparrow.

B–25.1—The Savannah River Plantations in Hampton County

Winter **
Spring **
Summer ***
Fall **

See letter C on Map B–25.1.

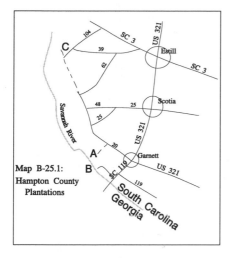

Map B-25.1:
Hampton County
Plantations

Along the Savannah River are several plantations which cater to deer and quail hunters. They are not normally open to the public, except for the James W. Webb Wildlife Center (see Section B-25.2). These hunting preserves are great private wildlife areas. The managers use controlled burning in the pinewoods, which improves quail, turkey, and deer habitat, and also provides excellent habitat for Red-cockaded Woodpecker and Bachman's Sparrow. The open fields provide feeding areas for American Swallow-tailed Kites as well as white-tailed deer.

It is possible to see much of these beautiful plantations from the public road. Do not wander from the road. If you wish to explore this type of habitat on foot, continue a few miles south to the Webb Wildlife Center.

Our tour starts on SC 3, at the Allendale County—Hampton County line. This is about 6.4 miles west of US 321 in Estill or about 15 miles southeast of the intersection of SC 3 and US 301. At the county line turn southwest (left if you are coming from Estill, right if you are coming from Allendale County). The first 2.2 miles of the road are in Allendale County but right on the county line. This same road becomes Road 39 when it enters Hampton County. At 2.5 miles from SC 3 the road with the Road 39 number turns left. Keep going straight ahead, now on Road 503.

At about 3 miles from SC 3 the road leaves the fields and enters an open pinewoods. Stop here for a minute. There are a few trees along the road in this area in which Red-cockaded Woodpeckers roost. Other species common in this open pinewoods are Red-headed Woodpecker, Eastern Bluebird, Brown-headed Nuthatch (found year-round), and Bachman's Sparrow, Summer Tanager, and Eastern Wood-Pewee (April though September). Keep an eye out for Wild Turkeys, which are common throughout the plantation country.

About 5 miles south of SC 3 the paved road ends at a T-junction of sand roads. The road to the right is private, so turn left onto a well-maintained public sand road. Just after the turn the road crosses over a small creek. The brush here is great for migrants, especially in the fall. The sand road goes up a slight hill and into an area of large fields. In winter look in the hedgerows along the road for sparrows; Chipping, Field, Vesper, Savannah, Fox, Song, Swamp, White-throated, and even White-crowned Sparrows and Dark-eyed

Juncos are found here. In summer look for Painted and Indigo Buntings, Blue Grosbeak, and Orchard Oriole. This area of open fields is good year-round for Northern Bobwhite, Loggerhead Shrike, Chipping and Field Sparrows, Red-shouldered and Red-tailed Hawks, and Eastern Meadowlarks. It is possible to find Common Ground-Doves here, but this pretty little dove is sadly rare despite the great habitat for it here.

About 7 miles from SC 3 the road becomes paved again. For the next few miles keep an eye for American Swallow-tailed Kites (late March through August; best in July and early August). These magnificent raptors breed in the swamps along the nearby Savannah River and often feed over the open fields near the community of Shirley.

This paved road is Road 20. About 15 miles from the beginning of the tour (about 3.9 miles south of the intersection of Roads 20 and 25 in Shirley), look for the well-marked entrance to the Webb Wildlife Center, on the right (west) side of Road 20. Unless there is a deer or quail hunt going on, you will probably want to explore the Webb Center, where you can hike about a bit in great pinewoods and swamps (see Section B-25.2).

From the Webb Center entrance road, the present tour continues southeast about 2.8 miles to the three-way intersection of Road 20, US 321, and SC 119 in the little town of Garnett. From Garnett you can go 8.3 miles north on US 321 and return to SC 3, or you can go 25 miles south to Exit 5 of I-95, in Hardeeville. Garnett is also a possible starting point of the tour of the Savannah River areas of Jasper County (see Section B-27) as well as the start of the side trip to Stokes Bluff Landing on the Savannah River in Hampton County (see Section B-25.3).

B–25.2—James K. Webb Wildlife Center

Winter   **
Spring   **
Summer ***
Fall   **

See letter A on Map B–25.1.

Named for a former executive director of the South Carolina Department of Wildlife and Marine Resources, the 5,741-acre Webb Wildlife Center has been state property since 1941. Due to careful management, this area is one of the best places in the state to observe the wildlife of the pinewoods and river swamps of the Coastal Plain. Except for a few weekends in the late fall and winter, when there are deer hunts here, the area is open to the public at all times. (No fishing is allowed on Sundays.) You can pick up a schedule of hunts at the Webb Center as part of the hunting and fishing regulations, available at any South Carolina Welcome Station, or write or call the Manager, Webb Wildlife Center, Garnett, SC 29922, telephone (803) 625-3637.

The entrance road passes through one of the most beautiful open pine forests in South Carolina. Keep an eye out for Red-cockaded Woodpecker roost trees on either side of the road. There are several families of this endangered woodpecker on the property. Bachman's Sparrows are common but difficult to find except when they are singing (late March through September). All of South Carolina's woodpeckers are relatively easy to find. Red-headed are common, as are Red-bellied. Pileated Woodpeckers prefer the hardwoods down by the Savannah River but may occur anywhere.

About a quarter mile from Road 20 you will see a sign for a nature trail on the right (west). This is the Upland Nature Trail, an unmarked trail on service roads. If you keep to the left at all junctions, you can walk about a mile through the pinewoods and rejoin the entrance road about a quarter mile to the south. During the spring and summer look for Painted Bunting as well as Indigo Bunting and Blue Grosbeak along this loop. It is difficult to walk this trail without flushing Northern Bobwhite, and Wild Turkeys are fairly common as well. The pinewoods along this trail is broken here and there by clearings planted for deer and other wildlife. This makes for excellent birding.

About 1.4 miles from Road 20 the entrance road reaches the headquarters area, the old plantation house. At the headquarters the road swings around to the left (east). Just past this left turn, look for a side road to the right. This is the road to the river swamp.

Follow the side road for about two miles. After passing some residences, the road first goes through pinewoods (which also have Red-cockaded Woodpeckers) and then reaches the flood plain of the Savannah River at Bluff Lake. Park at the picnic area, and proceed on foot.

From the open field near Bluff Lake scan the sky for hawks. Here you have an excellent chance of finding Mississippi Kite (late April through early September) and a fairly good chance of American Swal-low-tailed Kite (mid March through August). Both kite species breed on the property.

Walk to the left (east) around Bluff Lake (an oxbow of the Savannah) until you reach the Savannah River Swamp Trail. This trail into the flood plain is marked at first but deteriorates after a half mile or so. Even still, it is a great way to get into the flood plain forest of tupelos, bald cypresses, oaks, elms, and many other tree species. The forest, while not a virgin forest, is quite similar to that of the Congaree Swamp in Richland County (see Section B-40). You can expect the birds of the Coastal Plain swamp forest: Barred Owl, Wood Duck, Acadian Flycatcher (April to September), White-breasted Nuthatch, all woodpeckers except the Red-cockaded, Prothonotary (summer) and Yellow-throated (all year) Warblers, Northern Parula (summer), and others. The trail is quite grassy in part, so beware of chiggers during warm weather.

From Bluff Lake it is best to backtrack to the headquarters and then out the entrance road. There are other roads on the property, but they may not always be passable without four-wheel drive.

B–25.3—Stokes Bluff Landing

Winter	*
Spring	*
Summer	**
Fall	*

See letter B on Map B–25.1.

This boat-launching ramp on the Savannah River, just downstream from the Webb Wildlife Center (see Section B-25.2), is an excellent place to find American Swallow-tailed Kite (mid-March to mid-August) and Mississippi Kite (late April to early September). From the three-way intersection of US 321, SC 119, and Road 20 in Garnett, go south on SC 119. In 2.1 miles you will enter Jasper County. At 4.4 miles south of Garnett turn right (west) onto Road 119. (If you continue south on SC 119, you can either turn east onto Road 119 and go to the Tillman Sand Ridge Preserve, described in Section B-27, or you can cross the Savannah River into Georgia and reach I-16 about 36 miles south of the river.)

Once you have turned west onto Road 119, go 2.4 miles to the end of the road, which is back in Hampton County. The large parking area affords a good view of the river and the sky. Kites are most often seen after 10 A.M., after the thermals have developed and soaring is easier. If you watch for a while, you will also see Red-shouldered Hawk, Broad-winged Hawk, Wood Stork, Anhinga, White Ibis, and a variety of herons.

Winter   *
Spring   *
Summer **
Fall   *

See Map B–25.2.

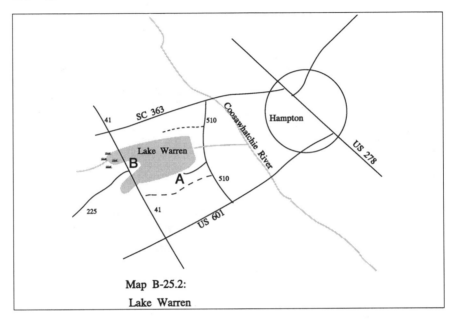

Map B-25.2:
Lake Warren

This beautiful area near the town of Hampton has just recently been upgraded to a state park, after having been a public fishing lake for many years. To reach the park from I-95, leave the interstate at Exit 68, and go northwest on SC 68 for about 20 miles to the intersection with US 601 in the center of the town of Hampton. Here turn south onto US 601. This route crosses the Coosawhatchie River in about 2.5 miles. At 4.7 miles from the center of Hampton US 601 reaches its intersection with Road 510 off to the right. Turn right (northwest) onto Road 510, and go about one mile to the state park entrance road, on the left (southwest). (See letter A on Map B–25.2.)

Currently (1992) facilities at the park are limited to a picnic ground and a community building, but trails and a camp-

ground will be developed in the near future. There is a fine mixed-hardwood forest near the picnic ground and a short trail down to the south shore of Lake Warren (actually part of the picnic ground).

To reach the boat ramp near the dam of the lake, return to Road 510, and turn left (northwest). Road 510 crosses the lake's dam and reaches the boat ramp just beyond the dam, on the left. From this point you can overlook most of the lake. Present year-round are Pied-billed Grebes, Anhingas, herons, Wood Ducks, and Common Moorhens. These residents are joined by a few coots and ducks in the winter. There are a number of alligators in the lake, most often seen during the summer.

Although there are no formal trails yet at

Lake Warren State Park, you can explore a bit of typical southern pine—oak woodland just beyond the boat ramp near the dam. From the boat ramp parking lot walk away from the dam on Road 510. In about two hundred yards you will see an old logging road off to the left, going into the pinewoods. This old road gives easy access on foot to the woods.

The best birding, however, is at the upper end of the lake. To reach this area, return to Road 510, and retrace your way to the park entrance road. But instead of entering the park, continue southeast toward US 601 for another 0.2 mile to the first unpaved county road to the right. Turn here, and follow the unpaved road southwest for about a mile. Here you will reach a T-junction with Road 41. Turn right (northwest) onto Road 41, reaching the upper end of Lake Warren in about a half mile.

Road 41 forms a causeway over the upper end of the lake, dividing it into two parts. To the east of Road 41 Lake Warren is somewhat deeper and mostly open. To the west of Road 41 the lake is essentially a huge freshwater marsh clogged with all manner of aquatic veg-

etation. From the Road 41 causeway you can overlook this marsh, keeping an eye out for herons, Anhinga, rails (Sora and Virginia in winter; King year-round), Least Bittern and American Bitterns, coots, moorhens, and even an occasional Purple Gallinule.

There is a picnic ground with a fishing pier off of Road 41 at the upper end of the eastern part of the lake (letter B on Map B–25.2). The marshy shoreline here is great for birds, including many herons year-round and migrant sandpipers in small numbers. In late winter or early spring you can find dozens of Common Snipe along the lakeshore here. The fishing pier makes an excellent platform from which to overlook the lake.

To return to the town of Hampton from the upper end of the lake, continue northwest on Road 41. In 2.0 miles from the picnic ground Road 41 crosses SC 363. Turn right (northeast) onto SC 363 to return to town in about six miles. Or from SC 363 you can continue straight ahead on Road 41 to the village of Gifford on US 321 in just 2.6 miles.

B–26—HORRY COUNTY

Horry (pronounced "ore-REE," with a silent "H") County is visited by thousands of tourists each year. Situated in the extreme northeast corner of the state, on the coast, this is the county which contains Myrtle Beach, the premier tourist attraction of the state. From the North Carolina state line at Little River Inlet and south into Georgetown County stretches one of the best sandy beaches on the Atlantic coast of the United States. This is the Grand Strand or, to South Carolinians, "the beach."

The highly developed sandy beach in Horry County is not a particularly good birding area. The only significant area of the beach which is not developed (and which is readily accessible without a

boat) is the mile or so of beach at Myrtle Beach State Park. Visitors to Myrtle Beach who wish to find birds are advised to go a few miles south to Huntington Beach State Park, just over the line in Georgetown County (see Section B-22.1 above).

There are two large Heritage Preserves in Horry County: Cartwheel Bay Heritage Preserve (568 acres in the northwestern part of the county) and Lewis Ocean Bay Heritage Preserve (6,422 acres east of Conway). Neither of these areas is covered in this section, because of lack of access. Both areas protect pocosin and longleaf-pine habitats with many interesting plants, including Venus's-flytrap and other carnivorous plants. Birds of interest include summer-resident Worm-eating

Warblers and breeding Red-cockaded Woodpeckers. For more information about Cartwheel Bay, Lewis Ocean Bay, or any of the twenty-seven South Carolina Heritage Preserves, write:

S.C. Wildlife and Marine Resources Department
Nongame and Heritage Trust Section
Post Office Box 167
Columbia, SC 29202

B–26.1—Myrtle Beach State Park

Winter	**
Spring	*
Summer	*
Fall	**

To reach *Myrtle Beach State Park* from the intersection of US 501 and US 17 Business in the center of Myrtle Beach, go south on US 17 Business (Kings Highway) for about 3.8 miles. The entrance to the park is on the left just south of the main gate of Myrtle Beach Air Force Base.

To reach the park from the south, go north on US 17 from Georgetown to the point where US 17 Business turns off from US 17 Bypass just north of the Horry County—Georgetown County line. Take US 17 Business, and go about 7 miles north to the park entrance, on the right.

The best birding in the park is along the beach (especially on the dunes south of the fishing pier) or along the mile-long Sculptured Oak Nature Trail. (This trail was severely damaged by Hurricane Hugo in 1989 and may not be reopened.)

The Sculptured Oak Nature Trail begins on the right (south) side of the entrance road, just beyond the entrance fee station. This trail wanders through an oak-hickory-pine forest for almost a mile before it emerges into the dunes near the fishing pier. In addition to the usual birds of Coastal Plain woods you may find wintering warblers (such as Yellow-throated, Black-and-white, or Orange-crowned Warblers). From late April until September you will find Painted Buntings in the thickets near the dunes. The dunes harbor wintering sparrows (mostly Savannah, Field, and Song Sparrows). Along the beach you will find Sanderlings, Willets, Red Knots, and Ruddy Turnstones. Over the ocean are various terns and Laughing Gulls in summer; in winter look for the usual ocean species, including Common and Red-throated Loons, Northern Gannets, Brown Pelicans, Double-crested Cormorants, and various gulls—Herring, Ring-billed, Great Black-backed, and Bonaparte's Gull.

Myrtle Beach State Park is not birded intensely (since most birders skip this park in favor of nearby Huntington Beach State Park, which offers a much wider variety of bird habitats). Thus you may turn up here an overlooked rarity, especially in fall migration. The park is extremely crowded during the summer beach season, but October through May is usually a good time to visit.

B–26.2—Cherry Grove Beach

Winter	**
Spring	**
Summer	*
Fall	**

The *Cherry Grove Beach* area of North Myrtle Beach has a few spots where you might find a few birds, especially in winter. A small salt creek flows into the Atlantic at the north end of Cherry Grove Beach at a minor inlet (Hog Inlet). Birding

130

here is not great, but you might check it out if you are in the area.

From US 17 or SC 9 in North Myrtle Beach or Little River follow the signs for Cherry Grove Beach. This will put you on SC 65, Sea Mountain Road. Follow Sea Mountain Road toward the beach until it ends at Ocean Boulevard. Here turn left (northeast) onto Ocean Boulevard. Go out Ocean Boulevard to 39th Avenue. Here turn left, and follow 39th Avenue about 2 blocks to where it crosses a small bridge. There is a good view of a salt creek and marsh here. Pull over and look around. At low tide there are usually a few common shorebirds on the exposed mud flats. At least you will find the Boat-tailed Grackle.

Return to Ocean Boulevard, and follow it to its northeastern end. If you can find a place to park, do so and look for the public beach access path, about one block before the end of the road. Cross over to the beach, and walk northeast along the beach to the inlet, where you should find a number of common gulls, terns, and shorebirds. The undeveloped island across the inlet (Waites Island) is accessible only by boat. Do not attempt to swim across the inlet, since currents are dangerous here.

B–26.3 – Waccamaw Bridges Heritage Preserve

Winter   **
Spring   **
Summer **
Fall   **

A new Heritage Preserve protects a bit of the floodplain forest along the Waccamaw River, near the North Carolina border. To reach this area from the intersection of US 17 and SC 9 in North Myrtle Beach, go west on SC 9 for 4.6 miles. Just before you reach the seafood restaurant on the east bank of the Waccamaw River you will pass a dike trail leading north into the swamp, along the border of the Heritage Preserve. To explore the preserve on foot, park at the entrance to this trail, or park at the restaurant and backtrack a hundred yards or so to the trail. The trail follows the property line for about a quarter mile, to the bank to the Waccamaw River. Birds found here are those typical of Coastal Plain floodplain forest.

B–27 – JASPER COUNTY

Jasper County is the southernmost county in South Carolina, just north of Savannah, Georgia. Interstate 95 runs through the middle of the county, past the town of Ridgeland (the county seat) and Hardeeville.

Jasper County is a coastal county, although the Atlantic Ocean in the county is not reached by any county roads. From the birder's point of view, Jasper County is dominated by the Savannah River. Jasper County includes portions of the Upper Coastal Plain and the Lower Coastal Plain. Interstate 95 runs roughly along the dividing line between these two natural regions.

In the northwestern part of the county (on the Upper Coastal Plain) the Savannah River runs through an extensive floodplain forest. Nearby are pine flatwoods and sandhills. This part of the county closely resembles neighboring Hampton County (see Section B-25 above). It is best explored at Tillman Sand Ridge Wildlife Management Area.

Downstream from about the I-95 bridge the Savannah River is influenced by the tides and so is considered part of the

Lower Coastal Plain. The upper reaches of the tidal estuary of the Savannah have extensive freshwater marshes, some of which were used as rice fields in the nineteenth century. This habitat is easily explored along the auto tour route at Savannah National Wildlife Refuge.

Savannah, Georgia, is a major port. To keep shipping channels open, the U.S. Army Corps of Engineers oversees a major dredging operation at Savannah. The spoil from this dredging is deposited in a huge spoil area just across the river from the city. This area, which is open to birders unless there is major construction going on, is one of the true birding hot spots of South Carolina.

B–27.1—A Western Jasper County Tour

Winter   *
Spring   ***
Summer ***
Fall   **

See Map B–27.1.

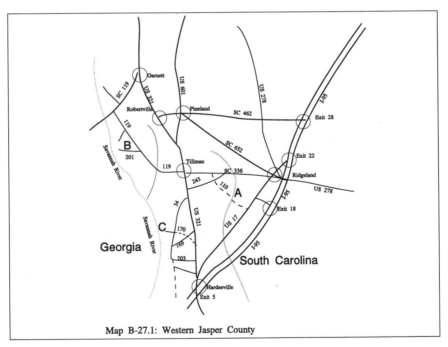

Map B-27.1: Western Jasper County

The following tour of the western part of Jasper County gives birders traveling on I-95 a chance to find most of the "Deep South" specialty species (including American Swallow-tailed Kite, Mississippi Kite, Wild Turkey, Brown-headed Nuthatch, Swainson's Warbler, and Bachman's Sparrow) during the course of a three-hour side trip from the interstate. Directions will be given for southbound travelers. Northbound birders can either follow the directions in reverse or drive a short stretch of I-95 twice.

Leave I-95 at Exit 18, just south of Ridgeland, and take the connecting road west for a few hundred yards to US 17. Turn left (south) onto US 17 and go 1.0 mile. Here turn right onto Road 110, an improved but unpaved road. Road 110 leads through the heart of *Okeetee Plantation*, a private quail-hunting plantation (letter A on Map B–27.1). Here be sure to keep to the public road, since this is all private property, and since there is a goodly population of eastern diamondback rattlesnakes on the plantation.

Road 110 goes through about five miles of Okeetee Plantation. Much of this land is a magnificent old-growth longleaf-pine forest. There are several clans of Red-cockaded Woodpeckers along the way. During spring and summer you can expect to hear the sweet song of the Bachman's Sparrow here and perhaps even a few Painted Buntings singing from scrubby areas. The buntings are here from mid-April until early October. The sparrows are permanent residents but are difficult to find outside of their song period (March through September).

Halfway through the plantation Road 110 crosses the Great Swamp, a fine floodplain forest, where you can find most of the species of such habitats.

Follow Road 110 westward to its end at SC 336. Here turn left (west) onto SC 336. You will reach US 321 in the town of Tillman in 2.4 miles. Here continue straight ahead across US 321. The road here is Road 119. Go west on Road 119 for 4.9 miles, until you come to a side road, Road 201, on the left (south).

The stretch of Road 119 between the town of Tillman and the intersection with Road 201 crosses Cypress Creek and a part of the Green Swamp. Here look for Prothonotary, Kentucky, and Swainson's Warblers in the floodplain forests in spring and summer. During this same season be alert for Mississippi and American Swallow-tailed Kites soaring over the clearcuts or the swamps.

The intersection of Roads 119 and 201 is roughly at the southeastern corner of *Tillman Sand Ridge Wildlife Management Area* (letter B on Map B–27.1). This 952-acre area of sandy pinewoods and

floodplain forest is primarily a refuge for the gopher tortoise. Gopher tortoise burrows are common in the sandy parts of the refuge, though the animals themselves are seldom seen. The floodplain forest portion of the refuge harbors nesting Mississippi and American Swallow-tailed Kites. To have a chance at seeing kites (mid-April through mid-August), turn onto Road 201 and follow it 1.7 miles to its end at a boat launch area, B & C Landing. This boat launch is some distance from the main channel of the Savannah River. A canal leads about a half mile through the swamp to the river. Swainson's Warbler breeds in the swamps near the landing and is often heard from the road. The clear-cuts along the road are good for Bachman's Sparrow and Painted Bunting.

From the boat launch parking lot, especially in midsummer, you might spy kites soaring and hunting at midday. Other soaring birds in summer may include Anhinga, various herons and egrets, White Ibis, Wood Stork, Black and Turkey Vultures, Red-shouldered Hawk, and even Broad-winged Hawk.

To explore the wildlife management area itself, return to Road 119 and turn left (northwest). Go about a mile until you find a gated sand road on the left with wildlife management area markings. Park along the paved road, and cross the gate on foot. There are no marked trails in this area, but you can readily use the sandy service roads to explore. This area has a few common birds of pinewoods and cutover areas, such as Northern Bobwhite, Carolina Chickadee, Tufted Titmouse, Northern Mockingbird, Northern Cardinal, and Rufous-sided Towhee. But reptiles are the key attraction here. You will see dozens of gopher tortoise burrows. Do not disturb the burrows, since they sometimes harbor snakes as well as tortoises. In fact, this is one of the best places in South Carolina to observe the eastern diamondbacked rattlesnake.

To continue the tour, backtrack along Road 119 to US 321 in Tillman. Here turn right (south), and follow US 321 for 1.9 miles to the intersection with Road 34, on the right. Turn right onto Road 34, which leads through more old-growth pine forest. This is a good area for Bachman's Sparrow and Wild Turkey.

After 7.1 miles on Road 34 turn right (west) onto Road 170. Follow this road for 0.3 mile to its end at another boat ramp, *Beck's Ferry* (letter C on Map B–27.1). This is another good spot for both kite species as well as Kentucky Warbler in the swamp.

After searching for kites and other soaring birds at Beck's Ferry, keep straight ahead on Road 170. When you cross Road 34, Road 170 becomes unpaved but is still a good road. Follow the un-

paved road for one mile to a crossroad intersection with Road 169. Here turn left (east), and go 0.5 mile to US 321. This is your last chance for Bachman's Sparrow and Red-cockaded Woodpecker on this tour.

Turn right (south) onto US 321, and follow it for 4.2 miles. Here you will reach US 17 in Hardeeville. Continue south on US 17 for another 0.7 mile to Exit 5 of I-95. Here you can either return to the interstate or continue ahead to the Savannah National Wildlife Refuge (see Section B-27.2) or the Corps of Engineers spoil area (see Section B-27.3).

B–27.2—Savannah National Wildlife Refuge

Winter	****
Spring	***
Summer	**
Fall	****

See letter A on Map B–27.2.

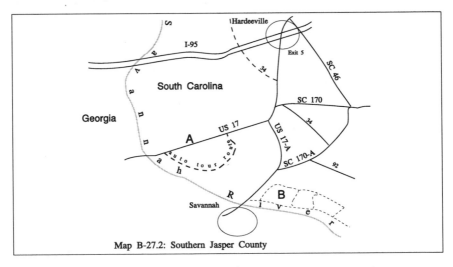

Map B-27.2: Southern Jasper County

To reach *Savannah National Wildlife Refuge* from I-95, exit at Hardeeville (Exit 5), and go south on US 17 toward Savannah, Georgia. At 6.1 miles south of the interstate you will reach a split in US 17. The road straight ahead is US 17 Alternate, which goes to the

Corps of Engineers spoil area and downtown Savannah. To the right is US 17, which goes toward the refuge and the Savannah Airport. Take the road to the right, and continue on US 17. Within a few hundred yards you will enter the refuge.

Within a mile of the US 17—US 17 Alternate split you will pass the end of the Laurel Hill Wildlife Drive on the left (south) side of US 17. This is a one-way road, so continue another 1.5 miles on US 17 to the beginning of the wildlife drive, on the left. About a mile past the beginning of the wildlife drive US 17 crosses into Georgia. There are several pulloffs along US 17 within the refuge, from which you may easily overlook refuge impoundments or hike out along refuge dikes.

The easiest way to bird Savannah National Wildlife Refuge is to drive along the four-mile wildlife tour road (the Laurel Hill Wildlife Drive), stopping frequently. The route follows dikes through numerous freshwater impoundments and along the edge of tidal freshwater marsh (part of the delta of the Savannah River).

Here and there along the tour road are small islands in the marsh called "hammocks," heavily forested with large live-oaks, hackberries, red maples, and other trees. These oak hammocks concentrate small birds and are especially good to bird during spring and fall migrations.

By carefully birding the tour road and perhaps exploring a few of the oak hammocks and side dikes, you should be able to find most of the birds of Coastal Plain ponds and freshwater marshes and also those of Coastal Plain mixed-hardwood forest.

Currently (1992) the best birding in the refuge is from the dike trail around Impoundment 18, which is at the southern edge of the refuge. To reach this area take the Laurel Hill Wildlife Drive for about 2.5 miles from its beginning at US 17. Here the drive takes a sharp turn to the left. Just before this turn is a side road, which crosses the main diversion canal of the refuge and dead-ends in about 250 yards. Turn right onto this side road, cross the canal, and immediately

park. Walk on the dike trail on the south side of the diversion canal. Go west for about a quarter mile to an oak hammock. Here take the left fork, and follow this trail as it loops about a mile around Impoundments 18 and 17.

Impoundment 18 is great for ducks, herons, ibis, shorebirds, and alligators. Rarities found here include a male Eurasian Wigeon (found in fall 1990).

The oak hammocks are good for migrant warblers, Scarlet Tanager, and Rose-breasted Grosbeak in April and May or September and October. Some of the rarities which have been found on the refuge include Red-necked Grebe, Fulvous Whistling-Duck, Tundra Swan, Oldsquaw, Golden Eagle, Yellow and Black Rails, Upland Sandpiper, Ruff, Groove-billed Ani, and Short-eared Owl.

Some favorite species bring South Carolina birders to the refuge annually. This is the most dependable place in the state to find Purple Gallinule (present mid-April through mid-October, common May through August). Look at the water lilies and other emergent aquatic vegetation in the impoundments, especially in those along US 17. The Painted Bunting is abundant in scrubby areas from mid-April until July or so. A few linger into the fall. Great Horned Owls nest in most of the oak hammocks and are often seen in daylight during the winter months. And, of course, alligators are to be seen year-round, but seldom in the cooler months.

Savannah Refuge is good for an hour stopover on your way to Florida or for an entire weekend of birding. There are rest rooms at the beginning of the wildlife drive. The gates are open during daylight hours. Since they are opened and closed automatically by a timer, be sure to note the posted hours and to get back to US 17 well before the closing time, or you risk being stuck behind a locked gate.

B–27.3—The Corps of Engineers Savannah Spoil Area

Winter   ***
Spring   ****
Summer **
Fall   ****

See letter B on Map B–27.2.

To reach the Corps of Engineers spoil area from I-95, exit at Hardeeville (Exit 5), and go south on US 17 toward Savannah, Georgia. At 6.1 miles south of the interstate you will reach a split in US 17. Straight ahead the road is US 17 Alternate, which goes to downtown Savannah. To the right is US 17 toward Savannah National Wildlife Refuge and the Savannah Airport. Continue straight ahead on US 17 Alternate for 6.5 miles. Just before you cross the flat bridge over the part of the Savannah River which is the Georgia-South Carolina state line, look for a dirt road on the left (east). This dirt road reaches a locked gate almost immediately. Park near the locked gate, being careful not to block the road, and proceed on foot into the Corps of Engineers property. The Corps does not mind birders here as long as they stay clear of ongoing construction projects and observe any restrictive signs that may be posted.

The area is huge. It stretches for ten miles or more along the Savannah River and inland from the river for about a mile. There are many miles of dikes (which may or may not be passable on foot) and service roads. The three main habitats to bird here are: (1) the Savannah River itself, together with adjacent mud flats and brackish marshes; (2) the main service road, which sometimes leads through grassy areas but which usually has a brushy edge of wax myrtle, baccharis, salt cedar, and other shrubs; (3) the spoil area proper, which consists of high dikes or levees enclosing a constantly changing area of salt-cedar scrub, brackish pools, freshwater marsh, mud flats, and drainage ditches (with and without standing water).

The Savannah River and its marshes attract a wide variety of coastal species.

Double-crested Cormorants are abundant (except in early summer), and you will usually find most of the following species (in season): Pied-billed and Horned Grebe (winter); Brown Pelican; various herons and egrets; Red-breasted Merganser (winter); Clapper Rail (marshes); Black-bellied and Semipalmated Plover; Greater and Lesser Yellowlegs; Willet; Spotted Sandpiper (except early summer); Semipalmated (spring and fall), Western, and Least Sandpiper; Dunlin (except early summer); Short-billed Dowitcher; Laughing, Bonaparte's (winter), Ring-billed, Herring, and Great Black-backed (winter) Gull; Caspian, Royal, Common, Forster's, and Least (summer) Tern; Black Skimmer (summer), and Marsh Wren.

The grassy and brushy areas along the main service road are great for spring and fall migrants. In summer the Painted Bunting is common. In winter look for Orange-crowned Warbler and perhaps other warbler species among the thousands of Yellow-rumped Warblers in the brush.

The spoil area proper may appear birdless at first, but this is the area which attracts the most rarities. If you walk the dikes long enough, you may flush a flock of Common Ground-Doves. Shorebirds can be found wherever there is water. Black-necked Stilt, Wilson's Plover, and Least Tern breed, and in winter look for such rarities as Long-billed Dowitcher and American Avocet among the more common Dunlin, also both species of yellowlegs, Black-bellied Plover, Killdeer, and Least Sandpiper. In recent years the avocets have been seen year-round here, raising the question of possible breeding.

The salt-cedar flats of the spoil area abound with rodents (mostly cotton rats), and as a result hawks are common here, especially in winter. On a good winter day you can expect to find most of the following hawk species: Black and Turkey Vulture; Osprey (except in the coldest winters); Bald Eagle; Northern Harrier; Sharp-shinned, Cooper's, and Red-tailed Hawk; American Kestrel; and Merlin. Other species may occur, including Peregrine Falcon (fairly common in migration) and Rough-legged Hawk (very rare, but to be hoped for in winter).

The Corps of Engineers spoil area at Sa-

vannah is a dynamic and exciting place to bird. Birders interested in finding rare species in South Carolina will return as often as possible. Rarities that have been found here include Ruff, Curlew Sandpiper, Wilson's Phalarope, Rough-legged Hawk, and many others. If you have a slow day here (which is not impossible), do not give up on the area. Conditions vary widely from month to month, and your next visit may be great.

B–28—KERSHAW COUNTY

Many counties in South Carolina have the same names as their principal cities. Kershaw County is a notable exception to this tendency, since its county seat is Camden. The city of Kershaw lies just north of Kershaw County, in neighboring Lancaster County.

Kershaw County lies along the Fall Line about twenty-five to forty miles east of Columbia. Like Richland County (Colum-

bia's county) Kershaw County contains portions of three different natural divisions: the Piedmont in the northwestern quarter of the county, the Sandhills subregion of the Upper Coastal Plain in the central portion of the county, and the Upper Coastal Plain proper in the southern part of the county and along the Wateree River. This geographic diversity means that Kershaw County has a wide variety of bird habitats.

B–28.1—Historic Camden Revolutionary War Park

Winter   *
Spring   **
Summer **
Fall   *

See letter A on Map B–28.1.

Historic Camden Revolutionary War Park is primarily a city park that tells the story of the British occupation of Camden during the American Revolution. The park has a half-mile nature trail, which is worth a short stop if you are visiting Camden or are passing by on nearby I-20 and wish to take a pleasant half-hour walk through a typical Upper Coastal Plain floodplain forest.

Leave I-20 at Exit 98, and go north on US 521 into the city of Camden. About 1.4 miles north of I-20 you will find the parking lot for the Revolutionary War Park on the right (east). The nature trail starts at

the far right (southeastern) corner of the parking lot, goes past a small pond, and then enters the floodplain forest along Big Pine Creek. The trail loops around to the left and emerges from the woods behind the ruins of the 1777 powder magazine, which are just a few dozen yards from the parking lot.

The birds encountered along the trail are those typical of floodplain woods in South Carolina. Breeding species of interest include Mississippi Kite, which breeds along Big Pine Creek and may be seen from the parking lot (May through August), and Swainson's Warbler, which is often heard (but seldom seen) in the thick undergrowth along the trail near Big

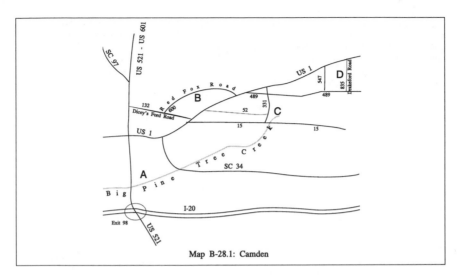

Map B-28.1: Camden

Pine Creek. Hooded Warblers are common, and a Louisiana Waterthrush is possible as well, so be sure that you are listening to a Swainson's Warbler. The Swainson's Warbler is a fairly common summer resident in thickets of floodplain forests in the Sandhills and Coastal Plain of South Carolina. Those at the Revolutionary War Park are very conveniently near an interstate highway.

B–28.2—Boykin Mill Pond and Vicinity

Winter	*
Spring	**
Summer	**
Fall	*

Boykin Mill Pond is a large millpond along Swift Creek, a tributary of the Wateree River about ten miles south of Camden. It is the site of one of the largest inland heronries in South Carolina, supporting hundreds of Cattle Egrets, Great Egrets, and White Ibis as well as small numbers of Anhingas, Little Blue Herons, Black-crowned Night-Herons, and Yellow-crowned Night-Herons. The aquatic vegetation of the pond shelters large numbers of Common Moorhens. There are a few Least Bitterns, Purple Gallinules, and alligators.

Boykin Mill Pond is not open to the public, but a visit to the neighborhood is interesting nevertheless. Herons, egrets, ibis, and Anhingas can be seen flying to and from their nests. There is spot where you can see part of the heronry and pond from the public road, but a telescope is necessary to see nesting birds.

Because of the heronry it is possible to seen many egrets and ibis feeding in the surrounding countryside. The following tour is recommended from May through August.

From I-20 exit at Exit 98, and go south on US 521 toward Sumter. At 2.8 miles south of I-20 bear right (southeast) onto SC 261 toward Stateburg. Go about 2 miles south on SC 261. Pass Broom Hill Church on the right, and start looking for an unpaved county road off to the right. This is Stockton Road. Follow Stockton Road west for about a mile, then turn left (south) onto Guy Road. Follow Guy Road south for a mile or so. It becomes paved and ends at a T-junction with Red Bank Road, Road 486. Turn right onto Road 486, and explore west for a mile or so, until the pavement ends. Then turn around, and follow Road 486 east back to SC 261.

This part of the tour leads you through an area of large fields and a few pastures bordering the floodplain woods of the Wateree River—a good example of Upper Coastal Plain farm country. In late spring or summer you should see most of the following species: Great Blue Heron, Great Egret, Little Blue Heron, Cattle Egret (often in flocks of a hundred or more), Green-backed Heron, White Ibis, Black and Turkey Vulture, Mississippi Kite, Red-shouldered and Red-tailed Hawk, Northern Bobwhite, Killdeer, Mourning Dove, Yellow-billed Cuckoo, Chimney Swift, Ruby-throated Hummingbird (look for trumpet creeper in flower), Red-bellied Woodpecker, Eastern Kingbird, Horned Lark (look for large, freshly plowed fields), Purple Martin, Barn Swallow, Blue Jay, American and Fish Crow, Carolina Wren,

Eastern Bluebird, Northern Mockingbird, Brown Thrasher, Loggerhead Shrike, European Starling, White-eyed Vireo, Prairie Warbler, Yellow-breasted Chat, Summer Tanager, Northern Cardinal, Blue Grosbeak, Indigo Bunting, Chipping and Field Sparrows, Red-winged Blackbird, Eastern Meadowlark, Common Grackle, Brown-headed Cowbird, Orchard Oriole, and House Sparrow.

Once you return to SC 261, turn right (south), and go 0.4 mile to the intersection with Road 2. Turn left (east) onto Road 2, drive in about two hundred yards, and park next to the country gift shop on the left. From this point you can overlook a part of *Boykin Mill Pond*, but resist the urge to trespass. You should be able to see many birds flying to and from nests, including Anhinga, Great and Cattle Egret, Little Blue Heron, and White Ibis.

To return to I-20, return to SC 261, and turn right (north). The interstate is about 7 miles north of the mill pond.

B–28.3—A Kershaw County Sandhills Tour

Winter   *
Spring   **
Summer **
Fall   *

See Maps B-28.1 and B-28.2.

The *Sandhills of Kershaw County* have little resemblance to the huge area of longleaf pines and turkey oaks that characterized this natural region two centuries ago. Nevertheless, today's mixture of small farms, horse ranches, pine plantations, and suburbs makes for pleasant roadside birding in any season. The following tour describes a meandering drive northeast of Camden which can be done as a half-day's outing or as an alternate route from Camden to the Carolina Sandhills National Wildlife Refuge in neighboring Chesterfield County (see Section 13.1).

From Exit 98 of I-20 go north on US 521 for 2.4 miles to the intersection with US 1 in

downtown Camden. Continue north on US 521 (Broad Street) for another 1.5 miles, and then turn right onto Dicey's Ford Road, Road 132. This is a tricky turn—very easy to miss. Look for the sign for the Camden Airport. If you get to the point where SC 97 turns off to the left, you have gone too far. Backtrack about 0.5 mile to Dicey's Ford Road. Once you have turned east onto Road 132, Dicey's Ford Road, go for about 2 miles, and then turn left onto Road 600, Red Fox Road. This turn is about a quarter mile before you get to a large water tower. If you get to the water tower, you have gone too far east on Dicey's Ford Road.

Red Fox Road leads for about 3 miles through beautiful suburbs and small horse farms. The longleaf pines along

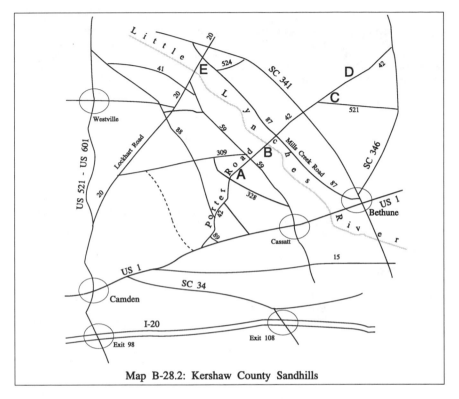

Map B-28.2: Kershaw County Sandhills

Red Fox Road are in beautiful open stands, the sort of habitat that would be suitable for Red-cockaded Woodpeckers, if there were enough of them. You will find birds typical of Upper Coastal Plain farms and suburbs.

After about a mile or so on Red Fox Road, the road runs along the *north side of the Camden Airport (Woodward Field)* (letter B on Map B–28.1). Scan the short grass for Horned Larks (most likely in winter and early spring, but possible any time). This is a good spot for Common Nighthawks in summer and hawks in winter.

Red Fox Road ends at US 1. (This point is about 5 miles northeast of the intersection of US 1 and US 521 in downtown Camden). Turn left (northeast) onto US 1, and go 0.2 mile to the intersection with Road 489. Here turn right, following the signs for N. R. Goodale State Park. Go

east 1.0 mile on Road 489, then turn right (south) onto Road 331 to the entrance to the state park.

Goodale State Park (letter C on Map B–28.1) is a small park with a swimming lake but with no family campground and no marked trails. The lake may attract a Pied-billed Grebe or two in winter, but not much more. There are no marked trails, but by exploring the numerous sand roads that crisscross the area to the left of the swimming beach, you may be able to find a few birds. The birdlife here is typical of second-growth pinewoods and bay-swamp thickets.

To continue the tour, leave Goodale State Park, and go north on Road 331 for 1.6 miles to the intersection with Road 489 (Cheraw Road). Turn right (east) onto Road 489, and go 1.7 miles. Look for an inconspicuous secondary road on the left. This is Road 835, Drakeford Road. (If

140

you miss this turn, you will reach the end of Road 489 at Road 549. Backtrack 1.2 miles to Road 835.)

Turn left (north) onto Road 835 (Drakeford Road), and go 0.3 mile. Just beyond the point where the road bends to the left, look for an inconspicuous sand road on the left (west). Turn into this sand road and park. This is the access point for *Savage Bay Heritage Preserve* (letter D on Map B–28.1), a 69-acre preserve of the Heritage Trust program of the South Carolina Wildlife and Marine Resources Department.

Savage Bay Preserve protects two Carolina bays. Carolina bays are elliptical basins ranging in size from an acre or so to several square miles. They are found in the Coastal Plain from Delaware to Georgia but are most common in North and South Carolina.

Walk west on the sand road for about two hundred yards to the edge of Savage Bay. The bay is bordered by red bay, sweet bay, titi, catbrier, and other thicket-forming plants. The interior of the bay is more open and consists of a pond-cypress swamp with an understory of myrtle-leafed holly. The part of the preserve outside of the bay consists of two main habitats: longleaf-pine—turkey-oak woods and old fields growing up in broom sedge and loblolly pines.

The best birding at Savage Bay Preserve is in or near the thicket surrounding the bay. Swainson's Warbler is an occasional breeder. You can expect to find most of the species typical of bay-swamp thickets. The oak-pine woods and broom sedge fields are less productive than the bay-swamp thicket, but you will find a few sparrows: Field and Chipping Sparrows year-round, and Song, White-throated, and Fox Sparrows and Dark-eyed Juncos in winter.

After exploring Savage Bay, turn left (north) onto Road 835, and go 0.6 mile to US 1. Turn right (northeast) onto US 1. Keep an eye out for an underpass under the railroad tracks. (This underpass is about 1.1 miles beyond Road 835.) Turn left onto Road 89 (Map B-28.2) immedi-

ately beyond where US 1 goes under the railroad tracks. This is Porter Road. Go north on Road 89 for 0.8 mile. Here bear right onto Road 42. This is still Porter Road. Continue on Road 42, heading northeast into a progressively more rural part of the Kershaw County Sandhills.

From mid-April through early September it is fairly easy to find Bachman's Sparrows in young pine plantations and overgrown clear-cuts along Porter Road. Look for a large cutover area with scattered turkey oaks and pines no more that six feet high. and listen for the sweet song of the Bachman's Sparrow. Often the singer is close enough to spy it as it sings from the top of a small pine, a brush pile, or a tall weed. Other common summer birds of this habitat include Chipping and Field Sparrows, Blue Grosbeak, Indigo Bunting, Northern Bobwhite, Yellow-breasted Chat, Prairie Warbler, Common Yellowthroat, Northern Cardinal, Brown Thrasher, and Rufous-sided Towhee. At dusk you will find that Whip-poor-wills and Chuck-will's-widows love these clear-cuts as well.

If you stop by a mature pine forest in spring or summer, do not be surprised if you hear the "tee-churr, tee-churr, tee-churr" of the Ovenbird. Ovenbirds are fairly common in dry pinewoods in the Sandhills of Kershaw County, even though they are rare or absent in the Piedmont to the northwest and the Lower Coastal Plain to the southeast.

About 4 miles from where you turned off of US 1, Road 42 passes a *small horse lot* at the intersection with Road 328 (letter A on Map B–28.2). During the summer of 1987 a pair of Common Ground-Doves frequented this lot. Ground doves are quite rare away from the coast, but cattle feedlots seem to be good places to look for them. Listen for their low plaintive call—"whooip, whooip, whooip." You will be lucky to find ground doves inland, but it is possible. About 3 miles beyond the cattle feedlot (7 miles from where you turned off of US 1), Road 42 descends into the *floodplain of Little Lynches River* (letter B on Map B–28.2). For a half mile the road cuts through mature floodplain forest, which often has very dense undergrowth. The road shoulder is good, and the traffic is usually very light. From mid-April until September this is an excellent area to hear (and often see) most of the species of Coastal Plain floodplain forests.

Soon after leaving the floodplain of the Little Lynches River, you will reach the intersection of Road 42 (Porter Road) and Road 87 (Mills Creek Road). If you are going on to the Carolina Sandhills National Wildlife Refuge, turn right (southeast) onto Road 87, which reaches SC 341 just north of US 1 in the town of Bethune, 7.0 miles away. To continue on the present tour, however, continue northeast on Road 42. In another 2.4 miles Road 42 crosses SC 341, about 7 miles north of US 1 in Bethune.

From the intersection of Road 42 and SC 341, continue ahead on Road 42. In 1.1 miles you will pass Road 521 on the right (east). Just beyond Road 521 you will pass through a large *egg farm* (letter C on Map B–28.2). The pastures on either side of the road here are great for breeding Horned Larks and Grasshopper Sparrows. Rarities seen here include Upland Sandpipers in early April, and in breeding season, American Kestrels.

Continue ahead on Road 42 for about another mile to a small bridge over Jumping Gully Creek, the outlet creek of *Horton Pond*, a small millpond just to the left of the road. In some years a pair of Eastern Phoebes nest under this bridge (letter D on Map B–28.2).

If you continue northeast on Road 42 after looking for phoebes at the Horton Pond outlet, you will reach SC 346 in another 2.4 miles. Here you can turn south and reach US 1 at Bethune in 9 miles. To continue the tour, turn around at Jumping Gully Creek and backtrack through the egg farm to SC 341. When you get back to SC 341, turn right (northwest), and go for another 4.2 miles. Here turn left onto Road 20, Lockhart Road.

Soon after turning onto Road 20, you will pass through another area of extensive pastures good for breeding Horned Larks and migrant Upland Sandpipers (April and August). At about 1.7 miles south of SC 341 you will descend to the floodplain of the Little Lynches River. A farm pond on the left often attracts a few ducks in winter or shorebirds during migration. Just before crossing the river, find a place to stop and overlook the wet pasture on the left. This is *Lockhart Road Marsh* (letter E on Map B–28.2). From the roadside you might see or hear numerous species of marsh birds here. King Rails, Virginia Rails, Soras, and Sedge Wrens have been found here in April. (Remember that this is private property, so do not leave the roadside.)

Continue south on Road 20, which reaches US 521—US 601 just north of Camden in about another 11 miles. Here turn left to return to Camden.

B–28.4—Lake Wateree Dam (West Side)

Winter	**
Spring	**
Summer	*
Fall	**

The area just below Lake Wateree Dam on the Wateree River is one of the most dependable places in the South Carolina Piedmont to observe Bald Eagles from late summer to early winter. At least one is usually around during the cooler half of the year, and often you can see four or more birds.

To reach this area from I-20, leave the interstate at Exit 92, and go north on US 601 toward Camden. In 2.1 miles US 601 merges with US 1. Continue north on US 1—US 601. This is the main strip of the town of Lugoff. At 1.5 miles northeast of where US 1 merges with US 601, turn left (north) at a traffic light. (This is opposite the main entrance to the Dupont plant. If you cross the Wateree River, you have gone too far.)

This left turn puts you on Road 5, Longtown Road. (You can reach this road from downtown Camden by following US 1 south and turning right at the first stoplight after you cross the Wateree River.)

Once you are on Road 5 (Longtown Road), go north for 5.6 miles. Here bear right onto Road 37 (Buck Hill Road). Go north on Buck Hill Road for 2.7 miles. Here turn right onto Wateree Dam Road (still Road 37). Go east on Wateree Dam Road for 0.7 mile until you see a sign that says, "End State Maintenance." Here turn right onto a good, unpaved road, and follow this road for one mile to a small park and boat launch area on the Wateree River just below the dam. This park is called Lugoff Access Area. Park in the parking lot. The eagles may sometimes be seen from this point, but they are most often seen about a quarter mile downstream. Look for a farm road that turns off from the southern end of the park, and walk downstream along this road, which parallels the river. There are numerous fishermen's trails over to the river. The eagles are often seen perching in the trees on the opposite (east) side of the river.

B–29–LANCASTER COUNTY

Lancaster County is one of three adjacent counties (along with York and Chester) which might be called the "Pennsylvania counties" of South Carolina, since emigrants from Pennsylvania named their county seats (the cities of Lancaster, Chester, and York) for places in southeastern Pennsylvania. Like their northern namesakes, these three counties lie in the Piedmont region, with the Catawba River substituting for the Susquehanna.

Lancaster County lies east of the Catawba River, just southeast of Charlotte, North Carolina. For the most part it is a county of small farms, woodlots, and forests of loblolly pines, various oaks, hickories, and other hardwoods typical of the Piedmont. There is quite a lot of sandy soil in the southeastern part of the county, which is on the edge the Sandhills subregion of the Upper Coastal Plain.

B–29.1–Flat Creek Heritage Preserve and Forty-Acre Rock

Winter   *
Spring   ***
Summer **
Fall   ***

Forty-Acre Rock is an area of about 150 acres of granite outcroppings overlooking the valley of Flat Creek in the eastern part of the county. This area has long been famous among botanists for its rare plants, including certain rock-loving plants which are found almost nowhere else. The rock outcroppings and nearby bluffs, ravines, and the floodplain of Flat Creek are protected by the Heritage Trust program of the South Carolina Wildlife and Marine Resources Department as *Flat Creek Heritage Preserve*. The preserve includes 1,436 acres of the best birding area in Lancaster County, which is indeed one of the best in the entire Piedmont of South Carolina.

Flat Creek starts in central Lancaster County and flows eastward into Lynches River, which is the eastern border of the county. Flat Creek Heritage Preserve lies about one mile north of the intersection of US 601 and SC 903, which is about 6 miles north of the town of Kershaw (on US 601) or about 16 miles east of the town of

Lancaster (on SC 903). From the junction of US 601 and SC 903 drive north on US 601. In 0.8 mile you will come to the new US 601 bridge over Flat Creek. A pair of Eastern Phoebes nests under this bridge, here near the eastern edge of their breeding range. To the left, on the south side of Flat Creek, is a small marsh and beaver pond. From the road you may see a pair of Wood Ducks in the marsh.

To reach the parking lot, cross the bridge, and turn left immediately onto Road 27. The parking lot is 0.25 mile north on the left (west) side of Road 27. On the way to the parking lot you will pass the old, abandoned roadway of old US 601. From the parking lot you can return to the old road and follow it to the old bridge over Flat Creek. The old road continues up the hill, but it is effectively blocked by blow-downs from Hurricane Hugo, which hit this area in September 1989.

The main trail to Forty-Acre Rock begins at the parking lot and winds its way up the hill for about a mile to the largest of the rock outcroppings. From the parking lot go west about a quarter mile. Here the trail splits. The main trail to the rock goes right and winds about a mile to the rock, going up a marvelous creek with good examples of oak-hickory and cove hardwood forest. The trail to the left goes to the big beaver pond and the flood-plain forest along Flat Creek.

From the big rock you can overlook the Flat Creek valley. Birding on the rock or in the nearby dry woods of various oaks, shortleaf pine, and eastern red cedar is usually not too good. In winter you may find a few sparrows or juncos. In summer look for breeding Prairie Warblers and Field Sparrows as well as the usual Carolina Wrens, Northern Mockingbirds, Northern Cardinals, and the like.

The beaver pond is one of the largest in the state. Many wood duck boxes have been set up here, with the result that Wood Ducks are common residents. The woodies are joined in winter by a few Mallards and American Black Ducks. Other residents of the pond include Eastern Bluebirds, various woodpeckers (in dead trees), and Red-winged Blackbirds.

Follow the beaver pond trail as it loops clockwise around the pond. The loop trail continues around the pond, then climbs the hill, crosses a power line right-of-way, and rejoins the trail coming down from the big rock. In all, the loop is about a three-mile walk.

Since Flat Creek Heritage Preserve was officially opened only in 1984, it is not yet well known among birders, but it should be good for most bird species found in the Piedmont. The combination of dry and moist woods, recently cut-over areas and mature forest, hillside and river bottom, pond and marsh makes for a remarkable mix of habitats.

This is a great area in April or early May, when wildflowers are abundant and the woods are filled with the songs of migrant and resident warblers, vireos, thrushes, and flycatchers. Scarlet Tanagers are rather common here, at the edge of their breeding range. They are most often found in the woods along the creek. The following species of warbler have been found on the preserve during the breeding season: the Northern Parula, Yellow-throated Warbler, Pine Warbler, Prairie Warbler, Black-and-white Warbler, American Redstart, Prothonotary Warbler, Ovenbird, Louisiana Waterthrush, Kentucky Warbler, Common Yellowthroat, Hooded Warbler, and Yellow-breasted Chat.

B–29.2—Andrew Jackson State Park

Winter *
Spring *
Summer *
Fall *

This small state historical park is just north of the intersection of SC 5 and US 521, on US 521. From I-77 exit on SC 5 just east of the city of Rock Hill, and go east about 14 miles to US 521. Turn left onto US 521, and look for the park entrance on the right. From the SC 9—US 521 Bypass in Lancaster go north on US 521 about 8 miles to the park entrance on the right.

Birding in the park is not very exciting,

since most of the park consists of rather typical loblolly-pine forest, with oaks, sweet gums, and other hardwoods mixed in. There is a short nature trail, which makes a good leg-stretching walk after viewing the historical exhibits. The park honors President Andrew Jackson, who was born nearby and claimed by both North and South Carolina as a native.

B–29.3—Tom G. Mangum Bridge over the Catawba River

Winter *
Spring *
Summer *
Fall *

SC 200 and SC 97 cross the Catawba River on the *Mangum Bridge* just below the Fishing Creek Dam. There is a good pulloff to view the area below the dam on the Lancaster County (east) side of the bridge. From the SC 97 exit of I-77 go east about 9 miles to the bridge. From the SC 200 exit of I-77 go northeast about 10 miles to the bridge. The bridge is just north of the town of Great Falls (Chester County).

From the parking area just north of the

Lancaster County end of the bridge, you can easily overlook the river just below the dam. Here, in the water or on the rocks, you will find in summer egrets and herons (mostly Great Egrets and Great Blue Herons) and in winter, gulls (mostly Ring-billed). A Double-crested Cormorant may be here any time.

Dozens of Cliff and Barn Swallows nest under the bridge. The swallows are common from mid-April until late August or September.

B–30—LAURENS COUNTY

Laurens County is in the Piedmont region in the central portion of the state. Here, in a single county, we can find aspects of the entire South Carolina Piedmont. The small cities along Interstate 385 from Fountain Inn (which is mostly in Greenville County) through Laurens and Clinton to Joanna are similar to the industrial areas of Greenville and Spartanburg. Adjacent to these cities are suburbs and open

farm country with pastures and peach orchards. This is also similar to much of rural Greenville and Spartanburg counties. On the other hand, the eastern edge of Laurens County is in the Sumter National Forest, similar to most of the rest of the Piedmont.

The Enoree River, a beautiful Piedmont stream, forms the northeastern border of

Laurens County, while the southwestern border is the Saluda River (including part of Lake Greenwood, which is an impoundment of the Saluda River).

Birding in Laurens County is not distinguished. There are no state parks or national forest recreation areas in the county, and Lake Greenwood is not usually considered a hot spot for wintering or migrating waterfowl. But the countryside has a few surprises. A pair of Scissor-tailed Flycatchers were found breeding in the northern part of the county for a couple of years in the early 1980s, the farthest east this species has been known to breed. While the scissor-tails have not been found in recent years, who knows where they may turn up next?

B—30.1—The Flat Ruff Area

Winter *
Spring **
Summer *
Fall *

See Map B—30.1.

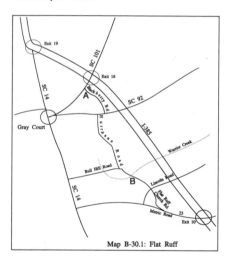

Map B-30.1: Flat Ruff

This seven-mile tour through Piedmont farmlands and apple orchards is a pleasant alternative route for birders traveling on I-385 south of Greenville. The roads described here have little traffic and lead through good birding country. This is not an area known for its rarities, but a Henslow's Sparrow was found here along the roadside in February 1988.

From I-385 southbound exit at SC 101 (Exit 16), and go southwest toward Gray Court. About a quarter mile from the exit look for a paved county road on the left (east). This is Blackberry Road. Turn left onto Blackberry Road.

The first good birding spot is immediately after you turn onto Blackberry Road. The thicket and wet woods along the road usually harbor quite a few birds. The most unusual resident of this thicket is a mammal, the eastern chipmunk, here found at the southeastern edge of its range (letter A on Map B—30.1).

After looking for the chipmunk, continue ahead on Blackberry Road. There are numerous thickets and hedgerows along this part of the route which are good for wintering sparrows. Soon you will emerge into an area of pastures and apple orchards. Stop anywhere that looks good and try your luck, but be sure to remain on the roadside, since this is all private property.

In about a mile Blackberry Road ends at SC 92. Turn right onto SC 92, and go about three hundred yards to the first county road to the left. This is Hurricane Road. Follow Hurricane Road southeast. In 1.5 miles it reaches a T-junction with Bull Hill Road. Bear left. At 1.6 miles from the junction with Bull Hill Road it crosses Lincoln Road and becomes Flat Ruff Church Road. Keep straight ahead on Flat Ruff Church Road until it ends at a stop sign at Road 23 (Metric Road). Turn left onto Road 23, and go about 1.2 miles to Exit 10 of I-385, the end of this side trip. The Flat Ruff side trip offers you a chance to find most birds of the Piedmont farmlands. Sparrows are especially common from late October until early April, with Chipping, Field, and Grasshopper Sparrows remaining to breed. In late winter look for Horned Larks in the orchard areas. This is a good road to drive at night. Great Horned Owls (year-round) and Whip-poor-wills (early April through September) are often heard, and there is a slight chance of finding a Barn Owl here.

An evening visit in February or March gives you the chance to observe the display flight of American Woodcocks. Woodcocks are common here, especially near streams. The road between Bull Hill Road and Lincoln Road (about 3.6 miles from where you leave I-386) crosses a small creek (*Warrior Creek*; letter B on Map B–30.2). Woodcocks do their sky dance display over the pastures near this creek just after sunset or just before sunrise.

B–30.2—Ware Shoals on the Saluda River

Winter	*
Spring	***
Summer	*
Fall	**

The rivers of South Carolina which rise in the Blue Ridge Mountains and then flow across the Piedmont and Coastal Plain to the sea are called *brownwater rivers*, because they often carry a heavy load of silt from the red clay soils of the Piedmont. Brownwater rivers are contrasted with *blackwater rivers*, which rise in the Coastal Plain and often have water colored by decaying vegetation and thus often looks black at a distance. One of the premier brownwater rivers of South Carolina Is the Saluda, which rises in the mountains along the North Carolina border and then flows southeast to Columbia, where it joins the Broad River to form the Congaree.

Brownwater rivers in the Piedmont occasionally flow through an area of more resistant rocks, resulting in what are called shoals, stretches of the river with large rocks strewn about in a shallow riverbed. The last of these shoals as you descend the river helps determine the Fall Line. Areas of shoals often have high bluffs or even minor gorges with steep slopes sometimes going up more than a hundred feet above the river. Such areas are great areas for plants and animals and are especially good areas for seeing migrating birds. Two outstanding examples of rocky shoals communities are the lower Saluda River near Columbia

(see Sections B-32 and B-40) and the Landsford Canal area of the Catawba River (see Section B-12). Another good shoals area along the Saluda River is in and near the town of *Ware Shoals*.

Ware Shoals is mostly in Greenwood County, on the southwest side of the Saluda River, though part of the town is just upstream in Abbeville County, and a small portion is across the river, in Laurens County. The best birding areas in Ware Shoals are in Laurens County, since this part is much less developed.

To reach the good birding areas in Ware Shoals, go to the intersection of SC 252 and US 25 Bypass, on the Laurens County (northeast) side of the Saluda River. (This intersection is about 15 miles west of Laurens on SC 252 or 17 miles north of Greenwood on US 25.) From SC 252 get onto US 25 Bypass and go south toward Greenwood. Take the first exit, about 2.0 miles south of SC 252. (If you are coming from the south, take the first exit after crossing the Saluda River, the first exit in Laurens County.) From the exit get onto Road 42, Powerhouse Road, and follow this road northwest, upstream along the east bank of the river.

For 1.1 miles Powerhouse Road skirts the river at the edge of a narrow floodplain with a high bluff to the right, away from the river. Most of the floodplain forest is gone, replaced by residential lots and second-growth woods. There are numerous informal pulloffs and fishermen's paths along the river. This is a great place for birds, especially in migration.

Soon Powerhouse Road runs along the edge of a riverside park, Irvin Pitts Memorial Park. This small park offers good bird-ing opportunities. At 1.1 miles from US 25 Bypass, Powerhouse Road crosses over the river to downtown Ware Shoals. Just before the bridge turn right onto Road 81, Cemetery Road. Road 81 winds its way up the high bluff and passes a cemetery before reaching US 25 Business in 1.4 miles. Turn right onto US 25 Business to return to the intersection of US 25 Bypass and SC 252.

B–31—LEE COUNTY

Lee County lies in the Upper Coastal Plain, about midway between Columbia and Florence. Interstate 20 bisects the county from east to west. Crossing I-20 at about a right angle is Lynches River. The floodplain forests of Lynches River are the main break in the general landscape of the county, which is one of broad culti-vated fields punctuated by small wood-lots of pine-oak forest and loblolly-pine plantations. The best birding in Lee County is along Lynches River, especially at Lee State Park. The Sandhills subregion in northwestern Lee County is worth a visit in late spring and early summer to look for unusual breeding species such as the Lark Sparrow (very rare).

B–31.1—Lee State Park

Winter   **
Spring   **
Summer *
Fall   **

See letter A Map B–31.1.

The 2,839-acre *Lee State Park* is located so that it is conveniently accessible from I-20; in fact, the interstate runs through a small part of the southern end of the park. Leave I-20 at Exit 123, and go north on Road 22 for 1.2 miles to the park entrance road, on the left (west). Follow the entrance road in to a T-junction.

At the T-junction you can go right toward the campground or left toward the picnic and swimming area. The best birding is on the road to the right, which soon becomes a one-way automobile loop road through the swamp.

A few yards from where you turned right you will pass the entrance to the Sandhill Nature Trail, a poorly marked footpath into a dry, sandy area of longleaf pines and turkey oaks. If you walk on this half-mile trail, be prepared to backtrack when you lose the trail.

The birds of the Sandhill Nature Trail are those species typical of longleaf pine-woods. Red-cockaded Woodpeckers have appeared here in past years, but since this area is protected from fire, and since no controlled burning is done, the area is no longer attractive to them, and they probably no longer come to the park. You will find the Northern Cardinal, Tufted Titmouse, Carolina Chickadee, Brown-headed Nuthatch, Pine Warbler, and Downy Woodpecker year-round, joined in winter by species such as the Dark-eyed Junco, both kinglet species, and Yellow-rumped Warbler. In summer expect the Eastern Wood-Pewee, Blue-gray Gnatcatcher, and Summer Tanager in the dry pinewoods. Bachman's Spar-

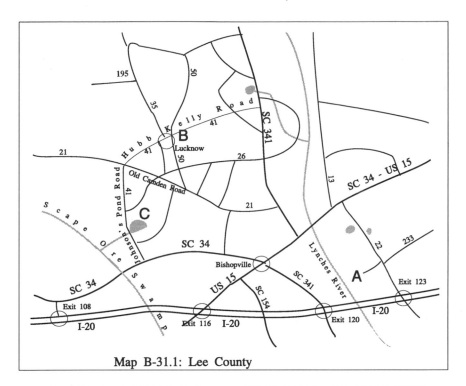

Map B-31.1: Lee County

rows may still occur, but like the Red-cockaded Woodpecker, this species is not found often in areas that have been protected from fire for many years.

The best birding in the park is along the auto tour road, which loops about two miles through the swamps and floodplain forests along Lynches River. If the river is in flood (as it often is in late winter and early spring), this road may be closed due to the flooding. If the road is open, it offers the best area in South Carolina to drive through a floodplain forest on public land.

This is not virgin forest, but it is mature and has many of the same species that you might expect in the Congaree Swamp National Monument (see Section B-40.8 below). Woodpeckers are common, including Red-headed, Red-bellied, Downy, Hairy, and Pileated Woodpeckers and the Northern Flicker (all permanent residents), and the Yellow-bellied Sapsucker in winter. Other permanent resi-

dents include the Wood Duck, Barred Owl (common and often seen in daylight), Red shouldered Hawk, Belted Kingfisher (along the river), White-breasted Nuthatch, Carolina Wren, Carolina Chickadee, Tufted Titmouse, Brown Thrasher, and Northern Cardinal.

In winter look for both kinglet species, Brown Creeper, Winter Wren, White-throated Sparrow, and Eastern Phoebe. In summer you can count on Acadian and Great Crested flycatchers; White-eyed, Yellow-throated, and Red-eyed vireos; and many warblers, including Northern Parula, Yellow-throated, Hooded, Kentucky, and Louisiana Waterthrush. This area looks like great habitat for Swainson's Warbler, but they are not usually found. Perhaps you will be lucky.

The auto tour loop rejoins the main park road near the T-junction where you originally turned right to go on the tour. Just after you emerge from the floodplain forest and before you reach the end of the one-way road, stop and look for a Red-cockaded Woodpecker roost tree on the right. The birds have used this area in the past, and hopefully they will continue to do so despite the deterioration due to the suppression of fires. The best times of day to look are early in the morning or late in the afternoon, when the woodpeckers are near their roost trees.

There is another foot trail in the park, the one-mile-long Artesian Nature Trail. From

the parking lot of the picnic ground look for the trail blazes near the dam of the swimming lake. The trail goes through pine-oak woods for the most part. The birds along this loop are the typical species of Coastal Plain woods. Wood Thrushes are especially common in summer, as are Northern Parula and Yellow-throated Warblers (nesting in the Spanish-moss—covered tree of the picnic area). In winter this is a good place for kinglets and Yellow-rumped Warblers.

B–31.2—The Lucknow Area

Winter   *
Spring   **
Summer **
Fall   *

See Map B–31.1.

The northern part of Lee County is in the Sandhills subregion of the Upper Coastal Plain, but little of the natural vegetation (longleaf pine and turkey oak) remains. In its place is a mosaic of pastures, hay-fields, fields of row crops, hedgerows, plum thickets, and small loblolly-pine plantations. Along the creeks you can still find a few bay-swamp thickets. Several creeks have been impounded into small ponds. This is a delightful area to visit at any time but is especially interesting from April through August, when several breeding species of interest may be found.

To tour the Lucknow area from I-20, leave the interstate at Exit 123, the Lee State Park exit, and go north on Road 22. You will soon pass the entrance to Lee State Park (see Section B-31.1, above; letter A on Map B–31.1). Continue north on Road 22 for 4.9 miles after leaving the inter-state. You will pass a series of roadside farm ponds in this section. These ponds are attractive to herons and White Ibis. Great Blue Herons are present year-round and are joined in the warmer part of the year by Green-backed Herons, Great Egrets, Cattle Egrets (common), and a few White Ibis (uncommon).

When you reach US 15—SC 34, turn left (west) toward the town of Bishopville. Go southwest on US 15—SC 34 for 2.3 miles until you reach SC 341, on the north side of Bishopville. Here turn right (north) onto SC 341 toward Bethune. Go north on SC 341 for 5.9 miles to Road 41 (Hubb Kelly Road). Before turning west (left) onto Hubb Kelly Road, go a hundred yards farther north on SC 341 to the bridge over Turkey Creek. Here you can inspect a typical Sandhills millpond, where you might find a Wood Duck at any time or swallows during migration.

From the bridge over Turkey Creek return to Road 41 (Hubb Kelly Road), and go west toward the small community of Luc-know, which is marked by an imposing water tower (letter B of Map B–31.1). You will reach the water tower about 4 miles from SC 341. Just before the tower turn right (north) onto Road 35 (Old George-town Road East). A short side trip north on Road 35 will lead you past pastures with breeding Grasshopper Sparrows. The field at the top of the hill one mile north of the water tower sometimes has breeding Horned Larks.

At 1.3 miles north of the water tower you will reach the intersection with Road 195, Mount Hebron Road. here to look for hawks (including breeding American Kestrel and Cooper's Hawk) and also Horned Larks in the open fields. To continue the tour, return to the water tower on Road 41 (Hubb Kelly Road).

After the side trip north from the water tower, turn right (west) onto Road 41. The next mile is a particularly interesting part of this road. Here, in 1987, Lark Sparrows were found during June and July, and they may be breeding. Other species to look for along this mile of road include Northern Bobwhite, Ruby-throated Hummingbird, Eastern Kingbird, Purple Martin, Gray Catbird, Loggerhead Shrike, Chipping and Field Sparrows, and Eastern Meadowlark.

About 1.4 miles west of the Lucknow water tower, Road 41 intersects Road 21, Old Camden Road. South of Old Camden Road, Road 41 continues, but with a new name, Johnson's Pond Road. Go south on Johnson's Pond Road. In a couple of miles you will pass *Johnson's Pond* (letter C on Map B–31.1), a rather large millpond where you might find a Wood Duck or a Green-backed Heron. At 3.9 miles south of Old Camden Road, Road 41 (Johnson's Pond Road) ends at SC 34. Here turn right (west), and go about 4 miles to Road 31, which is a short access road to I-20. Turn left onto Road 31, and enter I-20 at Exit 108.

B–32—LEXINGTON COUNTY

Like Richland County, Lexington County is part of the Columbia metropolitan area near the center of the state. Its busy cities (including Lexington, Cayce, and West Columbia) are commercial and industrial centers served by an excellent network of roads. As a natural area Lexington County straddles the Fall Line and contains Piedmont and Upper Coastal Plain habitats. Furthermore, much of the northern part of the county is in Lake Murray, a seventy-eight-square mile impoundment on the Saluda River (see Section B-32.1). Three other counties border on Lake Murray: Richland (see Section B-40), Newberry (see Section B-36), and Saluda (see Section B-41).

Downstream from the Saluda Dam (which

forms Lake Murray) the Saluda River rushes over a series of rapids for about eight miles until it joins the Broad River to form the Congaree River at Columbia. These rapids are the Fall Line. The rich Piedmont floodplain forest along this stretch of the Saluda is an outstanding area for spring and fall migrants (see Sections B-32.2 through B-32.5).

In addition to Lake Murray on the north, Lexington County is bordered on the east by the Congaree River and on the west by the North Edisto River. The bottomlands along the Congaree afford excellent birding all year long (see Section B-32.7).

B–32.1—The Lake Murray Area

Winter	**
Spring	**
Summer	*
Fall	**

Lake Murray is a fifty-thousand-acre impoundment on the Saluda River. Its dam in Lexington County, on SC 6 about 7 miles north of the town of Lexington. Most of the lake is in Lexington County, but Richland, Saluda, and Newberry counties

also have parts of Lake Murray. The best birding on the lake is at Dreher Island State Park (see Section B-36.1). There are, however, numerous public access points on the Lexington County side of the lake where you might see a few birds.

The South Carolina Electric and Gas Company (SCE&G) maintains eight public parks on Lake Murray, of which three are in Lexington County. Two of the three are at the dam which is known as Saluda Dam. To reach the dam from I-26, leave at Exit 102, and go west on SC 60 through the city of Irmo. In about four miles SC 60 joins SC 6 at the north end of the Saluda Dam. One park is here (Lake Murray Park No. 8), while the second park (Lake Murray Park No. 1) is a mile further at the south end of the dam. SC 6 uses the top of the dam to cross the Saluda River.

Lake Murray Park No. 8 is open all year. In summer there is a nominal admission charge. In winter you can usually just drive in. This park gives you a great view of the lower part of Lake Murray. In winter you might find species such as Common Loons, Horned and Pied-billed Grebes, a few ducks, American Coots, Ring-billed

and Herring Gulls, and little else. In summer there are usually no birds at all.

Lake Murray Park No. 1 is at the south end of the dam, and it is open only in summer, so it is of little interest to a birder.

Lake Murray Park No. 2 is a few miles west of the dam, on the road to Shull Island. The quiet coves here are more likely to have ducks in winter. To reach this park from the dam, go south on SC 6 for 7 miles to the north side of the town of Lexington. Here turn left (west) onto US 378, and follow US 378 out of town. US 1 joins US 378 for a short distance, then splits off to the left. Bear right, remaining on US 378, heading toward the town of Saluda. At 8.6 miles west of US 1 turn right (north) onto Road 115, and follow the signs to the park, which is about 4 miles from US 378.

B–32.2—The Saluda Hills Area on the Saluda River

Winter *
Spring ****
Summer *
Fall ***

The south side of the Saluda River near I-26 offers the best migration birding in the Columbia area. This abused area, where trash dumping and vandalism are rampant, may be closed and posted sometime in the future, but as long as the public may enter, Columbia birders will consider this *the* spot to look for migrants.

To reach the Saluda River bottomlands from I-26, leave the interstate at Exit 110 (US 378, Sunset Boulevard). Get onto the access road that runs along the east side of the interstate. (This road runs in front of the Ramada Inn. Lexington County Medical Center is on the other side of I-26 from the access road that you seek.)

Follow the access road north (downhill, toward the Saluda River). In 0.5 mile turn right (east) onto the first side street. This street has no name, but there is a sign for the Westover Hills neighborhood at this turn. Go east for one short block, and

turn left (north) onto Terrace View Drive. Follow Terrace View Drive north for about a half mile to its end. Here park on the side of the road, and explore the area in front of you on foot.

At the end of Terrace View Drive you will find two entrances to the undeveloped bottomlands along the Saluda River. Straight ahead is a sewage line right-of-way. To the left is a jeep trail. Either way will get you into the birding area.

For your first visit follow the jeep trail, which takes off to the left. In about two hundred yards you will come to a junction of jeep trails. Here turn right. You will quickly come to an old sewage treatment pond. Some of the best birding along the Saluda is around this old pond. Follow the jeep trail around the pond to the left.

Just before you get to the Saluda River,

you will encounter a path. To the left the path enters the woods. You may be able to follow this path upstream for almost a mile along the river to the I-26 bridge. Under the bridge breed numerous Barn Swallows and in some years a pair of Eastern Phoebes, here at the southern edge of their breeding range.

To the right the path goes along the north dike of the old sewage pond, par-alleling the river. Follow this path, which soon joins the sewage line right-of-way. Turn right (south) onto the right-of-way. (If you follow the right-of-way too far, you will return to the end of Terrace Drive, where you parked.)

Just before you reach Terrace Drive, look for a path off to the left. This path leads into a mature floodplain forest. By explor-ing this path (and side trails off of it), you will find a wide variety of habitats. It is easy to spend an entire morning here during migration.

This area is only so-so for breeding birds. The deeper woods harbor resident Barred Owls and most of the common species of Piedmont floodplain forests. But from mid-April through mid-May and again from late August through early Oc-tober, this area can be excellent.

The prime attraction is the wide variety of migrant warblers to be found here. In 1988, for example, at least thirty-three species of warbler (and a hybrid—Lawrence's Warbler) were found here in addition to numerous thrushes, vireos, fly-catchers, orioles, and other birds.

To whet your appetite, here is the Saluda warbler list:

Blue-winged Warbler—fairly common in spring and fall
Golden-winged Warbler—rare in fall
Tennessee Warbler—uncommon, spring and fall
Nashville Warbler—rare in fall

Northern Parula—common, spring and fall (a few breed)
Yellow Warbler—rare in spring
Chestnut-sided Warbler—fairly common, spring and fall
Magnolia Warbler—uncommon in spring, common in fall
Cape May Warbler—common in spring, uncommon in fall
Black-throated Blue Warbler—common, spring and fall
Yellow-rumped Warbler—common winter resident
Black-throated Green Warbler—rare, spring and fall
Blackburnian Warbler—rare, spring and fall
Yellow-throated Warbler—uncommon in spring (a few breed)
Pine Warbler—uncommon permanent resident
Prairie Warbler—uncommon in fall
Palm Warbler—uncommon, spring and fall
Blackpoll Warbler—fairly common in spring, rare in fall
Cerulean Warbler—rare in spring
Black-and-white Warbler—common, spring and fall
American Redstart—common, spring and fall
Prothonotary Warbler—uncommon sum-mer resident
Worm-eating Warbler—fairly common, spring and fall
Swainson's Warbler—uncommon in spring
Ovenbird—fairly common, spring and fall
Northern Waterthrush—fairly common, spring and fall
Louisiana Waterthrush—rare in spring
Kentucky Warbler—uncommon summer resident
Common Yellowthroat—uncommon, spring and fall
Hooded Warbler—uncommon summer resident
Wilson's Warbler—rare in fall
Canada Warbler—uncommon in spring, rare in fall
Yellow-breasted Chat—rare summer resi-dent

B–32.3—The Saluda River at Seminole Drive

Winter   *
Spring   ***
Summer *
Fall   **

There is good access to the Saluda River at the end of *Seminole Drive*. To reach this area from I-26, get off at Exit 110, the US 378 exit, and go east (toward Columbia) on US 378, Sunset Boulevard. At 1.9 miles from the interstate turn left at a stop light onto Seminole Drive. Follow Seminole Drive north for about a mile to its end by a softball field. Park here.

A power line right-of-way gives a good view northward over the Saluda River. Numerous trails and paths lead down a two-hundred-foot hillside to the river. A few hours spent exploring this area during April, May, September, or October will usually turn up many of the bird migrants

mentioned for the Saluda Hills area (see Section B-32.2). The advantage of the Seminole Drive area is that the trails here are not so likely to be overgrown, and there are fewer fire ants to contend with. For this reason you might consider coming to Seminole Drive rather than Saluda Hills, especially during fall migration, when the paths at Saluda Hills are particularly overgrown.

There are plans to build a footbridge over the river to this part of the Saluda River corridor from the Riverbanks Zoo (see Section B-40.3) immediately across, so by the mid-1990s you might be able to visit the corridor much more easily.

B–32.4—The Saluda River at Garden Valley Lane

Winter   *
Spring   ***
Summer *
Fall   **

Five places along the lower Saluda River offer good birding opportunities. One is Riverbanks Park in Richland County (see Section B-40); the second and third are the Saluda Hills area (see section B-32.2) and the Seminole Drive area (see Section B-32.3); the fourth is a one-mile stretch of the river on lands owned by the South Carolina Electric and Gas Company (SCE&G) readily accessible from a nice canoe launch area just west of I-20 at the end of *Garden Valley Lane*. (The fifth is the Hope Ferry Landing area; see Section B-32.5.)

To reach the Garden Valley Lane area from I-20, leave the interstate at Exit 62, and go northwest (away from Columbia) on Bush River Road. At 1.0 mile from I-20 turn left (south) onto Garden Valley Lane. Follow this street for 0.4 mile to a nice fenced-in parking lot along the Saluda

River. This SCE&G park is open from dawn to dusk. There is a trail along the river. Upstream the trail peters out in about two hundred yards, but the downstream trail follows the river for almost a mile to the I-20 bridge.

The downstream trail leads to a mature Piedmont floodplain forest. Also in the area are second-growth floodplain woods, a thick pine plantation, and brushy openings. Birding here is not quite as good as in the Saluda Hills area (which is about 2.5 miles downstream), but with the larger wooded area here at Garden Valley Lane species which prefer deep woods are more common than at Saluda Hills. For example, Wild Turkeys are seen in the swampy woods at Garden Valley Lane, but not in the more open woods at Saluda Hills.

B–32.5—The Saluda River at Hope Ferry Landing

Winter   **
Spring   ***
Summer **
Fall   ***

One of the wildest portions of the lower Saluda River is just a mile or so downstream from the Saluda Dam, especially on the north side of the river. This area is accessible from the public boat-launching area provided by SCE&G at *Hope Ferry Landing*. There are actually *two* Hope Ferry Landings, one on each side of the river. Here we are referring to the one on the north side of the river, where Bush River Road is.

To reach this area from I-26, go west from Exit 106 on Road 36, St. Andrews Road. Follow St. Andrews Road for 2.9 miles. Just beyond the Allied Chemical plant turn left (west) onto Road 107, Bush River Road, which is the road to the Saluda Dam on Lake Murray. Go west on Bush River Road for about 1.4 miles to an unpaved road on the left. (There is a sign here for a public boat ramp.) Turn left (south) onto this unnamed road, and follow it about a half mile to a parking lot by the river.

If you are coming from the Garden Valley Lane area (see Section B-32.4), turn west onto Bush River Road. In about 0.6 mile the street becomes Tram Road, which immediately comes to a stop light at St. Andrews Road. Here turn left, go about 1.1 miles to the intersection with another part of Bush River Road, and proceed as described above. In other words, there are *two different* Bush River Roads broken by a mile stretch of St. Andrews Road.

From the parking lot you will be able to find anglers' trails both upstream and downstream along the Saluda River. The downstream trail ends in about a half mile, but there is a rabbit's warren of paths and trails upstream from the parking lot. To reach the main network of trails, walk back toward Bush River Road for about a hundred yards from the river, and look for a trail into the woods on your left. This trail leads to numerous other trails and paths along the river, through Piedmont floodplain forest and loblolly-pine plantations. The whole complex is hemmed in by the Saluda River to the south and a large power line right-of-way to the north.

If you explore this area during spring or fall migration, you will find lots of birds, including many of the migrants mentioned for the Saluda Hills area. During summer or winter the Hope Ferry Landing area is much better than the other areas mentioned for the lower Saluda River, since it is the largest and least developed. You can expect to find most of the species typical of Piedmont floodplain forests and pine plantations. In addition to the woods, the power line right-of-way along the northern edge of this area harbors lots of birds, especially sparrows in winter.

In 1990 the landowner (SCE&G) put up a fence along the road to the boat landing in an attempt to protect the area from abuse by vandals and off-road vehicle enthusiasts. While this fence is up, the area will be closed to casual birders. Hopefully a plan can be devised in the near future to patrol the area so that nondestructive uses (such as fishing and birding) can resume. Until this happens, this area will not be of much interest to the casual birder, since the best parts are fenced off.

Winter   *
Spring   *
Summer *
Fall   *

The Nature Conservancy's three-hundred-acre *Peachtree Rock Nature Preserve* is well known to South Carolina's botanists as one of the best areas to observe many typical—and some unusual—Sandhills plants in a striking natural setting. A mile-long loop trail leads from the parking lot through a variety of habitats—loblolly-pine plantation, Piedmont-like hardwoods with an understory of mountain laurel, oak-pine scrub, longleaf-pine forest, turkey-oak barrens, and bay-swamp thicket. There is a waterfall, a rocky cliff, and of course Peachtree Rock. This is a twenty-foot-high sandstone boulder which is much broader at its top than at its base. This peach-tree-like shape gives it its name. The Peachtree Rock area is a hot, dry place with few birds, even in fall or winter. You can expect flocks of Tufted Titmice and Carolina Chickadees all year, joined in winter by Yellow-rumped Warblers and both kinglet species, and in summer by Blue-gray Gnatcatchers. The hotter, drier areas of blazing white sand are desertlike. Midday summer temperatures here are the hottest in the state, often exceeding a hundred degrees. It looks like good breeding habitat for Lark Sparrows, a species which has been found breeding in similar places in the Sandhills of North Carolina but which has not yet been found here at Peachtree Rock. If you hike the trail in summer, come early in the morning, and keep reminding yourself of the possibility of finding a rare sparrow.

To reach Peachtree Rock from I-26, use Exit 115, and go south on US 21—US 176—US 321 toward Gaston. Immediately south of the interstate is the intersection with Road 73 (Fish Hatchery Road) and the new Southeastern Expressway (SC 478), which will eventually be the southern end of I-77. At this intersection you could turn left to enter the expressway (and cross the new bridge over the Congaree River to go to SC 48 in Richland County). Do not turn left, however. Turn right onto Road 73.

If you are coming from Richland County, cross the Congaree River on the new bridge. From SC 48 the signs say, "To I-26." When you get to the end of the expressway, do not use either of the I-26 exits. Use the US 21 exit. You will come to a stoplight at US 21—US 176—US 321. Go straight ahead. This will put you on Road 73, Fish Hatchery Road.

Go west on Fish Hatchery Road through the community of Pineridge. You will reach a T-junction at 5.3 miles from US 21. Here turn right in order to continue on Road 73. Go west another 6.4 miles (11.7 miles from US 21). Here you will come to another stop sign at the intersection with Road 65, Meadowfield Road. Turn right (north) onto Road 65, and go 1.2 miles to a stop sign at SC 6. Turn right onto SC 6. Go just 0.7 mile northwest on SC 6, and look for a good sand road on the right. This county road is Peachtree Rock Road. Turn right onto Peachtree Rock Road and go a quarter mile to the parking lot, on the right.

If you are coming from the west on I-20, use Exit 39 to US 178. Turn right (east) onto US 178 toward Pelion. Follow US 178 through farm county for 15.4 miles to the intersection with SC 302 in the small town of Pelion. Turn left (northeast) onto SC 302 toward Columbia, and go just 1.1 miles. Here turn right (east) onto Road 73, Fish Hatchery Road. Go 3.6 miles on Road 73 to the stop sign at SC 6. Turn left onto SC 6, and go 1.7 miles to Peachtree Rock Road, a sand road off to the right. Go a quarter mile on Peachtree Rock Road to the parking lot.

B-32.7—Congaree River Bottomlands along Old State Road

Winter **
Spring ***
Summer **
Fall ***

Old State Road, as this area of Congaree River bottomland is known to birders, is one of the favorite birding areas in the Columbia metropolitan area and one of the best areas for birds year-round in the central part of the state. In past years this area has yielded breeding Grasshopper Sparrows and Dickcissels, but these are not to be expected. This area of cultivated fields, pine plantations, swamps, oak-pine woods, and a boat ramp on the Congaree River is great for sparrows and hawks in the winter, for migrant and breeding warblers, and for breeding Mississippi Kites in the summer.

While it is possible to reach Old State Road from New State Road in the city of Cayce, you will probably get lost doing it. If you are new to the area, get on I-26, and go to Exit 119, US 21—US 176. Go north on US 21 past the entrance to the truck stop. At 0.9 mile from I-26 turn right (east) onto Road 1258, Wire Road. Road 1258 crosses over I-26 (no exit here) and then descends into the floodplain of the Congaree River. The pavement ends. Continue east on Wire Road to a T-junction with another unpaved road. This is Old State Road. If you turn right, you will return to US 21 and I-26 in about a mile. Turn left (north). The habitat here is large

cultivated fields and pine woods. The hedgerows along the road here shelter numerous sparrows in winter, including Fox and White-crowned.

The land here is privately owned, so birding must be confined to the roadsides. Even with this limitation this is a worthwhile birding area. Soon after turning north onto Old State Road, you will reach two spots where power line rights-of-way cross the road. The brushy edge here attracts many birds. Just north of the second power line Old State Road passes through a half mile of swampy second-growth woods. This area is great for spring and fall migrants as well as for breeding warblers, including the Kentucky Warbler. In June 1990 a singing Cerulean Warbler was found along this part of the road. You will eventually reach the Cayce Boat Launch area, on the Congaree River. The riverside woods downstream from the parking lot are great for migrants. In summer be alert for Mississippi Kites, which breed here in good numbers.

From the boat launch it is best to retrace your path to I-26, though it is possible to reach downtown Cayce by continuing north along Old State Road.

B-33—MARION COUNTY

Marion County is a rural area in the Coastal Plain in the northeastern part of the state. By the classification used in this book, the county lies along the border between the Upper Coastal Plain and Lower Coastal Plain (SC 41 runs through the center of the county). Marion County has a typical mixture of croplands, pine plantations, and floodplain forests but lacks any notable birding destination, primarily due to the lack of public lands

in the county. Marion County is one of the few South Carolina counties without a state park, national forest, or national wildlife refuge.

Marion County is sandwiched between the Little Pee Dee River and the Great Pee Dee River, both of which have broad floodplain forests. These forests are great areas for breeding Mississippi Kite and Swainson's Warbler as well as other species typical of Coastal Plain floodplain forests. If you are traveling to the beach on US 378, take an hour to explore the

Britton's Neck area near the confluence of the Great and Little Pee Dee Rivers.

B–33.1—The Britton's Neck Area

Winter   *
Spring   **
Summer **
Fall   *

See letter B on Map B–33.1.

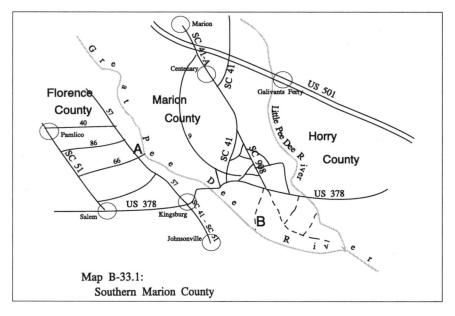

Map B-33.1:
Southern Marion County

Britton's Neck is the name given to the peninsula in southern Marion County between the Little Pee Dee River and the Great Pee Dee River. This area is easily explored as a side trip from US 378. The best birding is along a two-mile-long unpaved road from US 378 to a public boat launch area at *Dunham Bluff*, on the Great Pee Dee River (letter B on Map B–33.1). From late April until mid-August this road is a good place to find breeding Swainson's Warbler and Mississippi Kite. The kites are usually seen from the

boat launch area, while the warblers may be heard (and sometimes seen) in swamp thickets anywhere along the road to Dunham Bluff.

The road to the Dunham Bluff boat launch is just a few yards west of the T-junction of SC 908 and US 378. This junction is 7.5 miles east of the US 378 bridge over the Great Pee Dee River (the Marion County—Florence County line), or 3.0 miles west of the US 378 bridge over the Little Pee Dee River (the Marion County—Horry County line).

B–34—MARLBORO COUNTY

Marlboro County lies on the North Carolina border, in the northeastern part of the state. The northwestern part of the county is in the Sandhills subregion of the Upper Coastal Plain, but most of the county is part of the Upper Coastal Plain proper. Culturally speaking, Marlboro is part of the Pee Dee tobacco region. This is an apt name, since tobacco is an important crop here, and the Great Pee Dee River is the western border of the county.

The Great Pee Dee flows into South Carolina and becomes the border between Chesterfield and Marlboro counties. (In North Carolina it is known as the Yadkin River for most of its length, but it becomes the Pee Dee a few miles upstream from the South Carolina line). The Pee Dee river system is the northernmost area along the east coast of the United States where the Mississippi Kite is a common summer resident (although a few kites breed along the Roanoke River in North Carolina and may well be expanding northward into Virginia). Birders often visit the swamps and fields along the Pee Dee in late July or August to view concentrations of up to twenty Mississippi Kites. The Welsh Neck area of Marlboro county is a good place to look for kites in summer.

B–34.1—The Welsh Neck Area

Winter   *
Spring   **
Summer **
Fall   **

Although anywhere along the Great Pee Dee River below Blewett Falls Lake in North Carolina is a good place to find Mississippi Kites from late April until late August, the *Welsh Neck* area of Marlboro county is a better place than most, because of good access to the floodplain forest and adjacent fields. The best birding is along Road 167 (Welsh Neck Road), a paved secondary road that branches off to the northwest (upstream) from US 15–401.

From the town of Society Hill (in Darlington County) cross the river on US 15–401, and look for Road 167 just beyond the bridge. (The turn is to the left if you are northbound on US 15–401.) From Bennettsville follow US 15–401 south toward Society Hill. About 9 miles south of Bennettsville, just before the bridge over the Great Pee Dee River, look for Road 167 on the right.

There is a sign for Colonel Kolb's tomb at the turnoff. This historic site is about halfway to the end of Road 167, which reaches a dead end at 2.5 miles from the main highway. Because this is a dead-end road without a boat-launching ramp, traffic is very light. You can stop anywhere to bird from the roadside, but please do not enter the woods, since they are posted. There is a bit of public land at Colonel Kolb's tomb where you can get over to the river.

The kites can be anywhere along this road but are most easily seen soaring and kiting over the river or over one of the open fields or pastures. The floodplain forests along the road have many of the usual floodplain forest species. Breeding birds include Northern Parula, Yellow-throated, Hooded, Prothonotary, and Kentucky Warblers, Acadian Flycatcher, White-breasted and Brown-headed Nuthatch, and six species of woodpecker (Red-bellied, Red-headed, Hairy, Downy, and Pileated Woodpecker, and Common Flicker).

Wild Turkeys are common residents of the woods here and are most easily seen in early morning. Late summer is a good season to see turkeys, but they are to be found all year long. You need a bit of luck to see them, though, so don't get your hopes up too high.

Winter birds along the Welsh Neck Road

are similar to wintering species of fields and woodlands throughout most of the state. Look for Brown Creeper and Winter Wren in the woods, and be alert for a half-hardy lingerer such as an Orange-crowned Warbler, especially if the weather has not been too cold.

B–34.2—Lake Wallace in Bennettsville

Winter   ***
Spring   **
Summer   *
Fall   **

Lake Wallace, one of the South Carolina Wildlife and Marine Resources Department's public fishing lakes, is a three-hundred-acre lake lying on the northwest side of the city of Bennettsville. It attracts a surprising number of wintering waterfowl, including Canada Geese, various ducks, American Coots, and gulls.

To reach the causeway over the upper end of Lake Wallace from the intersection of US 15—401 and SC 9 on the east side of Bennettsville, go north on US 15—401 for 1.5 miles to Road 47, Beauty Spot

Road. Go left (west) on Road 47 for 1.3 miles to the causeway over the lake. There is room for parking at either end of the causeway. The lake is easily birded, either from the causeway or from the fishing dike, which runs the length of the southern part of the lake.

The more common ducks on Lake Wallace in winter are Wood Ducks, Mallards, Ring-necked Ducks, and Buffleheads. Other species occur from time to time, especially in spring and fall migration.

B–35—MCCORMICK COUNTY

Situated in the Piedmont region along the Georgia border, McCormick County is one of the most rural, least populated counties in South Carolina. The Savannah River and its seventy-thousand-acre impoundment, Lake Thurmond (formerly known as Clarks Hill Lake) dominate the natural scene in McCormick County. There are numerous access points along the lake, some run by the Corps of Engineers, some by the U.S. Forest Service, and some by the South Carolina Depart-

ment of Parks, Recreation, and Tourism. The visitor to McCormick County should seek out the Savannah River Scenic Highway (SC 28 and SC 81) and explore the lakeshore wherever seems best. Some good spots to try are mentioned below. In addition to the Lake Thurmond points, McCormick County has the Stevens Creek Heritage Preserve, which protects an extraordinarily rich woods on the eastern edge of the county.

B–35.1—Baker Creek State Park and Hawe Creek Campground

Winter *
Spring *
Summer *
Fall   *

See letters A and B on Map B–35.1.

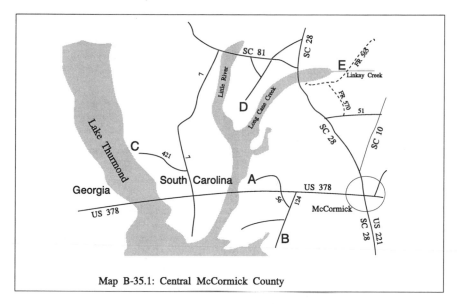

Map B-35.1: Central McCormick County

Baker Creek State Park (letter A on Map B–35.1) is a 1,305-acre park on the shores of Lake Thurmond. The park entrance is along US 378 about 4 miles west of the center of the town of McCormick or 3 miles east of the Georgia border.

The park is not a birding hot spot, but you can find most of the common species of Piedmont pine-oak forests along a mile-long nature trail loop called the Wild Mint Trail. This trail begins at Camping Area #2 and loops near the lake for part of its length. The trail is not worth a special trip, but give it a try if you are camping or picnicking at Baker Creek.

If you look carefully (such as along creeks), you will find a few dwarf palmettos (*Sabal minor*) in the park. Baker Creek is about as far up the Savannah River as this Coastal Plain plant is found.

Unless you have a boat, Baker Creek is not a good spot to look for water birds in the lake. You will probably find more birds at some of the other spots along the lakeshore.

The Corps of Engineers' *Hawe Creek Campground* (letter B on Map B–35.1) is just south of US 378 opposite Baker Creek State Park. To reach this area from the town of McCormick, go west on US 378 from SC 28 for 2.7 miles. Here turn left onto Road 124, which leads to the campground in about 3 miles. Or from the entrance to Baker Creek State Park turn right (west) onto US 378, then almost immediately turn left (south) onto Road 56. Follow Road 56 for 0.6 mile to a T-junction with Road 124. Here turn right, and follow Road 124 to the campground.

Hawe Creek Campground is of interest to birders because it has one of the last Red-cockaded Woodpecker colonies in the South Carolina Piedmont. To find the woodpeckers' roost trees, enter the campground area, and turn left at the fork opposite the ranger's residence. This leads to the loop of the campground with electric hookups. The woodpeckers' roost trees are right next to the shower building.

This is a marginal Red-cockaded Woodpecker colony and might well be abandoned by the time you read this, but there is a slim chance that you might find this endangered species here. If not, you can still enjoy a great campground (no picnicking) and a typical Piedmont southern-pine—oak forest.

There are no formal trails at Hawe Creek, but a good place to hike around and look for Red-cockaded Woodpeckers is along the gated forest service road that you pass on your right (west) about a half mile before you get to the campground. This old road goes about a mile to the shore of Lake Thurmond and is a great place to find birds of the pinewoods.

B–35.2—Hickory Knob State Park

Winter *
Spring *
Summer *
Fall *

See letter C on Map B–35.1.

Hickory Knob State Park is primarily a golfing park, but there are two short trails near the hotel where you might find a few common species. From the hotel parking lot cross the road, and walk toward the lake. You will see the beginnings of the Beaver Run Nature Trail (a half-mile loop through typical oak-hickory-pine forest), and the Turkey Ridge Trail, a short trail down to the shore of the lake.

To reach the park from the intersection of US 378 and SC 28 in McCormick, go west on US 378 for 5.9 miles to the turnoff for Road 7. (This intersection is 1.2 miles east of the bridge to the Georgia side of the lake on US 378.) Turn right (north) onto Road 7, and go 1.6 miles to the park entrance road (Road 421), on the left (west). Follow the entrance road to the hotel, where you can pick up a map of the park and a brochure for the nature trail.

Be aware that Hickory Knob State Park does not have a picnic area (but it does have a campground). If you wish to picnic, your best bet is nearby Baker Creek State Park (see Section B–35.1) or Elijah Clark State Park, which is just over the US 378 bridge on the Georgia side of Lake Thurmond.

B–35.3—Hamilton Branch State Park

Winter **
Spring **
Summer *
Fall **

See letters D and E on Map B–35.2.

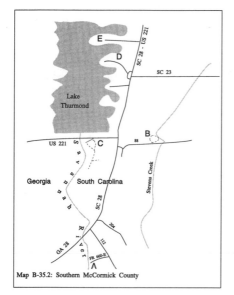

Map B-35.2: Southern McCormick County

Hamilton Branch State Park (letter E on Map B–35.2) is one of three South Carolina state parks on Lake Thurmond and

the one with the best view of the lake from shore. To reach the park from the intersection of SC 28 and US 378 in McCormick, go south on SC 28—US 221. In 14 miles you will come to the small town of Parksville. Just south of Parksville on SC 28 you will reach a roadside picnic area on the right (west). From this picnic area you can usually find a few ducks or Canada Geese on the lake. American Coots are common here in winter.

To reach the park, continue south on SC 28 for about 2 miles south of Parksville. The park road is on the right (west). Turn in and follow the road to the lakeside picnic area at the end of the road. This is a good place from which to overlook the middle portion of Lake Thurmond.

When you are done at Hamilton Branch State Park, return to SC 28 and turn right (south). In about 1.5 miles you will come to the turnoff for *Modoc Camp Recreation Area* (letter D on Map B–35.2), a Corps of Engineers park on the lake. The view of the lake from this recreation area is about the same as that from the state park. In winter you will probably find a few ducks, coots, and Canada Geese (introduced, permanent residents).

B–35.4—Clarks Hill Dam on Lake Thurmond

Winter **
Spring **
Summer *
Fall **

See letter C on Map B–35.2.

The best birding in the Lake Thurmond area is near its dam (Strom Thurmond Dam, also known as Clarks Hill Dam), at the south end of the lake. To reach this area from I-20, exit at exit 65 in Georgia, and go north on GA 28. In about 11 miles the road crosses into

South Carolina and continues as SC 28. (Two miles north of the bridge you will pass the turnoff for Fury's Ferry, on the McCormick County—Edgefield County line. See Section B-19.3.) To continue on to the Lake Thurmond Dam, go north on SC 28 for 7 miles from the Georgia border to the intersection with US 221. Turn left (west) onto US 221, and go about a mile. (Just before you get to US 221, you will pass the turnoff for Stevens Creek Heritage Preserve, described below in Section B-35.5.)

There are two birding spots in the vicinity of the dam. One is the Corps of Engineers Visitors' Center (a right turn if you are westbound on US 221.) Here you can overlook the deepest part of the lake, where you will have the best chance of finding a rare duck in winter. The other birding spot is the area just below the dam.

To reach the picnic area just below the dam, turn left from US 221, opposite the visitors' center, and follow the road downhill. Near the first sharp turn you will pass a rough logging road on the left. Continue down the paved road, ignoring any turnoffs to the right. After passing a grassy area just below the dam, the paved road enters the woods. Here look for an old road off to the left, which is now closed to vehicles by a barrier. Park and explore this old road on foot.

Follow the old road for a quarter mile or so as it passes through an excellent floodplain forest. Dwarf palmetto (*Sabal minor*) is abundant here at the northern edge of its range. This is a good place for Wild Turkey as well as other species of Piedmont floodplain forests.

In about a half mile the old road joins the jeep trail that you passed while driving along the paved road. Here you have a choice. You can turn sharply left and walk back to the main entrance road in about a half mile, or you can turn right and explore the jeep trail for about 0.7 mile.

The jeep trail soon emerges from the woods at the edge of the Corps of Engineers property and continues along the edge of a huge clear-cut. (This section of the trail is part of the Sumter National Forest.) The regenerating clear-cut will be up the hill to your left (east), while to your right you will pass a good Piedmont floodplain forest. There are numerous old logging roads into the forest, which you can use to explore the swamp (if you don't mind a bit of wading).

Continuing south along the jeep trail, you will reach private property in about 0.7 mile (marked by red blazes on trees and a chain across the trail). Here turn around, and backtrack to the main entrance road.

There are enough good spots near the dam to occupy you for a half day or more, if you have the time. Winter and spring are the best seasons, but even in summer you will find lots of birds here.

B–35.5—Stevens Creek Heritage Preserve

Winter   *
Spring   ***
Summer *
Fall   **

See letter B on Map B–35.2.

The rich wooded area along Stevens Creek in eastern McCormick county is famous among botanists for its large number of plant species. Here the cove hardwood forest of the Southern Appalachians meets the tupelo, bald cypress, and dwarf palmetto of the Coastal Plain. The preserve protects a good population of an extremely rare shrub, the Florida Gooseberry (*Ribes echinellum*). This low,

thorny shrub is found only in two places—here at Stevens Creek and near Lake Miccosukee in northern Florida.

In the spring the *Stevens Creek Heritage Preserve* has the finest wildflower display in the South Carolina Piedmont, including the only known colony of dutchman's breeches (*Dicentra cucullaria*) in the state. The wildflower show begins in mid-February and is at its peak during March and April.

The birdlife of the preserve is less remarkable, but this is still a good place to look for species of Piedmont floodplain forests. Perhaps the most interesting species at Stevens Creek is the American Woodcock, which is a permanent resident. Wander about in the woods along the creek for a while, and you just might flush one. The woodcock performs its famous "sky dancing" display flight at dawn and dusk in late winter and early spring.

To reach Stevens Creek Heritage Preserve, go to the point where US 221 and SC 28 split about 1.3 miles northeast of Clarks Hill Dam. To reach this point from I-20, leave the interstate at exit 65 in Georgia and go north on GA 28. In about 9 miles the road crosses the Savannah River and enters South Carolina as SC 28. Go north on SC 28 for another 7 miles. Just before SC 28 joins US 221, look for Road 88 on the right (east). Turn onto Road 88. (Note that Road 88 bears to the left just after crossing the railroad tracks next to SC 28.) Follow Road 88 east for 1.2 miles to an indistinct parking area on the left (north) side of the road. If you get to the bridge over Stevens Creek, you have gone 0.8 mile too far.

The trail into the preserve begins at the parking area and loops down the bluff to Stevens Creek and back (about 1.5 miles round trip). At one point you will reach a rocky outcrop at the top of a hundred-foot-high bluff above the creek. This is a good spot to observe migrating warblers and vireos in the spring or fall, since birds which are normally high above you in the treetops can be seen here at eye level.

The pinewoods along Road 88 outside of the preserve were clear-cut in the late 1980s and so provide a good place to observe birds of Piedmont old fields. This should be a good place to find the elusive Bachman's Sparrow until the mid 1990s. Undoubtedly, by then some other hillside in the neighborhood will have been cut over. To find Bachman's Sparrow (between April and September), look for large clear-cuts with brush between three and six feet high. When you find such an area, listen for the loud, clear song of the sparrow—a long high note followed by a musical trill or warble and then another long lower note. Bachman's Sparrows are best enjoyed from the roadside, since their brushy habitat is also conducive to ticks and chiggers.

B–35.6—John De La Howe Woods

Winter	*
Spring	**
Summer	*
Fall	**

See letter D on Map B–35.1.

In 1797 a local physician, Dr. John De La Howe, established an agricultural school for indigent children in what is now northwestern McCormick County. The school is still in operation, having been taken over by the State of South Carolina in 1918. Of interest to the naturalist is a tract of some two hundred acres surrounding the tomb of John De La Howe on the southern edge of the school property. These woods have not been logged in almost two hundred years, with the result that the tract supports a mature oak-hickory-pine forest that is similar to the original forest of the South Carolina Piedmont. There are many extremely large loblolly-and shortleaf-pines interspersed in a forest of white oak, southern red oak, and many other species.

The birdlife of the De La Howe woods is typical of Piedmont oak-hickory forests. Since it is a large area of mature woods, it is quite attractive to the thrushes: Wood Thrush in summer, Hermit Thrush in winter, and all of the woodland thrushes in migration.

The main entrance to the De La Howe School is on the south side of SC 81 about 8 miles north of McCormick or 8 miles south of Mount Carmel. To reach the woods, turn south onto the main school road, and follow it about two miles to its end. (Follow the signs for the De La Howe tomb.)

B–35.7—Linkay Creek

Winter *
Spring **
Summer *
Fall **

See letter E on Map B–35.1.

Mature floodplain forests are somewhat scarce in the South Carolina Piedmont, since most have been cleared for agriculture or covered by a lake. Whenever we can visit one of the remaining floodplain forests, we are in for a treat. One such spot in the Sumter National Forest is the floodplain of *Linkay Creek.*

To reach Linkay Creek from the town of McCormick, go northwest on SC 28. In 5.3 miles you will reach the intersection with Road 51 on the east (right). (This intersection is 1.7 miles southeast of the junction of SC 28 and SC 81, near the De La Howe School—see Section B–38.7.) Turn east onto Road 51, and go 1.7 miles. Here turn left (north) onto Forest Road 570. Follow Forest Road 570 one mile to a T-junction at Forest Road 565.

There are good birding spots both left and right on Forest Road 565. First turn left, and follow Forest Road 565 about 2.5 miles to its end near the Long Cane Creek arm of Lake Thurmond. The parking area here is about two hundred yards from the lakeshore. Between the parking area and the lake is a field planted for wildlife. This is a great spot for birds, including sparrows in all seasons and an occasional flock of Wild Turkeys.

After exploring the lakeshore area, retrace your path along Forest Road 565. At 0.5 mile east of Forest Road 570 you will reach the low bridge over *Linkay Creek.* Park and explore the floodplain forest here. The woods here are full of birds in all seasons, especially species such as woodpeckers, titmice, and other hole-nesting species. This is one of the few places in the South Carolina Piedmont where you can find resident White-breasted Nuthatches, a species indicating mature forests.

After exploring Linkay Creek, you may either retrace your path back to SC 28, or you may go straight ahead (east) on Forest Road 565, which reaches the town of Troy (in Greenwood County) in about 4 miles. At Troy you can pick up SC 10 about 7 miles north of McCormick or 18 miles south of Greenwood.

B–36—NEWBERRY COUNTY

Newberry County lies in the Piedmont region, roughly forty miles northwest of Columbia along I-26. The northeastern portion of the county is largely within the Sumter National Forest and is characterized by loblolly-pine plantations on the uplands and hardwood floodplain forests along larger creeks and rivers. The Broad River is the eastern border of the county, and one of its major tributaries, the Enoree, flows through the northeastern part of Newberry County to join the Broad.

The southern and western parts of Newberry County are dominated by dairy and chicken farms, giving rise to Newberry County's slogan "The Dairy and Egg Capital." The town of Newberry has a water tower near I-26 shaped like a giant egg cup with an egg in it! This heavily agricultural area has no large forests but rather a mosaic of pastures, hayfields, woodlots, and small pine plantations.

The western and southwestern border of Newberry County is the Saluda River and two of its main impoundments—Lake Greenwood and Lake Murray. The best birding spot on Lake Murray is in Billy Dreher Island State Park. Other good birding spots are found along the Broad River and Enoree Rivers in the eastern part of the county, along county roads in the heart of the dairy and egg producing farmlands northwest of the town of Newberry, and at Lynches Woods Park on the southeastern edge of the town.

B–36.1—Billy Dreher Island State Park

Winter	**
Spring	*
Summer	*
Fall	**

Billy Dreher Island State Park occupies a 340-acre island in the northern portion of Lake Murray. Its 12 miles of shoreline afford opportunities for various sorts of water-oriented recreation, including birding. To reach Dreher Island from I-26 westbound, get off at the Chapin exit in northern Lexington County (Exit 91). Go west on Road 48 for about 2 miles until you reach US 76 in Chapin. Turn right (northwest) onto US 76, and go for a half mile until you reach Road 29, St. Peter's Church Road. Here turn left (west), following signs for the state park. At 3.6 miles west of US 76 turn left (southwest) onto Road 231, Dreher Island Road. In another 2.4 miles Road 231 crosses an arm of Lake Murray (Camping Creek) and enters Newberry County. The same road continues in Newberry County as Road 15. Go west on Road 15 for 0.6 mile to Road 571, a turnoff to the left. Follow Road 571 south for about 2 miles to the state park. (This rather complicated route is marked with state park direction signs at every major turn.)

The directions to Dreher Island from I-26 eastbound are a bit simpler. Leave I-26 at any of the Newberry exits, and go west to US 76. Follow US 76 southeast from Newberry to the town of Prosperity, about 5 miles from Newberry. Here turn right (south) onto SC 391, which becomes Main Street in Prosperity. In downtown Prosperity, SC 391 turns off to the right, but you should go straight ahead, following the signs for Lake Murray and the state park. Here Main Street becomes Road 26.

Follow Road 26 for about 8 miles to the intersection with Road 15. Here turn left (following the sign to the state park), and go east on Road 15 for just 0.6 mile, where you will turn right onto Road 571, which leads to the state park in about 2 miles.

When you get to the park, you will cross a short causeway before you get to the entrance station. Just beyond the entrance station is a second, longer causeway. Some of the best birding in the park is along the second causeway, which connects the island to the mainland. To bird the causeway, drive into the park, and park your car in the small parking lot beside the entrance station, then walk a few yards more to the second causeway.

From mid-April until mid-July Cliff Swallows breed under the bridge in the middle of the second causeway. The causeway area is a fairly good place to look for waterfowl in winter. Common Loons and Horned Grebes are common; sometimes dozens are here. Other water birds seen here in winter often include Mallards, American Black Ducks, Ring-necked Ducks, Buffleheads, Hooded Mergansers, and American Coots. Other duck species are possible but not to be expected. You will see mostly loons and

gulls: Ring-billed, Herring, and a few Bonaparte's Gulls.

Once you have checked out the birds of
the second causeway, return to your car,
and drive onto the island. You will immediately come to a large parking lot and
the state park marina. This area gives you
another look at the lake and lakeshore.

Dreher Island has a short nature trail,
from which you can overlook most of the
central part of Lake Murray. To reach the
trail from the marina area, drive over the
short one-lane bridge that is just beyond
the marina, and keep to your right, following park signs for the nature trail, picnicking area, and community building.

Park in the lot next to the community
building.

The nature trail winds for a quarter mile
through second-growth mixed oak-pine
woods, which harbor the usual common
species of Piedmont woods. The trail
loops along the lakeshore, then returns to
the parking lot.

Billy Dreher Island State Park juts out into
the lake, so that from there you can observe most of the central portion of the
lake, including the widest part of it. For
this reason Dreher Island is probably the
best birding area in the Lake Murray
area.

B–36.2—The Broad River Area (From Peak to SC 34)

Winter   *
Spring   **
Summer *
Fall   **

See Map B–36.1.

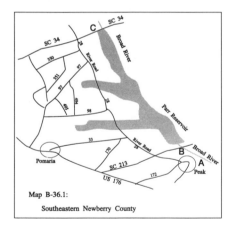

Map B-36.1:

Southeastern Newberry County

The back roads of southeastern Newberry
County offer a delightful alternative to
Interstate 26 for birders who are not in a
hurry. From I-26 leave at Exit 97, and follow US 176 northwest. At 6.5 miles from
the interstate turn right (north) onto Road
32. In 1.5 miles Road 32 enters Newberry
County, where it continues as Road 28. In
less one mile from the county line, Road

28 enters the *village of Peak*, a quiet and
beautiful old town on a hillside above
the Broad River (letter A on Map B–36.1).
Be alert for birds at feeders in town. In
winter this is a good place to find
Evening Grosbeaks, and in summer hummingbird feeders often attract a Ruby-
throated Hummingbird or two.

Road 28 winds around to the left and
then goes along a railroad track on the
north side of town. briefly at the point
where Road 28 passes under the railroad
trestle. There are always birds here or
around the nearby bridge over Rocky
Creek.

Continue north on Road 28. At two miles
north of the county line Road 28 crosses
SC 213.

To visit Lake Monticello or other birding
spots in Fairfield County, turn right here,
and go about 4 miles to the town of
Jenkinsville. See Section B-20 for more
details. If you go on SC 213 in late spring
or early summer, stop at the *bridge over
the Broad River* (letter B on Map B–36.1).
Cliff Swallows breed under this bridge

and are readily seen from the west end of the bridge (in Newberry County).

To continue the tour of the Newberry County side of the Broad River, continue north on Road 28 from its intersection with SC 213. You will pass over two arms of Parr Reservoir, which is an impoundment of the Broad River. The first arm is about 3 miles north of SC 213, and the other is about 6 miles north of SC 213. Each has a small SCE&G (South Carolina Electricity and Gas Company) park, with boat launching, pit toilets, picnicking, and primitive camping.

Parr Reservoir is not a particularly good place to see birds, but you will find Canada Geese on the lake year-round. Under either of the two bridges over the reservoir look for nesting Eastern Phoebe, Barn Swallow, and Cliff Swallow. Purple Martins and Eastern Bluebirds breed in

dead trees in the shallow parts of the lake.

Continue north on Road 28 for 11.2 miles from SC 213 to the intersection with SC 34. Here turn right for a 1.2 mile side trip to the *SC 34 bridge over the Broad River* (letter C on Map B–36.1). Park on the Newberry County side of the bridge, and walk out onto the wide bridge, being careful to avoid the traffic. The SC 34 shoulder on the bridge gives you a chance to overlook the bluffs and floodplain of the Broad River. The floodplain has been cleared of large trees, with the result that it is now a melange of marsh, willow thicket, canebrake, and mud flats. Canada Geese breed here, and there is always something interesting flying up or down the river. This is an excellent place to look for hawks, including Bald Eagle, which has bred nearby.

B–36.3—The Broad River Area (From SC 34 to Enoree Waterfowl Management Area)

Winter	*
Spring	**
Summer	*
Fall	**

See Map B–36.2 and B–44.1 (p. 216).

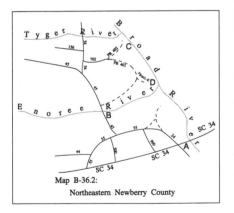

Map B-36.2:
Northeastern Newberry County

This tour begins at the intersection of SC 34 and Road 28 in the northeast part of Newberry County (letter A on Map B–36.2). This is the ending point

of the route described in Section B-36.2. To reach this intersection from I-26, leave the interstate at Exit 74 in Newberry, and go east on SC 34 for 10.9 miles.

From the intersection of SC 34 and Road 28, go north on Road 28. In about a mile the road swings left (west) and changes its number to Road 55. The open pinewoods at this point are in Sumter National forest. These woods have a good variety of birds, including Solitary Vireos year-round (breeding and wintering). At 3.7 miles from SC 34 you will reach the intersection with Road 45 on the right (north). Turn right onto Road 45.

At 2.2 miles from where you left Road 55 the route crosses the Enoree River at *Keitt's Bridge* (letter B on Map B–36.2). The Enoree is a beautiful, wild Piedmont

169

stream popular with canoeists. A brief stop by the bridge will net you Barn Swallows in summer. (They breed under the bridge.) Keep an eye out for Wild Turkey in this area. They are common here, but you need a bit of luck to find one.

Continue north on Road 45. At 4.0 miles from Road 55 you will pass an unpaved road to the right (east). This is the back way in to the Enoree Waterfowl Management Area. Keep straight ahead on Road 45. At 4.4 miles north of Road 55 you will reach a paved road to the right. This is Road 54. Turn right (northeast) onto Road 54, and go 1.1 miles. Here look for Road 702 off to the right. Turn right onto Road 702. In 1.0 mile the pavement ends.

At the end of the pavement of Road 702 you have a choice. The right fork leads to the entrance road for Enoree Waterfowl Management Area, which we will cover below. The left fork (Forest Road 402) leads to the *Broad River Scenic Area of Sumter National Forest* (letter C on Map B–36.2).

To reach the Broad River Scenic Area, turn left onto Forest Road 402, following signs to the hunt camp. At about 1.0 mile in from the end of the pavement you will pass Scenic Area Hunt Camp on the right. At 1.6 miles from the end of the pavement, look for a old logging road off to the right (southeast). This is the best way into the scenic area. If you reach the dead end at the Broad River, you have gone about 1.1 miles too far.

There is no marked trail into the scenic area. Park along Forest Road 402, and walk east along the logging road. In about a quarter mile you will reach a large clearing. Keep left at the clearing, and gradually walk downhill. The oak-pine woods here are interesting for possible breeding Solitary Vireo, here near the southern edge of its breeding range. Since the Solitary Vireo is uncommon in winter in this area as well as in summer, this is one of very few places where it is possible to find a Solitary Vireo at any time of year. For the most part birding is fair along this road. Expect the common species of Piedmont oak-pine woods.

At about 0.5 mile in from Forest Road 402 you will reach a second clearing. Continue steeply downhill and a bit to the right. You will soon reach the edge of the Scenic Area, a nice Piedmont floodplain forest. The Broad River is about one mile in from where you left Forest Road 402. After exploring the Scenic Area, backtrack to Forest Road 402, and return to the end of the pavement of Road 702.

Early April is a good time to visit the Broad River Scenic Area. Most of the summer resident bird species have returned by April 15, and the spring wildflowers here are extraordinary.

To reach *Enoree Waterfowl Management Area* (letter D on Map B–36.2; also letter A on Map B–44.1), take the right fork at the end of the pavement of Road 702. Road 702 becomes Forest Road 401. Follow Forest Road 401 for about two miles to the intersection with Forest Road 401-E, which comes in from the left. Follow Forest Road 401-E to a parking lot for the waterfowl management area, which you will reach in about a half mile. (This area is closed during the season when it is most used by migrant ducks—October 1 through February 1.)

If the waterfowl area is open, continue on foot downhill along the service road from the parking lot. You will soon reach the floodplain bottomlands near the confluence of the Enoree and Broad Rivers. The service road winds through fields planted with grain for wildlife as well as through floodplain forests. The main impoundment lies a bit to the right of the service road at the point where the road goes through the woods along the Broad River, but if you keep on going, you will eventually come to a pond with standing dead trees. Wood Ducks are common breeders here along with a few Mallards. Other duck species are rarely seen, but keep an eye out for a rare breeder. This is the sort of place that might get a pair of breeding Hooded Mergansers from time to time.

Woodpeckers are common in the dead trees. Six species breed here: Red-bellied, Red-headed, Hairy, Downy, Pileated, and Northern Flicker. The woods and fields attract a wide variety of migrant and breeding land birds, including most species of Piedmont floodplain forests and agricultural fields. If you visit in late winter or spring, be alert for American Woodcocks and Common Snipe in the wet fields.

When you are done with the Enoree WMA, backtrack along Forest Road 401-E to where you turned off of Forest Road 401. Here you have a choice; either to turn right to backtrack to Road 702 or to

continue to the left on Forest Road 401, which winds its way for about three miles and eventually rejoins Road 45 at a point 1.8 miles north of the bridge over the Enoree River.

Whichever way you return to Road 45, go south on Road 45 to its end at Road 55. Here you may return to SC 34 by turning either left or right. From the south end of Road 45 it is 3.6 miles to SC 34 if you turn right (west) or 3.7 miles to SC 34 if you turn left (east).

B–36.4—Lynches Woods Park

Winter	*
Spring	***
Summer	*
Fall	**

Cannons Creek rises on the southeastern side of the city of Newberry and flows generally eastward to the Broad River near Parr Dam. About 360 acres of the upper reaches of the Cannons Creek watershed are protected in a beautiful Newberry County park, *Lynches Woods Park*. Much of the park consists of a mature cove hardwood forest along the creek with a mature oak-hickory forest on the sleeper slopes uphill from the creek. The woods seem more like those of the lower slopes of the Blue Ridge Mountains than those of the Piedmont. Birders have only recently discovered Lynches Woods, so not much is known of its birding potential, but it should be quite good. Lynches Woods is an island of mature hardwoods in an otherwise heavily developed part of Newberry County, so it should be excellent in spring and fall migration.

To reach Lynches Woods Park from I-26 westbound, leave at Exit 76 and follow SC 219 west into the city of Newberry. In 3.4 miles you will reach US 76 Bypass. Turn left (southeast) onto US 76 Bypass.

From I-26 eastbound leave at Exit 74, and follow SC 34 southwest for 2.6 miles to US 76. Here turn left (southeast), and follow US 76 Bypass. You will reach the intersection of SC 219 and US 76 Bypass in just 0.2 mile. Continue southeast on US 76 Bypass.

In 0.8 mile from the intersection of SC 219 and US 76 Bypass you will reach the point where SC 34 Bypass turns west (right). Directly across US 76, on the left, you will find the old National Guard Armory. Turn into the old armory grounds, and park either in the lot in front of the old armory or near the trash boxes at the left rear of it.

A well-maintained trail for horses and hikers begins just behind the old armory. This trail (which is a really a service road) winds for about 4 miles through the park, until it emerges behind the right (southeastern) edge of the armory grounds. A morning spent hiking this trail should provide good birding, especially in spring and fall. Sometimes the service road is open to vehicles, in which case you can drive around the four-mile loop.

B—37—OCONEE COUNTY

Oconee County lies in the northwestern-most part of South Carolina in the Piedmont and Blue Ridge natural provinces. Elevation in Oconee County ranges from about 660 feet at Lake Hartwell in the southern part of the county to 3294 feet at the top of Fork Mountain in the Andrew Pickens Ranger District of Sumter National Forest.

The best birding in Oconee County is along the shores of Lake Hartwell or Lake Keowee (best in winter) and in the mountains (best from late April through October). One good place to observe birds on Lake Hartwell is Lake Hartwell State Park (see Section B-37.1). Lake Keowee is covered in Section B-37.2. The best mountain birding is along SC 107 in the Sumter National Forest (see Section B-37.3).

B—37.1—Lake Hartwell State Park

Winter **
Spring **
Summer *
Fall **

Lake Hartwell State Park is a relatively new park (established in 1986) on the shores of Lake Hartwell, in the extreme southwestern part of the county. From Exit 1 of I-85 go north on SC 11 (the Cherokee Foothills Scenic Highway). About a half mile from the interstate look for the entrance to the park on the left (west). at the Trading Post, which is just a few dozen yards from SC 11, for park information.

The lake is best viewed from a boat, but you can see some of it from the boat launch area. There are few birds to be seen in summer, but in migration or winter you may find a Common Loon or two, Pied-billed and Horned Grebes, and a few ducks. (Better areas for birding Lake Hartwell are in Anderson County—see Section B-4).

A walk along the half-mile-long *Beech Bluff Nature Trail* will give you a chance to explore typical Piedmont pine-oak woods. Birding here is not great, but you may turn up something good in spring or fall. In summer look for breeding Solitary Vireos, a species normally thought of as a mountain species but which is to be found in pinewoods in the Piedmont. Listen for its song, which is slower and sweeter than that of the more common Red-eyed Vireo. White-eyed and Yellow-throated Vireos are here as well, which means that you can find all of the common breeding vireo species of South Carolina on one short walk.

B—37.2—Lake Keowee

Winter **
Spring ***
Summer *
Fall ***

Lake Keowee (pronounced "KEE-oh-wee"), an 18,750-acre impoundment in the eastern part of Oconee County, is a bit unusual in that it has two dams, Keowee Dam on the Keowee River (which is the eastern border of the county) and Little River Dam on the Little River, about four miles southwest of Keowee Dam. In other words, Lake Keowee is really two different impoundments which are connected.

This deep, clear lake, constructed by Duke Power Company to provide cooling water for the Oconee Nuclear Power Plant, is a popular spot for fishing and boating. It also is a good birding area in the cooler part of the year, especially during waterfowl migration periods (late October—early December and late February—early April).

Duke Power Company and Oconee County maintain several parks and boat ramps along the lake. (You can pick up a free map of Lake Keowee and nearby Lake Jocassee at any South Carolina Welcome Station.) We will mention a few of the better spots for birds, but bear in mind that any place where you can get down to the lake might have a good duck or gull during migration.

Probably the best birding area on Lake Keowee is at Little River Dam. There is no park or boat ramp here, but since SC 130 runs on top of the dam, it is fairly accessible. From the intersection of US 76—US 123 and SC 130 on the north side of Seneca, go north on SC 130 for about two miles. (If you are coming from the Issaqueena area of Pickens County, as described in Section B-39.7, you will reach SC 130 in this area about one mile south of the Little River Dam.) As you approach the dam, you will see a wide expanse of the lake on your left (northwest). Park on the side of the road just before the dam,

and overlook the lake. A telescope is useful here. With luck you will see a few ducks and gulls in winter or migration. The Canada Geese here are mostly introduced residents, but they are joined in winter by a few migrant geese from the north, including an occasional Snow Goose. During migration in late winter you might find scores of Common Loons or Horned Grebes.

From Little River Dam continue north on SC 130. At 6.9 miles north of US 76—US 123 you will reach a junction where SC 183 comes in from the east. (If you turn right here you will reach the town of Pickens in about 15 miles.) Continue north on SC 130—SC 183. In another mile turn right onto the entrance road of Duke Power Company's Keowee-Toxaway Visitors' Center, also known as the World of Energy. This area includes an attractive picnic ground in a Virginia-pine grove on the lakeshore. From the picnic ground you can overlook a wide expanse of the lake just north of the Keowee Dam.

To reach a third birding spot on Lake Keowee, return to SC 130—SC 183 and continue north. You will cross over Lake Keowee and in 0.6 mile reach the point where SC 130 and SC 183 split. Here take the left fork, and follow SC 183 westward toward Walhalla. Go west for 2.0 miles, and then turn left (south) onto Road 574, which leads in about a mile to High Falls County Park. This small park has camping, picnicking, and a fishing pier from which you can overlook a small arm of the lake.

B–37.3—An Oconee County Mountains Tour

Winter	*
Spring	***
Summer	**
Fall	***

See Map B–37.1.

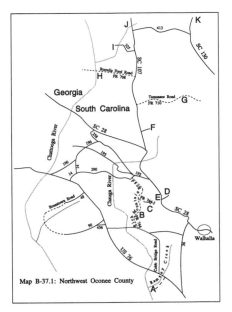

Map B-37.1: Northwest Oconee County

The following tour will lead you through or near some of the best birding spots in the foothills and mountains of Oconee County. The mountains are not quite a high as those in Caesar's Head State Park in Greenville County or Sassafras Mountain in Pickens County, but many of the characteristic breeding species of the Greenville and Pickens County mountains may also be found in Oconee County. At least two species (Red-breasted Nuthatch and Golden-crowned Kinglet) are currently found regularly in South Carolina only in Oconee County during the breeding season.

From Exit 11 of I-85 (in Anderson County; see Section B-4) go northwest on SC 24 for about 19 miles to the junction with US 76—US 123 in the small city of Westminster. Here turn left (west) onto US 76—US 123, and follow these combined routes through town. On the west side of the city the routes split; US 123 bears left (west) toward Toccoa, Georgia, while US 76 bears right (northwest) toward Clayton, Georgia. Bear right onto US 76.

At 2.2 miles from the US 76—US 123 split you will pass the entrance road to *Chau Ram County Park* (letter A on Map B–37.1) on your left. This is a good camping and picnicking spot with birds typical of Piedmont pine-oak woods. To continue the tour, keep going on US 76 for another 0.3 mile. Here you will reach Cobb Bridge Road.

Follow Cobb Bridge Road north. At 2.2 miles from US 76 you will reach a major junction. Bear left, keeping on Cobb Bridge Road. At 2.8 miles from US 76 turn right onto an unpaved road, Forest Road 744 (Rich Mountain Road). This road soon enters the Sumter National Forest, ascending from the Piedmont countryside of small farms and suburban development into the foothills of the Blue Ridge Mountains. The road gradually climbs the side of Rich Mountain, with good views to the south and southwest, across the Piedmont of South Carolina and into Georgia.

At 4.3 miles north of US 76 you will reach the top of *Rich Mountain* (letter B on Map B–37.1), elevation 1,546 feet. There is an informal parking area along the side of the road here. A few dozen yards beyond the parking area along the road is a vista to the east. The drop-off here is about 700 feet to the Piedmont countryside. Rich Mountain is covered with a magnificent, mature cove hardwoods forest. Here you can expect to find most of the species typical of Blue Ridge cove hardwood forests. Common breeding birds include various woodpeckers, Scarlet Tanager, Red-eyed Vireo, and several species of warbler. Keep an eye out for Cerulean Warblers here. This species is rare in South Carolina and has not yet been found breeding on Rich Mountain, but the habitat is similar to its breeding habitat in nearby North Carolina mountains.

From the top of Rich Mountain continue north on Forest Road 744. At 7.1 miles north of US 76 you will reach a spur road to the right, Forest Road 744-I. This road leads for about two miles to a dead end on the side of Buzzard Roost Mountain, an area protected by the Nature Conservancy and the State of South Carolina as *Buzzard Roost Mountain Heritage Preserve* (letter C on Map B–37.1). The habitat here is much drier than on Rich Mountain, with a dry oak-hickory forest giving way to stands of pitch pine with a thick understory of mountain laurel and other shrubs. Typical breeding birds here include Solitary Vireo and five warbler species: Pine Warbler, Black-and-white Warbler, Hooded Warbler, Worm-eating Warbler, and Ovenbird. This area is best in fall migration.

After exploring Forest Road 744-I, return to Forest Road 744, and continue north. At 10.2 miles north of US 76 you will reach a T-junction with a paved road: Road 290, Stumphouse Road. Here turn right (northeast), and follow Road 290 for 0.9 mile to a second T-junction. Here turn right onto Road 193, Whetstone Road, which reaches SC 28 in another 0.6 mile.

At SC 28 you can go right for 0.7 mile to two fairly good birding areas; one is *Stumphouse Tunnel* and *Issaqueena Falls* (see Section B-37.4; letter D on Map B–37.1) on the left (east), and the other, two hundred yards down the road, is *Yellow Branch Picnic Area* on the right (west) (letter E on Map B–37.1).

If you are coming up the hill from Walhalla on SC 28, the Yellow Branch Picnic Ground is the first developed area in the Sumter National Forest that you reach. A short loop nature trail starts at the picnic area and goes for a half mile through typical oak-hickory woods with an understory of mountain laurel. While this is not a birding hot spot, you will be able to find many of the common species of Blue Ridge oak-hickory forest. Elevation here is about 1,600 feet above sea level.

To continue the tour, turn left (north) onto SC 28. In 2.0 miles you will come to an important fork in the road. To the left SC 28 continues north toward the Chattooga River, where it crosses into Georgia as GA 28. This part of northeastern Georgia is birdy and is well worth exploring. However, to continue the tour, bear right (northeast) onto SC 107.

About 2.5 miles north of SC 28 the tour (now on SC 107) reaches the main entrance to *Oconee State Park* (see Section B-37.5; letter F on Map B–37.1). Elevation here is about 1,800 feet above sea level. To continue the tour, keep on going north on SC 107.

About 3.6 miles north of the entrance to Oconee State Park you will reach a parking area for the Foothills Trail at the intersection with the *Tamassee Road (Forest Road 710)*, also known as Winding Stairs Road. (*Tamassee* is pronounced "tuhMAS-See.") Elevation at the upper end of Forest Road 710 is about 2,100 feet. (letter G on Map B–37.1).

Tamassee Road goes east, down the mountain to Cherokee Lake (1,200 feet elevation). It is a relatively quiet road down the side of the escarpment, offering excellent birding (see Section B-37.6). Even if you are not going down Tamassee Road, you may wish to explore the overgrown clear-cut area just south of Forest Road 710 and east of SC 107. In the breeding season you will find the usual Indigo Buntings, Common Yellowthroats, Yellow-breasted Chats, and other species common to clear-cuts anywhere in South Carolina. In migration this is a great area for migrant warblers and other species. And while no one has found Golden-winged Warblers breeding in South Carolina since 1890, brushy areas at relatively high altitudes, such as this one, are good places to look.

To continue the tour, go north on SC 107. About 2 miles north of the Tamassee Road you will reach Cherry Hill Campground (a developed Forest Service campground) on the right (east). About 0.2 mile north of Cherry Hill Campground is Moody Spring picnic area, on the left side of SC 107. Elevation here is about

2,300 feet. Common Ravens cruise this area, looking for a meal along the road or at the picnic grounds.

About a mile north of Moody Springs, look for a pulloff on the left (west) for a scenic vista of Ridley Mountain (elevation 2930; elevation at the scenic vista is about 2,700 feet). This vista (or its companion vista, which is about a half mile farther north on SC 107) is a great place to look for birds. Common breeding species at the vistas include Indigo Bunting, Scarlet Tanager, Hooded, Worm-eating, and Black-and-white Warblers, and Common Yellowthroat. These brushy areas are too low in elevation to attract breeding Chestnut-sided or Canada Warblers, but these are common in migration.

About 0.2 mile north of the first scenic vista look for a side road on the left (west). This is Forest Road 708, which descends to *Burrell's Ford* on the Chattooga River within about two miles of SC 107 (see Section B-37.7; letter H on Map B–37.1).

To continue the tour, go north on SC 107 from Burrell's Ford Road. You will pass a scenic view on the right in about 0.2 mile and reach a picnic area on the right in about a half mile. This is Burrell's Place Wayside Picnic Area. Elevation here is about 2,800 feet.

Continue north on SC 107. About 1.5 miles north of Burrell's Ford Road (and about 10 miles north of the entrance road to Oconee State Park), you will come to the junction with Road 325 on the left (west). This road leads 1.8 miles down to the *Walhalla Fish Hatchery*, one of the best birding spots in Oconee County (see Section B-37.8; letter I on Map B–37.1). A visit to the fish hatchery is often the high point of the Oconee County mountain tour.

To continue the tour from the junction of SC 107 and Road 325, go north on SC 107 for 2.4 miles. Here you pass a paved road to the right, Road 413. Continue north on SC 107 for another 0.2 mile. Here you will reach *Sloan Bridge Picnic Ground* (letter J on Map B–37.1) on the left. From this parking area you can explore the Foothills Trail along Jack's Creek all the way to the North Carolina state line, which is 0.8 mile farther by road.

When you are done at Sloan Bridge, turn around and backtrack for 0.2 mile to Road 413, which goes down Chattooga Ridge for 2.3 miles to SC 130. There is a good overlook near the beginning of Road 413, near the top of the mountain, and an interesting beaver pond at the bottom of the hill, just before you get to SC 130. Check this area carefully in migration, since Willow Flycatchers have been reported from Oconee County beaver ponds in May.

When you get to SC 130, you have a choice. You can turn left (north) and enter North Carolina in 0.7 mile. About a half mile into North Carolina you will reach *Upper Whitewater Falls* in the Nantahala National Forest (letter K on Map B–37.1). Here you can hike downhill on the Foothills Trail back into South Carolina to view Lower Whitewater Falls. If you do not go to Upper Whitewater Falls, from Road 413 turn right (south) onto SC 130, which will get you back to SC 11 at Salem in about 10 miles. This is the end of the Oconee mountains tour.

B–37.4—Stumphouse Tunnel and Issaqueena Falls

Winter   *
Spring   **
Summer *
Fall   **

See letter D on Map B–37.1.

In the 1850s the Blue Ridge Railroad Company had a grand plan for a railroad to connect South Carolina with Knoxville, Tennessee. The plan called for a mile-long tunnel through Stumphouse Mountain. A tunnel was begun and 4,363 feet later abandoned. The tunnel to nowhere is now one of two main attractions at Stumphouse Tunnel Park, the other being Issaqueena Falls, a 220-foot waterfall.

Stumphouse Tunnel Park is operated by the Pendleton District Historical and Recreational Commission, is open during daylight hours, and has free admission.

The birds here are those typical of low altitude Blue Ridge cove hardwood forests and rhododendron thickets. With luck you may find a Swainson's Warbler along the creek, but you will probably have to settle for the usual cardinals and chickadees.

B–37.5—Oconee State Park

Winter   *
Spring   ***
Summer **
Fall   ***

See letter F on Map B–37.1.

Oconee State Park, with 1,165 acres of pine-oak forest and two small lakes, is one of the oldest and most popular units of the South Carolina state park system. From spring through fall the park is crowded with campers and picnickers, especially on the weekends. The park also has a restaurant and cabins for rent.

Oconee State Park is a good place to take a hike into the woods, where you will find most of the species of Blue Ridge foothills pine-oak forests, including species such as Ruffed Grouse (year-round) or Black-throated Green Warbler (April through October). You can hike for an hour, a day, or a week (since the park is at the western end of the hundred-mile-long Foothills Trail).

For a short hike that will give you a taste of the park, try the Wormy Chestnut Nature Trail. Enter the park on the main entrance road. Soon after passing the fee station you will reach a Y-junction. Keep left at this split. In a few yards you will

pass the parking lot for the restaurant and the bath house, on the right. At 0.6 mile from the Y-junction you will reach a small parking lot on the left side of the road. Park here and follow the marked nature trail around a quarter-mile loop. There is an old pond along this trail, now overgrown into an alder swamp. This swamp is fairly good for common birds, including Worm-eating Warbler (late April through August).

For a good half-day hike, try the Tamassee Knob Trail, which leads for about 2.1 miles to Tamassee Knob, an 1,800-foot high mountain with good views to the south and north. To reach the Tamassee Knob Trail, return to the main Y-junction near the beginning of the main park road, and go 0.5 mile to the western terminus of the Foothills Trail, on the left side of the road. (There is no formal parking lot here, but you can usually find a place to park along the side of the road.)

Follow the Foothills Trail north for 0.4 mile. Here the white-blazed Foothills Trail continues north, while the rust-blazed Tamassee Knob Trail turns right (east). Follow the rust blazes for another 1.7 miles to an overlook on Tamassee Knob, a low peak that juts out eastward from the main north-south ridge. From the overlook there is a good view northward over the valley of Tamassee Creek. On a good day you can see the line of Chattooga Ridge all the way to the North Carolina border.

The trail to Tamassee Knob is an out-and-back trip. Return to Oconee State Park by backtracking. Along the way you will go through northern-pine—oak forest on the drier ridge top and well developed cove hardwoods on the slopes.

B–37.6—Tamassee Road and Tamassee Creek

Winter   *
Spring   ***
Summer **
Fall   ***

See letter G on Map B–37.1.

In about three miles, starting from SC 107, Forest Road 710 (Tamassee Road or Winding Stairs Road), a well-maintained unpaved road, winds down the Chattooga Ridge escarpment from SC 107 (elevation 2,100 feet) to the Lake Cherokee development (elevation 1,100 feet). The road passes through excellent cove hardwoods and pine-oak habitats with lots of breeding birds. The best time of year to try the Tamassee Road is late April or early May, when you will find many migrant warblers, vireos, and thrushes along the way.

At the bottom of the hill you will leave the Sumter National Forest and reach a T-junction with the road around the west side of Lake Cherokee (labeled on some maps "Lake Isaquenna"). Turn right at the T-junction, and follow the road around the lake. This is private property, so do not leave the roadside. There are a couple of places where you can stop and overlook the lake from the roadside. Expect a few ducks or a Common Loon during migration or winter.

Follow the lakeside road (a good paved road) southeast. At about two miles from the end of the Tamassee Road look for Forest Road 715-A on the right (southwest). Turn right and go about a half mile to Tamassee Creek. Park on the right, just before the bridge.

This portion of Tamassee Creek runs through an attractive cove hardwood forest which has been partially cleared for wildlife. This is part of the Sumter National Forest and is a great place for birds and wildflowers from April through September.

Just downstream from the bridge over Tamassee Creek is a beaver pond where the Willow Flycatcher has been found in May. After looking over the beaver pond, follow the horse trails upstream through the wildlife clearings and cove hardwood forests along the creek. This is an outstanding area for migrants in early May.

After exploring Tamassee Creek, return to the paved road. Here you have a choice. If you wish to return to the mountains, retrace your route back up the hill, up Tamassee Road to SC 107.

To leave the mountains and go east to SC 11, turn right. You will reach a stop sign in a bit more than a mile. Here turn left onto Road 95. Follow Road 95 northeast for a mile to a stop sign at Road 375. Turn right (south) onto Road 375, and go 1.1 miles to yet another stop sign. Here turn right onto Road 172, and go 1.4 miles to SC 11 in the community of Tamassee, about 6 miles north of Walhalla.

B–37.7—Burrell's Ford and the Chattooga River

Winter   *
Spring   ***
Summer **
Fall   ***

See letter H on Map B–37.1.

The Chattooga River begins in the high mountains of southwestern North Carolina and flows for about fifty miles until it reaches Tugaloo Lake. It leaves North Carolina at Ellicott Rock and then is the South Carolina–Georgia border for about thirty-five miles. The river is famous for whitewater canoeing and rafting, and also for trout fishing. It has been designated a National Wild and Scenic River.

The Chattooga River offers some of the best birding in South Carolina. It is not high—the river drops from about 2,200 feet at Ellicott Rock to about 900 feet at Tugaloo Lake—but the falling water in the deep gorge keeps the forests along the river much cooler than you might expect for such a relatively low elevation. The result is that from Burrell's Ford (elevation 2,000 feet) upstream to Ellicott Rock there is a five-mile stretch of the river that has an extensive forest of eastern hemlock and white pine, mixed in with cove hardwoods and rhododendron thickets. This cool coniferous forest provides breeding habitat for bird species that you would ordinarily expect at much higher altitudes (or much farther north): Red-breasted Nuthatch, Golden-crowned Kinglet, and perhaps Red Crossbill.

An excellent network of hiking trails provides access to this part of the Chat-

tooga River, which is part of the Ellicott Rock Wilderness Area of Sumter National Forest. The trailhead is at the Burrell's Ford parking lot. This parking lot is 2.6 miles down Forest Road 708 from SC 107. Note that the parking lot is 0.2 mile before you get to the bridge over the river.

To explore this area, try the following half-day hike: From the parking lot cross the road, and go north on the Foothills Trail (white blazes). The trail winds up the mountain by easy switchbacks. At 0.6 mile from the parking lot turn left onto the Chattooga Trail (black blazes). Follow the Chattooga Trail until it reaches a relatively flat area near the river at about 1.7 miles from the parking lot. Here turn left and follow an unnamed spur trail downstream along the edge of the river. You will return to Forest Road 708 in 0.8 mile. When you get to the road, turn left and go 0.2 mile uphill to the parking lot.

This 2.7-mile loop can be easily extended by following the black-blazed Chattooga Trail upstream from the point where you reach the unnamed return trail instead of going back immediately. The Chattooga Trail reaches the East Fork of the Chattooga River in another 1.0 mile, and it reaches Ellicott Rock in 2.7 miles, so you can easily add 2.0 miles or 5.2 miles to your hike. All of these trails are rated easy.

B–37.8—The Walhalla Fish Hatchery

Winter   *
Spring   ****
Summer **
Fall   ***

See letter I on Map B–37.1.

There are three good areas in which to look for birds of the middle elevations of

the Southern Appalachian Mountains in South Carolina: Caesar's Head State Park in Greenville County (see Section B-23.1), Sassafras Mountain in Pickens County (see Section B-39.1), and the *Walhalla Fish Hatchery* of Oconee County. From SC 107, Road 325 to the hatchery and a U.S. Forest Service picnic ground winds 1.8 miles at elevations from 3,000 feet down to 2,500 feet. Along the way you will pass through a mature cove hardwoods forest with an understory of mountain laurel.

To explore this forest a bit more closely, park at the Foothills Trail parking area (about 0.3 mile on Road 325 from SC 107), and walk a bit in either direction along the Foothills Trail. In May or June you will be able to find most of the common breeding birds of Blue Ridge cove hardwoods along this trail. Black-throated Blue Warblers are especially common here, closely followed in numbers by Black-and-White Warblers, Hooded Warblers, Worm-eating Warblers, Ovenbirds, and others. Be alert for a rarity such as a Canada, Cerulean, or Blackburnian Warbler, or a Rose-breasted Grosbeak.

The road to the fish hatchery is great for birds, especially in spring migration, but there are not too many spots where you can safely pull off, since the shoulder is quite narrow. One good spot to explore is just before you get to a small bridge (the bridge over the East Fork of the Chattooga River). Park and explore the area to the right (upstream of the bridge). About a hundred yards from the road is a small pond surrounded by beautiful white pines. This area around this pond is great for birds. Look for Black-throated Blue Warblers in the rhododendron thickets and Red-breasted

Nuthatch in the pines. Least Flycatcher has been seen in spring migration and should be looked for as a breeding species in late May or June. Least Flycatchers have not yet been found breeding in South Carolina but may appear here. Other high-mountain species to look for include Red Crossbill (especially from August through November) and Common Raven.

Continue down the road to the picnic area. Here be alert for species such as Golden-crowned Kinglet (in the ornamental spruce trees near the entrance to the fish hatchery), Black-throated Green Warbler (common in hemlocks), Cerulean Warbler (rare), and Red-breasted Nuthatch (uncommon; in hemlocks).

Although the Walhalla Fish Hatchery is only 2,500 feet above sea level, it lies in the gorge of the East Fork of the Chattooga River. The river helps keep this area cooler in summer than you might expect, which encourages high-mountain bird species.

Along the East Fork of the Chattooga is a beautiful forest of eastern hemlock and white pine with an understory of rhododendron and mountain laurel. To explore this forest, hike a bit on the East Fork Trail. This trail begins at the picnic ground and follows the river downhill for 2.5 miles, where it joins the Chattooga Trail near the point where the East Fork flows into the main branch of the Chattooga River (see Section B-37.6). This is a birdy trail, although you might have a bit of trouble hearing the birds above the roar of the river.

B–37.9—Oconee Station

Winter	*
Spring	**
Summer	*
Fall	**

Oconee Station State Park is a small historical park which preserves a fortified trading post built in 1760. The park is undeveloped but is known among South Carolina naturalists as the trailhead for

the Station Falls Trail, a one-mile trail to the falls on Station Creek. This easy trail goes through one of the most beautiful cove hardwood forests in the state. From mid-March through early May the rich woods harbor an amazing display of wildflowers. The waterfalls themselves provide a cool, moist habitat for many unusual plants, including the rare walking fern.

Along the trail you can find most of the birds of the cove hardwood forest, including many woodpeckers, White-breasted Nuthatches, Wood Thrushes, Black-throated Green Warblers, Louisiana Waterthrushes, and many others.

To reach the trailhead, go to the intersection of SC 11 and SC 183 just north of the town of Walhalla. Here go north on SC 11 for 2.1 miles, where you will find the intersection with Road 95. (There should be a sign for Oconee Station State Park at this intersection.) Turn left (northwest) onto Road 95, and go another 2.1 miles to the old trading post on your right (east). Continue north past the old trading post for another three hundred yards or so until you see a pulloff on your left (west). Park here and follow the trail into the woods. You will reach Station Falls in less than a mile of relatively easy walking.

B–38—ORANGEBURG COUNTY

Many visitors to South Carolina pass through Orangeburg County, because the intersection of two busy interstate highways—I-95 and I-26—is in the southeastern part of this large, predominately rural county. Lake Marion forms its northern border and offers some of the best birding in the county at Santee State Park and in the Eutaw Springs area. The North Edisto River and South Edisto River flow through the county, providing further birding opportunities.

B–38.1—Santee State Park

Winter   **
Spring   **
Summer *
Fall   **

See letter G on Map B–9.2 (p. 48).

Santee State Park is a large (2,364-acre) park on the south shore of Lake Marion. Though best known for its fishing and camping, the park offers fairly good birding year-round, either from the lakeshore or along one of three nature trails.

To reach the park from I-95, leave the highway at Exit 98 (Santee), and follow SC 6 west for 1.2 miles. Here turn right onto Road 105. In another 2.4 miles Road 105 reaches a stop sign at the main park intersection. If you continue straight ahead, the road becomes Road 82, which leads to the western end of the park. If you turn hard to the right instead, this road leads to the east end of the park. To continue on Road 105 out of the park and toward the town of Elloree, turn to the left. (This route is described in Section B-9.2, Calhoun County farmlands tour; see Map B–9.2.)

Most of the developed part of Santee State Park is in the western section of the park, which is open year-round. This is the area for the cabins, a restaurant, fishing pier, tackle shop, boat launch ramp, and campground. The one-mile-long Oak Pinolly Nature Trail is in this area. The eastern end of the park is open to cars in the summer and has a campground, boat ramp, picnic area, swimming area, and two nature trails, the Limestone Nature Trail and the Lakeshore Nature Trail.

The Oak Pinolly Nature Trail is a one-mile loop trail through a mature oak-hickory-pine woods. The trailhead is in the picnic area in the west end, near the tennis courts. This trail winds through rather ordinary open woods, where you might see a few birds typical of oak-pine woodlands. The best birding, however, is probably from the fishing pier. Here you overlook a wide expanse of Lake Marion. This view is best in winter, when there are numerous cormorants and gulls as well as a few Common Loons and ducks. During the warmer parts of the year keep an eye out for Great Egret, Osprey, and Anhinga. In summer a few Laughing Gulls come up from the coast, even though this spot is sixty miles inland. A Bald Eagle is possible any time but most likely in winter.

The eastern end of the park is less developed and offers better birding. In winter the road to the eastern end is gated, but you can still walk in. It is about a mile from the gate to the picnic grounds at the east end of the park.

The east-end picnic grounds are a great place for woodpeckers. The open pine-oak woods attract all the species of woodpeckers you can find in South Carolina. A few Red-cockaded Woodpeckers still occur here. Look for a well-marked Red-cockaded Woodpecker breeding area just beyond the turnoff for the east-end campground. Currently the woodpeckers are using cavity trees a few hundred yards farther on, closer to the campground.

The east-end picnic grounds are the trailhead for the Limestone Nature Trail. This 1.5-mile loop trail is the best of the three nature trails in the park for birding. The trail leads along the edge of a creek (an arm of the lake, really), then crosses the

creek on a boardwalk. Then the trail winds through a mature southern mixed-hardwoods forest and loops back to the picnic ground. This is a good place to find most species of the southern mixed hardwoods. Fall is the best season for birding here, since many migrant warblers occur in September and October. Early spring is good for wildflowers. This is an especially good area for viewing the flowers of the red buckeye (*Aesculus pavia*) in March and early April.

The unpaved road to the east-end campground turns off from the paved road to the east-end picnic area. At the eastern end of this campground is the trailhead for the 1.5-mile Lakeshore Nature Trail, which runs through a rather ordinary southern pine—oak forest. This trail is not a loop trail—you must backtrack to the trailhead. Birding along this trail is unexceptional, except that you will be near the lakeshore. Scanning the lake might turn up something of interest.

The park woods harbor many owls—mostly Great Horned and Eastern Screech-Owls, but also a few Barred Owls. Camping here (or staying in the cabins) will give you a chance to hear Great Horned Owls calling, especially in winter and early spring. Eastern Screech-Owls call year-round, but especially in late summer and fall. From March through September the owls are joined by a chorus of Chuck-will's-widows (and perhaps a Whip-poor-will or two). These night birds are often heard, but seldom seen. You may luck upon an owl in daytime along one of the trails, especially in winter and early spring.

B–38.2—Eutaw Springs

Winter	**
Spring	**
Summer	*
Fall	**

Eutaw Springs is a small community on the south shore of Lake Marion, in eastern Orangeburg County. From I-95 exit at Exit 98, and go 9 miles southeast on SC 6

to the intersection with SC 45 in Eutawville. Here turn left, keeping on SC 6, and go another 2.5 miles to the *Eutaw Springs battlefield memorial*, on the north (left) side of the road, at the intersection with Road 137. Eutaw Springs battlefield was the site of the last major battle of the American Revolution in South Carolina, on September 8, 1781. Birders will find the memorial grounds of interest as a breeding area for American Robins, a scarce breeder so close to the Lower Coastal Plain.

From the battlefield memorial turn left (northeast) onto Road 137. Within a quarter mile you will reach an area with water on both sides of the road. The water on the left is a backwater of Lake Marion; that on the right is a shallow pond cut off from the big lake by the road. This is a good area for herons and egrets in summer and a few ducks in winter. Mallards and Wood Ducks breed here.

About 0.3 mile from SC 6 look for an unpaved county road off to the left toward Lake Marion. This is Ferguson Landing Road, which leads to the lakeshore in about a mile. About a half mile down Ferguson Landing Road is the entrance to *Santee-Cooper Wildlife Management Area*. This area is an important deer- and duck-hunting area. It is closed to casual entry between October 1 and March 1. From April through September it is a good birding area very similar to parts of Santee National Wildlife Refuge (see Section B-14, Clarendon County).

To explore the wildlife management area, turn left off of Ferguson Landing Road onto a service road at the management area sign about a quarter mile in from Road 137. After a quarter mile on the service road you will reach a junction, near an equipment shed. Here keep to the left, and go another half mile to the end of the service road. Park and explore the dikes and sloughs on foot.

Santee-Cooper Wildlife Management Area is almost never birded, so you might turn up something good overlooked by the crowd. More likely are the usual species of Upper Coastal Plain freshwater marshes and ponds. This is an excellent area for herons, egrets, and Wood Ducks. Bobolinks are common in late April and early May. September brings a wide variety of migrant land birds. Be prepared for heat, humidity, insects, and chiggers.

After exploring Santee-Cooper Wildlife Management Area and Ferguson Landing Road, return to Road 137, and turn left. Go about 0.5 mile on Road 137 to the intersection with Road 139 (unpaved). Here turn right (east) onto Road 139, and follow it to its end in about 3 miles. This road is a county lane through oak-hickory woods and farm country. It is very lightly traveled and so is a good birding road, especially in the fall or winter. At the end of Road 139 turn right to return to SC 6 at a point some 3.1 miles east of the Eutaw Springs battleground.

B–38.3—Orangeburg National Fish Hatchery

Winter   *
Spring   **
Summer   *
Fall   **

The *Orangeburg National Fish Hatchery* headquarters area is just south of the city of Orangeburg. This part of the hatchery has a small aquarium and a picnic ground (open Monday through Friday, 9 A.M. to 4 P.M.—closed on federal holidays). To reach this area, go to the intersection of US 310 and SC 4 on the south side of the city of Orangeburg. If you are southbound on US 301 in the city of Orange-

burg, you will reach SC 4 on your left just before you reach the entrance to Edisto Gardens on your right. (If you cross over the North Edisto River, you have gone too far.) Turn left (south) onto SC 4, and follow it for about 1.6 miles to the entrance to the headquarters area of the fish hatchery.

There may be a few herons at the ponds

by the headquarters, but the best birding is in another unit of the hatchery, several miles away. To reach the *Hundred Acre Pond* portion of the hatchery, leave the city of Orangeburg on US 301 southbound. About 0.3 mile after you cross over the North Edisto River, turn left (south) onto Road 49. Go south on Road 49 for 4.0 miles to the entrance to the fish hatchery on your right (west). An unpaved road leads past several hatchery pools and ends at a boat launch area on the shore of Hundred Acre Pond. This pond is covered mostly by water lotus and other aquatic vegetation. Birds found year-round here include a variety of herons and egrets, Anhingas, Wood Ducks, and Common Moorhens. The pond is easily scanned from the parking lot or from the rough angler's trails along the bank. Keep an eye out for reptiles as well, including alligators and snakes.

B–38.4—The Orangeburg Sod Farms

Winter   *
Spring   **
Summer   ***
Fall   ***

Sod farms along Interstate 26 a few miles east of the city of Orangeburg offer birders the chance to look for rare shorebirds during migration as well as permanently resident Horned Larks. From late March through early May and again during August and September you might be lucky enough to find here a Pectoral Sandpiper, Upland Sandpiper, Lesser Golden-Plover, or some other good shorebird species. Up to eight Buff-breasted Sandpipers were in this area in September 1991.

To reach the main part of the sod farms, leave I-26 at Exit 154, and follow US 301 southwest toward the city of Orangeburg. At 0.5 mile from the interstate look for the office of the Supersod Company on the left (south) side of US 301. If the office is open, stop by and ask for permission to bird on the sod farm. Birders are welcome, but please stay well away from farm activities, and stay on the roads or on well-sodded areas. Please stay off any bare area. The best time to visit the sod farms is on the weekends (especially Sunday), when there is less human activity and more birds. The best birding is often along the private road that starts behind the office (Supersod Boulevard).

In addition to the main sod farms west of I-26, there are smaller areas on the other side of I-26 which also attract good birds. Return to US 301, and follow it northeast toward Santee. At 0.9 mile from the interstate turn right (south) onto Road 196. (There may be a sign at this turn for Pioneer Equipment Company, a farm equipment supplier.) Follow Road 196 south back toward I-26. Soon after passing the Pioneer Equipment Company sales lot, you will begin passing a sod farm.

Road 196 crosses over I-26 (no interchange), but do not cross over the interstate. Instead, turn left onto the paved perimeter road just before the bridge over the interstate. Follow the perimeter road east. In less than a mile you will reach "Road Ends" signs. But at the end of the paved perimeter road you will find the beginning of an unpaved road, Orangeburg County Road 4226. Follow this good sand road as it winds through another mile of sod farms. Here it is easy to scan the fields from the roadside, searching for shorebirds, Horned Larks, and migrant swallows.

At 3.6 miles from I-26 the unpaved road ends at Road 36 (a state-maintained paved road). To return to I-26, turn right onto Road 36, which reaches Exit 159 in 3.2 miles. To return to US 301, turn left onto Road 36.

B–39—PICKENS COUNTY

Pickens county is one of three mountain counties of South Carolina (along with Oconee County to the west and Greenville County to the east). The northern third of Pickens County is in the Blue Ridge region, a part of the southern Appalachian mountains, while the remainder of the county lies in the Piedmont.

The most exciting birding in the county is in the mountains, especially since Sassafras Mountain, the highest point in the state, lies on the North Carolina line in northern Pickens County. In the southwestern part of the county is the delightful university town of Clemson, seat of Clemson University, which has had a strong graduate program in ornithology for years. For this reason the good bird-ing spots near Clemson area are quite well known and include good Piedmont habitats in nearby Anderson and Oconee counties as well as in Pickens county.

The best way for a traveler to get a feeling for the South Carolina mountains is to spend a day or two driving along SC 11, the Cherokee Foothills Scenic Highway, taking side trips along the way. This highway runs roughly at the foot of the mountains from I-85 at the Georgia border, then east to I-26, and then on to Exit 92 of I-85 near the North Carolina border. SC 11 runs through northern Pickens county and will be the baseline for our description of most of the birding areas of the county.

B–39.1—Sassafras Mountain

Winter	*
Spring	****
Summer	***
Fall	****

See Map B–39.1.

At 3,548 feet above sea level the top of *Sassafras Mountain* is the highest point in South Carolina. It is not surprising, then, that Sassafras Mountain offers some of the best birding in the state during the warm part of the year. The area is good in migration and is—along with Caesar's Head State Park in Greenville County (see Section B-23.1) and the Walhalla Fish Hatchery area in Oconee County (see Section B-37.8)—one of the best areas in South Carolina in which to find many of the typical breeding species of the middle altitudes of the southern Appalachian Mountains. Above 3,000 feet on Sassafras Mountain you might find breeding species such as Ruffed Grouse, Common Raven, Black-throated Blue Warbler, Chestnut-sided Warbler, and Dark-eyed Junco. Other mountain species, such as Worm-eating Warbler and Solitary Vireo, are quite common on Sassafras, and there is always the chance of finding a first or second breeding record for the state. Species such as Least Flycatcher, Veery, Golden-winged Warbler, and Rose-breasted Grosbeak have not been known to breed in South Carolina (or are very rare breeders); if any of these are found breeding in the state, it will probably be on Sassafras Mountain or some nearby peak.

Our tour of Sassafras Mountain begins at the *intersection of US 178 and SC 11* (letter A on Map B–39.1), in Piedmont habitat at the foot of the mountains. Go north on US 178. You will soon leave the farm country and begin following a mountain stream (the upper Oolenoy River) up the hill. There are few places to pull off along US 178, so when you see a good pulloff, you should use it.

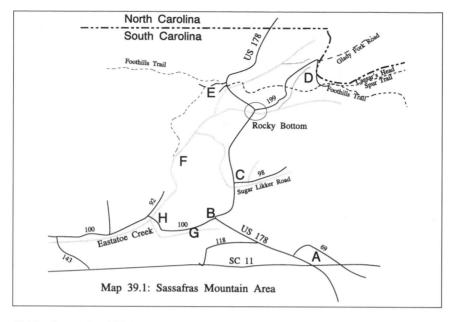

Map 39.1: Sassafras Mountain Area

At 4.3 miles north of SC 11 you will reach a divide, where you will leave the Oolenoy River and begin traveling through lands drained by Eastatoe Creek (pronounced "eestuhTOEwee"). There is a country store here (letter B on Map B-39.1) and also a road to the left (Road 100). This is the beginning of the *lower Eastatoe Creek* tour (see Section B-39.3).

After passing Road 100, the Sassafras Mountain tour continues north on US 178, quickly gaining altitude, though still under 2,000 feet. In 1.6 miles you will reach another side road, *Road 98*, Sugar Likker Road, on the right (letter C on Map B-39.1). Sugar Likker Road goes about a mile up a small creek through a heavily wooded area. Since this is a dead-end road, there is little traffic and may be worth a quick side trip. Cerulean Warblers have been found here in July and may breed. There is a slight chance of Swainson's Warbler here, but beware; Hooded Warbler and Louisiana Waterthrush are both common here and have songs which sound a lot like that of the Swainson's Warbler.

Once back on US 178, continue north up

the hill. You will pass Camp McCall, a Baptist boys' camp, on the left. A mile or so up US 178 from Camp McCall you will reach a good pulloff on the left by some trash containers. Here you will have a chance to listen to the songs of typical breeding birds such as Black-and-white Warbler, Hooded Warbler, and Black-throated Green Warbler. There is usually a Swainson's Warbler or two along the creek here. In fact the Swainson's Warbler is fairly common along the rest of US 178 from the trash containers all the way north to the North Carolina border and beyond.

When you reach the community of Rocky Bottom (7.4 miles north of SC 11 on US 178), turn right (northeast) onto Road 199, also known as the *F. Van Clayton Memorial Highway* (letter D on Map B-39.1), which goes from Rocky Bottom store (elevation 1,750 feet) to the parking lot near the top of Sassafras Mountain (elevation 3,500 feet). Along the way you will pass through some of the best and most accessible birding areas in the South Carolina mountains. Road 199 goes for 4.8 miles from US 178 to the top of Sassafras. Most of the land here is owned by the

Duke Power Company and is open to the public, but be sure to observe any "No Trespassing" signs you may find and to stay clear of logging operations.

A mile or so up the hill from Rocky Bottom store you will reach Chimneytop Gap (elevation 2,400 feet), where the Foothill Trail crosses Road 199. There is a parking area for trail hikers just over the crest of the gap. This is a great area to explore on foot.

A mile up the road from Chimneytop Gap there is a clearing with an old house site on the left. The creek here is good for breeding Swainson's Warbler. From here the road up the mountain becomes much steeper. At three miles from US 178 the road reaches another gap. This is the Tennessee Valley Divide and also the North Carolina state line. A gravel road (Glady Fork Road) continues straight ahead into Transylvania County, North Carolina. (Glady Fork Road is good for breeding Swainson's Warblers.) To stay in South Carolina, keep right on the paved road. The elevation here is 2,800 feet. For the next mile the road follows the state line as it ascends the western flank of Sassafras Mountain. From here to the top of the mountain you will have the best chance of finding the high-elevation breeding bird species such as Ruffed Grouse, Common Raven, Chestnut-sided Warbler, and Dark-eyed Junco.

Once you reach the parking lot near the top, you can easily explore the South Carolina "high country" by hiking east or west on the well-marked Foothills Trail. The following loop hike takes about an hour: From the parking lot follow the Foothills Trail uphill to the top of Sassafras

Mountain. Keep on the Foothills Trail as it descends the west side of the mountain, reaching Road 199 in 0.4 mile. Here leave the trail, and follow the paved road left back to the parking lot. This loop trail is excellent for mountain birds.

Two trails go east from the parking lot; the main branch of the Foothills Trail leads to Table Rock State Park, and a spur of the Foothills Trail goes to Caesar's Head State Park. The main branch starts a few yards downhill along the paved road from the spur trail. For a good half-day hike follow the main branch of the Foothills Trail southeast from the Sassafras Mountain parking lot. The first two miles or so of the trail here are nearly level and over 3,200 feet elevation. This is a fairly easy way to get into the highest mountain country in South Carolina. At about 1.8 miles from the parking lot you will reach Hickorynut Gap. Here the trail cuts sharply to the left and starts steeply downhill. This is a good point to turn around.

The Foothills Trail to Hickorynut Gap leads through a good variety of forest types: northern pine—oak forest, cove hardwoods, and rhododendron thickets. Look for Blackburnian Warblers in the pitch pines. They have been found in summer and may breed here. This is also a good area for Ruffed Grouse, especially in March or early April.

Once you have finished with the top of Sassafras Mountain, retrace your route back to Rocky Bottom store, on US 178. This is the starting point of the tour of the Eastatoe Creek Heritage Preserve (see Section B-39.2).

B–39.2—Eastatoe Creek Heritage Preserve

Winter   *
Spring   **
Summer **
Fall   **

See letters E and F on Map B–39.1.

Eastatoe Creek begins at the Tennessee Divide (near the North Carolina border just uphill from the community of Rocky Bottom) and then descends over 1,000 feet in seven miles to farmlands at the foot of the mountains. About five miles of this pristine mountain stream have been protected by the Nature Conservancy and the State of South Carolina in *Eastatoe Creek Heritage Preserve* (373 acres). The gorge of Eastatoe Creek is a wild and wonderful place, difficult to reach and seldom visited. It is the only North American station for the Tunbridge filmy fern, *Hymenophyllum tunbrigense*, a fern of the South American mountains.

Birding is good along the trail to Eastatoe Creek gorge. During the breeding season the Worm-eating Warbler is especially common, but bear in mind that a visit to the gorge is fairly difficult, more of a wilderness experience than a casual stroll.

To reach the preserve, go to the community of Rocky Bottom on US 178 just south of the North Carolina border (see Section B-39.1). Instead of turning off of US 178 to follow the road up Sassafras Mountain, continue north on US 178 for another 0.9 mile. Here you will reach Road 237 on the left, a short spur road to a small mountain motel and restaurant (Laurel Valley Lodge). Turn left onto Road 237, and then immediately turn right onto an unpaved road, Laurel Fork Road. Follow Laurel Fork Road for about 0.3 mile to a parking lot for the Foothills Trail (letter E on Map B–39.1). Park here and continue along the road (not the Foothills Trail). At about 0.2 mile from the parking lot you will reach the Eastatoe Gorge Trail on your left (south).

Follow the trail south for about 1.5 miles through a large clear-cut area. Eventually you will reenter the woods and reach the edge of the Heritage Preserve (letter F on Map B–39.1). Here the trail turns sharply right and follows an old logging road for a few hundred yards. This part of the trail is easy, but soon you will get to the place where the trail descends steeply into the gorge of Eastatoe Creek. In about another mile the trail reaches the creek, though you might not go that far. The habitat here is rather different from anyplace else in South Carolina— rugged and mountainous but at the same time dark from the shade of giant trees and humid. The soft sandstone here is easily eroded, creating a wonderland of cliffs, grottoes and ravines. You might not find many birds here, but the experience of being a part of this eery place is worth the effort of visiting it.

B–39.3—Lower Eastatoe Creek

Winter   *
Spring   **
Summer **
Fall   **

See letters G and H on Map B–39.1.

Once Eastatoe Creek emerges from its gorge (see Section B-39.2), it is joined by other streams and forms a beautiful mountain cove at about 1,000 feet above sea level. This portion of the Eastatoe Creek valley is mostly farmland; pastures, small cultivated fields, hedgerows, and small woodlots. This is a delightful place to look for birds, especially during spring and fall migration.

To reach this area from the intersection of SC 11 and US 178, go northwest (uphill) on US 178 for 3.3 miles to the junction with Road 100. Here turn left (west) onto Road 100, which immediately starts to descend steeply. At about 0.4 mile downhill from US 178 look for an informal pulloff on the left shoulder of the road. This is the place to park for a small waterfall (letter G on Map B–39.1), a lovely mountain cascade that begins just below the pulloff. The habitat here is typical of Blue Ridge foothills cove-hardwoods forest, with quite a few eastern hemlocks and white pines and an understory of rhododendron. Typical breeding birds here include Black-throated Green Warblers and American Redstarts.

After overlooking the waterfall, continue down the hill on Road 100. In a bit more than a mile you will reach the valley floor and emerge into the farmlands. by the *bridge over Eastatoe Creek* (letter H on Map B–39.1) at about 1.7 miles from US 178. The roadside hedgerows here are great for birds, especially in migration. This is a good spot for species of farmlands in the Blue Ridge foothills.

Turn left at the T-junction at 2.0 miles from US 178, keeping on Road 100. In another 3.3 miles you will reach a Y-junction. Here turn left (south) onto Road 143. Follow Road 143 for 2.5 miles to return to SC 11 at a point 4.9 miles west of US 178 or 3.6 miles east of Keowee-Toxaway State Park (see Section B-39.4).

B–39.4—Keowee-Toxaway State Park

Winter	*
Spring	*
Summer	*
Fall	*

Keowee-Toxaway State Park is a thousand-acre park on the shores of Lake Keowee in the western part of Pickens County. SC 11 runs through the park about 8.5 miles west of US 178. The park has facilities for picnicking and camping as well as cabins for rent and a short trail that highlights the history of the Cherokee Indians.

This is a low-key park, a great place for a picnic or for camping. The habitat is Piedmont pine-oak forest. A good place to explore these woods is the picnic area on the south side of SC 11 in the center of the park, where you will find the Cherokee Interpretive Trail, a sort of outdoor

museum with exhibits again pertaining to the history of the Cherokee Indians.

Just west of the park, SC 11 crosses over Lake Keowee and enters Oconee County. To overlook the lake, stop at an informal pulloff just before you get to the bridge. Lake Keowee here is deep and clear—popular with scuba divers, but not attractive to birds. During the breeding season look for Barn Swallows breeding under the SC 11 bridge and Northern Rough-winged Swallows breeding along nearby cliffs. There may be a loon or duck during winter or migration. (For better birding spots on Lake Keowee, see Section B-37.)

B–39.5—Table Rock State Park

Winter   *
Spring   ***
Summer *
Fall   **

See letter G on Map B–23.1 (p. 113).

Table Rock is a huge granite monolith which rises from the Blue Ridge foothills at about 1,200 feet above sea level and reaches an elevation of 3,157 feet. Table Rock dominates the landscape for miles around and is the focus for *Table Rock State Park* (3,069 acres), one of the state's oldest and best-loved parks. The main entrance to the park is on SC 11 (4.4 miles east of US 178 or 4.7 miles west of US 276).

Trails in the park begin behind the nature center, which is on the main park road near the swimming area. Here you can hike the trail to the top of the mountain (7 miles round-trip, rated extremely strenuous), or you might opt for the moderate 1.8-mile loop nature trail, Carrick Creek Trail. This is an extremely popular trail, so plan to hike it early in the morning if you wish to avoid the crowds. The habitats along the trail include oak-hickory forest, cove-hardwood forest, and rhododendron thickets.

B–39.6—Pumkintown

Winter   *
Spring   **
Summer *
Fall   **

See letter H on Map B–23.1 (p. 113).

Pumkintown is a delightful area for many reasons besides its colorful name. For the birder it is an area of productive roadside birding, especially in the spring. The attractions are the birds of small farms and open country, and also one of the best wetlands in the Piedmont of South Carolina—the floodplain of the Oolenoy River, a tributary of the Saluda.

From the intersection of US 178 and SC 11 go east on SC 11 for just 0.8 mile. You will pass over the Oolenoy River (here hardly more than a creek). Immediately after the bridge look for Road 69 to the right (east). Follow Road 69, which parallels the river for 2.4 miles. A stop anywhere along here will yield most of the bird species of Piedmont farmlands, but stay on the roadside. This is all private property.

After a couple of miles of farmlands, Road 69 bends right (south) and goes through a wooded gap between two hills. The Oolenoy River is close to the road at this point. Stop here in spring or summer to find species of Piedmont streamsides such as Louisiana Waterthrush and Northern Parula.

At 2.4 miles from SC 11, Road 69 ends at SC 288. Here turn left (east) onto SC 288, and follow it for 3.5 miles to the crossroads in "downtown" Pumkintown, where SC 288 intersects SC 8. This stretch of SC 288 is birdy. The Yellow Warbler is common in spring and summer. Broad-winged Hawks breed on nearby forested hillsides. Goldfinches and Song Sparrows are to be seen year-round. The pines here are Virginia pines, giving the area the feel of the Piedmont of Maryland or northern Virginia. A species to keep an eye out for here is the Willow Flycatcher. This species has not yet been found breeding here, but this countryside is similar to its breeding areas in nearby parts of North Carolina.

When you get to SC 8 in Pumkintown, turn right (south) onto SC 8, and go about a third of a mile. You will cross the Oolenoy River, but there is no parking along this part of SC 8, because the shoulder is too narrow. Keep going until you reach a country store a few dozen yards south of the river. Park at the store, and retrace your route on foot. In early spring the Oolenoy River floods the fields along its northern bank here. This forms a transient marsh and mud flat area, which is attractive to migrant birds. Species to look for here in April or early May include Great Blue Heron, Green-backed Heron, Canada Goose, Wood Duck (breeds), Mallard, Blue-winged Teal, and many species of shorebirds. Common spring shorebirds here include Killdeer (breeds), Semipalmated Plovers, Greater Yellowlegs, Lesser Yellowlegs, Solitary Sandpipers, Spotted Sandpipers, Pectoral Sandpipers, and Common Snipes. If the fields have not completely dried up, you will find something good here.

This is the end of the Pumkintown tour. To return to SC 11, go north on SC 8 for about four miles.

B–39.7—Issaqueena

Winter	*
Spring	***
Summer	**
Fall	***

Just four miles north of the town of Clemson lies a portion of *Clemson University's experimental forest near Lake Issaqueena*, which offers great Piedmont woodland birding opportunities. To reach the area, start at the intersection of US 123 and SC 133, on the northern edge of the town of Clemson, and go north on SC 133. At 0.9 mile from US 123 you will pass the entrance for Twelve Mile Recreation Area, a Corps of Engineers picnic area on Twelve Mile Creek, an arm of Lake Hartwell. Continue north on SC 133. At 3.8 miles north of US 123 turn left onto Old Six Mile Road at Lawrence Chapel Church. (There is also a water tower at this intersection.) In just 0.1 mile turn right (west) at the entrance of Clemson Experimental Forest, Lake Issaqueena Area. Follow the gravel road into the preserve.

The main road leads past many side trails and gated roads, which invite you to hike a bit into the woods. At a half mile from the entrance you will reach a parking area for the Indian Creek Hiking Trail. At 1.1 miles is Willow Springs Picnic area.

At 1.6 miles from the entrance the road passes a marsh on the left and a road up the hill on the right. The marsh is a backwater of Lake Hartwell and may produce some interesting birds. Prothonotary Warblers sometimes breed here. The hill behind you has a great oak-hickory forest. Worm-eating Warblers breed in mountain laurel thickets on this hillside.

The gravel road winds for 4.3 miles past other picnic areas and good birding areas in Piedmont floodplain forest, cove-hardwood forest, and southern-pine—oak forest. This is a great area during migration. You might find twenty species of warblers in a few hours in early May.

The gravel road ends at Road 225. Here you can turn left (south). In 0.4 mile this road crosses the Seneca River and enters Oconee County, where it continues as Road 27. Go southwest on Road 27 for two miles to a T-junction at Road 1. Here you have a choice. If you turn left (east), you will soon rejoin US 123 just west of the town of Clemson. If you turn right (west) onto Road 1, you will reach SC 130 just one mile south of the Little River Dam on Lake Keowee. To visit Lake Keowee, turn right and follow the directions given in Section B-37.2.

B–40—RICHLAND COUNTY

Columbia, the capital of South Carolina, is near the center of the state at the junction of three major interstate highways (I-20, I-26, and I-77). The Columbia metropolitan area lies in two counties, Richland (covered here) and Lexington (see Section B-32).

Richland County is centrally located in terms of natural, as well as cultural, geography. It lies on the Fall Line—the eastern border of the Piedmont region. Here two major Piedmont rivers, the Broad and the Saluda, join to form the Congaree. At the southeastern corner of the county the Wateree River joins the Congaree to form the Santee River. One main stream flows more or less northwest to southeast through the county but has three different names: the *Broad*, the *Congaree*, and the *Santee*.

Richland County contains parts of three natural regions. The northwestern third of the county is in the Piedmont. This area of small farms, suburbs, loblolly-pine plantations, and oak-hickory-pine forests is quite similar to the Piedmont in Newberry County (see Section B-36). The central third of the county is in the Sandhills subregion of the Upper Coastal Plain. This includes most of the city of Columbia, the Fort Jackson military reservation, and some adjacent areas. The southeastern third of the county lies in the Upper Coastal Plain proper. This natural area is most evident along the Wateree and Congaree Rivers.

In each of the three natural regions in Richland County there is an important tract of public land where birders may get to know the some of the typical birds of those three regions. In the Piedmont portion of Richland County there is Harbison State Forest; in the Sandhills there is Sesquicentennial State Park; and in the Upper Coastal Plain there is the Congaree Swamp National Monument.

B–40.1—Harbison State Forest

Winter *
Spring **
Summer *
Fall **

Harbison State Forest consists of about two thousand acres of loblolly-pine woods and floodplain forest in the northwestern portion of Richland County. It is close enough to Columbia that it is surrounded by suburban housing developments and to be a convenient place for Columbia birders to enjoy typical Piedmont woods.

To reach Harbison State Forest from I-20, exit at the US 176 or Broad River Road exit (Exit 65), which is just one mile east of I-26. Go northwest on US 176 (Broad River Road) for 4.1 miles, passing the state forest headquarters on your right (east). Keep going on US 176 until you reach the turnoff for Road 674, Lost Creek Road.

Here turn right (east). Road 674 runs through the state forest for more than a mile.

Follow Road 674 (Lost Creek Road) for 1.1 miles from US 176. Here look for a gated logging road on your right (east). Park here (being careful not to block the gate), and follow the logging road on foot into the state forest.

The logging road goes for about a mile through typical loblolly pine-woods. Here and there you will find other species of pine, notably the longleaf pine (characteristic of the Coastal Plain) and the shortleaf pine (characteristic of the Piedmont). This overlapping of pines reminds us that we are at the southeastern edge of the Piedmont, almost in the Coastal Plain.

The birds of the first part of the trail are those species typical of Piedmont pine-oak forests. Do not expect rarities, but keep alert for species such as Red-breasted Nuthatch in winter and breeding Solitary Vireo in summer. Ovenbirds are uncommon breeders here.

After about a mile the logging road descends to the floodplain of the Broad River. This is the best area in the state forest for birding, especially in spring and fall migrations, since many migrants follow the river. The road ends at a wildlife clearing next to the river. The clearing is about fifty to a hundred yards wide and three hundred yards long, and it provides just the sort of opening in the woods which makes for good birding in the migrations for warblers, vireos, flycatchers, and other small birds. If you come here before dawn or at dusk in late winter or early spring, you will have a good chance of observing the display flight of the American Woodcock, which is an uncommon breeder here.

Follow the clearing to your left (upstream). It ends at Nicholas Creek. A major portion of the floodplain forest along Nicholas Creek lies within the state forest. There are no trails here, but it is possible to make your way up the south side of Nicholas Creek and into the floodplain forest. This is best done in winter, since from early spring through the fall this area is overrun by poison ivy. Wild Turkeys are rather common in this woods.

After exploring the floodplain and admiring the view of the Broad River, backtrack along the logging road to Road 674.

Back at Road 674 you can drive ahead for 1.5 miles to a bridge over Nicholas Creek, outside of the state forest. This area is especially good in spring migration for warblers. When you reach a T-junction at 2.7 miles from US 176, turn around and backtrack to US 176. Here you can backtrack to I-20, or you can turn right and go northwest to Exit 102 of I-26 in about 2.2 miles.

B–40.2—Riverbanks Park along the Saluda River

Winter	*
Spring	***
Summer	*
Fall	**

From the Saluda Dam at Lake Murray to the confluence of the Saluda and Broad Rivers to form the Congaree River in downtown Columbia, the lower Saluda River is one of South Carolina's most scenic. The Saluda has deep pools, rapids, and rocky shoals as the water flows by high bluffs as well as low floodplain woods. Most of the lower Saluda is in Lexington County (see Section B-32), but from the I-26 bridge downstream to the confluence with the Broad River, the river follows the county line, with the northeast bank in Richland County and the southwest bank in Lexington County.

Almost all of the Saluda in Richland

County is also within the city limits of the city of Columbia, but the river nevertheless maintains a wild aspect, with high bluffs, rocky shoals and rapids. Here you can see the falls in the Fall Line (the border between the Piedmont and the Coastal Plain). Fortunately there is excellent public access to this portion of the Saluda at *Riverbanks Park*.

Riverbanks Park is best known as the site of Columbia's Riverbanks Zoo, a delightful zoo well worth several visits a year. But the park also gives access to an outstanding stretch of the lower Saluda River. To reach Riverbanks Park, get onto I-126 (the Lester Bates Freeway from I-26 into downtown Columbia; this is also US 76), and go to the zoo exit at Greystone Boulevard. Follow the signs to the Riverbanks Zoo. Park in the northern (right-hand) part of the Zoo parking lot, and look for the entrance to the picnic area just north of the zoo.

The Riverbanks Park picnic area is along the Saluda River and offers good birding, especially in early morning during spring or fall migrations. From the picnic area you will find a trail along the river. You can go upstream for about two hundred yards to an open area with a good overlook of the river. A power line right-of-way

here is good for sparrows in winter and House Wrens in spring migration. In September keep an eye out for migrating hawks coming down over the river.

The best birding, however, is downstream from the picnic area. A trail leads downstream for about three-quarters of a mile to the point where the Saluda flows into the Broad to form the Congaree. This stretch of trail goes through good Piedmont floodplain forest and is excellent for spring and fall migrants. In winter look for an occasional Bald Eagle over the river. In summer look for breeding Prothonotary Warblers.

B–40.3—Columbia Canal Park

Winter	*
Spring	**
Summer	*
Fall	**

It is possible to get the feeling of a little bit of wilderness in the heart of downtown Columbia at the *Columbia Canal Park*. To reach the park from I-20 or I-26, take either freeway to the junction of I-20 and I-26. If you are on I-20, get onto I-26 eastbound toward Charleston, but immediately move to the left lanes to take I-126 (also US 76) toward downtown Columbia. If you are on I-26 westbound, take the I-126 exit toward downtown Columbia. Once on I-126, follow the freeway to its end, where you should exit to the right onto Huger Street. Once on Huger Street, get in the right lane, and turn right at Laurel Street, at the first stop light. Follow Laurel Street west one block to its end, which is the parking lot for Columbia Canal Park.

A three-mile-long hiking and bicycle trail

leads from the parking lot along the dike that separates the Columbia Canal from the river. The river at the beginning of the trail is the Congaree River, but following the trail upstream, you soon reach the confluence of the Saluda and Broad Rivers. This is the beginning of the Congaree River. The trail continues upstream, along the Broad River, to a diversion dam, which provides water for the Columbia Canal.

This hike can be good for spring and fall migrants, and for herons and egrets in late summer. You will get a good look at a rocky shoals habitat and see why the Fall Line is so called. In winter you might even luck upon a Bald Eagle. (A pair attempted to nest along this part of the Broad River in the late 1980s and may try again.)

B–40.4—Sesquicentennial State Park and Vicinity

Winter *
Spring **
Summer *
Fall **

Established in 1937 to celebrate the sesquicentennial of the founding of the city of Columbia, *Sesquicentennial State Park* provides a 1,445-acre haven for outdoors activities in the sandhills of the northeastern suburbs of Columbia. From Exit 74 of I-20 take US 1 (Two Notch Road) north toward Camden. In about three miles turn right onto the well-marked park entrance road. Soon after the entrance station the road goes over the top of a sizable sand hill and descends through typical dry longleaf-pine and turkey-oak scrub to a large parking lot by the bathhouse.

One good way to bird "Sesqui" is to hike the two-mile Jackson Creek Nature Trail around the lake, which starts at a parking lot just to the left of the bathhouse (as you face the lake). From the parking lot follow the trail to the left (clockwise around the lake).

Bird species at Sesqui are the usual woodland species that can be found readily in most parts of the state. But in these woods—especially the bay-swamp thickets along the creek and along the lake shore—birders do turn up a few unusual species, especially in the fall migration (late August to early October). Then you can keep an eye out for more unusual warblers, such as Blue-winged, Golden-winged, Chestnut-sided, and Bay-breasted, as well as common migrants such as Magnolia Warblers.

Sesquicentennial State Park is good for common woodland birds. A nearby spot where you can add open-country species to your list is the Sandhill Experiment Station of Clemson University. To reach this spot, return to US 1 (Two Notch Road), and turn right (north) toward Camden. Go north on US 1 for about 2.8 miles from the entrance road to Sesquicentennial State Park. Keep an eye out for a sign indicating the station. At the sign turn left (west) onto Road 52 (Clemson Road). Road 52 runs through the station for about three-quarters of a mile. This is a research area and not normally open to the public for birding, but Road 52 has wide, grassy shoulders where you can easily pull over and examine the fields and peach orchards of the research station. Here you can expect open-country and grassland species such as Eastern Meadowlark (year-round), Blue Grosbeak (summer), Eastern Kingbird (summer), Northern Harrier (winter), Vesper Sparrow (best in November and March), Savannah Sparrow (winter), and others. In late winter and early spring this is a good spot for Horned Larks, which probably breed here. The most unusual species ever found here was a Snowy Owl (November 1986).

From the Sandhill Experiment Station return to US 1 (Two Notch Road). To return to Columbia, you can backtrack by turning right (southwest) onto US 1. Or to return to I-20 by a quicker route, go south on Clemson Road for about two miles to Exit 80 of I-20.

B–40.5—The Screaming Eagle Road Area

Winter   *
Spring   **
Summer **
Fall   *

See Map B–40.1.

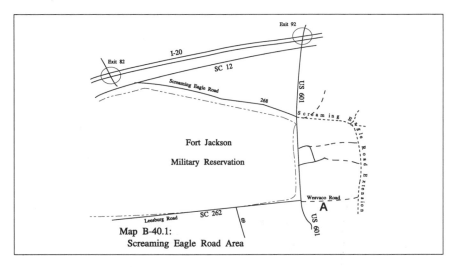

Map B-40.1:
Screaming Eagle Road Area

This tour is best during the breeding season from late April until about July but can be good at any season. During the winter this area is not different from most other places in the countryside of central South Carolina. During the breeding season, however, this area is a delight, especially before dawn or just after sunset.

The Sandhills of eastern Richland County were originally covered by an old-growth longleaf-pine and turkey-oak forest. This forest has been cut over to the point where no large areas of mature longleaf pines remain. The Red-cockaded Woodpecker, for example, is no longer found here (except on portions of the Fort Jackson Military Reservation which are closed to the public), but many distinctive Sandhills plants still occur, even on the clear-cut areas of the paper companies' pine plantations.

From I-20 northeast of Columbia leave at Exit 82, the Pontiac exit. Instead of going north (toward the community of Pontiac), go south. Within 0.2 mile you will reach SC 12 (Percival Road). Turn left (east) onto SC 12 toward Camden, and go 0.5 mile to the junction with Road 268, Screaming Eagle Road. Turn right (southeast) onto Screaming Eagle Road, which parallels the edge of the Fort Jackson Military Reservation. Go 7.9 miles east on Screaming Eagle Road, until it intersects with US 601 at the eastern edge of Fort Jackson. (This intersection is 9.3 miles south of I-20 on US 601.) Go straight across US 601, leaving the paved road and continuing east on a sand road known as Screaming Eagle Road Extension.

About 0.2 mile east of US 601 on the sand road you will come to a fork. To the left is Pilgrim Church Road. The tour route bears right, which is still Screaming Eagle Road Extension. This road goes east a mile or so along the top of a sand ridge. Soon you will come to a television broadcast tower. Chipping Sparrows are common all year long in this area, and the guy wires of the tower are attractive to Eastern Bluebirds.

Soon after passing the television tower, Screaming Eagle Road Extension comes to the edge of the ridge, and there is a great overlook to the east over the valley of the Wateree River. You can easily see ten miles to the east or twenty miles to the southeast, beyond the edge of the Sandhills and into the floodplain of the Wateree and Congaree Rivers.

If it has rained recently, or if you are faint of heart, turn around here, since the road deteriorates beyond this point. But normally the road is passable to ordinary passenger cars, although there are some areas of deep sand where you may become stuck if you slow down or stop. Cars with little ground clearance should turn around at the television tower.

The adventuresome (or foolish) can continue east on Screaming Eagle Road Extension down a rather steep hill (which is slippery in wet weather). At the bottom of the hill (about a mile east of the television tower) you will come to a crossroads. Here turn right (south). This will keep you on Screaming Eagle Road Extension. The other two roads soon lead to locked gates.

Follow the sand road south from the crossroads. You will encounter three main intersections, about 1, 2, and 4 miles south of the crossroads where you turned south. If you turn right (west) at any of these intersections, you will return to US 601.

Turn right at the third intersection. This is Wesvaco Road (letter A on Map B–40.1; also letter A on Map B–40.2), also a sand road. Follow Wesvaco Road west for about 2 miles until you rejoin US 601. At US 601 turn right (north) to return to I-20.

The area traversed by Screaming Eagle Road Extension and Wesvaco Roads is typical sandhills planted in loblolly pines at various stages of growth. From time to time you will cross small creeks. In these wetter areas the vegetation is a bay-swamp forest similar to parts of Sesquicentennial State Park (see Section B-40.4). Birding should be confined to the roadside, since this is private land, much of it highly posted.

The star birds of this loop through the back roads of the Sandhills are Bachman's Sparrow (fairly common April through August) and night birds: Whippoor-will (abundant), Chuck-will's-widow (common), and Common Nighthawk (uncommon). The whips and chucks are here from late March until mid-September, while the nighthawks are to be found from early May until mid-September. A drive along this stretch of road in May or June at dawn or dusk will give counts of twenty to thirty Whip-poor-wills, five to fifteen Chuck-will's-widows, three to four Common Nighthawks, and three to six Bachman's Sparrows.

The sparrows are easy to hear but tougher to spot when they are singing from perches in clear-cut areas or grassy fields with scattered pines. During May and June the Bachman's Sparrows sing throughout the day, even when it is hottest.

Most of the night birds will be heard only, but with a bit of luck you will be able also to spot two or three Whip-poor-wills and a Chuck-will's-widow displaying somewhere along the sand road. Nowhere are Whip-poor-wills more common in the breeding season than in the brushy hillsides and overgrown clear-cuts of the Piedmont and Sandhills of South Carolina, even though this place is near the southern edge of their breeding range.

B–40.6—Eastern Richland County along US 601

Winter   *
Spring   **
Summer **
Fall   *

See Map B–40.2.

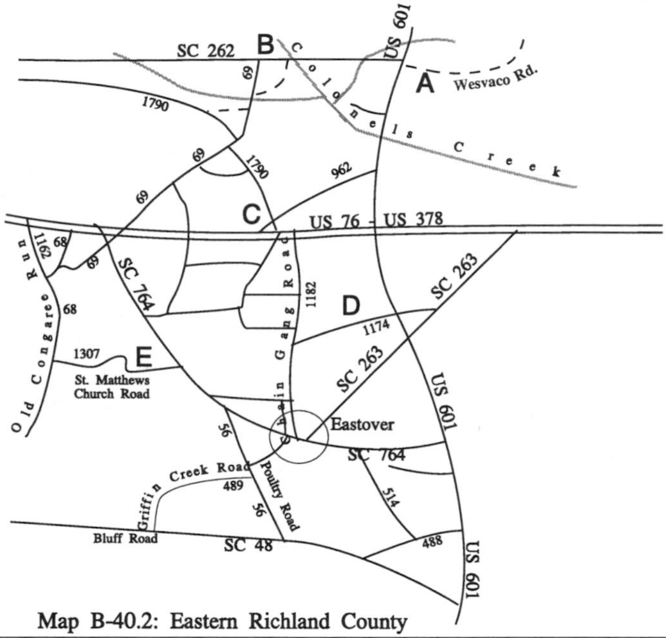

Map B-40.2: Eastern Richland County

US 601 is the main north-south road through the eastern portion of Richland County. It crosses I-20 just north of Richland County, near the community of Lugoff in Kershaw County (at Exit 92 of I-20). After US 601 goes south from I-20 for 7.8 miles through typical Sandhills habitat, it gets to the Richland County line. Then just 1.5 miles south of the county line it is crossed by Screaming Eagle Road. (A side trip into the Sandhills along Screaming Eagle Road Extension is detailed in Section B-40.5).

The end of the Screaming Eagle Road side trip is 3.5 miles further south, at the junction with SC 262. Here SC 262 goes westward to Columbia along the southern edge of Fort Jackson. Across from SC 262, to the left (east), is Wesvaco Road, a sand road that leads to Screaming Eagle Road. This is where you will emerge if you follow the directions outlined in Section B-40.5. (See Map B–40.1 and letter A on Map B–40.2.)

To follow the present tour, turn right from US 601 (west) onto SC 262. You will immediately find yourself in a moist woods. There is a wide shoulder a few yards from US 601 where you can pull off. Do not leave the roadside. The area to the north is in a part of Fort Jackson that is closed to the public, and to the south is posted private land. But from the road during the late spring and summer you can usually find several species of warbler, including Northern Parula, American Redstart, and

Louisiana Waterthrush. In winter you may find a Rusty Blackbird, if you are lucky.

Continue driving west toward Columbia. At the top of the hill, opposite the South Carolina National Guard Training Area, is a cutover area. From the roadside you can see or hear Bachman's Sparrow (April through August), Loggerhead Shrike (all year), and Red-headed Woodpecker (all year).

Down the hill from the National Guard area SC 262 crosses another swampy creek (Colonels Creek—see letter B on Map B–40.2). This is about 1.8 miles west of US 601. There is a wide shoulder to pull off onto just before the bridge over the creek. The prime attraction here is a Swainson's Warbler, which can be heard singing in the swamp from mid-April until July. Don't expect to see the bird, however, unless you are lucky. If you use a tape recording of the Swainson's Warbler's song to attract the bird, please do not overuse it, since this will drive the bird off.

At 2.3 miles west of US 601 turn left (south) onto Road 69. This is the first paved road to the left as you go west on SC 262. Road 69 goes south through typical Sandhills woods and farmlands. At 1.9 miles south of SC 262, Road 1790 comes in from the right (northwest), and 0.1 mile farther (2.0 miles south of SC 262) Road 1790 branches off to the left. Turn here and follow Road 1790 southeast. In 3.6 miles Road 1790 ends at a four-lane highway, US 76—US 378, the main road from Columbia to Sumter.

The 5.6 miles of back roads between SC 262 and US 76—US 378 offer good birding in the spring and summer. Purple Martins and Northern Rough-winged Swallows are common. Cattle Egrets can usually be seen in the horse pastures along with Eastern Kingbirds, Eastern Meadowlarks, and Chipping Sparrows. Road 1790 goes through a large clearcut, which is used year-round as a hunting area by American Kestrels and Red-tailed Hawks. There is usually a Loggerhead Shrike or two on a roadside power line or wire fence.

To continue the tour, turn left (east) onto US 76—US 378 (letter C on Map B–40.2). If you wish, you can continue on this highway east toward good birding areas in Sumter County (see Section B-43) or turn right (west) to go to Columbia (about 15 miles away). But the present tour goes east just 0.4 mile. Here turn off of the four-lane highway at the second paved road (Road 1182, Chain Gang Road) to the right. If you miss the turn onto Chain Gang Road, you will reach the overpass intersection with US 601 in 1.4 miles.

Go south along Chain Gang Road for 2.1 miles from the four-lane highway. There turn left (east) onto the first paved road. This is Road 1174, Community Pond Road (letter D on Map B–40.2). Go down the hill on Community Pond Road for about a third of a mile. At the bottom of the hill is the outlet creek of Community Pond. Park on the wide shoulder on the left side of the road, and examine Community Pond.

Community Pond was a rather typical country pond, common in the Sandhills region. But at some point the pond was drained, producing a large marshy area of *Juncus* and other water-loving plants. From October through late April this marsh is filled with Swamp Sparrows. Common Yellowthroats are found year-round, and this is a good spot to listen to American Woodcocks displaying at dawn or dusk (late winter to early spring). But the best birds appear during the migrations. This looks like excellent habitat for rails (though none have been found here yet). In April this is a fair spot to find migrating Sedge Wrens, an uncommon species this far from the coast. If they are around, the wrens can be heard singing (and sometimes seen as well), especially at dawn.

To continue the tour, continue east on Community Pond Road. At 1.3 miles from Chain Gang Road you will rejoin US 601. Here turn right (south). The tour goes directly south on US 601 all the way to the county line, which is the bridge over the Congaree River. This is about 13 miles from the intersection with Community Pond Road or 14.5 miles from US 76—US 378.

A mile or so south of Community Pond Road, US 601 leaves the Sandhills and enters the Coastal Plain proper. Here are large grain and vegetable fields, pastures, and scattered woodlots—a much more open habitat than that of the Sandhills. Open-country birds are abundant all year long. In winter look for hawks, sparrows, and shrikes. During the warmer part of the year you will find species such as Eastern Kingbird, Orchard Oriole, Blue Grosbeak, and Indigo Bunting mixing in with permanent residents such as Loggerhead Shrike, Northern Mockingbird, Brown Thrasher, and Northern Bobwhite. The common breeding sparrows are Field and Chipping Sparrows, but there may be a few Grasshopper Sparrows in the hayfields. When you stop the car, be sure to pull well off of the road, since this is a busy highway.

About 9 miles south of Community Pond Road (10.5 miles south of US 76—US 378), SC 48 comes into US 601 from the left (west). This is the start of the Congaree Swamp tour (see Section B-40.8). But to continue the present tour, keep going south on US 601. About 0.2 mile south of the junction with SC 48, US 601 crosses railroad tracks by the Wateree Country Store. The remaining 4 miles to the bridge over the Congaree River are different from the farmlands to the north. Here US 601 traverses 4 miles of the floodplain of the Congaree River. The causeway has several pulloffs and a wide, grassy shoulder. It is possible to stop just about anywhere and overlook the swamp without getting your feet wet.

The Congaree floodplain offers great birding all year long. Just south of the railroad tracks a power line right-of-way parallels the highway. The drier parts of this right-of-way are great for sparrows in the winter. You will easily find Swamp, Song, Savannah, and Field Sparrows. If you spend an hour tramping around here in winter, it is always possible that you will scare up a Henslow's Sparrow or a Grasshopper Sparrow. These species

have not yet been found here, but the habitat looks great for them.

The wooded swamp itself harbors lots of birds. Woodpeckers are especially common. You can spend a lot of time waiting for an Ivory-billed Woodpecker to fly over the road. Rumors of Ivory-bills here crop up from time to time, but there have been no authenticated sightings here in at least twenty years. If the Ivory-bill survives in South Carolina, it is probably somewhere in the Congaree Swamp, but don't get your hopes up.

The spring and summer are a great time to visit this area. Early in the day you can listen to a great chorus of breeding birds: Northern Parula, Prothonotary Warbler, Acadian Flycatcher, Barn Swallow (breeding under the highway bridges), and many others. By midmorning the soaring birds will be up. Look for Mississippi Kite (common), Red-shouldered Hawk, Anhinga (common), Great Blue Heron, White Ibis (uncommon), and Wood Stork (rare; mostly seen in August). The main night bird heard here is the Barred Owl, which is common. You may hear one calling in broad daylight.

When you finally get to the bridge over the Congaree River, cross over into Calhoun County, and park on the right (north) side of the road. Here, on the south side of the river, is a fifty-foot bluff which gives you a good platform from which to overlook the Congaree floodplain to the north. This is the best spot for spying Mississippi Kites (late April through late August or early September).

From the bridge over the river, US 601 continues south through Calhoun County (see Section B-9). It intersects with I-26 (Exit 145) in about twenty miles. You may choose to backtrack north to SC 48. This is the fastest way back to Columbia. It is also the way to the best birding area in Richland County, the Congaree Swamp National Monument, described in section B-40.8.

B—40.7—St. Matthews Church Road

Winter ⁕⁕
Spring ⁕⁕
Summer ⁕
Fall ⁕

See letter E on Map B—40.2.

St. Matthews Church Road in eastern Richland County is the closest place to Columbia where it is relatively easy to find Horned Larks in late winter or early spring. The larks are around all year long but are difficult to find when they are not singing. The habitat along St. Matthews Church Road is one of huge open fields. Typical winter birds of this area include American Pipit, Savannah Sparrow, American Kestrel, and Red-tailed Hawk. In spring migration this is a good area for migrating Bobolinks, and a few Grasshopper Sparrows breed in weedy or fallow fields. The Eastern Meadowlark is common year-round.

To reach St. Matthews Church Road from Columbia, go east on US 76—378. About 11 miles east of downtown Columbia you will pass McEntire Air National Guard Base on your right (south). Look for the first paved road to the right once you have passed the air base (about 0.7 mile beyond the air base entrance). This is Road 1162, Old Congaree Run.

Turn right (south) onto Road 1162, and follow it for 1.1 miles, where it merges with Road 68. Continue south on Road 68, which is still Old Congaree Run, for another 0.8 mile. Here turn left (east) onto Road 1307, St. Matthews Church Road. You will reach the open fields in about a mile.

Follow Road 1307 for 3.0 miles until it ends at SC 764. To return to US 76—378, turn left (northwest) onto SC 764, and go for 3.8 miles. This will put you about a mile east of where you originally turned off of US 76—378.

B—40.8—Congaree Swamp National Monument

Winter ⁕⁕
Spring ⁕⁕⁕
Summer ⁕⁕
Fall ⁕⁕⁕

See Map B—40.3.

Congaree Swamp National Monument protects more than fifteen thousand acres of the floodplain forest of the Congaree River in southeastern Richland County. The greater part of the National Monument's forest has never been cut. This is an area of great diversity of trees—more than eighty-five species. Some of the trees are true giants. More than 150 trees are larger than twelve feet in circumference. Some ancient loblolly pines are more than a hundred feet tall.

This outstanding natural area is great for birds. Since so much of the National Monument is mature floodplain forest, the diversity of birds may be somewhat less than in areas outside of the park, which have a mosaic of woods, ponds, and fields. But the birdlife of the park is impressive and abundant. Species which rely on tree cavities, such as woodpeckers, nuthatches, and chickadees, are especially common.

In 1990 the park service acquired several hundred additional acres, mostly on the edge of the park. Much of this new land was clear-cut in the late 1980s. At present (1992) this land offers good birding in an old-field habitat. These old fields will almost certainly revert to pinewoods and eventually hardwood forests. It will be interesting to observe the changing bird-

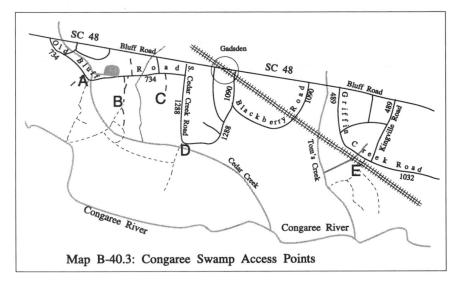

Map B-40.3: Congaree Swamp Access Points

life in these regenerating clear-cuts over the next few decades.

First-time visitors to the National Monument should go first to the ranger station to get a trail map and ask the rangers questions about the park. The turnoff from SC 48 for Old Bluff Road (Road 734) as well as the turnoff from Old Bluff Road for the park entrance are both well marked. The following directions may be helpful to get to the general neighborhood of the park.

The approach from the east begins at the junction of US 601 and SC 48, which is about 25 miles north of the exit from I-26 for US 601 (Exit 145) or about 28 miles south of the exit from I-20 for US 601 (Exit 92). (See Section B-40.6 for more details on birding along US 601 in Richland County).

Go about 9.0 miles west along SC 48 until you see the sign for the Congaree Swamp National Monument. This turn is 0.7 mile west of the railroad crossing in the little community of Gadsden. Along the way keep an eye out for Logger-head Shrikes, which are fairly common all year long along SC 48. Turn left onto Road 1288 (South Cedar Creek Road). Follow South Cedar Creek Road south only 0.1 mile to Road 734 (Old Bluff

Road). From the eastern end of Old Bluff Road to the entrance road of the National Monument is 2.4 miles. Turn left (south) at Caroline Sims Road, the entrance road to the National Monument (a good sand road). Go about a mile south to the entrance gate, the *ranger station*, and the main trailhead for the park (letter B on Map B–40.3).

If you are coming on I-26 from the northwest, take Exit 116, which is a left exit if you are eastbound. This exit is currently (1992) marked only by the words *To SC 48*, but it is actually the exit for the Southeastern Expressway, most of which is under construction. The highway that exits from I-26 is a limited-access freeway marked "I-326" on some maps and called "SC 478" on some highway signs. This will eventually be part of I-77 (scheduled completion is 1995). Take this freeway east, crossing the Congaree River. In about 6 miles you will reach the exit for SC 48.

After leaving the freeway, turn right (east) onto SC 48, and follow it about 8.4 miles. Here turn right onto Road 734 (Old Bluff Road) where you see the sign for the National Monument. Follow Old Bluff Road east for 4.5 miles to Caroline Sims Road, the entrance road for the National Monument (marked by a sign).

About 3 miles east of SC 48, Old Bluff Road passes along the side of Duffies Pond, a large farm pond with a sizable bald-cypress swamp at one end. From the public road you can overlook the pond. The common ducks here are Wood Ducks and Mallards, but other species sometimes appear in migration. The standing dead trees at the eastern end of the pond attract numerous Red-headed Woodpeckers. In late summer you may find an Anhinga or a Wood Stork soaring overhead or perched in the bald cypresses. This is a fairly good spot for Bald Eagle in winter or spring.

The easiest way to bird the National Monument is to go to the trailhead near the ranger station, study the trail map, and hike as much or as little of the over 25 miles of marked trail as you want. During late winter and early spring many of the trails are often flooded. Ask the ranger where you can go and remain dry. Even if the swamp is flooded, you can walk the three-quarter-mile-long boardwalk or the mile-long Bluff Trail, which stays on high ground. The boardwalk was heavily damaged by Hurricane Hugo in September 1989, but it has now been repaired.

To get the flavor of the swamp, walk on the boardwalk to its end at Weston Lake, then take the Weston Lake trail to the right (east). You will soon hit a service road. Go right onto the service road to the parking lot. This is a loop of about two miles and goes through some of the best areas for birds near the ranger station. It is the best area in the park for Red-headed Woodpeckers, which like to use the standing dead pines for feeding and nesting.

To add about another mile to your walk, turn left onto the service road from the Weston Lake trail instead of right. Follow the service road to the old hunt club area, which is on Cedar Creek. There is a small clearing around the old clubhouse, which makes this a good area for wintering sparrows. In summer this is a good area to see Mississippi Kites soaring above, since there is a good view of the sky from the clearing. In 1988 a pair of Eastern Phoebes nested under the old clubhouse (which is built on pilings to keep it above the flood). Phoebes are rare breeders in the South Carolina Coastal Plain but may be regular here.

The old clubhouse is at the trailhead for several other trails. You could spend a week walking on them looking for the Ivory-billed Woodpecker, but there have been no good records of this species from the area for at least twenty years. Once you are through looking around the old clubhouse, follow the service road back north for a mile or so to the main parking lot.

Aside from the trails which begin near the ranger station, four other areas of the National Monument are good for birding. These are (1) the Garrick Road area, (2) the Iron Bridge Trail, (3) the Griffin Creek Road area, and (4) the Old Boat Launch Road.

(1) The only Red-cockaded Woodpeckers which are regularly found on lands protected by the National Park Service are in a pinewood area of the National Monument, *the Garrick Road area* (letter C on Map B–40.3). To reach the area, return to Road 734 (Old Bluff Road) from the ranger station, and turn right (east). Go east on Old Bluff Road for 1.7 miles, and turn right (south) onto a county-maintained dirt road called Garrick Road. (The intersection of Old Bluff Road and Garrick Road is 0.7 mile west of the point where Old Bluff Road ends at Road 1288, South Cedar Creek Road.)

Follow Garrick Road south for about a mile to its end. There is a wide spot or turnaround where you can park, on the edge of the National Monument. At present there are no marked trails in this area. Straight in front of the parking area you will see an old logging road going into the National Monument. Cross the cable motorcycle barrier, and follow this old road. It goes for a few yards through a thick grove of young loblolly pines and then enters a more open area with mature loblolly- and longleaf-pines. This is the beginning of the area where the Red-cockaded Woodpeckers might be found. There is currently (1992) only one known family group of these fascinating woodpeckers in the area, and they may well die out soon. You do not have a good chance of finding the birds, but you may be lucky.

This open area is the best place in the Congaree National Monument for Bachman's Sparrow. Listen for their songs between mid-March and early September. They may also be around in winter, but they are virtually impossible to find when they are not singing. The other pine-woods birds are also common here: Brown-headed Nuthatch and Pine Warbler (year-round), Summer Tanager and Eastern Wood-Pewee (summer).

Look in the area to your left (east) for several hundred yards for trees in which Red-cockaded Woodpeckers actively roost, which are easily recognized by the copious pine sap running from the sap wells excavated by the birds. There are numerous roost trees in the area, but only three to six birds. As with Red-cockaded Woodpeckers anywhere, these birds are easiest to find at dawn or late afternoon, when they are near their roost trees and calling. The easiest time of year to find them is May or June, when there may be young in the nest.

(2) Perhaps the best birding in the National Monument is along the Iron Bridge Trail (also known as the Old Dead River Trail, the Avian Trail, the New Road, and the Lower Road). This trail follows an old logging road in the eastern part of the park. To reach the Iron Bridge Trail from the Garrick Road area, return to Old Bluff Road and turn right (east). Go 0.7 mile to the T-junction with South Cedar Creek Road. (This is 2.4 miles east of the main entrance road of the National Monument.) Go right (south) onto Cedar Creek Road (Road 1288) for 1.8 miles. You will approach a point where the paved road bears to the left (east). Look for a dirt road that goes straight ahead. Go straight on this dirt road for about twenty yards and park (letter D on Map B—40.3). This parking lot is often used by canoeists. Directly south of the parking lot is a trail into the National Monument. Follow this trail to a footbridge over Cedar Creek and onto the old logging road beyond. This logging road (Iron Bridge Trail) is sometimes overgrown with black-

berries and impassable, but if the trail has been mowed recently and the area is not flooded, it offers excellent birding. The trail goes south about 2.5 miles into the swamp.

After following the Iron Bridge Trail south for about a mile, you will reach a maintained side trail off to the right. This trail (presently unnamed) parallels a slough for about 1.5 miles and eventually joins the eastern portion of the Kingsnake Trail at a point about 3 miles from the main parking lot near the ranger station. There are several old clearings along this connector trail which make this area extremely good for birding, especially in migration.

The area along the Iron Bridge Trail has been logged, so it is more open than the virgin forest near the ranger station. Some bird species, such as Yellow-breasted Chat, are found here, but not in the deep woods that characterizes most of Congaree Swamp National Monument.

The Iron Bridge Trail is the best place in the park to find Swainson's Warblers (mid-April through mid-August). But here as elsewhere, it is much easier to hear a Swainson's Warbler than to see one. Be careful in your song identification, since both Louisiana Waterthrush and Hooded Warbler are also common here. Listen for the "whip-whip-whip-poor-will" of the Swainson's, the "weetoe-weeteeoh" of the Hooded, and the jumble of notes of the waterthrush's song.

(3) Some of the most interesting birding in the National Monument is in the regenerating clear-cuts, on land acquired in 1990. The best place to explore these clear-cuts is along Griffin Creek Road, in the extreme eastern portion of the park (letter E on Map B—40.3). To reach this area from just about any other area of the park, find your way back to SC 48 (Bluff Road), and go east. You will soon reach the village of Gadsden, where the railroad crosses SC 48. From the railroad grade crossing of SC 48 in Gadsden continue east on SC 48. At 2.5 miles east of the railroad crossing turn right (south) onto Road 489 (Griffin Creek Road). Fol-

low Griffin Creek Road southeast for 3.8 miles. Here look for National Park property line signs and an unpaved road to the right (south). If you get to a stop sign (at the intersection of Griffin Creek Road and Kingville Road), you have gone 0.3 mile too far.

The unpaved road is an old logging road which crosses the railroad in about a hundred yards from Griffin Creek Road. Here the old logging road is gated, so you will have to explore this area on foot.

About fifty yards beyond the railroad track another old logging road turns off to the left (east). You can follow this old road for about three miles, until it finally peters out.

If you continue straight ahead on the old road you started on, you will reach a turnoff to the right in about a half mile. If you take this right turn, this old road reaches the floodplain forest along Tom's Creek in about another half mile.

If you continue ahead on the road you started on, this road goes for about two miles but eventually becomes impassable.

Whichever way you go, you will encounter much the same habitat—mature floodplain forest interspersed with old-field habitats. For the next ten years or so these old fields will give you the chance to observe most of the species of Coastal Plain old-field habitats. These old fields are especially good for night birds, including numerous Whip-poor-wills and Chuck-will's-widows in spring and summer, and American Woodcock, Eastern Screech-Owl, Great Horned Owl, and Barred Owl year-round.

None of the old roads mentioned offer a loop hike. Explore as long as you want, then return to Griffin Creek Road.

(4) One last place in the Congaree National Monument deserves special mention, Old Boat Launch Road (also known as the Upper Road). From the main entrance road (Caroline Sims Road), turn left (west) onto Old Bluff Road, and go about 2.1 miles. Immediately after cross-

ing the bridge over Cedar Creek, turn left (south) onto the first sand road, and park in the small lot used by canoeists (letter A on Map B-40.3). (If you reach Roger Myer Road, you have gone fifty yards too far.) Do not drive further than this parking lot. Follow the sand road south on foot. This is on private property just outside of the National Monument. After about a three-minute walk you will come to an overgrown road off to the left, which leads two hundred yards to the National Monument property line. Ignore this side road and keep going straight ahead on the main road.

You will soon reach a three-way fork in the road, with each of the forking roads blocked by a metal gate painted orange. Here turn left, and walk around or under the orange gate. Follow this sand road for about five more minutes' walk, and you reach a second gate at the edge of the National Monument. Cross this gate onto the public land. From here you can walk about two miles along the dirt service road to a primitive boat-launching ramp on the Congaree River. Along the way you will pass two roads or trails off to the left (east). The first is a service road to a pistol range. (Do not enter if you hear gunfire.) The second is a marked trail—the River Trail—which leads back to the trailhead parking lot near the ranger station. The distance back to the ranger station is about 5 miles.

Along the way to the river, the service road passes through excellent habitat for birds. The birds here are much the same as are found near the ranger station. But since this area is much more remote, it is much easier to find species such as Wood Duck and Barred Owl along this service road. You will probably be completely alone for the entire five-mile hike to the river and back.

One species which is best found in this area is the Yellow-crowned Night-Heron. Several pairs nest here and are easily observed from early April until July. You will probably not find this species near the ranger station.

This is also the easiest place to hike to the river in the National Monument. From the boat-launching area you will see Mississippi Kites (late April through mid-August) as well as other hawks. This area is great for breeding American Redstarts.

Once you reach the river, you have an option. You may wish to retrace your path back to the parking area. Or you may follow the River Trail for a short distance downstream. From the boat launch area the River Trail cuts through a dense canebrake for about a third of a mile. This is an excellent spot for Swainson's Warbler in late spring and early summer. Eventually the River Trail leaves the canebrake and takes a sharp left turn. If you go straight ahead instead of following the trail, you will soon reach (in about two hundred yards) a large sandbar area in the river. When the river is low,

this is an excellent area to bird. In summer it is about the best place in the park to find Mississippi Kites. A singing Warbling Vireo was found here in June 1991. In winter it abounds with sparrows, including Song and Swamp Sparrows. In migration anything might turn up. Rangers have reported Bald Eagles flying along the Congaree River, and this is as good a spot as any to look for one.

When you finish at the sandbar, rejoin the River Trail. The River Trail soon joins an old road which is a good spot for American Woodcock in winter. If you turn left onto this old road, you will return to the Old Boat Launch Road, near the boat launch area. From here retrace your path back to the parking area.

B–41—SALUDA COUNTY

Saluda County is a rural county along the Fall Line mostly in the Piedmont about thirty to sixty miles west of Columbia. Birding in Saluda County is best along the Saluda River, which forms the northern border of the county. The river in the eastern part of the county is really the upper end of Lake Murray. For more on birding Lake Murray, see Section B-32 (Lexington County) and Section B-36 (Newberry County).

All directions to birding areas in Saluda County are given from the traffic circle intersection of US 378 and SC 391 in the eastern part of the county. This intersection is 18 miles west of the town of Lexington, 14 miles east of the town of Saluda, or 19 miles south of the town of Newberry.

B–41.1—The SC 391 Bridges over Lake Murray

Winter   **
Spring   *
Summer *
Fall   *

Starting about 2 miles north of the traffic circle intersection of US 378 and SC 391, SC 391 goes over three causeways or *bridges over Lake Murray*. Find a place to stop where the shoulder is a bit wide, and overlook the lake. In winter you may see Ring-billed, Herring, or Bonaparte's Gulls, Common Loon, American Coot, Mallard, or Ring-necked Duck. From late summer through the fall you will find a

number of egrets, mostly Great Egrets, as well as Great Blue Herons.

The most sought-after species along this stretch of SC 391 is the Cliff Swallow, which nests under most of the bridges over Lake Murray or over the Saluda River in Saluda County. The swallows return in early April (about April 10 or so), and are here through the summer, though they are tough to find after they finish breeding in early July. Barn Swallows, Northern Rough-winged Swallows, and Purple Martins are also common breeders in the area. Tree Swallows are common in early spring and in late summer. A few Bank Swallows may occur in late summer.

B–41.2—The SC 395 Bridge over the Saluda River at Kempson's Ferry

Winter **
Spring *
Summer *
Fall *

The *SC 395 bridge over the Saluda River* crosses the extreme upper end of Lake Murray. When the lake is low, extensive mud flats are visible from the road. This is a good place to look for herons and egrets from July through December, for Cliff Swallows (mid-April through mid-July), and for migrant or wintering shorebirds (especially Killdeer and Common Snipe).

To reach this area, go north on SC 391 from the traffic circle at the intersection of US 378 and SC 391. In about 3.5 miles turn left (west) onto SC 194. Follow SC 194 for 4.6 miles to SC 395. Turn right (north) onto SC 395, and go 3.4 miles to the bridge. There is a small pulloff on the south side of the bridge (in Saluda County), where you can overlook the mud flats or look for Cliff Swallows (which nest under the bridge). There is a paved boat launch on the north side of the bridge (in Newberry County). The Newberry County shore is part of a wildlife management area, which you may explore on foot following a fishermen's path upstream from the boat launch area.

B–42—SPARTANBURG COUNTY

Spartanburg County has a typical Piedmont mixture of manufacturing towns, small farms, and pine plantations centering on the city of Spartanburg. The city of Spartanburg has a population of approximately fifty thousand and lies at the intersection of two major interstate highways, I-26 and I-85.

The main birding opportunities in Spartanburg County are at Croft State Park (just southeast of the city of Spartanburg) or from the roadsides of the rural parts of the county. Although the county has neither mountains nor vast swamps nor huge lakes, many common species can be found, and spring and fall migration can be good.

B–42.1—The Farmlands near Landrum

Winter **
Spring **
Summer *
Fall **

See letter A on Map B–42.1.

Excellent birding is possible from roadsides in the farm county just east of Landrum, which is just south of the North Carolina border. Leave I-26 at Exit 1, the Landrum exit, and go northeast (away from Landrum) on Road 128. In 1.3 miles

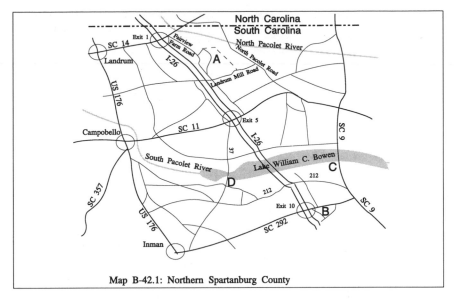

Map B-42.1: Northern Spartanburg County

you will enter Polk County, North Carolina, where Road 128 becomes Secondary Road 1520. Keep straight ahead to the first main intersection, which is 0.3 mile into North Carolina. Here turn right onto Secondary Road 1519 (Jackson Grove Road). Follow Jackson Grove Road for 1.9 miles to the South Carolina state line. Here keep straight ahead on what is now called North Pacolet Road.

At 0.8 mile south of the North Carolina border the road crosses the North Pacolet River. Park by the bridge. In late spring and summer you should find many birds here, including breeding Yellow Warblers. In the summer of 1991 Willow Flycatchers were found nesting along the river here.

After looking for breeding Willow Flycatchers, continue south on North Pacolet Road for 0.5 mile. Here turn right (west) onto Landrum Mill Road. Follow this road west for 2.2 miles to Racetrack Road, on the edge of Fairview Farms. This is a good spot for breeding Grasshopper Sparrows and for wintering Lincoln's and White-crowned Sparrows.

Turn right (north) onto Racetrack Road, and go 1.2 miles to the point where Racetrack Road merges with Fairview Farms Road. Here bear left, keeping on the paved road. You will reach a T-junction with Road 128 in another 0.6 mile. Here turn left for just a few dozen yards to return to I-26 at Exit 1.

B–42.2—William C. Bowen Lake

Winter   *
Spring   **
Summer *
Fall   **

See Map B–42.1.

William C. Bowen Lake is the main reservoir of the city of Spartanburg. It is a

long, narrow lake, an impoundment of the South Pacolet River about fifteen miles north of the city. Interstate 26 crosses the lake, but to get a good look, you must leave the interstate and drive some of the lakeshore roads. The following tour begins at Exit 10 of I-26 and loops around the main part of the lake.

From I-26 leave at Exit 10, and go east on SC 292. About two hundred yards from the interstate turn right (south) onto a paved county road, which parallels the interstate for a quarter mile, then turns back to the left (northeast) until it rejoins SC 292. This bit of county road skirts a large hayfield where the Grasshopper Sparrow often breeds (letter B on Map B–42.1).

Once back to SC 292, follow this road to the right (east) until it ends at SC 9. This T-junction is 1.6 miles east of Exit 10 of I-26. Turn left (north) onto SC 9. In about a mile look for a small county park on the left just before the bridge over Lake Bowen (letter C on Map B–42.1). Turn into this park, and drive around until you find a good view of the lake. Look for ducks and Canada Geese in winter. Late April brings large flocks of swallows (mostly Barn and Tree), but all eastern swallows are possible here. Barn Swallows breed under low bridges near the park, and a few Cliff Swallows breed under the I-26 bridge over the lake, but you will need a boat in order to see the nests.

After checking out the park, return to SC 9 and turn left (north), soon crossing the lake on a short bridge. About 0.6 mile north of the bridge turn left (west) onto a paved county road. Follow this road west for several miles, paralleling the north shore of the lake. The road will cross over I-26 (no exit here). Soon after crossing over the interstate, you will reach a stop sign at Road 37. Turn left (south) at this stop sign, and follow Road 37, which soon crosses over the lake on a short bridge. Just beyond the bridge is a fishing pier on the left. Park on the wide shoulder here, and overlook the lake from the pier. This is a good spot from which to spy a few ducks in winter or in migration (letter D on Map B–42.1).

After checking out the lake from the Road 37 fishing pier, continue ahead (south) on Road 37. About a half mile south of the bridge turn left onto the first paved county road. Follow this road south for about two miles to a T-junction. Here turn left (east) onto Road 212. Follow Road 212 east. This road soon crosses over I-26 and then skirts the south shore of Lake Bowen. In 2.8 miles Road 212 ends at SC 9. Here turn right (south), and go just 0.1 mile to the intersection with SC 292. Here turn right onto SC 292, returning to Exit 10 of I-26 in 1.6 miles.

B–42.3—Croft State Park

Winter	*
Spring	***
Summer	*
Fall	**

Croft State Park is a seven-thousand-acre former military base just south of the city of Spartanburg. Its rolling hills are covered mostly with second-growth oak-hickory-pine forest, but also with a few mature oak-hickory areas. There are also two small lakes and a bit of Piedmont floodplain forest along Fairforest Creek and its tributaries. This is the largest natural area in Spartanburg County and one of the best birding spots in the Piedmont of South Carolina, especially in spring and fall.

To reach Croft State Park from I-26, leave the interstate at Exit 22, and go east on SC 296. In one mile turn right (southeast) onto SC 295, and follow this road for 6.0 miles to SC 56. Here turn right (south), and go another 2.3 miles to Road 394 (Dairy Ridge Road) on the left (east). Follow Dairy Ridge Road east for 0.3 mile to the main park entrance road. Here turn right (south), and follow the main park road into the park for 3.2 miles to the park headquarters. Turn left at the headquarters, and follow the road to its end at a parking lot on the shore of Lake Tom Moore Craig, one of two park lakes.

The best birding in the park is found along the six-mile-long Lake Johnson Trail. From the lakeshore parking lot pick up the trail, which goes over a short boardwalk along the shore of Lake Craig to the right of the parking lot. In about a quarter mile this hiking trail joins a horse trail. (To make a short two-mile loop, turn right onto the horse trail, and follow it to the stables, then up the hill to the entrance road and back to the starting point.) The main trail goes left at the horse trail downhill to the Lake Craig dam. Here you will get a good view of the lake. In winter there may be a few ducks and Pied-billed Grebes on the lake, but this is not a major concentration point for waterfowl.

Follow the trail over the dam and up the hill beyond. In a mile or so you will reach a paved road, the road to Lake Johnson, the other park lake. Lake Johnson is to the left (downhill) along the paved road. The loop trail turns right, however, and goes up the hill for a quarter mile to a road off to the right, which passes an old fire tower and then a TV tower.

From the TV tower the trail enters the woods again and winds its way downhill to the floodplain of the Fairforest Creek. Here it crosses Kelsey Creek on a steel bridge and then turns sharply uphill and to the right at a trail junction. (The path leading straight ahead goes to a ford of Fairforest Creek.)

Soon after turning uphill, the trail joins the road to the park's stables. Here keep left, and continue uphill past the horse show ring to the park headquarters, where you turn right to get back to your car, parked by Lake Craig.

This is a fairly long hike, but an easy one. During spring and fall migration you will find a lot of migrants on this trail, especially in the floodplain of Fairforest Creek, but also near the Lake Craig dam. Birding is less exciting in summer and winter, but the walk is a nice half day's outing at any time of year.

The other main birding area in Croft State Park is Lake Johnson, the other park lake. You may reach this lake by following the trail outlined above, or you may drive. To drive to Lake Johnson, leave the main part of the park and return to Dairy Ridge Road, just outside the main entrance. Here turn right, and go about 3 miles to SC 295. Turn right onto SC 295, and go two miles, past the White Stone post office. Turn right onto Road 359, which is the first state road to the right once you have passed the post office. Follow this road into the park and to its end at a picnic area on Lake Johnson.

The small swamp at the upper end of Lake Johnson, where the road crosses the creek, is a good place to look for migrant warblers.

B–43—SUMTER COUNTY

Sumter County is in the Upper Coastal Plain at the geographic center of South Carolina. Its county seat is Sumter, a pleasant city of twenty-five thousand, that is forty-five miles east of Columbia on US 76—378. Interstate 95 cuts through the eastern edge of the county.

While Sumter County is entirely within the Upper Coastal Plain, it is not without physiographical variety. The eastern portion of the county is mostly flat, dominated by broad agricultural fields punctuated with woodlots and pine

plantations. But west of the city of Sumter one finds a somewhat different topography. The Citronelle Escarpment runs through the western edge of the county. This formation is most visible along US 76—378 west of Sumter. As one travels west, the country is quite flat until the western edge of Shaw Air Force Base, just west of Sumter. Then from Shaw to the historic village of Stateburg there is a gradual rise. The open fields of the eastern part of the county give way to forested hills, until just west of Stateburg the highway plunges two hundred feet to the bottomlands along the Wateree River.

This sandy ridge or hilly area is considered by some naturalists to be a part of the Sandhills, since it is rather sandy, and many plants typical of the Sandhills are found there. For our purposes we will call this area the Red Hills of Sumter County, an area of sand hills disjunct from the true Sandhills subregion, which begins a

dozen or more miles north of Sumter County, in Kershaw and Lee counties.

The Wateree River bottomlands and the Red Hills, which separate the bottomlands from the agricultural plains to the east, are the most interesting areas in the county for birding (see Sections B-43.1 through B-43.3). Poinsett State Park is an especially pleasant stop for birding in any season.

B—43.1—The Wateree River Bottomlands near Stateburg

Winter   **
Spring   **
Summer   *
Fall   **

See letter A on Map B–43.1.

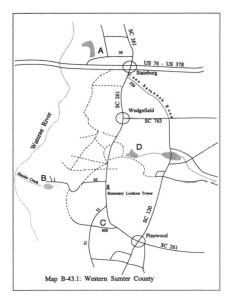

Map B-43.1: Western Sumter County

These directions begin from the intersection of US 76—378 and SC 261, which is 13 miles west of Sumter or 32 miles east of Columbia. Go north on SC 261 toward Camden for 1.1 miles to the first state road to the left (west). This is Road 39, Old Garner's Ferry Road. Turn left onto Road 39, and follow it down the hill into the bottomlands of the Wateree River. In 1.2 miles you will cross a railroad track. There

is a road to the right (north) just beyond the railroad track, Road 346. Ignore this road, and keep going straight ahead on Old Garner's Ferry Road.

The area on either side of the road just west of the tracks is great for small land birds, especially in winter. A bit of squeaking here in winter will soon attract a mob of chickadees, kinglets, sparrows, and the like. The pastures and plowed fields on the north side of the road will have open-field species such as Eastern Meadowlark (year-round), Cattle Egret (summer), and blackbirds (mostly in winter). This is a good spot for Rusty Blackbird in winter. Be alert for the rare Brewer's Blackbird as well. Telling a Brewer's from a Rusty can be tricky. To be sure you have a Brewer's, look for the dark eye of the female. Male Brewer's (and both sexes of Rusty) have a light eye.

About 0.3 mile west of the railroad tracks the road passes a large farm pond. In winter this pond sometimes has an amazing variety of ducks, mostly diving ducks such as Bufflehead, Ruddy Duck, Canvasback, Redhead, Ring-necked Duck, and scaup (usually Lesser Scaup).

In warm weather the ducks are gone (except for a few Wood Ducks), but the herons and egrets take over. Most common are Great Blue Heron, Great Egret, and Green-backed Heron, but other species of egret, as well as Anhinga and White Ibis, are seen regularly. Many of these birds come from the large heronry at Boykin Mill Pond in Kershaw County, which is about 12 miles north (see Section B-28.2).

Continue past the farm pond. About a mile beyond the railroad tracks Old Garner's Ferry Road ends at US 76—378, a four-lane, divided highway. Here you can go left (east) back to Stateburg or right toward Columbia. For the best birding go west toward Columbia. For three miles US 76—378 goes through the floodplain swamp of the Wateree River. It is easy to find a place to pull over on the shoulder and overlook the swamp. This is a good spot for Mississippi Kites in summer and Red-shouldered Hawks year-round. The area is very similar to the US 601 crossing of the Congaree Swamp in Richland County (see Section B-40 for a list of birds along US 601; most of the same species are found in the Wateree Swamp as well).

The bridge over the Wateree is the county line. Here you can continue west into Richland County (see Section B-40) or turn around and return to Stateburg, which is the jumping-off place to visit Poinsett State Park and Manchester State Forest (see Sections B-43.2 and B-43.3).

B—43.2—Poinsett State Park

Winter	*
Spring	**
Summer	*
Fall	**

See letter B on Map B—43.1.

From the intersection of US 76—378 and SC 261, which is 13 miles west of Sumter or 32 miles east of Columbia, go south on SC 261 (toward Pinewood) for 10.2 miles to the intersection with Road 63. Turn right (west) onto Road 63, and go about two miles to the entrance to the state park. Road 63 becomes the main park road and ends at the main picnic area, by a small lake.

Poinsett State Park is located along the bluff on the east side of the Wateree River. A small creek (Shanks Creek) creates a large system of ravines and wooded hollows. At the bottom, near the western edge of the park, is a small lake, which was constructed in the eighteenth century to provide a constant source of water for rice fields along the Wateree River. The rice fields are long gone, overgrown with a typical Upper Coastal Plain floodplain forest, but the lake remains.

Poinsett State Park has about a thousand acres to explore. The park was established in 1934 and is named for a nineteenth-century naturalist and diplomat from nearby Stateburg, Joel Robert Poinsett. Poinsett is famous for introducing a popular Christmas plant, the poinsettia.

Poinsett State Park is best known for its early spring wildflowers and its display of mountain laurel in May, but it is worth a visit in any season. The best birding is along the trails above the lake. From the parking lot at the end of the road look for the beginning of the Coquina Nature Trail near the bathhouse. The trail crosses the dam of the lake and then wanders up the hill on the far side (south side) of the lake. You will encounter a rain shelter in about a mile. Shortly beyond the shelter there is a split in the trail. The Coquina Nature Trail turns left toward the upper end of the lake. The Hilltop Hiking Trail goes to the right, wandering along the slope of the ravine formed by Shanks Creek. In about a mile this trail descends to the creek, passing a good stand of mountain laurel. The Hilltop Hiking Trail ends at the main park road about a mile after breaking off from the Coquina Nature Trail. Turn left onto the park road and walk along the road for about a mile or so to the parking lot where you began.

The birds along these trails are the usual species of Upper Coastal Plain oak-hickory-pine woods and floodplain forest, but they are very common and easily seen here. Special birds include the Louisiana Waterthrush, which breeds along the creek below the dam, and possibly also breeding Solitary Vireos, here at the extreme southeastern edge of their breeding range. Birding is best here in spring and fall migration, when numerous migrant warblers are around. This is an excellent place for migrant Worm-eating and Black-throated Blue Warblers (especially in fall), and other species are possible. In winter you may well find all three of South Carolina's nuthatch species here; the White-breasted and Brown-headed Nuthatch are common year-round, while the Red-breasted is found here most winters, sometimes in good numbers.

One other birding spot in the park deserves special mention—the overlook of the Wateree valley. There are two park roads going north from the main park road. The first one encountered (as you enter the park) is the road to the cabin area. The second goes to the campground and hilltop picnic area. Walk or drive up this second road, which leads in less than a mile to a picnic area. Here is a shelter from which there is a great view to the west across the floodplain of the Wateree River to the Richland County hills on the far side about 5 miles away. This overlook is a great spot to watch birds flying high over the floodplain. In summer you can expect Anhinga, several species of heron and egret, White Ibis, and Mississippi Kite. Keep an eye out for rarities such as Wood Stork and American Swallow-tailed Kite, which are rare but regular in late summer. At any time of year you will see Black and Turkey Vulture, and hawks—mostly Red-shouldered and Red-tailed.

B–43.3—Manchester State Forest

Winter	*
Spring	**
Summer	*
Fall	*

See Map B–43.1.

Manchester State Forest is a large area of pinewoods, small creeks with bay-swamp thickets, and small lakes next to Poinsett State Park (see Section B-43.2). Birders often combine a visit to Poinsett with one or two stops in the state forest, which has habitats that are rare or not found in the park. Manchester State Park has a very accessible Red-cockaded Woodpecker colony, which means that a winter trip to Poinsett State Park and Manchester State Forest might yield all of South Carolina's woodpeckers (except for the Ivory-billed, of course). The Red-cockaded Woodpecker colony was heavily damaged by Hurricane Hugo in September 1989 and it is no longer easy to find the species at Manchester State Forest. But a few of the woodpecker's spectacular roost trees have survived the storm, and perhaps the colony will also survive, although the prospect for these particular birds is rather grim.

To reach the *Red-cockaded Woodpecker colony* (letter C on Map B–43.1), start at the intersection of Road 63 (the entrance road for Poinsett State Park) and SC 261. Go south (a right turn if you are coming from the state park) toward Pinewood. At 5.0 miles from Road 63 the main highway passes Road 808 to the right (southwest). Turn right onto Road 808 and go 0.2 mile. Red-cockaded Woodpecker roost trees are on both sides of the road here, well-marked by the white pine sap flowing down the sides of the trees. The woodpeckers were formerly easily found in early morning and late evening while they were going from and returning to their roost trees.

Another good birding area in Manchester State Forest is at *Elliot Lake* (letter

D on Map B–43.1), one of several small lakes which dot this forest. To reach Elliot Lake from the intersection of Road 63 (the entrance road to Poinsett State Park) and SC 261, turn north on SC 261 (toward Stateburg), and go 2.9 miles. Here look for a sand road to the right (east) opposite a sign for solid waste containers. Turn right onto the sand road, and go straight ahead for 1.2 miles, where you will find a turnout and small parking area on the left (north). This is the parking area for the Elliot Lake dam.

Elliot Lake is about a third of a mile long, with very clear water and lots of emergent vegetation. This clean, clear lake does not attract many birds, but you may find Pied-billed Grebes in winter and Great Blue Herons or Wood Ducks year-round. The birding attraction is the swamp below the dam, a typical bay-swamp thicket such as you might find in the Sandhills or Upper Coastal Plain of South Carolina. By walking along the dam, you can find ways to get into the swamp, at least a little way. Here you will find birds typical of floodplain forests in the Sandhills. The star attraction here is Swainson's Warbler, which is around from mid-April until late summer (though difficult to find after it quits singing in early July). Here, as elsewhere, the Swainson's Warbler is easily heard but hard to see-.Other species whose songs resemble the "whip-whip-whip-poor-will" song of the Swainson's are also here—Hooded Warbler and Louisiana Waterthrush—so be cautious in your identification.

There are many other areas in the Manchester State Forest, which are best explored using a county map or a topographic map. This is an interesting area to visit, whether for a rest stop on your way to Lake Marion or for a two-day camping trip.

B–44.4—Woods Bay State Park

Winter	**
Spring	**
Summer	*
Fall	**

Woods Bay State Park is a 1,541-acre park which protects one of the more spectacular and least disturbed Carolina bays in South Carolina. A Carolina bay is a geographic and natural feature: an oval-shaped depression in Coastal Plain or Sandhills soils that ranges in diameter from a few feet to several miles. Carolina bays are found from Delaware to north Florida but most common in the Coastal Plain of North and South Carolina.

Woods Bay State Park is easily reached from I-95, so interstate travelers have a chance to take a two-hour to half-day stop in order to explore a rare natural area. Exit from I-95 at Exit 141, and go northeast on SC 53 for 1.3 miles. Here turn right (south) onto Road 597, and go south for 1.6 miles to a T-junction. At the T-junction turn left (east) onto Road 48. Follow Road 48 for 1.7 miles to the park entrance road on the right (south).

Note: Days of operation vary a lot at South Carolina State Parks. Currently (1992) Woods Bay State Park is open only five days a week (closed Tuesdays and Wednesdays). If you want to visit the park in the middle of the week, it is a good idea to call ahead to check on days and hours of operation or to stop by a South Carolina Welcome Center and pick up a state park brochure with the current operating schedule for all state parks. The telephone number for Woods Bay State Park is (803) 659-4445.

You can explore some of the park on foot, but the best way to get into the Carolina bay itself is by canoe. The park ranger has canoes for rent at a very reasonable rate. Stop by the ranger's residence at the park entrance and inquire.

There are two trails you can use to explore the park. A half-mile-long nature trail begins to the left of the parking lot and winds around a small millpond before leading to a boardwalk into the Carolina bay itself. The boardwalk goes for a quarter mile into a beautiful water-tupelo—bald-cypress swamp. If your visit falls between mid-April and early July, you will think that every Prothonotary Warbler in the world is at Woods Bay. Other abundant breeders include Northern Parula and Yellow-throated Warbler. In winter expect the usual species of Upper Coastal Plain swamps.

The second trail at Woods Bay is unmarked but leads to a very different habitat and is well worth a half-hour walk. From the parking lot follow the service road to the right. In about two hundred

yards the service road turns right. (If you go straight ahead, you will leave the park and reach private property.) Follow the service road to the right, where it soon reaches a broad open corridor between mature oak-hickory woods on the left and a dense pine plantation on the right. In another two hundred yards or so this corridor ends. Here keep to the right on a mowed trail that encircles the pine plantation before rejoining the service road. The whole walk thus goes in a figure-9 pattern.

The mowed trail around the pine plantation leads through an area of thick brush and briars that is great for birds, especially in fall and winter.

B–44—UNION COUNTY

Union County is a rural area in the Piedmont in the north-central part of the state. Its seat is the small city of Union. The southeastern half of Union County is mostly in the Sumter National Forest, an area devoted primarily to loblolly-pine plantations. The northwestern half of the county has small farms and woodlots. The Broad River is the eastern border of the

county, and the Enoree River is the southwestern border. The floodplains of these important Piedmont rivers provide some of the more interesting habitat for birding in the county. Additional birding opportunities include Lake Long, an eighty-acre public fishing lake a few miles east of the city of Union.

B–44.1—The Cross Keys Area

Winter   *
Spring   **
Summer *
Fall   *

See letter B on Map B–44.1.

A delightful alternative to I-26 for birders going from Spartanburg to Columbia is to travel on the excellent back roads in Spartanburg, Union, and Newberry counties.

Directions from the southeast:

(If you are coming from the southeast—that is, from Columbia—see Section B-36.3.) From the junction of US 176 and SC 72 in Whitmire, cross the Enoree River

on US 176—SC 72—SC 121. The highway signs indicate US 176 west here, but you are actually heading northeast at this point. One mile north of the bridge, SC 72—SC 121 turn off to the right. Continue on US 176. One mile beyond the split (two miles beyond the Enoree River) turn left (northwest) onto Road 18. Follow Road 18 through the Sumter National Forest. At 4.8 miles from US 176 you will come to Road 16, the southern turnoff for Rose Hill State Park. (See Section 44.2 if you wish to make a side trip to the park. See letter C on Map B–44.1.)

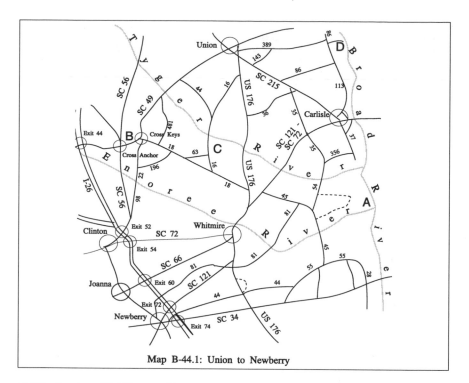

Map B-44.1: Union to Newberry

At 7.7 miles from US 176 you will pass Road 63, the northern turnoff for Rose Hill State Park. (This is where you rejoin the present tour, if you made the side trip.) Soon after this junction you will emerge from the woods into farm country. At 10.8 miles from US 176 there is an interesting farm pond on the left (south). At 12.8 miles you will reach the historic crossroads of Cross Keys and pass by the old tavern (still standing). At 13.0 miles northwest of US 176 you will reach SC 49. Continue west (left) on SC 49. One mile west of Cross Keys you will pass a public dove field on the right (north). At 3.7 miles west of Cross Keys you enter Spartanburg County. From here go west on SC 49 for 5 miles to Exit 44 of I-26.

Directions from the northwest:

From Exit 44 of I-26 go east on SC 49 through the town of Cross Anchor. Five miles from I-26 you will enter Union County. At 2.6 miles into Union County you will pass a public dove field on the

left (north). At 3.9 miles bear right onto Road 18. This is the old crossroads community of Cross Keys. At 2.2 miles southeast of SC 49 you will pass an interesting farm pond on the right (south). At 5.3 miles you will reach the northern turnoff for Rose Hill State Park (see Section B-44.2). If you wish to visit the park, turn left onto Road 63. At 8.2 miles southeast of SC 49 you will pass the southern turnoff for Rose Hill State Park. (This historical park has a short trail through typical pine-oak woods.) Continue straight ahead on Road 18. At 13.0 miles you will reach a T-junction with US 176. Turn right onto US 176, and go south 2 miles to the bridge over the Enoree River at Whitmire (see Section B-36.)

The tour outlined above leads through farmlands and pinewoods. While good at any time of year, it is best in the spring and early summer. The hayfields of the area near *Cross Keys and Cross Anchor* (letter B on Map B–44.1) harbor numerous Grasshopper Sparrows in summer. The best place to find breeding Grasshopper Sparrows is at the public dove field on SC 49 between Cross Anchor and Cross Keys. Bird this area only in the spring and summer. In fall and winter it is best left to the dove hunters. If you venture into this area in summer, beware of chiggers and ticks. This is a good area for the common breeding species of open fields: Mourning Dove, Blue Grosbeak, Loggerhead Shrike, Northern Bobwhite, Eastern Meadowlark, and the like.

The farm pond east of Cross Keys on Road 18 is a hot spot of bird activity. From the road look for Green-backed Heron, Great Egret, Killdeer, Belted King-

fisher, Grasshopper Sparrow, and many other species. The fields north of Road 18, opposite the pond, are sometimes good for Horned Lark. This is all private land, so stay on the public road.

Road 18 through the Sumter National Forest is fairly good for Wild Turkey, which are common but seldom seen. When you pass a clear-cut area, in summer, stop and listen for the sweet song of the Bachman's Sparrow, among the more common Chipping and Field Sparrows. While Bachman's Sparrow prefers open pinewoods in the Coastal Plain, it is found in brushy fields in the Piedmont.

B–44.2—Broad River Recreation Area, Sumter National Forest

Winter *
Spring **
Summer *
Fall **

See letter C on Map B–12.1 (p. 69); also letter D on Map B–44.1 (p. 215).

The Broad River floodplain on the eastern border of Union County is one of the few places in South Carolina where you can explore a good Piedmont floodplain forest. Most such forests have either been cleared for farmland or flooded by reservoirs, or they are on private property. The Broad River floodplain in the Sumter National Forest is a happy exception. Two excellent places to explore the floodplain forest are *Broad River Recreation Area* and Woods Ferry Recreation Area in Chester County (see Section B-12.1).

To reach Broad River Recreation Area from Union, follow SC 215 Bypass southeast to its junction with SC 215 Business, then go 1.8 miles southeast on SC 215 to Road 143. Turn left (northeast) onto Road 143, and go 2.2 miles from SC 215 to a T-junction with Road 389. Turn right (east) onto Road 389, and follow it 2.1 miles to Road 86. To keep on Road 389, you have to jog right (south) a short distance on Road 86. Follow Road 389 to its end at the recreation area.

If you are coming from Chester County on SC 49, follow SC 49 west for 2.4 miles from the SC 49—SC 9 bridge over the Broad River at Lockhart, then turn left (south) onto Road 86. Go south on Road 86 for 5.4 miles, then turn left (east) onto Road 389 to go down the hill to the riverside.

If you are coming from Chester County on SC 215, turn right (north) onto Road 113 at 1.2 miles west of the SC 215—SC 72—SC 121 bridge over the Broad River at Carlisle. Go north on 113, which becomes Road 86. At 8.7 miles north of SC 215 turn right (east) onto Road 389, which ends at the recreation area.

From the parking area there is a quarter-mile trail (one way) downstream through the riverside forest. This area is best during the breeding season and during the spring and fall migration, when many migrant warblers can be found. This is a good area for all species of Piedmont floodplain forests.

As you follow the trail downstream from the parking lot, peer through the woods to your right, away from the Broad River.

You may spy a way to bushwhack through a hundred yards or so of floodplain forest to reach an area of ponds and marshes. This is a waterfowl hunting area. After the duck season ends in January, you might find a few ducks here. Mallards and Wood Ducks breed. Other puddle duck species are here from late January through early April. A few Blue-winged Teals may linger into May. If you can find a way over to this area, you may also find a few herons and perhaps a migrant American Bittern or some other migrant marsh species. Be prepared for mud, briars, and biting insects.

B–44.3—Lake John D. Long and Vicinity

Winter   **
Spring   **
Summer   *
Fall   **

See letters D and E on Map B–12.1 (p. 69).

Lake Long is an eighty-acre lake managed by the South Carolina Wildlife and Marine Resources Department as part of its State Fishing Lake Program. While this is primarily a program for anglers, it also benefits birders by providing public access to small ponds and the surrounding lakeshore areas.

Lake Long has two access points. The main access is from SC 49. From downtown Union follow SC 49 eastward toward Lockhart and Chester. At about 4.5 miles east of downtown Union you will reach the bridge over *Little Browns Creek* (letter D on Map B–12.1). There is an excellent freshwater marsh along this creek, easily visible from the roadside. Here you will find resident Canada Geese, Wood Ducks, and perhaps other marsh-loving species. (If you are coming from the east, this point is about 5 miles west of the town of Lockhart on SC 49).

About 1.2 miles east of Little Browns Creek you will reach the intersection with Road 26 to the left (north). This is the turnoff for the northern access point of Lake Long, which we will cover in a moment. For now continue east on SC 49 for another 1.2 miles to Road 467. Here turn left (north), and go 0.3 mile to a parking lot at the *south end of Lake Long* (letter E on Map B–12.1). Here you will find picnic tables, pit toilets, and a short trail along the dam of the lake. From the dam you can easily overlook the lake. There may be a few ducks in winter or in migration. This is an excellent area for migrant swallows in April and May and again in August and September. On a good rainy day in April or September you might find all six of South Carolina's swallow species hawking for insects over the lake.

To reach the *north end of Lake Long*, return to SC 49, and turn right (west, toward Union). Go 1.2 miles to Road 26. Here turn right (north), and go 2.4 miles to a T-junction with SC 9 in the village of Adamsburg. (Adamsburg is 5 miles west of Lockhart on SC 9.) Turn right onto SC 9, and go 0.3 mile to a county road off to the right (south). Turn right, and follow this road one mile to a parking lot by the lake. The road leads through an area of pastures and hedgerows which is great for sparrows, including breeding Grasshopper Sparrows. From the parking lot at the north end of Lake Long you can follow anglers' trails along a bit of the lakeshore. The thick brush along the lake to the left of the parking lot is great for migrant land birds in spring and fall.

B–45—WILLIAMSBURG COUNTY

Williamsburg County is a typical part of South Carolina's Coastal Plain— agricultural, sparsely populated, and mostly flat. The Santee River forms the southern boundary and provides the best birding in Williamsburg County.

B–45.1—The Santee River Floodplain near US 52

Winter   *
Spring   *
Summer *
Fall   *

See Map B–45.1.

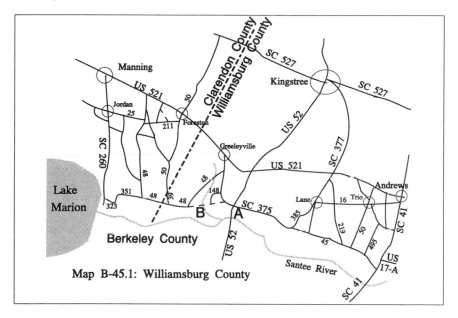

Map B-45.1: Williamsburg County

This is not a primary birding area, but it is worth a stop if you are in the neighborhood. Columbia-area birders often pass this way on their way to the coast.

We start this tour at the US 52 bridge over the Santee River (letter A on Map B–45.1), which is some 23 miles north of Moncks Corner or 17 miles south of Kingstree US 52. There is a primitive boat-launching area on the north side of the river (in Williamsburg County) just east of US 52. This is a good spot to observe Mississippi Kite (late April though mid-August). You may spy an American Swallow-tailed Kite here as well, since one may stray up the Santee from its breeding area a few miles downstream, but this is not likely.

From the bridge go north on US 52 for 1.3 miles to SC 375. Here it is possible to go right (east) onto SC 375 (which farther along is designated Road 45), paralleling the Santee River until you reach US 17A and SC 41 at the Georgetown County line. (See Map B–45.1) This is an interesting back road to take if you are going to the coast.

To continue the tour, however, turn left (northwest) onto SC 375. Go about 1.7 miles on SC 375 to the first county road on the left, a sand road with a sign for Mount Zion Church. Turn here, and follow this unpaved road west (to letter B on Map B—45.1).

Immediately after you turn onto the unpaved road, you will be in an area of open loblolly-pine woods heavily damaged by Hurricane Hugo in September 1989. This is a great place for birds. Woodpeckers are common: Red-headed, Red-bellied, Downy, Hairy, and Pileated as well as other species typical of open pinewoods. This is a good area to visit at night to hear owls. Barred and Great Horned Owls are common, and you may get an Eastern Screech-Owl to answer a whistled imitation of its call, if you are lucky. Chuck-will's-widows are common here as well (from late March through early September), and you may well see one on the road, especially in spring.

In about a mile the unpaved road will pass Road 148 (paved) on the right. Keep straight ahead on the sand road. A half mile west of Road 148 (or about 1.5

miles west of SC 375) the road will pass over a small creek, Mount Hope Swamp. This is an excellent birding area. Here you should be able to find most of the species typical of floodplain forests such as woodpeckers, the Carolina Chickadee, Tufted Titmouse, White-breasted and Brown-headed Nuthatches, and Northern Cardinal (all year). These permanent residents are joined in summer by species such as Yellow-throated, Northern Parula, Prothonotary, and Hooded Warblers, Blue-gray Gnatcatcher, Acadian and Great Crested Flycatcher, Eastern Wood-Pewee, Yellow-billed Cuckoo, and many others. In winter look for Ruby-crowned and Golden-crowned Kinglet, Brown Creeper, Yellow-rumped Warbler, Winter Wren, White-throated Sparrow, Yellow-bellied Sapsucker, Eastern Phoebe, and many other species typical of floodplain forests.

From the bridge over Mount Hope Swamp continue west on the sand road. In another mile you will join a paved road, Road 48. Here you can either turn right to rejoin SC 375 just south of its intersection with US 521 in Greeleyville, or you can keep straight ahead on Road 48, which eventually enters Clarendon County and joins SC 260 just north of the Santee Dam on Lake Marion. (See Map B—45.1.)

B—46—YORK COUNTY

York County lies in extreme north-central South Carolina, just south of the city of Charlotte, North Carolina. Interstate 77, the main highway from Charlotte to Columbia, runs through the county. Much of the county is suburban, with lots of lakefront development on Lake Wylie, an impoundment of the Catawba River. Away from the housing developments you will find a pleasant mix of rolling hills with farms, pine woodlots, and oak-hickory forests—typical Piedmont countryside.

While York County lies in the Piedmont, the northern half of the county shows definite similarities to the Blue Ridge Mountains. In the northwestern part of the county is a series of low ridges with ele-

vations of up to 1,100 feet above sea level. The highest of these ridges is Kings Mountain (see Section B-46.2). This area is the home of the Virginia pine, a scrubby, short pine with short twisted needles in bundles of two. Virginia pines do not self-prune their lower limbs as readily as most other pine species do. A Virginia pine grove on an abandoned field may be almost impenetrable.

The southern part of York County is more typical of the South Carolina Piedmont. Here are old fields grown up with loblolly pines, eastern red cedars, winged elms, and sweet gum. Virginia pines are still found, but large groves of them are uncommon.

Winter **
Spring **
Summer *
Fall *

See Map B–46.1.

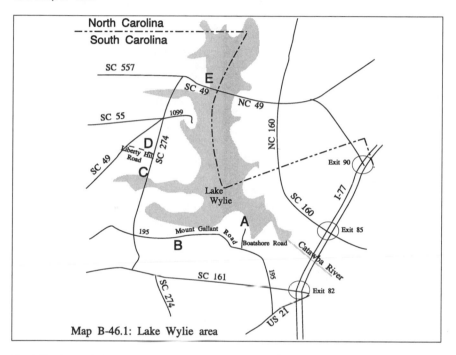

Map B-46.1: Lake Wylie area

The following tour touches on some of the better birding areas on those portions of Lake Wylie that are in South Carolina. The northeastern shore of this impoundment of the Catawba River is in Mecklenburg County, North Carolina. This area includes suburbs of Charlotte and Rock Hill. It is crowded, especially on weekends. The constant motor boat activity makes any birds other than Ring-billed Gulls rather unusual on the lake. The roads in the area are usually narrow and crowded, with little shoulder to pull off onto. Be careful birding along the roads described here.

From I-77 exit west onto SC 161 at the northeastern corner of the city of Rock Hill. Follow the signs for the Museum of York County. About 1.2 miles west of I-77 turn right (north) onto Road 195, Mt. Gallant Road. You will still follow signs for the museum. About 4.3 miles from SC 161 look for a sign indicating the turn for *Ebenezer Landing* (letter A on Map B–46.1). Turn right (north) at this sign, onto Boatshore Road. Follow Boatshore Road north 0.7 mile to a boat launch area and small park. From the park you can get a good view of much of Lake Wylie to the west, north, and east. In winter there may be a Common Loon or perhaps a Ring-necked Duck. This area is extremely crowded in summer and on weekends all year long.

221

Return to Road 195, and turn right (west). You will come to the *Museum of York County* (letter B on Map B–46.1) in 1.3 miles from Boatshore Road (5.6 miles from SC 161). This is a fine small museum, combining natural history exhibits with visual arts. Just behind the museum is a half-mile-long nature trail with many labeled trees. The trail winds through second-growth mixed Virginia-pine and hardwood forest, and it has an observation deck overlooking a small creek. The birding here is not exceptional, but you will find lots of the common birds of second-growth woods, such as Carolina Wrens, Carolina Chickadees, Tufted Titmice, and Northern Cardinals. From early April through July look for a Louisiana Waterthrush along the creek.

Return to Road 195, and go west 1.9 miles to the intersection with SC 274. Turn right (north) onto SC 274. In about 2.7 miles you will cross over *Calabash Creek*, an arm of Lake Wylie (letter C on Map B–46.1). There is a small boat-launching area and a park just north of the bridge. In summer many Barn Swallows nest under the bridge. Check also for nesting Cliff Swallows, which often nest elsewhere in the Lake Wylie area and which may nest here from time to time.

Continue north on SC 274. About one mile north of Calabash Creek look for a county-maintained dirt road on the left (west). This is Liberty Hill Road. (You may also see a sign for Liberty Hill Church marking this intersection.) Turn left (west) onto Liberty Hill Road. Go 1.4 miles (from SC 274), at which point another dirt road comes in from the right. Turn right onto this unnamed road, and follow it up the hill to the fire tower at the top of *Ferguson Mountain* (letter D on Map B–46.1). This hill is a miniature version of Kings Mountain, jutting about 300 feet above the surrounding countryside. There is a good view here, especially in winter, when the trees are bare. To the east you can see Lake Wylie and the suburbs of

Charlotte. To the west you can see the higher ridges of Kings Mountain. Ferguson Mountain is best in spring and fall, when many migrating warblers, vireos, thrushes, and flycatchers can be seen.

From the fire tower return to Liberty Hill Road (in 0.6 mile), and turn right. You will reach SC 49 at 1.2 miles from the fire tower. Here you may notice a sign for the state-operated fire tower. This is a good landmark if you are trying to find the road up Ferguson Mountain from SC 49.

Go north on SC 49 about one mile to a five-point intersection. Here SC 274 comes in from the south and merges with SC 49. SC 55 begins here and goes west toward the town of Clover and Kings Mountain State Park (see Section 46.2). Road 1099 goes east to a development on the shore of Lake Wylie. To continue the tour, go north (straight ahead) on SC 49—SC 274.

At 2.1 miles north of the five-point intersection, SC 49 and SC 274 split. Turn right (east) onto SC 49. In just under three miles from where you turn right you will approach Lake Wylie. If you wish to examine the lake, park at the *Hungry Fisherman Restaurant* just before you get to the bridge (letter E on Map B–46.1). There is an unimproved dirt road from the restaurant to the left side of the bridge, about two hundred yards away. Here you can find Cliff Swallows from mid-April until mid-August or so.

The middle of the lake here is the state line. To return to I-77, cross the bridge into North Carolina, where the road becomes NC 49 in Mecklenburg County. Follow NC 49 northeast for about 3 miles to the intersection with NC 160. Turn right (south) onto NC 160. In 2 miles you will reenter York County, South Carolina, near the lakeside town of Tega Cay. Here the highway becomes SC 160. Follow SC 160 south for 3 miles to I-77.

Winter   *
Spring   **
Summer *
Fall   **

A traveler on I-85 between Greenville and Charlotte will notice that near the North Carolina—South Carolina border the highway runs through a wide valley between a series of low ridges. These northeast-to-southwest ridges reach a height of about 1,700 feet above sea level, or about 1,100 feet higher than the surrounding countryside. This high point, the Pinnacle of Kings Mountain, is in North Carolina. The area can be explored at Crowders Mountain State Park, near Gastonia, North Carolina. The highest point of these ridges in South Carolina is about 1,100 feet above sea level.

The most famous of these low mountains and the easiest to explore is Kings Mountain. Here, in October 1780, the rebel mountain men won a decisive victory over loyalist and British troops, one of the most important battles of the American Revolution in the southern colonies. This battle is memorialized by Kings Mountain National Military Park and Kings Mountain State Park, South Carolina. Together these parks protect about ten thousand acres of outstanding Piedmont oak-hickory-pine forest, so that these are natural parks as much as they are historical.

From I-85 take the southernmost exit in North Carolina, and go southeast on NC 216. In about one mile you will enter South Carolina, where the road becomes SC 216. Keep straight ahead. In about one mile this road enters *Kings Mountain National Military Park*. Here the road is called Main Park Drive. This is in Cherokee County, South Carolina, but since almost all of the parks are in York County, we cover them here. Follow Main Park Drive east about 2.5 miles to the *National Park Visitor Center*. Here is a good museum, and you can pick up a park brochure and a map of hiking trails.

The easiest trail in the park and a good one for birds as well is the *Kings Moun-tain Battlefield Trail*, a 1.5-mile loop trail that begins behind the visitor center. Kings Mountain battlefield is not an open field area like the great Civil War battlefields such as Gettysburg. The battle was fought in the woods, and the area is mostly wooded today. Along this trail (or elsewhere in the park, in less crowded areas) you can find all the birds of the Piedmont forests.

Mountain influences among breeding birds are few, but you can find Scarlet Tanager (more common than Summer Tanager; both are easily found in summer) and occasionally breeding Solitary Vireo and Worm-eating Warbler. Warblers that commonly breed in the park include Northern Parula, Yellow Warbler (more common in farmlands just outside the park), Yellow-throated, Pine, Prairie, Black-and-white, Prothonotary (along streams), Worm-eating (a few), Kentucky, Hooded Warblers, American Redstart, Ovenbird, Louisiana Waterthrush (streams), Common Yellowthroat (open areas), and Yellow-breasted Chat (briar thickets).

The best time for birding Kings Mountain is during the migrations, especially from about late April to early May and late August to October. At these times migrant warblers abound. Common migrants (in addition to the breeding species) include Blue-winged (a few), Tennessee, Chestnut-sided (more common in fall), Magnolia (fall), Cape May, Black-throated Blue, Yellow-rumped (a few winter), Black-throated Green, Blackburnian, Palm (more common in fields outside of the park), Bay-breasted (fall), Blackpoll, Cerulean (a few; late April or early August), Northern Waterthrush (streams), and Canada Warblers. The migration is usually not as heavy at Kings Mountain as it is in the Blue Ridge Mountains a few miles to the west, but with a bit of luck, you can have a good day at Kings Mountain.

From the visitor center you can back-track to I-85, so you can continue east on Main Park Drive. A mile or so east of the visitor center you will enter *Kings Mountain State Park*. Here are facilities for camping, picnicking, and swimming as well as other trails. A favorite attraction of the State Park is the "Living Farm," a working replica of an 1846 South Carolina frontier farm.

Main Park Drive leaves the state park and joins SC 161 just 0.2 mile south of the North Carolina line. Turn left to go to I-85 near the city of Kings Mountain, North Carolina, or turn right to go to the city of York, South Carolina. If you wish to visit Lake Wylie, turn left onto SC 161, and go south for 2.8 miles to SC 55. Turn left (east) onto SC 55, which goes through the town of Clover and eventually ends at SC 49—SC 274 at the five-point intersection near Ferguson Mountain (see Section B-46.1).

Here are some suggestions (given in taxonomic order) for finding some of the more sought-after bird species in South Carolina. If a South Carolina species is not in this list, then it is either fairly common at some time of year in some part of the state, or it is so rare that you have little chance of finding it anywhere here.

Red-throated Loon—fairly common in winter along the coast. Easy to find in the ocean at Huntington Beach State Park (B–22.1), Sullivans Island (B–10.3), Folly Beach (B–10.11), Edisto Beach (B–15.4), and Hunting Island State Park (B–7.6). Rare on inland lakes.

Common Loon—common in winter along the coast and on inland lakes. Along the coast try those areas mentioned for Red-throated Loon as well as Charleston Harbor (B–10.1). Inland try any of the larger lakes, especially Lake Murray (B–32.1, B–36.1), Lake Monticello (B–20.2), Lake Hartwell (B–4.1, B-4.2, B-4.3, B-37.1), and Lake Keowee (B–37.2).

Pied-billed Grebe—common and widespread in winter on fresh water throughout the state. Much less common during the breeding season. In summer look for it at Bear Island (B–15.1), Magnolia Gardens (B–10.13), Savannah NWR (B–27.2) and elsewhere on ponds in the Coastal Plain. Rare breeder in the Piedmont.

Horned Grebe—common in winter along the coast and on inland lakes. See Common Loon and Red-throated Loon.

Red-necked Grebe—rare in winter in salt creeks along the coast. Try Charleston Harbor (B–10.1), Beaufort (B–7.4), or Pinckney Island NWR (B–7.2).

Cory's Shearwater—uncommon far offshore in summer and fall. Try from a party boat out of Little River, Murrell's Inlet, or Charleston.

Greater Shearwater—see Cory's Shearwater.

Audubon's Shearwater—see Cory's Shearwater.

Wilson's Storm-Petrel—see Cory's Shearwater.

Northern Gannet—uncommon winter visitor along the coast. Try Huntington Beach State Park (B–22.1), Sullivans Island (B–10.3), Folly Beach (B–10.11), Edisto Beach (B–15.4), or Hunting Island State Park (B–7.6).

American White Pelican—rare winter visitor to the coast. Has been seen recently at Moore's Landing (B–10.5), Savannah NWR (B–27.2), Bear Island (B–15.1), and in the Ashley River in Charleston (B–10.1).

Brown Pelican—common permanent resident along the coast. During the breeding season this species is more local. Try Charleston Harbor (B–10.1), Folly Beach (B–10.11), and Moore's Landing (B–10.5).

Great Cormorant—scarce winter visitor along the coast. The best spot to look is at the jetty at Huntington Beach State Park (B–22.1).

Double-crested Cormorant—abundant in winter and in migration along the coast and at Lake Marion; less common on large lakes in the Piedmont. Breeds in small numbers at Lake Marion (B–14.1, B-14.2, B-14.3, B-38.2).

Anhinga—common at ponds and rivers throughout the Coastal Plain in summer; much less common in winter. In summer try at Boykin Mill Pond (B–28.2), Santee NWR (B–14.1, B-14.2, B-14.3), Bear Island (B–15.1), Santee Coastal Reserve (B–10.7), Magnolia Gardens (B–10.13), Savannah NWR (B–27.2), Hilton Head Island (B–7.3), and many other locations. In winter your best bets are Savannah NWR, Hilton Head Island, and Magnolia Gardens.

Magnificent Frigatebird—very rare summer visitor along the coast. Your best bets are Hilton Head Island (B–7.3), Hunting Island (B–7.6) and Folly Beach (B–10.11). Do not count on seeing this species in South Carolina.

American Bittern—uncommon to rare winter visitor to marshes throughout the state; very rare breeder. Try the marshes at Savannah NWR (B–27.2), Bear Island (B–15.1), Magnolia Gardens (B–10.13), Brookgreen Gardens (B–22.2), or Huntington Beach (B–22.1).

Least Bittern—summer resident in marshes throughout the state; rare in the Piedmont, but common in the Lower Coastal Plain. Most easily seen at Savannah NWR (B–27.2), Bear Island (B–15.1), or Magnolia Gardens (B–10.13)

herons and egrets—many species are seen year-round along the coast with little difficulty, including Great Blue Heron, Great Egret, Snowy Egret, Little Blue Heron, and Tricolored Heron. Inland these species appear mostly in summer and fall, with the exception of the Great Blue Heron, which is found throughout the year. Herons and egrets are seen easily at Huntington Beach (B–22.1), Brookgreen Gardens (B–22.2), Santee Coastal Reserve (B–10.7), Bulls Island (B–10.5), Magnolia Gardens (B–10.13), Bear Island (B–15.1), Savannah NWR (B–27.2), Pinckney Island NWR (B–7.2), and many other places. During the summer and fall the following sites in the Upper Coastal Plain are also excellent for herons and egrets: Boykin Mill Pond (B–28.2), Santee NWR (B–14.1, B–14.2, B–14.3), and Silver Bluff Audubon Sanctuary (B–2.6).

Reddish Egret—rare late summer visitor to the coast. Most often seen at Huntington Beach (B–22.1).

Cattle Egret—common summer visitor to the Coastal Plain; rare in winter. Look for it near the spots mentioned above for herons and egrets, and in pastures throughout the Coastal Plain.

Green-backed Heron—common summer resident of ponds throughout the state; rare in winter. In winter try at Savannah NWR (B–27.2) or Hilton Head Island (B–7.3).

Black-crowned Night-Heron—fairly common permanent resident in marshes along the coast; rare breeder inland. Fairly easy to find at dusk at Huntington Beach (B–22.1), Bear Island (B–15.1), Sa-

vannah NWR (B–27.2) and many other places along the coast. Inland your best bet is Boykin Mill Pond (B–28.2), where the species has recently been found breeding in small numbers.

Yellow-crowned Night-Heron—uncommon summer resident of salt marshes along the coast and floodplain forests inland. A few breed in the Piedmont, but most are found in the Coastal Plain. Most easily seen from the Marsh Boardwalk at Huntington Beach State Park (B–22.1) or at Pinckney Island NWR (B–7.2), where there is a large breeding colony. There is a small breeding colony in Washington Park in downtown Charleston (just east of Meeting Street between Queen Street and Cumberland Street). Inland try B & C Landing on the Savannah River (B–27.1), Congaree Swamp National Monument (B–40.8), or Francis Beidler Forest (B–18.1) at dusk in late spring or early summer.

White Ibis—common along the coast from late summer through early spring. During the breeding season this species is much more local. In late summer a few wander up into the Piedmont. During the breeding season try Boykin Mill Pond (B–28.2), Francis Beidler Forest (B–18.1), Santee Coastal Reserve (B–10.7), Santee Delta WMA (B–22.3), Bear Island (B–15.1), Pinckney Island NWR (B–7.2), Hilton Head Island (B–7.3), B & C Landing (B–27.1), and Savannah NWR (B–27.2). At other times try any of the places mentioned for herons and egrets.

Glossy Ibis—uncommon and decreasing permanent resident of coastal marshes, especially freshwater marshes. Most frequently seen at Bear Island (B–15.1), Magnolia Gardens (B–10.13), Santee Coastal Reserve (B–10.7), and Savannah NWR (B–27.2). Rare in the Upper Coastal Plain and Piedmont.

Roseate Spoonbill—very rare visitor along the coast. Recently seen from the causeway at Huntington Beach State Park (B–22.1), the Savannah Spoil Area (B–27.3), and near Beaufort (B–7.4).

Wood Stork—uncommon and local breeder in the ACE Basin of Colleton

County (B–15.5); fairly common summer visitor along the coast, less common inland. Easy to find in late summer at Silver Bluff (B–2.6), Savannah NWR (B–27.2), Pinckney Island NWR (B–7.2), and Bear Island (B–15.1).

Fulvous Whistling-Duck—rare winter visitor to old rice fields in the Lower Coastal Plain; most often seen at Magnolia Gardens (B–10.13) or Bear Island (B–15.1).

Tundra Swan—uncommon but increasing winter visitor to the Coastal Plain; fairly easy to see at Santee NWR (B–14.1). Has appeared at Huntington Beach (B–22.1), Bear Island (B–15.1), and elsewhere.

Greater White-fronted Goose—very rare except at Santee NWR (B–14.1), where it is a regular winter visitor.

Snow Goose—uncommon winter resident at Santee NWR (B–14.1); rare elsewhere on the Coastal Plain.

Brant—rare winter visitor along the coast. Not here every winter. Most likely in the Charleston Harbor (B–10.1), at the Pitt Street Causeway in Mount Pleasant (B–10.2), and at Moore's Landing (B–10.5).

Canada Goose—migratory Canada Geese are common in winter at Santee NWR (B–14.1); introduced, nonmigratory geese are common and increasing in many parts of the state, and are easily seen at Carolina Sandhills NWR (B–13.1), Lake Monticello (B–20.2), Lake Thurmond (B–35.3), Lake Hartwell (B–4.1), and many other places.

wintering puddle ducks—there are a number of areas, mostly in the Lower Coastal Plain, where you can usually find all of the common species of puddle ducks in winter: Green-winged Teal, American Black Duck, Mallard, Northern Pintail, Blue-winged Teal, Northern Shoveler, Gadwall, and American Wigeon. The best of these areas are Huntington Beach (B–22.1), Magnolia Gardens (B–10.13), Bear Island (B–15.1), Savannah NWR (B–27.2), and Santee NWR (B–14.1). Farther inland you can find many of the same species, but not so often, at Carolina

Sandhills NWR (B–13.1) and Broad River Waterfowl Area (B–20.1).

Mottled Duck—between 1975 and 1982 Mottled Ducks were released in the Santee Delta and along the Combahee River. Breeding in the wild was first noted in 1980. Now (1992) there are probably at least a thousand Mottled Ducks in South Carolina. Easily seen at the Savannah spoil area (B–27.3), Santee Coastal Reserve (B–10.7), and Bear Island (B–15.1), where they are permanent residents.

Mallard—migratory Mallards are fairly common winter visitors wherever there are large numbers of puddle ducks. In addition, there are numerous resident Mallards, descendants of domestic birds, found on small ponds throughout the state.

Canvasback—uncommon winter resident throughout the state; decreasing. Most often seen at Huntington Beach (B–22.1), Magnolia Gardens (B–10.13), Santee NWR (B–14.1), and Savannah NWR (B–27.2).

Redhead—rare winter resident throughout the state. Look for this species wherever you find Canvasbacks.

Ring-necked Duck—our most common bay duck. Common to abundant in winter at Savannah NWR (B–27.2), Santee NWR (B–14.1), Carolina Sandhills NWR (B–13.1), Magnolia Gardens (B–10.13), Huntington Beach (B–22.1), and many other places. Often seen on Piedmont reservoirs.

Greater Scaup—scarce winter resident, mostly along the coast. Sometimes seen in large flocks in the ocean at Huntington Beach (B–22.1), Folly Beach (B–10.11), and Hunting Island State Park (B–7.6).

Lesser Scaup—fairly common winter resident throughout the state. Look for this species wherever puddle ducks are found or in the ocean (see Greater Scaup).

Common Eider—rare winter visitor to rock jetties along the coast. Most often seen at Huntington Beach (B–22.1).

King Eider—rare. See Common Eider.

Harlequin Duck—very rare. See Common Eider.

Oldsquaw—rare winter visitor to the nearshore ocean and to large reservoirs in the Piedmont. Has been seen at Huntington Beach (B–22.1), Lake Murray (B–36.1), Lake Keowee (B–37.2), and elsewhere throughout the state.

scoters—all three scoters are occasionally found along the coast in winter in the same places mentioned for Greater Scaup. Most common is the Black Scoter, followed by Surf Scoter. White-winged Scoter is rather rare. Sometimes a few scoters winter in Charleston Harbor (B–10.1) or on large reservoirs in the Piedmont, where they are quite rare.

Common Goldeneye—uncommon to rare winter resident throughout the state. Has been found recently in Charleston Harbor (B–10.1), at Huntington Beach (B–22.1), and at Bear Island (B–15.1).

Bufflehead—uncommon to abundant winter visitor throughout the state. Migrants are often found in the Piedmont, even at small ponds. Hard to miss at Huntington Beach (B–22.1) and many other places along the coast.

Hooded Merganser—common winter resident and rare summer resident throughout the state. Most easily seen in salt marsh creeks along the coast such as at Huntington Beach (B–22.1), Folly Beach (B–10.11), Hunting Island State Park (B–7.6), and many other places. Has bred at Huntington Beach, Lake Wallace (B–34.2), Savannah NWR (B–27.2), and elsewhere.

Common Merganser—rare winter visitor, mostly found on salt water. Try at Huntington Beach (B–22.1), Charleston Harbor (B–10.1), or some other coastal location.

Red-breasted Merganser—common to abundant winter visitor throughout the state on the ocean or on large lakes. A few nonbreeders may linger into the summer. Hard to miss at Huntington Beach (B–22.1) or Folly Beach (B–10.11).

Ruddy Duck—uncommon winter visitor throughout the state. Good locations to look include Huntington Beach (B–22.1), Santee NWR (B–14.1), Savannah spoil area (B–27.3), Lake Wallace (B–34.2), Lake Oliphant (B–12.5), and many other locations.

American Swallow-tailed Kite—uncommon to rare summer resident of the lower Santee and Savannah River valleys. Most often seen at Santee Delta WMA (B–22.3), Wambaw Creek (B–10.8), B & C Landing in Jasper County (B–27.1), and along the Savannah in Hampton County (B–25).

Mississippi Kite—common summer resident of Coastal Plain river swamps and agricultural areas near rivers. Rather easy to see along the Congaree River (B–40.8, B-32.7), the Savannah River in Hampton County (B–25), B & C Landing in Jasper County (B–27.1), the Great Pee Dee River (B–33.1, B–34.1), and many other places. Often breeds in towns and cities (for example, Moncks Corner, Society Hill, Camden, and Columbia).

Bald Eagle—locally common resident along the coast; rarer inland. Most often seen in winter or early spring. Most easily seen at Bear Island (B–15.1), Savannah NWR (B–27.2), and Santee NWR (B–14.1). Often abundant in late summer along the Wateree River in Kershaw County (B–28.4). Can be found at many other places.

Merlin—uncommon to rare winter visitor, mostly on the coast. Your best bets are Bear Island (B–15.1), Savannah NWR (B–27.2), Magnolia Gardens (B–10.13), and Huntington Beach (B–22.1).

Peregrine Falcon—uncommon, but increasing, winter visitor, mostly along the coast. Try any of the spots mentioned for Merlin. Efforts are being made to reintroduce this species in the South Carolina mountains.

Ruffed Grouse—uncommon and local resident of the Blue Ridge region. The best spots are Sassafras Mountain (B–39.1) and Caesar's Head (B–23.1). Most easily located in early spring, when the males are drumming.

Wild Turkey—fairly common and increasing. Found throughout the state, but most often seen in national forests in the Piedmont and Coastal Plain. Try Santee Coastal Reserve (B–10.7), Francis Marion National Forest (B–8.2, B-10.8), Webb Wildlife Center (B–25.2), and Woods Ferry (B–12.1).

Yellow Rail—rare winter visitor to wet old-field habitats in the Coastal Plain. You might be able to hear one respond by your clicking pebbles on the edge of wet fields or marshes at dusk on warm winter evenings. Has been found at Huntington Beach (B–22.1), Santee NWR (B–14.1, B-14.2, B–14.3), and elsewhere. Don't expect to see the bird, even if you can hear one calling.

Black Rail—rare summer resident of marshes, mostly along the coast. Has been found at Bear Island (B–15.1), Magnolia Gardens (B–10.13), Huntington Beach (B–22.1), and near Townville (B–4.3). This species is most vocal in May and June, even calling at midday. If you actually want to see one, you will have much better luck in coastal North Carolina.

Clapper Rail—common to abundant permanent resident of salt and brackish marshes along the entire coast. Easily found at Huntington Beach (B–22.1), Folly Beach County Park (B–10.11), Hunting Island State Park (B–7.6), Pinckney Island NWR (B–7.2), and many other places.

King Rail—fairly common permanent resident of freshwater marshes in the Lower Coastal Plain; uncommon to rare summer resident inland. Most easily found at Savannah NWR (B–27.2), Bear Island (B–15.1), Magnolia Gardens (B–10.13), and Brookgreen Gardens (B–22.2).

Virginia Rail—uncommon to rare winter visitor to marshes throughout the state. Try the same spots as for King Rail. Very rare in summer at Savannah NWR (B–27.2) and Townville (B–4.3).

Sora—fairly common in winter and during migration in marshes throughout the state. See King Rail.

Purple Gallinule—common summer resident at Savannah NWR (B–27.2). Uncommon to rare elsewhere in the Coastal Plain on ponds with lots of water lilies.

Sandhill Crane—rare visitor in winter and during migration, mostly along the coast. Has been seen recently at Savannah NWR (B–27.2), Huntington Beach (B–22.1), and in the Santee Delta (B–22.3).

migrant and wintering shorebirds—there are a few places inland which are good during migration. Except during early summer you should find good numbers of shorebirds at Huntington Beach (B–22.1), Moore's Landing (B–10.5), Pitt Street (B–10.2), Folly Beach (B–10.11), Beachwalker County Park (B–10.12), Hunting Island (B–7.6), the Port Royal flats at Hilton Head (B–7.3), and the spoil area near Savannah (B–27.3). Other spots can be very good when the water is low, such as during late summer and early fall. These include Santee NWR (B–14.1), Santee Coastal Reserve (B–10.7), and Bear Island (B–15.1). Species typically seen at these sites include the Black-bellied Plover, Semipalmated Plover, Killdeer, Greater Yellowlegs, Lesser Yellowlegs, Solitary Sandpiper (migration only), Willet, Spotted Sandpiper, Ruddy Turnstone, Red Knot, Sanderling, Semipalmated Sandpiper (migration only), Western Sandpiper, Least Sandpiper, Dunlin, Short-billed Dowitcher, and Common Snipe.

Lesser Golden-Plover—this species is seen mostly in migration at airports and other grassy areas. Often found inland in April or August, especially after a rain. Try the Anderson airport (B–4.5), the turf farms near Blackville (B–6.1) and Orangeburg (B–38.4), Barnwell airport (B–6.2), East Cooper airport (B–10.10), Santee NWR (B–14.1), Huntington Beach (B–22.1), Savannah spoil area (B–27.3), and Camden airport (B–28.3).

Wilson's Plover—uncommon and local summer resident along the coast. Most easily found at Huntington Beach (B–22.1) and the Savannah spoil area (B–27.3).

Piping Plover—uncommon to rare winter visitor along the coast. Currently the best spot is Huntington Beach (B–22.1). This species is decreasing in South Carolina. Has bred on undeveloped barrier islands in Horry County, near the North Carolina border.

American Oystercatcher—common resident of salt marshes along the coast. Most easily seen at Huntington Beach (B–22.1), Moore's Landing (B–10.5), Pitt Street (B–10.2), Hunting Island (B–7.6), and Pinckney Island NWR (B–7.2).

Black-necked Stilt—fairly common but local summer resident in freshwater marshes near the coast. Easy to find in summer at Bear Island (B–15.1) and the Savannah spoil area (B–27.3).

American Avocet—rare in winter and during migration. May breed at South Island in Georgetown County and at the Savannah spoil area (B–27.3). Your best bet for this species at any time of year is the Savannah spoil area.

Upland Sandpiper—uncommon to rare migrant, found in the same areas as Lesser Golden-Plover.

Whimbrel—common migrant and rare winter resident in salt marshes all along the coast. Most easily seen at Huntington Beach (B–22.1), Moore's Landing (B–10.5), Folly Beach (B–10.11), Hunting Island (B–7.6), and Pinckney Island NWR (B–7.2).

Long-billed Curlew—rare visitor to salt marshes, mostly during migration. Look for them in the same places that you find Whimbrels.

Marbled Godwit—uncommon to locally common winter visitor to salt marshes and mud flats along the coast. Most easily seen at Moore's Landing (B–10.5), Pitt Street (B–1.2), and the Port Royal flats at Hilton Head (B–7.3).

White-rumped Sandpiper—uncommon migrant, mostly in freshwater mud flats near the coast. Look for this species in

late May or early June at Bear Island (B–15.1), the Savannah spoil area (B–27.3), or Santee Coastal Reserve (B–10.7). Possible anywhere in the state in early June.

Pectoral Sandpiper—fairly common migrant, found in muddy areas throughout the state, mostly in early April or late August. Try the Orangeburg sod farms (B–38.4), Santee NWR (B–14.1, B–14.2), East Cooper Airport (B–10.10), or Huntington Beach (B–22.1).

Purple Sandpiper—common winter resident on the jetty at Huntington Beach State Park (B–22.1); rare elsewhere on rock jetties. Sometimes lingers into early May.

Ruff—rare visitor in migration and winter along the coast. Has been seen in the Santee Delta (B–22.3) and at the Savannah spoil area (B–27.3).

Long-billed Dowitcher—uncommon to rare winter visitor to freshwater marshes near the coast. Your best bet is probably at the Savannah spoil area (B–27.3).

Red Phalarope—fairly common winter resident offshore; rarely seen from dry land. Try one of the party boats out of Charleston (or any other port).

Laughing Gull—permanent resident along the coast; abundant in summer, uncommon in winter. Fairly common at Lake Marion in late summer (B–14.1).

Little Gull—very rare winter visitor along the coast. Has been seen offshore and at Huntington Beach (B–22.1). Look for a large flock of Bonaparte's Gulls and then start sorting through them for a Little Gull. The ratio of Little Gull to Bonaparte's Gull in North Carolina is about 1 to 2,000. In South Carolina your chances might be about the same. The trick is to find a flock of 2,000 Bonaparte's Gulls.

Bonaparte's Gull—fairly common winter visitor to the coast and to large inland lakes. Easy to find at Huntington Beach (B–22.1). This gull often appears at sewage treatment plants, such as the one in Georgetown (B–22.5).

Ring-billed Gull—found year-round on the coast. Winter visitor to large lakes, landfills, and shopping centers throughout the state. Abundant in winter; uncommon in summer.

Herring Gull—resident along the coast and a winter visitor to large lakes inland. More common in winter. Easy to find on any beach in winter.

Lesser Black-backed Gull—rare winter visitor along the coast. Most often seen at Huntington Beach (B–22.1).

Great Black-backed Gull—uncommon to rare winter resident along the coast. Most often seen at Huntington Beach (B–22.1), in Charleston Harbor (B–10.1), or at Folly Beach (B–10.11).

Gull-billed Tern—uncommon summer resident of salt marshes. Most often seen at Moore's Landing (B–10.5), Huntington Beach (B–22.1), the Savannah spoil area (B–27.3), and Bear Island (B–15.1). Possible at any good salt marsh area.

Caspian Tern—uncommon along the coast from late summer to early spring; seen annually at large lakes inland during migration. Rare breeder along the coast. Not hard to find in winter at Huntington Beach (B–22.1), Moore's Landing (B–10.5), Pitt Street (B–10.2), Folly Beach (B–10.11), Bear Island (B–15.1), Hunting Island (B–7.6), Savannah NWR (B–27.2), and many other places.

Royal Tern—common to abundant permanent resident of ocean beaches and salt marshes throughout the state. Hard to miss at any beach.

Sandwich Tern—fairly common summer resident found along sandy beaches all along the coast. Not hard to find at Huntington Beach (B–22.1), Sullivans Island (B–10.3), Folly Beach (B–10.11), Hunting Island (B–7.6), and many other places.

Common Tern—uncommon to rare migrant and summer visitor along the coast. Your best bets are Huntington Beach (B–22.1) and Folly Beach (B–10.11).

Forster's Tern—common permanent resident all along the coast. Also fairly common on large inland lakes in summer and fall.

Least Tern—fairly common summer resident along the coast; rare inland to about the Fall Line. Easily seen in summer at Huntington Beach (B–22.1), Folly Beach (B–10.11), Bear Island (B–15.1), and many other places.

Bridled Tern—fairly common summer visitor to offshore waters; rarely seen from land. Most full-day party boats out of Charleston in the summer will turn up a few.

Sooty Tern—very rare summer visitor along the coast; more common offshore. Try Folly Beach (B–10.11), or go out on a party boat from Charleston.

Black Tern—uncommon to very common summer visitor to marshes along the coast; also a fairly common summer visitor to large inland lakes. Hard to miss at Bear Island (B–15.1) in August.

Black Skimmer—common on sandbars and mud flats along the coast in summer; scarce in winter. Easy to find in summer at Huntington Beach (B–22.1), Pitt Street (B–10.2), Folly Beach (B–10.11), Hunting Island (B–7.6), and many other coastal locations. Very rare inland.

Common Ground-Dove—uncommon and decreasing permanent resident of dunes and brushy areas along the coast; rare inland as far as the Fall Line. Good spots for this species include Huntington Beach (B–22.1), Sullivans Island (B–10.3), Folly Beach County Park (B–10.11), and the Savannah spoil area (B–27.3).

Barn Owl—uncommon to rare resident throughout the state. This species is seldom seen. The best way to see one is to drive back roads in farm country late at night. Try Calhoun County (B–9) or any other rural area.

Common Nighthawk—fairly common but decreasing summer resident; sometimes abundant in August or September. Breeds in cities and also in pine-oak forest, especially in areas that have been recently burned. Common in summer at Bear Island (B–15.1) and the Savannah spoil area (B–27.3), where it breeds on the dikes.

Chuck-will's-widow—common summer resident throughout the state except in the mountains. You can hear a chuck almost anywhere in the countryside on a warm night between April and September. To see one, try driving back roads on the Coastal Plain at night. One good spot is the Screaming Eagle Road area (B–40.5), but just about anywhere in the pinewoods will do.

Whip-poor-will—common and increasing summer resident throughout the state, although rare on the Lower Coastal Plain. Clear-cut pine plantations throughout the state seem to have the highest concentrations of this species, followed by pine-oak woods. To see one, drive a back road in the Piedmont on a warm evening in May or June. Screaming Eagle Road is an excellent place for this species (B–40.5), but just about any back road in the Piedmont or Upper Coastal Plain will do.

Red-cockaded Woodpecker—locally common, but very restricted in distribution. Found only in old-growth pine forests in the Coastal Plain. Francis Marion National Forest in Berkeley and Charleston counties is a stronghold of this endangered species, though a large number of the birds were wiped out by Hurricane Hugo in September 1989. Look for the roost trees (live pine trees covered with sap oozing from the roost hole area). The birds are most easily found in early morning or late afternoon while they are leaving or returning to their roost trees. Aside from the Francis Marion National Forest (B–8 and B-10), look for this species at Carolina Sandhills NWR (B–13.1), Cheraw State Park (B–13.3), Santee Coastal Reserve (B–10.7), Okeetee Plantation (B–27.1), and Webb Wildlife Center (B–25.2).

Willow Flycatcher—rare migrant and very rare summer resident in the Piedmont. A nesting pair was found along the North Pacolet River during the 1991 breeding season (B–42.1).

Gray Kingbird—rare summer visitor along the coast; very rare breeder. Can turn up anywhere in the Lower Coastal Plain in fall migration, but most are seen on power lines near salt water. Try Hilton Head (B–7.3), Pinckney Island NWR (B–7.2), Bear Island (B–15.1), Folly Beach (B–10.11), Sullivans Island (B–10.3), Bull's Island (B–10.5), and the Santee Delta (B–22.3).

Horned Lark—uncommon to rare resident in the Piedmont and Upper Coastal Plain; rare in sand dunes along the coast in winter. Most commonly found at airports or in large, cultivated fields in late winter or early spring. Look for this species at the Anderson County airport (B–4.5), in overgrazed pastures at Townville (B–4.3), turf farms near Blackville (B–6.1) and Orangeburg (B–38.4), Calhoun County farmlands (B–9.2), Flat Ruff (B–30.2), Lucknow (B–31.2), St. Matthew's Church Road (B–40.7), and many other places.

Tree Swallow—common migrant throughout the state; uncommon to rare winter resident along the coast. Found every month (with the possible exception of June) at spots such as Bear Island (B–15.1) and Savannah NWR (B–27.2). Increased field work may find this species breeding at Bear Island, or some similar coastal location.

Bank Swallow—found throughout as a migrant; rare to uncommon in spring but common in August and September. Very rare breeder. Found all summer long at Bear Island (B–15.1), raising the possibility of breeding nearby.

Cliff Swallow—uncommon migrant throughout. Fairly common and increasing summer resident of large lakes in the Piedmont, where it nests under bridges. Rare breeder on the coast. Easy to find from early April through early July at Lake Hartwell (B–4), Lake Russell (B–1.4), Lake Murray (B–36.1), Parr Reservoir (B–36.2), Lake Wylie (B–46.1), along the Catawba River in Lancaster County (B–29.3, B-29.4), and along the Saluda River in Saluda County (B-41.2, B-41.3).

Common Raven—uncommon visitor and rare breeder in the mountains. Most often seen at Caesar's Head (B–23.1), Camp Greenville (B–23.2), Sassafras Mountain (B–39.1), and above 2500 feet in Oconee County (B–37.3).

Red-breasted Nuthatch—uncommon to rare winter visitor throughout, mostly seen in pinewoods in the Piedmont. Fairly common year-round in white-pine—hemlock forests in Oconee County (B–37.7, B–37.8); rare in summer in pitch- and Virginia-pines along Persimmon Ridge Road (B–23.3).

House Wren—rare to common winter resident of the Coastal Plain and Piedmont, most common near the coast. Locally common breeder in cities in the Piedmont, but rarely found away from town. Has bred in Greenville, Greer, Union, Chester, Saluda, Winnsboro, and other Piedmont towns. Listen for its song in older residential areas where there are small vegetable gardens.

Sedge Wren—uncommon to rare winter resident throughout the state. Most easily found in grassy fields and the edges of salt marshes in the Coastal Plain. Try Huntington Beach (B–22.1), Santee Coastal Reserve (B–10.7), Magnolia Gardens (B–10.13), Bear Island (B–15.1), or Savannah NWR (B–27.2).

Golden-crowned Kinglet—common to abundant winter resident throughout the state. Rare in summer at the Walhalla Fish Hatchery (B–37.8), where it may breed.

migrant thrushes—of the five species of spotted thrushes of eastern North America, one (Wood Thrush) breeds in South Carolina, while one other (Hermit Thrush) is a common winter resident. The other three species (Veery, Swainson's Thrush, and Gray-cheeked Thrush) are found only in migration, mostly late April through mid-May or mid-August through early October. They are mostly easily found at migrant traps in the Piedmont or Upper Coastal Plain. Veery and Swainson's Thrush are fairly common; Gray-cheeked Thrush is uncommon to rare. Try river bottom areas in the Piedmont or Upper Coastal Plain such as Long Cane

Natural Area (B–1.2), Rivers Bridge State Park (B–5.1), Woods Ferry (B–12.1), Worthy's Ferry (B–12.2), Landsford Canal State Park (B–12.4), Carolina Sandhills NWR (B–13.1), Kalmia Gardens (B–16.1), Little Pee Dee State Park (B–17.1), Fury's Ferry (B–19.2), Broad River Waterfowl Area (B–20.1), Lake Wateree State Park (B–20.3), Lynches River State Park (B–21.1), Caesar's Head State Park (B–23.1), Jones Gap State Park (B–23.5), Flat Creek (B–29.1), Ware Shoals (B–30.2), Lee State Park (B–31.1), the lower Saluda River (B–32.3 through B–32.5), Old State Road (B–32.7), Britton's Neck (B–33.1), Thurmond Dam area (B–35.4), Enoree WMA (B–36.3), Lynches Woods (B–36.4), Walhalla Fish Hatchery (B–37.8), Sassafras Mountain (B–39.1), Harbison State Forest (B–40.1), Sesquicentennial State Park (B–40.4), Congaree Swamp (B–40.8), Croft State Park (B–42.3), Poinsett State Park (B–43.2), Broad River Recreation Area (B–44.2), and Kings Mountain (B–46.2).

Solitary Vireo—common migrant throughout the state. Fairly common in winter in the Coastal Plain; uncommon to rare in winter in the Piedmont. Many out-of-state birders are surprised to find this species breeding not only in the mountains but also at scattered locations throughout the Piedmont and Upper Coastal Plain. In summer look for this species anywhere in the mountains and also in mature loblolly-pine forests in the Piedmont, such as at Woods Ferry (B–12.1), Lick Fork Lake (B–19.1), Broad River Waterfowl Area (B–20.1), Broad River Natural Area (B–36.3), Lake Hartwell State Park (B–37.1), and Issaqueena (B–39.7).

Warbling Vireo—very rare migrant and summer resident. Has been found during June in recent years (1989—1991) at the Bluff Unit of Santee NWR (B–14.1), which is probably your best bet for finding this rare species. Has appeared in Spring in Congaree Swamp National Monument in willows along the Congaree River (B–40.8).

migrant warblers—the spring and fall migrations of warblers through South Carolina may be rated poor to good in comparison to the concentrations that birders find at warbler hot spots in the northeastern United States and eastern Canada. In general the migration is better in the Piedmont or Blue Ridge than in the Coastal Plain, although fall can be good anywhere in the state. Look for migrant warblers just about anywhere, but especially at those spots mentioned for migrant thrushes (above). The following species are regularly found in South Carolina during migration: Blue-winged, Golden-winged, Tennessee, Orange-crowned, Northern Parula, Yellow, Chestnut-sided, Magnolia, Cape May, Black-throated Blue, Yellow-rumped, Black-throated Green, Blackburnian, Yellow-throated, Pine, Prairie, Palm, Bay-breasted, Blackpoll, Cerulean, Black-and-white, American Redstart, Prothonotary, Worm-eating, Swainson's, Ovenbird, Northern Waterthrush, Louisiana Waterthrush, Kentucky, Common Yellowthroat, Hooded, Canada, and Yellow-breasted Chat.

Orange-crowned Warbler—fairly common in winter in the Lower Coastal Plain, becoming rarer inland and to the north. A few winter in the Piedmont. Look for this species from mid-October through early April in thick underbrush at areas such as Savannah NWR (B–27.2), Hilton Head (B–7.3), Magnolia Gardens (B–10.13), Brookgreen Gardens (B–22.2), and many other spots.

Yellow Warbler—this species is common from August through October throughout the state but is very local as a breeder. In June look for it near Townville (B–4.3), along the lower Eastatoe Creek (B–39.3), near Landrum (B–42.1), or in farmlands along the Middle Saluda River near Jones Gap State Park (B–23.5).

Chestnut-sided Warbler—sometimes found during the breeding season at brushy areas above 3,000 feet, such as Caesar's Head (B–23.1) and Sassafras Mountain (B–39.1).

Black-throated Blue Warbler—fairly common summer resident of rhododendron thickets above 2,600 feet in the mountains. Easily found at Caesar's Head (B–23.1), Sassafras Mountain (B–39.1), or the Walhalla Fish Hatchery (B–37.8).

Black-throated Green Warbler—fairly common summer resident of hemlocks above 1,800 feet in the mountains; also a rare breeder in bald cypress swamps along the coast. This species is easily found from early April through July at just about any suitable habitat in the mountains. The Coastal Plain birds are much harder to find. Try I'on Swamp (B–10.6) and other areas in the Francis Marion National Forest. There have been reports of this species in summer in swamps in the Sandhills of Lexington County.

Blackburnian Warbler—very rare in the breeding season in pines and hemlocks above 3,000 feet. Try the pitch-pine groves along the Foothills Trail near Sassafras Mountain (B–39.1).

Cerulean Warbler—rare in the breeding season in mature hardwoods in the mountains. Has been found recently at Caesar's Head (B–23.1) and the Walhalla Fish Hatchery (B–37.8). In June 1990 one singing male was found in the Upper Coastal Plain along Old State Road (B–32.7). Since this species breeds in the Coastal Plain of North Carolina, we can hope that there may be a few breeding in the Coastal Plain of South Carolina as well. The Cerulean Warbler is an early fall migrant and may be found just about anywhere in the state in August.

Worm-eating Warbler—common summer resident of rhododendron and mountain laurel thickets in the mountains. Easily found at Sassafras Mountain (B–39.1), Jones Gap State Park (B–23.5), the Walhalla Fish Hatchery (B–37.8), and many other places. Rare (but perhaps overlooked) summer visitor or breeder in bay-swamp thickets in the Coastal Plain. Try Carolina Sandhills NWR (B–13.1), Woods Bay State Park (B–43.4), and other similar areas. The Worm-eating Warbler is quite common in the Coastal Plain of North Carolina and should appear regularly in counties near the North Carolina border (such as Horry). By late summer this species is found throughout the state as a migrant.

Swainson's Warbler—fairly common summer resident of swamp thickets in the Coastal Plain; locally common in rhododendron thickets in the mountains. From mid-April until early July it is fairly easy to hear Swainson's Warblers singing at Congaree Swamp (B–40.8), Francis Beidler Forest (B–18.1), near B & C Landing (B–27.1), and many other places in the Coastal Plain. This species is a bit harder to find in the mountains but is regular at Jones Gap State Park (B–23.5) and along streams near Sassafras Mountain (B–39.1).

Canada Warbler—very rare in summer above 3,000 feet. In June you might find one at Sassafras Mountain (B–39.1). By mid-August migrants are found throughout the mountains and Piedmont.

Rose-breasted Grosbeak—rare summer visitor to mountains above 3,000 feet. Not yet found breeding. In June be alert for this species near the Walhalla Fish Hatchery (B–37.8), Caesar's Head (B–23.1), and especially Sassafras Mountain (B–39.1).

Painted Bunting—uncommon to common summer resident of thickets throughout the Coastal Plain, inland as far as Columbia and North Augusta. Easily found at Huntington Beach (B–22.1), Santee Coastal Reserve (B–10.7), Sullivans Island (B–10.3), Folly Beach (B–10.11), Santee NWR (B–14.1), Savannah NWR (B–27.2), and many other places, especially along the coast.

Dickcissel—sporadic and local, rare summer resident, mostly in the Piedmont. The most consistent breeding area for this midwestern species is at Townville (B–4.3). May turn up anywhere in migration or in winter.

Bachman's Sparrow—uncommon to rare permanent resident, breeding throughout the Piedmont and Coastal Plain. This species is very hard to locate except by song. It is found in two different types of habitats—very large regenerating clearcuts or power line rights-of-way and open mature pinewoods. Listen for this species' song from late March until September at large clear-cuts in the Piedmont or at any of the following Coastal Plain locations: Silver Bluff (B–2.4), Cainhoy (B–8.1), Witherbee Road (B–8.2), Santee Coastal Reserve (B–10.7), near Hampton Plantation (B–10.8), Carolina Sandhills NWR (B–13.1), the Webb Center (B–25.2), Tillman Sand Ridge WMA (B–27.1), Kershaw County Sandhills (B–28.3), Screaming Eagle Road (B–40.5), and Manchester State Forest (B–43.3).

Henslow's Sparrow—very rare, but possible at any time of the year in the Piedmont or Coastal Plain. Most likely in winter along power line rights-of-way in Coastal Plain pinewoods. Try the power line near the south end of Santee Dam (B–8.6). Henslow's Sparrows are fairly common breeders in the Coastal Plain of North Carolina and have even been found breeding in Brunswick County there, which borders Horry County, South Carolina. This species might breed in Carolina bays in Horry County, but it has not yet been discovered there. Very rare breeder in weedy fields in the Piedmont.

Le Conte's Sparrow—rare winter resident of broom sedge fields and the edges of salt marshes in the Coastal Plain. Has been found recently at Huntington Beach (B–22.1), Pitt Street in Mount Pleasant (B–10.2), and Bear Island WMA (B–15.1). When looking for Le Conte's Sparrow, be alert for Sedge Wren, Henslow's Sparrow, and Grasshopper Sparrow in the same habitat.

Dark-eyed Junco—common winter resident throughout the state; uncommon to rare breeder at Caesar's Head (B–23.1), Sassafras Mountain (B–39.1), and the Walhalla Fish Hatchery (B–37.8).

House Finch—common permanent resident of cities and large towns throughout the Piedmont, rapidly spreading toward the coast. As of 1991 this species was well established as far downhill as Darlington, Sumter, Columbia, Aiken, and North Augusta. By the end of the century it should be common throughout the state, even on the coast.

Red Crossbill—rare permanent resident in the mountains; very rare winter visitor elsewhere. Has bred at Caesar's Head (B–23.1). Most easily found in pines and hemlocks in the mountains of Oconee County in August and September (B–37.3 through B–37.8).

List of Maps

List of Maps

List of Maps

List of Maps

Species Index

Species Index

Hooded, 5–6, 48–50, 65–66, 72,
79–81, 91–93, 102–3, 113–15,
137–38, 144, 148–50, 153, 159–60,
174–76, 180, 185–87, 201–6, 213–14,
219–20, 223, 234
Kentucky, 6, 30–31, 72, 79–81, 91–93,
102–3, 132–34, 144, 148–50, 153,
157, 159–60, 223, 234
Lawrence's, 153
Magnolia, 72, 74–75, 79–81, 91–93,
102–3, 153, 195, 223, 234
Myrtle. *See* Yellow-rumped
Nashville, 153
Orange-crowned, 18–19, 35–36, 54,
72, 107–8, 130, 136–37, 159–60, 234
Palm, 18–19, 30–33, 35–36, 48–50,
64–65, 79–81, 107–8, 153, 223, 234
Parula. *See* Parula, Northern
Pine, 4–6, 18–19, 35–36, 41, 48–50, 56,
72, 79–81, 97, 102–3, 107–9, 144,
148–50, 153, 174–76, 201–6, 223,
234
Prairie, 8, 54, 67, 79–81, 105–7,
138–39, 140–42, 144, 153, 223, 234
Prothonotary, 15, 23–24, 30–31, 45,
65–66, 69–70, 72, 79–81, 91–93, 95,
102–3, 126–27, 132–34, 144, 153,
159–60, 191, 194, 198–200, 215,
219–20, 223, 234
Tennessee, 72, 102–3, 153, 223, 234
Yellow, 6, 26–27, 72, 79–81, 117–18,
121–22, 153, 190–91, 209, 223, 234
Swainson's, 5–6, 42–43, 45, 48–50, 57,
60–61, 79–81, 91–93, 95, 109–10,
113–15, 117–18, 125, 132–34,
137–38, 140–42, 148–50, 153,
157–158, 177, 185–87, 198–200,
201–6, 213–14, 235–35
Wilson's, 153
Worm-eating, 5–6, 72, 91–94, 102–3,
113–15, 115, 129–130, 153, 174–77,
180, 185–88, 191, 213, 223, 234
Yellow-rumped, 18–19, 30–31, 35–36,
39–40, 54, 65–66, 72, 79–81, 88,
102–3, 107–8, 136–37, 148–50, 153,
156, 219–20, 223, 234
Yellow-throated, 18–19, 30–31, 35–36,
45, 65–66, 72, 79–81, 91–93, 102–3,
105–8, 126–27, 130, 144, 148–50,
153, 159–60, 215, 219–20, 223, 234
Waterthrush: Louisiana, 17, 47–50, 71–72,
79–81, 113–15, 117, 137–38, 144,
148–50, 153, 181, 185–87, 190–91,
198–206, 213–14, 221–22, 223, 234;

Northern, 39–40, 72, 102–3, 153, 223,
234
Waxwing, Cedar, 53, 72
Whimbrel, 38–39, 62–63, 64–65, 230
Whip-poor-will, 57, 140–42, 146–47, 182,
196–97, 201–6, 232
Whistling-Duck, Fulvous, 65–66, 135, 227
Wigeon: American, 65–66, 74–75, 77–81,
99–100, 105–8, 227; Eurasian, 81–82, 135
Willet, 38–39, 105–7, 130, 136–37, 229
Wood-Pewee, Eastern, 4, 30–31, 48–50, 72,
79–81, 83–86, 125–26, 48–50, 201–6,
219–20
Woodcock, American, 6–8, 30–31, 69–70,
72, 79–81, 146–47, 165, 169–71, 193,
198–200, 201–6
Woodpecker(s), 3–6, 41–42, 45, 48–50, 72,
79–81, 95, 97, 123, 126–27, 144, 148–50,
159–60, 169–71, 174–76, 181–182,
198–200, 201–6, 213–14, 219–20
Downy, 30–31, 72, 79–81, 107–8,
148–50, 159–60, 169–71, 219–20
Hairy, 30–31, 48–50, 72, 79–81,
148–50, 159–60, 169–71, 219–20
Ivory-billed, 198–200, 201–6
Pileated, 30–31, 45, 60–61, 72, 79–81,
126–27, 148–50, 159–60, 169–71,
213–14, 219–20
Red-bellied, 30–31, 45, 72, 79–81,
107–8, 126–27, 138–39, 148–50,
159–60, 169–71, 219–20
Red-cockaded, 4, 41–42, 48–50,
56–61, 73–77, 79–81, 97, 125–27,
129–30, 132–34, 148–50, 162, 182,
201–6, 232
Red-headed, 14, 20–23, 34, 47–50,
60–62, 79–81, 91–93, 123, 125–27,
148–50, 159–60, 169–71, 198–206,
219–20
Wren, Carolina, 8, 30–33, 72, 79–81, 95,
105–8, 138–39, 144, 148–50, 221–22;
House, 30–33, 79–81, 117–18, 194, 233;
Marsh, 8, 39–40, 51–52, 83–86, 105–8,
111–12, 136–37; Sedge, 54, 60–62,
105–7, 140–42, 198–200, 233; Winter,
30–31, 95, 148–50, 159–60, 219–20

Yellowlegs: Greater, 31–32, 77–81, 83–86,
110–11, 136–37, 190–91, 229; Lesser,
31–32, 77–81, 83–86, 110–11, 136–37,
190–91, 229
Yellowthroat, Common, 7–8, 31–32, 35–36,
72, 79–81, 102–3, 107–8, 140–42, 144,
153, 174–76, 198–200, 223, 234

246

General Index

General Index

General Index